An Improper Profession

An Improper Profession

WOMEN, GENDER, AND JOURNALISM

IN LATE IMPERIAL RUSSIA

Barbara T. Norton & Jehanne M Gheith, editors

Duke University Press   Durham & London   2001

© 2001 Duke University Press

All rights reserved

Printed in the United States of America on acid-free paper ∞

Designed by C. H. Westmoreland

Typeset in Sabon by Keystone Typesetting, Inc.

Library of Congress Cataloging-in-Publication Data appear on the last printed page of this book.

To the memory of my parents, Frances Jacobson Norton and Clyde DeWitt Norton, and our shared love of Russia. BTN

For my parents: my father, Mohamed Gheith, whose strength, constancy, smartness, and sense of humor matter more than I can say; Aida Gheith, whose warmth and intelligence have created a refuge for me; and Dorothy Gheith, whose gifts of writing and bread have provided sustenance on many levels. JMG

Contents

- ix *Abbreviations*
- xi *List of Terms*
- xiii *Note on Dates, Transliteration, and Archival Citations*

- 1 Introduction   JEHANNE M GHEITH
- 26 "A Larger Portion of the Public": Female Readers, Fiction, and the Periodical Press in the Reign of Nicholas I   MIRANDA BEAVEN REMNEK
- 53 Redefining the Perceptible: The Journalism(s) of Evgeniia Tur and Avdot'ia Panaeva   JEHANNE M GHEITH
- 74 The Development of a Fashion Press in Late Imperial Russia: *Moda: Zhurnal dlia svetskikh liudei*   CHRISTINE RUANE
- 93 "Provid[ing] Amusement for the Ladies": The Rise of the Russian Women's Magazine in the 1880s   CAROLYN R. MARKS
- 120 Anna Volkova: From Merchant Wife to Feminist Journalist   ADELE LINDENMEYR
- 140 Meeting the Challenge: Russian Women Reporters and the Balkan Crises of the Late 1870s   MARY F. ZIRIN
- 167 Writing for Their Rights: Four Feminist Journalists: Mariia Chekhova, Liubov' Gurevich, Mariia Pokrovskaia, and Ariadna Tyrkova   ROCHELLE GOLDBERG RUTHCHILD
- 196 Mariia Pokrovskaia and *Zhenskii vestnik*: Feminist Separatism in Theory and Practice   LINDA EDMONDSON
- 222 Journalism as a Means of Empowerment: The Early Career of Ekaterina Kuskova   BARBARA T. NORTON

249 Sources for the Study of Russian Women Journalists:
    A Bibliographic Essay   JUNE PACHUTA FARRIS

281 *Appendix: Checklist of Women Journalists in Imperial Russia*

311 *List of Contributors*

313 *Index*

Abbreviations

The following abbreviations are used in the chapter notes and in the appendix:

BdCh	Biblioteka dlia chteniia
BVed	Birzhevye vedomosti
ChNS	Chital'nia narodnoi shkoly
DCh	Detskoe chtenie
DO	Detskii otdykh
DS	Detskii sad
DZh	Drug zhenshchin
IuCh	Iunii chitatel'
IV	Istoricheskii vestnik
LO	Listok ob"iavlenii
MirB	Mir bozhii
MM	Modnyi magazin
MS	Modnyi svet
MSMM	Modnyi svet i modnyi magazin
MVed	Moskovskie vedomosti
NRB	Novyi russkii bazar
NRS	Novoe russkoe slovo
NV	Novoe vremia
NZ	Nasha zhizn'
NZh	Novyi zhurnal
NZhdV	Novyi zhurnal dlia vsekh
OZ	Otechestvennye zapiski
PIOR	Perevody otdel'nykh (inostrannykh) romanov
PZhK	Pervyi zhenskii kalendar'
RB	Russkoe bogatstvo
RM	Russkaia mysl'
RSlovo	Russkoe slovo
RStar	Russkaia starina
RVed	Russkie vedomosti
SemV	Semeinye vechera

SevV	Severnyi vestnik
SS	Sem'ia i shkola
SPVed	Sankt-Peterburgskie vedomosti
SZh	Soiuz zhenshchin
TvK	Teatr v karikaturakh
VE	Vestnik Evropy
VM	Vestnik mody
VO	Vospitanie i obuchenie
VV	Vestnik vospitaniia
ZhD	Zhenskoe delo
ZhO	Zhenskoe obrazovanie
ZhV	Zhenskii vestnik
ZhivO	Zhivopisnoe obozrenie

Terms

Duma. Local legislative body after 1870, and also national legislative body (State Duma) after 1905.

estates. Legal categories into which Russian society was organized *(soslovie/sosloviia)* — including nobility, clergy, peasantry, townspeople (usually divided into merchants and *meshchane*, or lower townspeople), among others.

feuilleton. Newspaper feature article (human interest story, in factual or fictional form) printed across the bottom six inches of all six columns of the first and second pages, occasionally running onto the third page.

gimnazium (gimnaziia). Approximate equivalent of a high school.

Great Reforms. Wide-ranging political, economic, and social reforms undertaken during the 1860s and 1870s by Alexander II.

intelligentsia. Educated segment of Russian society that adopted a critical approach to the world and protested against the existing order.

Kadets. Members of the liberal Party of People's Freedom (Partiia Narodnogo svoboda), known colloquially as the Constitutional Democratic Party; Russia's main liberal party.

Liberation movement. Network of left-of-center liberals and moderate socialists, formed at the beginning of the twentieth century.

Provisional Government. Democratically oriented government of Russia following the 1917 (February) revolution.

Slavophiles. Moscow-centered group of romantic intellectuals (landowners and gentlemen-scholars) who felt that Russia should respect and build on its own historical experience rather than follow Western patterns of social and economic development. Flourished in the 1840s and 1850s. Opponents of the Westernizers.

thick journals. Monthly publications, divided into a half dozen or so sections: Russian literature, foreign literature, science and art, industry and agriculture, criticism, literary chronicle, miscellany *(smes')*. Typically about 300 pages; included discussion of world events and serialized books.

Socialist Revolutionaries. Members of the populist Socialist Revolutionary Party (Partiia Sotsialist-revoliutsionera); Russia's main peasant party.

Westernizers. Socially diverse group of intellectuals who maintained that the Western path of social and economic development was the model that Russia should follow. Flourished in the 1840s and 1850s. Opponents of the Slavophiles.

Zemstvo. After 1864, institution of local self-government concerned with finance, administration (including education and public health), and justice.

Note on Dates, Transliteration, and Archival Citations

The Julian calendar (Old Style) was used in Russia until 1918, when it was replaced by the Western Gregorian calendar (New Style). Dates in the Julian calendar were thirteen days behind the Gregorian in the twentieth century, twelve days behind in the nineteenth century, and eleven in the eighteenth century. The dates given in this volume are Old Style unless otherwise indicated (that is, when presented as dual dates [e.g., 6 January 1877/18 January 1877] or designated as New Style [NS]).

A modified Library of Congress system of transliteration has been employed (except in the case of names of Russian rulers and the cities St. Petersburg and Moscow, which appear in their more familiar English forms). All Russian titles (and most names) have been modernized; however, it is important to note that most library cataloging systems use a pre-1918 orthography (e.g., *Otechestvennye zapiski* is cataloged as *Otiechestvennye zapiski*).

Russian archival citations in this volume include the following abbreviations:

f. *fond* (an archival collection)
o. *opis* (a list of materials in a *fond*)
d. *delo* (a packet of materials in a *fond*; ed. khr. [*edinitsa khraneniia*] is an older way of referring to a *delo*)
l. *list* (a page; or ll. for pages)

Introduction

JEHANNE M GHEITH

When we have mentioned the topic of this book, people have often looked puzzled, as if the topics of women and journalism could not go together, as if something didn't quite add up. We have become used to the furrowed brow and puzzled look as we talk about women, journalism, and Russia. Yet in Russia today, women journalists are becoming increasingly important: the number of female journalists is growing, and organizations of women journalists are being formed. So on one level, this volume provides a genealogy and history for Russian women journalists working today. Equally important, this collection rewrites some of the common ways journalism in Russia has been conceptualized. To take just one example, journalism is usually thought of as a public discourse, and on one level, it was (is). Yet as several of the essays here demonstrate, the intersections of public and private were constantly being explored in published journals as well as personal diaries in late imperial Russia. Examining women's journalism, then, helps to untangle and reimagine the lines of the public and private, not just in women's journalism, but in Russian journalism in general.

Women, gender, journalism: each of these much-debated constructs has been acknowledged as central in the development of Russian history and literature, yet the relationships between them have rarely been examined. Although the issues around women and gender — to which we will return shortly — have been the subject of considerable recent scholarship, the nature and status of journalism have received much less attention.[1] This despite the fact that the periodical press is widely credited with being a major force in Russian culture; in particular, journalism has played a major role in formulating, defining, and reflecting the opinions of Russia's literate classes and, through them, has affected other sectors of Russian society. In fact, journalism has long been one of the most influential factors shaping Russian history, letters, and society, certainly from the second third of the nineteenth century to 1917, and arguably beyond. Yet considering its acknowledged importance, journalism has been narrowly studied. Moreover, scholarship on the subject tends to be obscure, so that it has not had as much impact on the profession of Russian history and literature as the topic warrants. Despite recent excellent work, the significance of journalism and scholarship on it are disproportionate.[2]

If relatively little is known about journalism in general, then women's involvement in journalism is almost completely uncharted territory. Since at least the late eighteenth century, women have participated in nearly every aspect of the journalistic process, functioning as editors and publishers,[3] authors of literary criticism and publicists, and readers of the periodical press. Yet women's involvement in Russian journalism remains virtually unexamined;[4] women as producers and consumers of journalism are rarely mentioned in major studies of the topic.[5] This is true even of very recent work: *Literary Journals in Imperial Russia,* a new collection that substantially enhances the scholarship of Russian journalism, makes almost no reference to the activities of female journalists. In *An Improper Profession,* we aim to address this lacuna, both by recovering the contributions of women to journalism in Russia and by exploring how such a recovery complicates traditional understandings of both journalism and gender in late imperial Russia. The essays in this volume demonstrate that journalism has been not only too narrowly studied but also too narrowly defined. An argument implicit in many of the chapters — and explicit in some — is that journalism is more than the sum of its visible products; that is, journalism is here considered not primarily as a commercial or historical phenomenon but rather as a complex cultural, historical, and social process.

In investigating women's contributions to Russian journalism, we are most interested in three related areas: first, recovering the work of individual female journalists; second, providing a set of contexts for this work; and third, exploring the significance of these discoveries. This introduction focuses both on how the essays that follow challenge some common assumptions about gender current in Western feminist scholarship and on how integrating the work of female journalists and the "women's press" into a conception of Russian letters adds to and changes received notions about Russian journalism, professions, and society.[6] We are not proposing a countertradition of women's journalism; rather, we place this journalism within the larger field of journalism in Russia and relate it to studies of gender and journalism in the West.

Exploring women's participation in journalism necessitates asking new kinds of questions both about Russia and about journalism. As the authors of this volume recover the work of women journalists and journalism directed at women, they are also discovering and (re)creating the contexts for these phenomena. Because the patterns of women's journalism often do not fit the established contexts and because the questions that have been asked about (men's) journalism often do not fit the realities of women's journalism, *An Improper Profession* concentrates as much on raising questions (and working out what are the most fruitful questions to ask of women's journalism) as on providing answers. In a field that is as new as women and journalism in Russia, it is both more honest and potentially more generative to define questions than to shape answers too early.

Because question asking can be interpreted in many and contradictory ways (as a form of tentativeness or as a sign of confidence), it is important to state our rationale for the following section. This introduction proposes a set of provisional views of the subject of women and journalism and offers concrete conclusions that are summed up at the essay's end. Yet we begin with an extended series of questions because we believe that asking questions is as vital in knowledge production as is finding answers, and that the kinds of questions that a study is based on are at least as illuminating as the answers provided. We offer these questions in the hope both that they will guide the reader through the volume and that they will generate more questions.

First, there is the deceptively simple query: What do we mean by a "Russian woman journalist"? A woman who published in the periodical press? A female reporter? A female editor-publisher? Because studying women and journalism in Russia has the potential to provoke a radical reconceptualization of all three categories ("women," "journalism," "Russia"), it is important not to narrow the field prematurely but rather to leave open as many options and avenues for further work as possible. Therefore our definition of a "Russian woman journalist" (and, by analogy, "women's journalism") is inclusive, encompassing any woman who was involved in any aspect of Russian journalism. In addition, by using a definition that makes diversity one of its constituent elements, we hope to avoid creating the impression of "women's journalism" as a monolithic entity.[7]

A related set of questions is about individual female journalists. Given that for most of the period under consideration here (the 1820s to the early twentieth century) women did not have access to higher education, nor could they hold government posts, how did they become involved in journalism? Because journalism was one of a very few ways that women could earn money in the imperial period, for how many of the journalists discussed were finances an issue, and how did this affect their journalistic efforts? Since social progress has long been an important aspect of Russian journalism, (how) did women's journalistic work express or reflect social concerns? Did it do so in ways similar to, or different from, men's? What influence did women's journalism have and on whom? How will focusing on periodicals and works for and by women disrupt conventional ideas about what constituted the major concerns of Russian society in the late imperial period? The work of female journalists often centers on women—in fiction, on exploring the lives of female characters; in nonfiction, on issues such as women's education, labor, and health. Do female journalists' descriptions of women differ from the better-known ones by men? What will an exploration of these works reveal about women's perceptions and representations of the issues important to women?

A third set of questions revolves around the development, functions, and significance of the women's press. How, in particular, did this press reflect the concerns of gender? Memoirs and essays indicate that published descriptions of women were taken as role models: What kinds of role models, then, did periodicals set up for women? Was this a conscious concern of the editors? And a related issue: As early as the late eighteenth century, many periodicals were directed at women, indicating the existence of a female readership (or at least a perception of one).[8] At what point did a female readership develop in Russia? How extensive was it? Who made up this readership? Was it mainly women of a certain age or geographic location (urban or rural) or a particular *soslovie* (estate)?[9]

And finally, how will understanding women's role in journalism contribute to the ongoing discussion about professions in Russia? As the triple entendre of our title suggests, we believe that it is too early to decide whether Russian journalism in the late imperial period can accurately be described as a profession. Yet it is important to raise this as an issue, both to better understand Russian journalism and to place our volume within the growing body of work on the professions in Russia. The term "profession" continues to be problematic when applied to Russian contexts: despite recent research, much of it excellent, no one has adequately defined what a profession means in the Russian setting. Furthermore, little of this work has focused either on journalism[10] or on women.[11] And the scholarship that does exist on the topic of women in Russian professions, for the most part, has not been effectively incorporated into the broader scholarship on the topic. The ambiguous—and in this period shifting—position of journalism (occupation, profession, calling, vocation) makes it both particularly difficult to incorporate journalism into a discussion of Russian professions and particularly important to do so: the anomalous status of journalism reflects the complex nature of journalism itself and of the professions in Russia. *An Improper Profession*, we hope, will both provide information about and stimulate further research on women's involvement in professions and the development of journalism as a profession in Russia.

The essays in this volume begin to address the questions we have raised, suggesting, for example, that financial need did motivate many women to take up or to continue on in journalism and also that there was a definable female readership at least from 1825 (and probably before). While these facts may reinforce some common assumptions (female journalists were in it for the money, they wrote primarily about women's issues), the chapters ultimately work against such assumptions, showing that the women discussed here did not compromise their principles for financial gain and that their journalism covered a wide range of topics, including, but not restricted to, issues of particular concern to women.

The chapters also address important theoretical issues. Many of these essays, for example, attempt to define and problematize a Russian feminism, something that has proven difficult for most Western researchers of Russia's women. (It may be anachronistic to speak of "feminism" before the 1890s, yet Russians were widely aware of something usually called the "emancipation of women" as early as the 1830s.)[12] While a number of the women discussed here may be "feminist" in (some) present-day Western definitions, it is also true that most of these women emphatically refused the term for themselves. This disjuncture is partly due to a difference in interpretation: Russians usually considered feminism to be a narrow movement, a Western import that necessarily built barriers between men and women, and, especially in the early twentieth century, a bourgeois phenomenon that deflected energy from the larger cause of transforming Russian society. The authors of this volume have a different, broader understanding of feminism. Yet even with this caveat, the difficulty remains: is naming these women "feminist" an act of appropriation of the kind that much feminist and postcolonialist theory works against? On the other hand, not calling them "feminist" seems to be less than true to the work these women did to advance the cause of women. While it is possible to dispense with the question of definition (a productive strategy for some projects),[13] we think there is also a value to (re)opening the question, to leaving it as a tension, an area that demands further exploration: What does feminism mean in the Russian context? And how might understanding the workings of Russian "feminism" affect Western conceptions of gender and of feminism? The essays presented here are part of that ongoing exploration, as they illuminate, both directly and indirectly, what constitutes (or may be called?) Russian feminism in different periods. In addition, this scholarship suggests some of the ways that Russian feminisms differ from Western varieties of feminism.[14] Taken as a whole, the scholarship in this volume provides new and multiple outlooks on Russian feminism as it indicates the need for a reinterpretation of the term both in Russianist and other circles.

An Improper Profession also encourages comparison of women's journalism in Russia with that in other countries, particularly in Western Europe and the United States. Because of different historical conditions in Russia, gender is differently constructed there than in countries such as England, France, and the United States, which have been the primary foci of feminist criticism.[15] Some differences between women's position in Russia and the West can easily be identified (such as the fact that women in Russia early had the right to hold property, and that female suffrage was necessarily a different kind of issue in Russia, where men, too, were denied national enfranchisement until the early twentieth century). But the deeper divisions of gender construction remain difficult to define. By exploring the development of the women's press (created by both men and women), as well as Russian women's individual efforts in journalism, the following essays demonstrate the workings of gender in Russia. In so doing, they not only add to (and challenge) recent Russianist discussion of the topic but also raise important questions for Western feminist scholars about issues such as oppression and resistance as well as the formation and function of gender.[16]

To take one concrete example: While the discussion of women's participation in journalism in Britain has largely centered on the creation of new forms of feminine subjectivity or on inscriptions and contestations of feminine ideologies,[17] in Russia, women's journalism appears to have been at least as much an outlet for social or political activity as it was an avenue for new understandings of feminine subjectivity. And where, in Britain, women have been described as first participating in journalism in ways that generally supported (but also subverted) the domestic status quo,[18] when Russian women began to publish, they—much more quickly than in the British case—moved into all forms of journalism. As the essays that follow reveal, Russian women not only focused on fashion and the domestic world but also wrote for professional journals and radical publications (Ruthchild and Norton) and even served as war correspondents (Zirin). Further, Russianists have tended to focus on women who were journalists rather than on inscriptions of feminine ideologies; in British contexts, there is less emphasis on female journalists. While these dissimilar approaches say as much about the different scholarly fields as they do about the countries of study, they also indicate the distinct roles that journalism played in the two countries.[19] In Russia, ruled by an autocracy (somewhat mitigated after 1905), journalism's role in changing society was primary; in England, ruled by constitutional monarchy, journalism had different functions.[20] In any event, it is worth noting that in Russia, journalism early provided a venue for social action for women in a way that was not true of the English case.

Historians have noted that from at least the 1820s, literate Russians considered improving the polity to be one of journalism's most important functions and that the emphasis on the social realm was one of the main factors influencing Russian journalism in the nineteenth century and into the twentieth.[21] Their studies have concentrated on the work of male journalists; the essays in this volume demonstrate that women's journalistic work, too, made transforming society a high priority.

As the following essays illustrate (see especially those by Linda Edmondson, Rochelle Ruthchild, and Barbara Norton), the connections between political causes and journalism are more often overt in the work of the early-twentieth-century journalists (for example, Mariia Chekhova, Liubov' Gurevich, Ekaterina Kuskova, and Ariadna Tyrkova) than in women's journalism of the first two-thirds of the nineteenth century, as the former regularly addressed acknowledged social issues in their articles. Many female journalists at and after the turn of the century intertwined feminist and other progressive causes in their writing.

Other essays detail more subtle but no less powerful social and political effects: Miranda Remnek's essay makes explicit the complex relationship of fact and fiction in Russian journalism. Journalism is today usually thought of as dealing primarily in fact (or sensationalist fiction of the *National Enquirer* variety) and the polity rather than in imagination and literature. Yet in imperial Russia (and elsewhere in the nineteenth century), this division was not so easy to make: not only was fiction widely considered to participate in social and political action, it was also regularly published in periodicals together with scholarly essays and articles on contemporary political developments. By taking fiction published in journals as her subject, Remnek indicates the interpenetration of the realms of fiction and fact in Russian journalism. Jehanne Gheith continues this delineation of the blurred boundary as she argues that the study of journalism is more than an exploration of its perceptible products.

Gheith's essay addresses the connections between women's journalism and the social in another way as well. She notes the vital role that salons (and later circles) played in the creation and maintenance of journalism; salons provided spaces in which people could meet, discuss ideas, and make the personal connections essential to founding and continuing any journalistic enterprise. And women, of course, were often central to the functioning of salons. Facilitating connections between people is one form of activism (or at least a factor without which activism cannot be enduring or collective). Personal empowerment may be another form of activism, especially if it empowers others as well; several of the essays indicate that women used journalism in just this way (e.g., Lindenmeyr, Norton). In addition, as Adele Lindenmeyr indicates in her discussion of the merchant woman journalist Anna Volkova, the rhythms of the personal and political could be very close. Through her journalism and private writing, Volkova created an alternative gender script; it is probable that other women (both as readers and writers) used journalism in a similar way.

Carolyn Marks, in fact, suggests that the women's press often did provide women with just such alternative scripts. Specifically, throughout the 1880s, the repertoire of roles made available to women in the "women's magazine" increased, and these magazines provided venues for women to move beyond traditional domestic occupations, certainly a political move in Russia of the late nineteenth century. In this way, the women's magazine both mirrored and helped to create changing gender roles in Russian society. Further, as Christine Ruane demonstrates, the fashion press engaged important social issues, such as Russia's relationship to the West, in ways different from those that have usually been studied.

Examining the women's press reveals largely unexplored aspects of Russian society and culture (e.g., by focusing attention on publications on fashion or for/about children). Such periodicals have not been considered important until quite recently,[22] but they had a formative influence on certain groups in Russian society (see Ruane, Marks). Further, study of women's role in journalism raises important questions about historiography: that such publications have not been considered important (and are now beginning to be) reveals that in concentrating only on certain kinds of journals, scholarship on Russia throughout the nineteenth and twentieth centuries has left out a great deal of material important for understanding Russian life and letters. And in discussing the ways that researching women's journalistic work enhances this scholarship, it is important to make two points that are in uneasy relation to each other. First, periodicals aimed at children and those concentrating on fashion should be taken more seriously than they have been, as they are important cultural and social indicators. And second, although many women did contribute to fashion and children's journals, they published in other venues as well. It is vital, then, both to examine Russian women's participation in all varieties of journalism and to reevaluate the significance of publications for children and those on upbringing *(vospitanie)* and fashion. Studying what are usually considered "secondary" journals not only reveals new facets of Russian society but also recontextualizes prior knowledges and allows for new conceptualizations of Russian history and journalism.

A corollary of the social effects of women's journalism is, of course, censorship, the controls placed on writings perceived to have the potential to upset the status quo. The history of censorship in Russia, its ebbs and flows in terms of relative strictness and permissiveness, should be kept in mind in reading *An Improper Profession,* for in each period, censorship partly determined what it was possible to publish and how publications were interpreted.

Periods of increased restrictions were usually related to external events (such as the tightening of censorship after the European revolutions of 1830 and 1848, or in 1881 after the assassination of Alexander II); there were also periods of relative permissiveness, as after the press reforms of 1865 (part of the Great Reforms of Alexander II) or during the Russian Revolution of 1905.[23] This fact provides important background for the essays in this volume, as it indicates why, for instance, political matters could be discussed more directly in the press after 1905 than in the 1850s. At the same time, though, the research in this collection demonstrates that taking women's journalism into account means that the effects of censorship must be read differently than they have been to date, and that, in many cases, periods of repressive censorship actually led to increased opportunities for women journalists and the women's press. The 1850s, for example, represented a flowering of Russian women's writing. And Carolyn Marks argues that the 1880s, generally seen as a time of great repression (and rightly so for certain periodicals and for certain populations), also allowed new possibilities.[24] Thus in that decade the increased restrictions on journals that the government perceived as a potential threat allowed for the proliferation of women's magazines, which were (inaccurately) perceived as nonthreatening or apolitical.[25] Anna Volkova also made her entrance into journalism in the 1880s, as did the three reporters Mary Zirin discusses: Ol'ga Novikova, Anastasiia Kairova, and Varvara Mak-Gakhan. The latter three began careers in journalism as a direct result of the Balkan crises, which may seem only tenuously related to issues of censorship. And yet there is a connection: in times when men are otherwise occupied (as in war) or when their activities (such as publishing) are restricted, new opportunities are opened to women.

The major studies of censorship, too, have focused on male journalists,[26] so that the relationship between women and censorship in Russia is almost entirely unexplored. Important questions to raise in this regard include, Did censorship operate differently in the case of women? That is, did censors, because of their understanding of gender properties, prohibit women from publishing on topics that were not off-limits for men? And did censorship affect women differently from men?

The essays in this volume (particularly those by Marks, Zirin, and Norton) provide answers to some of these questions. The limited available evidence suggests that though censorship affected everyone, censors were influenced by societal norms of what constituted proper language and topics for women and so, at least occasionally, would impose different restrictions on women than they did on men.[27] In addition, women were often refused the right to become editors (and sometimes publishers) of journals on the basis of their limited "literary experience."[28] Because men had many more opportunities to gain such experience, this amounts to a gender-based distinction. It is important to note here that, as far as we are aware, there were no female censors, and given the structure of state service in which, by law, only men could participate, it is unlikely that a woman could have been appointed to an official government post in late imperial Russia. But we are suspicious of this conclusion, as the common wisdom has long held that there were no Russian female journalists or writers. Further, women were occasionally appointed to government positions—and even served in the military (Dashkova, Durova).[29] Following our general model, then, regarding censorship, too, this volume both proposes answers about the relation of censorship and women and raises questions for future scholarship.

Like the maps of the world that reverse the placement of countries, thereby foregrounding unconscious political assumptions, one could retell the story of Russian journalism focusing primarily on women. In such a retelling, the history of Russian journalism would look very different from traditional accounts. One could easily make a case for the "feminization" of Russian journalism from its inception, by exploring Princess Dashkova's or Catherine II's achievements as central to the development of Russian journalism.[30] Or one could point to women's involvement in *Vestnik Evropy* (*European Herald*, 1802–1830), founded by Nikolai Karamzin and one of the most important periodicals of the first quarter of the nineteenth century.[31] A further result of reversing the journalistic map would be to emphasize debates other than those that are usually rehearsed—rather than focus on Karamzin's role in elaborating a Russian literary language, for example, we might instead view Dashkova's insistence that women become literate in Russian (rather than French) as a central fact in the development of a Russian reading public. But we are not interested in simple reversal, salutary as that may be; rather, we want to analyze women's involvement in journalism as an integral part of the history of journalism in Russia.

An Improper Profession accomplishes this reintegration in a number of ways. Beginning in the mid-1820s and 1830s, a time that represents not only a flowering of Russian journalism but also a period when women were becoming increasingly visible in Russian letters (two perhaps related developments), the chapters tell the story of women's role in shaping journalism—as publishers, authors, readers, and sometimes in more subtle ways. The essays do not follow a consistent trajectory, or a narrative of progress, but rather an account of various moments and movements in Russian women's journalism and an exploration of their significance for Russian letters and society. Although the essays may be read separately, they are connected to one another and build on each other: there is a dialogue among the essays (this does not, of course, imply a unified viewpoint or a single methodology).

The essays in this volume cover approximately a century (from the early nineteenth to the early twentieth century), and they follow a more or less chronological order. One caveat: we decided to focus on *Russian* women journalists in part because of our own fields of expertise, but also our sense that, at this time, in-depth scholarship of Russian women's journalism has more transformative potential than would a broad overview of female journalists of all the nationalities in the Russian empire. This latter—deeply important—work must remain a task for future scholarship.

Moving to the essays: Miranda Remnek discusses female readers from 1825 to 1840, suggesting both that the Russian reading public was larger than has usually been thought and that women made up a sizable component of those readers. Further, focusing mainly on the readership of serialized novels, Remnek also shows that whereas

INTRODUCTION 13

many female readers were, as one would expect, from the upper nobility, a significant proportion were from the middle estates. Remnek is one of the few scholars to explore readership in this period, and she is the first to make female readers a primary focus.

Jehanne Gheith's essay examines the work of the early journalists Avdot'ia Panaeva and Evgeniia Tur. These two women represent different aspects of what it meant to be both female and journalist in the middle of the nineteenth century. Panaeva was active in the circle around the leading journal *Sovremennik (The Contemporary)*, as a contributor, facilitator, and informal member of the editorial board, and Tur worked in an editorial capacity for Mikhail Katkov's *Russkii vestnik (Russian Herald)* and later edited and published a periodical of her own, *Russkaia rech' (Russian Speech)*. Gheith shows how an exploration of the journalistic activities of these two women necessitates an understanding of Russian journalism that goes beyond material factors such as funding, authors, editors, and censorship, and she encourages an exploration of all these terms.

Christine Ruane begins with a brief history of the development of the fashion press in Russia, analyzing *Moda: Zhurnal dlia svetskikh liudei (Fashion: A Journal for High Society,* 1851–1861). Although Ruane focuses mainly on one journal and its female editor, Nadezhda Utilova, providing a detailed accounting of the journal's evolution, she also indicates the broader implications of the fashion press for Russian society. The Russian fashion industry developed in relation to the West, specifically France, and Ruane's study reveals new aspects both of the process of defining a Russian sense of nationality and of the relationship between Russia and France as Russia worked to develop native fashion traditions. The fashion press, in her analysis, is a means of entering modernity as well as a way of making connections both socially and geographically, that is, both between the different social estates and between the provinces and the capitals. Finally, Ruane demonstrates the links between the development of the fashion press and larger social issues such as serfdom and the woman question.

Carolyn Marks discusses yet another aspect of women's journalism in Russia: the trajectory, in the 1880s, of the women's magazine (that is, a magazine not necessarily edited by a woman but one that was aimed at a primarily female audience). Marks shows how by creating and reflecting certain images of women in their pages, these magazines directly and indirectly influenced women; she also discusses the women's magazine as a larger social and economic indicator. By focusing on material concerns (including how advances in printing technology affected women's publications) and other societal factors, Marks demonstrates that while the 1880s were a period of increased censorship and repression, for women this decade was, in many ways, a time of expanding professional and domestic possibilities. Further, her biographies and analyses of editors of women's magazines, both men and women, are an example of the kind of reintegration we are attempting in and by this volume: Marks details some of the specific ways that women and men together created the journalistic field in Russia.

Marks's discussion of the merchant journalist Anna Volkova provides a link to Adele Lindenmeyr's essay, which explores Volkova's journalistic career and private life in other contexts and in greater detail. Volkova edited both *Drug zhenshchin* (*Woman's Friend,* 1882–1884) and *Drug zhivotnykh* (*Animal's Friend,* 1899)—an oddly ironic coincidence of title—and also published regularly in the periodical press. Lindenmeyr uses Volkova's writings, both her semi-private diaries and her published articles, to show how she perceived and represented herself as a female journalist, arguing that Volkova employed both kinds of writing to develop different scripts for what it meant to be a woman in Russian society. Lindenmeyr also details the ways that writing and editing for Volkova (as for many others of her generation) was personal and yet also had a larger social significance. Particularly in the 1880s, these activities were both a "psychological outlet" and a means of constructing an alternative and positive vision for Russia's future.

In her essay on three women reporters in the Balkan crises of 1875–1880, Mary Zirin explores how wartime needs for up-to-the-minute reporting, technological advances (the telegraph), and personal circumstances made it possible for Ol'ga Novikova, Anastasiia Kairova, and Varvara Mak-Gakhan to report on current developments—even from the front, in Kairova's case. These journalists were engaged in different kinds of work, but for all three, the Balkan crises served as a catalyst for journalistic careers, and their time abroad proved crucial for their development as journalists. This suggests that times of upheaval or crisis, as well as changes of scene, may afford possibilities for women that are not available in times of relative stasis. Finally, the three women's careers all contributed to the advancement of women in general and women journalists in particular (whether or not Novikova, Kairova, and Mak-Gakhan intended this). As Zirin puts it, they proved that they were "up to the challenges of international journalism," thus moving the question of whether women could do this kind of reporting out of the realm of the theoretical.

Both Rochelle Ruthchild and Linda Edmondson explore Mariia Pokrovskaia's work, though in different contexts, and both authors illustrate the problematic nature of (re)constructing feminism in late imperial Russia. Ruthchild discusses Pokrovskaia as a feminist activist and journalist, whereas Edmondson places her in the history of Russian women's journalism and explores the significance of Pokrovskaia's *Zhenskii vestnik* (*Women's Herald*, 1904–1917) for the Russian women's movement.

By considering four very different journalists (Pokrovskaia, Mariia Chekhova, Liubov' Gurevich, and Ariadna Tyrkova), Ruthchild highlights the diversity of the feminist movement in Russia at and beyond the turn of the century. She argues convincingly that there was much more to early Russian feminism than the bourgeois element with which it is often identified, and, conversely, that not all Russian feminists subsumed the cause of women to larger social and political goals. Ruthchild also reveals the increased opportunities available for women journalists after 1905 and shows the multiple ways women were involved in writing, editing, and activism, as well as the linkages between these activities.

Where Ruthchild discusses Pokrovskaia in the context of a study of the lives and careers of three other female and feminist journalists, Edmondson treats Pokrovskaia separately. In her chapter, Edmondson situates *Zhenskii vestnik* as being both important for and peripheral to the women's movement in Russia. She argues that although the journal was openly concerned with women's health and position in society, it was not identified with the liberal-radical Liberation movement at a time when many feminists saw such an alliance as crucial. Isolated from these feminists, Pokrovskaia was also one of the few to claim the term "feminist" as positive, and this resulted in her being further marginalized. Throughout her essay, Edmondson raises important questions about the nature of influence and how working from the margins may limit audience. As with Marks's and Lindenmeyr's discussions of Volkova, the different angles from which Ruthchild and Edmondson view Pokrovskaia serve as a concrete reminder of the multifaceted nature of these women's lives and careers, and the concomitant need to explore them from a variety of perspectives.

Barbara Norton also focuses on an activist-journalist of the late nineteenth and early twentieth century. In her essay, she explores the journalism of Ekaterina Kuskova, revealing the many ways in which it was a means of both personal and political empowerment. While Kuskova, in her later years, may be described as a feminist, the issue of her feminism is a vexed one, as Norton indicates. Initially, Kuskova seemed uninterested in feminism, and although she gradually developed a feminist consciousness and openly advocated women's rights, feminist concerns were not paramount in her journalism, a fact that probably helped her to avoid becoming marginalized like Pokrovskaia. Norton's essay ties together many of the themes that other essays in the volume address, such as financial need, the connections between journalism and activism, and those between journalism and gender.

The volume ends with June Pachuta Farris's bibliographic essay and, in the appendix, her checklist of women journalists in imperial Russia (compiled with the assistance of Rhonda Clark, Barbara Norton, and Mary Zirin). Farris's essay, which identifies and discusses sources for the study of Russian women journalists, provides a starting point for all further research on the subject. It comprises a comprehensive and detailed guide through the (mainly Russian and English) sources, including information on archival finding aids and electronic information services. Her checklist, although still a work in progress, as Farris notes, constitutes the most extensive compilation of information about Russian women journalists to date.

By offering new interpretations, based on both archival and published sources, about individual female journalists and the contexts within which they worked, *An Improper Profession* makes possible both more informed discussions of women's role in journalism and a more accurate view of Russian journalism as a whole. Women, as the essays in this volume demonstrate, contributed to Russian journalism in many areas, including fashion, education, foreign affairs, and social and political activism. And women helped to define and reflect public opinion in a variety of ways—as publishers, editors, reporters, writers, and readers.

Yet many important issues remain unresolved: it is unclear, for example, whether we can accurately speak of a "tradition" of Russian women's journalism.[32] As several of the contributors point out (e.g., Gheith, Zirin), it appears that many of Russia's female journalists were unaware of one another.[33] Conscious imitation of, or departure from, one's predecessors is one of the essential elements in most definitions of "tradition," so this lack of awareness indicates that female journalists did not make up a "tradition" in any usual sense.[34] Although scholars may, in time, discover that these women were in fact aware of one another, even if that turns out not to be the case, each female journalist made it easier in some sense for those who followed—if not in providing role models, then in making journalistic work socially acceptable. In addition, women's participation in journalism calls into question the idea of tradition itself, its importance as an indicator of influence or value. That is, as this volume makes clear, women were actively engaged in creating the field of Russian journalism, and whether their work constitutes a conscious tradition is less important than examining their activities and influence. Such exploration is the project of this volume, a project that indicates the limitations of traditional understandings of journalism.

The essays in *An Improper Profession* demonstrate, first, that women participated in nearly every level of journalism; this in itself is major new information. The volume delineates the nature of this participation, showing that journals were an outlet for social and political activity for female journalists as much as they were a vehicle for self-expression and, further, that "trivial" periodicals such as journals on fashion had significant social and political content. The chapters also trace the trajectories of women journalists and demonstrate that a life career as a journalist offered women an alternative to more traditional gender roles. Career trajectories differed by gender: for example, women journalists were affected differently from men by intensified censorship partly because, during times of increased censorship, women were offered and claimed new opportunities in seemingly nonthreatening venues such as women's magazines. Finally, *An Improper Profession* makes it clear that women's journalistic work cannot fully be understood in a separate context, since there is no tradition of women's journalism that can be extracted from the larger context of Russian journalism. The counterstatement is also true: journalism by men did not exist separately from journalism by women. By reclaiming fashion and mediation as important political measures, by showing that restrictive periods of censorship for men could open up opportunities for women, by exploring the varieties of activism in women's journalism, *An Improper Profession* reveals that the scope of Russian journalism was much wider and richer than has previously been imagined.

Notes

1 I use "we" and "our" throughout, as many of the ideas developed in this introduction grew out of conversations with my coeditor, Barbara Norton.
2 *Literary Journals in Imperial Russia,* a recent collection (Cambridge, 1997) edited by Deborah Martinsen, is a notable and welcome exception. For other works that directly address the development of journalism in Russia, see Effie Ambler, *Russian Journalism and Politics: The Career of Aleksei S. Suvorin, 1861–1881* (Detroit, 1972); B. I. Esin, *Istoriia russkoi zhurnalistiki XIX v.* (Moscow, 1989); Gary Marker, *Publishing, Printing, and the Origins of Intellectual Life in Russia, 1700–1800* (Princeton, 1985); Louise McReynolds, *The News under Russia's Old Regime: The Development of a Mass-Circulation Press* (Princeton, 1991); Charles Ruud, *Russian Entrepreneur: Publisher Ivan Sytin of Moscow, 1851–1934* (Montreal and Kingston, 1990); Mark Steinberg, *Moral Communities: The Culture of Class Relations in the Russian Printing Industry, 1867–1907* (Berkeley, 1992).
3 Publisher *(izdatel'/nitsa)* refers to the person who backed the periodical financially; editor *(redaktor),* to those who solicited contributions, read and edited them, and were responsible for the daily running of the journal. In some instances, one person fulfilled both functions.
4 Rhonda Lebedev Clark's recent pioneering dissertation provides a great deal of important information on Russian women journalists. See Clark, "Forgotten Voices: Women in Periodical Publishing of Late Imperial Russia, 1860–1905" (Ph.D. diss., University of Minnesota, 1996). There is one other full-length work on the topic, G. S. Lapshina, *Sila slovoiu zhivogo* (Moscow, 1992), and several shorter pieces: B. I. Esin, *Puteshestvie v proshloe: Gazetnyi mir XIX veka* (Moscow, 1983), 59–64; Gitta Hammarberg, "*Zhurnal dlia milykh,* or Sex and the Single Girl-Reader," paper presented at the AAASS Convention, Philadelphia,

1994; Louise McReynolds, "Female Journalists in Prerevolutionary Russia," *Journalism History* 14, no. 4 (winter 1987): 104–10; and Mary Zirin, "Aleksandra Ishimova and *The Captain's Daughter:* A Conjecture," *Pacific Coast Philology* 15, no. 2 (December 1980): 41–47. These essays and monographs represent a tremendous achievement, as it is still difficult to find even very basic information such as birth and death dates for many female journalists. We also want to stress that taken together, the works listed discuss only a small percentage of the female journalists working in Russia in the late imperial period, and none of these studies attempts an overarching structure for understanding women, gender, and journalism in late imperial Russia. Rhonda Clark's dissertation begins this important work.

5 See, for example, Daniel Balmuth, *Censorship in Russia, 1860–1905* (Washington, D.C., 1979); *Russkaia periodicheskaia pechat' (1702–1894): Spravochnik,* ed. A. G. Dement'ev, A. V. Zapadov, and M. S. Cherepakhov (Moscow, 1959); V. Evgen'ev-Maksimov, *"Sovremennik" pri Chernyshevskom i Dobroliubove* (Leningrad, 1936); *Russkaia periodicheskaia pechat', 1703–1900 gg.,* comp. N. M. Lisovskii (Petrograd, 1915); Marker, *Publishing;* Ruud, *Fighting Words: The Imperial Censorship and the Russian Press, 1804–1906* (Toronto, 1982), and *Russian Entrepreneur.* See note 4 for scholarship that does focus on women's participation in the journalistic world.

6 We define the "women's press" as those periodicals created with a primarily female audience in mind or for whom women were the primary readers (these periodicals were founded and edited by both men and women).

7 We generally agree with the large body of recent scholarship on gender that argues that "woman" is a culturally constructed category, and that definitions of "women" are complex, culturally specific, and often problematic. For the purposes of this discussion, we use the term "woman" to mean those who were defined as such in nineteenth- and early-twentieth-century Russia. For several examples of scholarship that problematizes the concept "woman," see Judith Butler, *Gender Trouble: Feminism and the Subversion of Identity* (New York, 1990); Patricia Hill Collins, *Black Feminist Thought: Knowledge, Consciousness, and the Politics of Empowerment* (1990; New York, 1991); Marjorie Garber, *Vested Interests: Cross-Dressing and Cultural Anxiety* (New York, 1992); and Linda Nicholson, "Interpreting Gender," *Signs* (autumn 1994): 79–105.

8 See, for example, Nikolai Novikov's *Modnoe ezhemesiachnoe izdanie, ili Biblioteka dlia damskogo tualeta* (1779) and *Aglaia,* which came out in two variants. N. M. Karamzin edited *Aglaia,* a yearly almanac that appeared in 1794–1795 and 1796; P. Shalikov published *Aglaia,* a

monthly journal, from 1808 to 1810 (and a further six issues in 1812). For the early nineteenth century, see also *Zhurnal dlia milykh* (1804) and *Damskii zhurnal* (1823–1833).

9 Although the Russian *soslovie* (plural *sosloviia*) does not translate cleanly into Western understandings of class or estates, "estates" gives the closest approximation to the legal divisions in Russian society. See Gregory L. Freeze, "The *Soslovie* (Estate) Paradigm and Russian Social History," *American Historical Review* 91, no. 1 (1986): 11–36.

10 Scholarly opinion about the professionalization of journalism varies widely, which indicates both the difficulty of discussing professions in the Russian context and the fluid status of journalism in late imperial Russia. Louise McReynolds argues that as late as the 1890s, journalism had not attained the status of a profession, while Gary Marker seems to imply a profession already emerging in the late eighteenth century. See McReynolds, *News,* 147, 153–59, and Gary Marker, "The Creation of Journals and the Profession of Letters in the Eighteenth Century," in *Literary Journals,* 26. In *Russia's Missing Middle Class: The Professions in Russian History,* ed. Harley Balzer (Armonk, N.Y., 1996), Balzer assumes that journalism is a profession. Aside from one mention, however, he does not discuss it as such directly, and none of the essays in the volume is on the topic of journalism. In *Between Tsar and People,* another recent discussion of Russia's "middle," focusing on the notion of an emerging public identity and civil society (and including discussions of professions as part of that process), there are several references to journalism and one essay on the topic (the issue of journalism as a profession is not the topic of the essay). See Louise McReynolds, "V. M. Doroshevich: The Newspaper Journalist and the Development of Public Opinion in Civil Society," in *Between Tsar and People: Educated Society and the Quest for Public Identity in Late Imperial Russia,* ed. Edith W. Clowes et al. (Princeton, 1991), 233–47.

11 Scholarship on Russian women in the professions includes Toby W. Clyman, "Women Physicians' Autobiography in the Nineteenth Century," in *Women Writers in Russian Literature,* ed. Toby W. Clyman and Diana Greene (Westport, Conn., 1994), 111–25; Mary Schaeffer Conroy, "Women Pharmacists in Russia before World War I: Women's Emancipation, Feminism, Professionalization, Nationalism, and Class Conflict," in *Women and Society in Russia and the Soviet Union,* ed. Linda Edmondson (Cambridge, 1992), 48–76; Ann Hibner Koblitz, *A Convergence of Lives: Sofia Kovalevskaia, Scientist, Writer, Revolutionary* (Boston, 1983); Christine Ruane, *Gender, Class, and the Professionalization of Russian City Teachers, 1860–1914* (Pittsburgh, 1994);

Jeanette E. Tuve, *The First Russian Women Physicians* (Newtonville, Mass., 1984).

12 Initially, this "emancipation" was seen as a Western phenomenon and was closely associated with the novels of George Sand. For a discussion of the use of the term "feminism" in the West, see Jane Rendall, *The Origins of Modern Feminism: Women in Britain, France, and the United States, 1780–1860* (Hampshire and London, 1985).

13 See Linda Harriet Edmondson, *Feminism in Russia, 1900–1917* (Stanford, 1984), ix.

14 As an example of the differences, in the United States, feminists have tended to make the project of feminism primary, and also to advocate for legislated change. Russians who have focused on improving the position of women have usually argued that legislated change is meaningless without shifts in individual attitudes and have placed their concerns within the context of larger social change. While it has often been argued that such positions mean that few positive changes have actually been made in Russian women's lives, the fact that in the United States today we are seeing how laws may be revoked or threatened (e.g., abortion laws) should make us seriously consider the value of, and possibilities offered by, this more integrationist approach.

15 A growing body of work challenges the primacy of "the West" in (feminist) criticism. These include *Scattered Hegemonies: Postmodernity and Transnational Feminist Practices*, ed. Inderpal Grewal and Caren Kaplan (Minneapolis, 1994); Françoise Lionnet, *Postcolonial Representations: Women, Literature, Identity* (Ithaca, 1995); *Third World Women and the Politics of Feminism*, ed. Chandra Talpade Mohanty, Ann Russo, and Lourdes Torres (Bloomington, 1991); Rajeswari Sunder Rajan, *Real and Imagined Women: Gender, Culture, and Postcolonialism* (London, 1993).

16 Of the numerous recent works that help to define and describe the workings of gender in the Russian context, those we have found particularly illuminating include *Engendering Slavic Literatures*, ed. Pamela Chester and Sibelan Forrester (Bloomington, 1996); *Russia through Women's Eyes: Autobiographies from Tsarist Russia*, ed. Toby W. Clyman and Judith Vowles (New Haven, 1996); *Sexuality and the Body in Russian Culture*, ed. Jane T. Costlow, Stephanie Sandler, and Judith Vowles (Stanford, 1993); Barbara Alpern Engel, *Mothers and Daughters: Women of the Intelligentsia in Nineteenth-Century Russia* (1983; Cambridge and New York, 1987); Laura Engelstein, *The Keys to Happiness: Sex and the Search for Modernity in Fin-de-Siècle Russia* (Ithaca, 1992); Barbara Heldt, *Terrible Perfection: Women and Russian Litera-*

ture (Bloomington, 1987); *Russia, Women, Culture,* ed. Helena Goscilo and Beth Holmgren (Bloomington, 1996); *Gender Restructuring in Russian Studies,* ed. Marianne Liljeström, Eila Mäntysaari, and Arja Rosenholm (Tampere, 1993); *Gender and Russian Literature,* ed. Rosalind Marsh (Cambridge, 1996); Richard Stites, *The Women's Liberation Movement in Russia: Feminism, Nihilism, and Bolshevism, 1860–1930* (1978; Princeton, 1990). See also the works, cited elsewhere in these notes, by Linda Edmondson, Catriona Kelly, and Christine Ruane, as well as the *Dictionary of Women Writers,* ed. Marina Ledkovsky, Charlotte Rosenthal, and Mary Zirin (Westport, Conn., 1994).

17 See Alison Adburgham, *Women in Print: Writing Women and Women's Magazines from the Restoration to the Accession of Victoria* (London, 1972); Kathryn Shevelow, *Women and Print Culture: The Construction of Femininity in the Early Periodical* (New York, 1989); Cynthia L. White, *Women's Magazines, 1693–1968* (London, 1970).

18 See especially Shevelow, *Women and Print Culture.* Shevelow argues that English women entered journalism mainly through writing letters to the editor; their topics tended to be marriage, children, and domestic responsibilities. Thus the subversive act of women's entering the world of publication was accomplished through reinforcing cultural norms regarding femininity.

19 One of the main differences is that in Russia, people were working from a model of general oppression, and this demanded different strategies of resistance from the English case, in which political struggles tended to be against particular oppressions. This view is supported by the fact that the Russian case is similar to those of the Arab world and of marginalized groups within the United States. See Beth Baron, *The Women's Awakening in Egypt: Culture, Society, and the Press* (New Haven, 1994); and *Southern Horrors: The Anti-lynching Campaign of Ida B. Wells, 1892–1900,* ed. Jacqueline Jones Royster (Boston, 1997).

20 It is true that the progression in England may simply have been more gradual, as, with time, increasingly activist kinds of periodicals were founded there. Russian journalism in general developed later and more rapidly than did the English, so that we may discover that this compression is the main reason for the differences described.

21 See Balmuth, *Censorship in Russia;* Esin, *Istoriia;* McReynolds, *News;* Ruud, *Fighting Words.*

22 Several articles in *Russia, Women, Culture* indicate a growing awareness of the importance of fashion periodicals in Russia during the last several centuries. See, especially, the essays by Helena Goscilo and Ol'ga Vainshtein. See also the forthcoming book by Christine Ruane, *The*

Empire's New Clothes: A History of the Russian Fashion Industry, 1700–1917.

23 Censorship issues and press reform are discussed in several of the essays. For a detailed examination of these matters, see Balmuth, *Censorship in Russia,* and Ruud, *Fighting Words.*

24 Rhonda Clark argues along these same lines in "Forgotten Voices," 28. And Louise McReynolds notes: "The 1880s, generally slighted in the historiography as little more than a decade of repression, stand out as the decade when commercially based, mass-circulation newspapers began to establish themselves as public institutions" ("V. M. Doroshevich," 236).

25 The "entertainment" or "mass-circulation" press also flourished in and after the 1880s. On the growth of this press in the late nineteenth and early twentieth centuries, see Jeffrey Brooks, *When Russia Learned to Read: Literacy and Popular Literature, 1861–1917* (Princeton, 1985); Daniel R. Brower, "The Penny Press and Its Readers," in *Cultures in Flux: Lower-Class Values, Practices, and Resistance in Late Imperial Russia,* ed. Stephen P. Frank and Mark D. Steinberg (Princeton, 1994), 150; and McReynolds, *News.*

26 See, for example, Balmuth, *Censorship in Russia;* Ruud, *Fighting Words.*

27 Rhonda Clark's work shows convincingly that women did not have an easier time than men becoming editors and publishers, so we do not address questions along these lines. See Clark, "Forgotten Voices," 79. For examples of gendered censorship, see Tur to A. A. Kraevskii, MS Division, Saltykov-Shchedrin Library, f. 391, d. 689, ll. 3, 12, 29, 35, 53, 56, and Tur to E. V. Petrovo-Solovovo, Rossiiskaia gosudarstvennaia biblioteka (RGB), MS Division, ll. 93 and 95.

28 See Clark, "Forgotten Voices," 57–62; Clark does not consider this differentiation to be based on gender.

29 Princess Ekaterina Dashkova (1743–1810, née Vorontsova) was, after Catherine II, the most prominent female journalist of her day. In 1763 Dashkova helped publish *Nevinnoe uprazhnenie* and later established and published regularly in two scholarly monthlies, *Sobesednik liubitelei rossiiskogo slova . . .* (1783–1784) and *Novye ezhemesiachnye sochineniia* (1786–1796). Dashkova's writings also appeared in various other periodicals. Furthermore, as director of the Academy of Sciences and founding president of the Russian Academy (she held both posts coextensively from 1783 to 1796), Dashkova was in a position to wield a great deal of influence on the development of Russian letters. Nadezhda Durova (1783–1866) was an officer in the Napoleonic Wars. After her retirement, she published a series of autobiographical writings based on her diaries from these times; she wrote fiction as well.

30   Catherine the Great (reigned 1762–1796) was a significant figure in the history of Russian journalism in several ways. Among them was the fact that she made the important move of allowing a (temporary and limited) separation of state and printing by permitting private printing presses in 1783. She was also active in the running of *Vsiakaia vsiachina* (*All Sorts,* 1769), a satirical-moral periodical. As these activities indicate, Catherine fostered a culture in which journalism could be valued. Additionally, many women were involved in various aspects of journalism during Catherine's reign, suggesting that even if she did not directly encourage women's participation, she created a climate in which women felt relatively free to take up journalism. For more information, see Marker, *Publishing;* Kevin J. McKenna, "Empress behind the Mask: The *Persona* of MD Vsiakaia vsiachina in Catherine the Great's Periodical Essays on Morals and Manners," *Neophilologus* 74 (1990): 1–11.

31   Because, as several of the contributors note (e.g., Gheith, Zirin, Norton), women's journalistic labor is often not recorded in the usual sources on journalism, it is important to detail women's contributions where information is available. Regarding *Vestnik Evropy,* Karamzin's second wife and his daughter, Sofiia, hosted a salon, a crucial factor in fostering journalistic connections. And from 1808 to 1809, A. P. Elagina (1789–1877) copyedited and published translations in the journal—work similar to that done by Evgeniia Tur for Nadezhdin's *Teleskop* in the 1830s. These facts suggest that future research may discover that other women, too, collaborated on periodicals. On Elagina, see Lina Bernstein, "Women on the Verge of a New Language: Russian Salon Hostesses in the First Half of the Nineteenth Century," in *Russia, Women, Culture,* 216. On Tur, see E. V. Sukhovo-Kobylina [Tur], *Dnevnik* (November 1834–February 1834), Institut Russkoi Literatury, 25.495, *tetrad'* 3, ll. 2, 11, 29, entries of November 1834 (no day given), 7 January, and 7 February 1835.

32   In a pioneering article, Louise McReynolds has argued that in the case of female reporters, there was no "tradition" in Russia. See her "Female Journalists," 109.

33   These and related questions may be answered in the near future. There is a new interest in contemporary female journalists, as evidenced by the recently founded Russian Association of Women Journalists and a seminar on women journalists run by Nadezhda Azhgikhina and Irina Iurna (under the auspices of the Journalism Department at Moscow State University).

34   Some well-known studies on the topic of literary tradition are Harold Bloom, *The Anxiety of Influence* (New York, 1973); *The Invention of Tradition,* ed. Eric Hobsbawm and Terence Ranger (1983; Cambridge, 1994); Sandra M. Gilbert and Susan Gubar, *The Madwoman in the*

Attic: The Woman Writer and the Nineteenth-Century Literary Imagination (1979; New Haven, 1984); Iu. N. Tynianov, *Arkhaisty i novatory* (Leningrad, 1929). For a recent reimagining of tradition, see Daniel Cottom, *Ravishing Tradition: Cultural Forces and Literary History* (Ithaca, 1996). The term "reimagining of tradition" is a coinage from Terence Ranger, "The Invention of Tradition Revisited: The African Case," in *Legitimacy and the State in Twentieth-Century Africa*, ed. Terence Ranger and O. Vaughan (London, 1993).

"A Larger Portion of the Public"

Female Readers, Fiction, and the Periodical Press in the Reign of Nicholas I

MIRANDA BEAVEN REMNEK

The involvement of women in Russian journalism—as readers as well as producers of periodicals—did not occur suddenly after the Great Reforms of Alexander II. During the reign of Nicholas I (1825–1855), many cultural initiatives laid the groundwork for developments later in the century. By then, as the following essays by Christine Ruane and Carolyn Marks show, women's magazines sought to attract readers in various ways. One was by providing fiction, which under Nicholas I (as this essay seeks to demonstrate) brought increasing numbers of women to the reading of periodicals. Yet the extent of cultural diffusion in Nicholaevan Russia— and the role of women—continue to be underrepresented; a recent summary of the period from 1689 through the 1860s concluded that "literature and journals very much reflected an exclusive, largely noble, and generally male preserve in which the vast majority of Russians did not in any way participate." An earlier study by Donald Fanger articulated the same notion: "Through the 1820s and early 1830s, readers of current literature with any pretensions to seriousness were largely concentrated in the capitals. . . . More often than not they knew each other socially, since both the production and consumption of literature . . . tended to be very much a class affair."[1]

Even so, Fanger went on to note, "in 1827 . . . this situation was drawing to a close." In other words, the reading public was expanding from a single, male, largely noble (that is, aristocratic) audience;[2] as suggested by a chorus of observations in the memoirs and journals of the period, it now included a series of increasingly "middle-class" publics differentiated according to class and sex.[3] Indeed, historians have affirmed that the number of subscribers commanded by journals rose from an average of 600 to 1,200 per title in the 1820s to figures like 7,000 for Senkovskii's popular *Biblioteka dlia chteniia (Library for Reading)* by 1837.[4] It thus seems probable that reading audiences were expanding in the early reign of Nicholas I.[5] But there needs to be further inquiry into the dimensions of the individual publics.[6] Female readers, in England and elsewhere, have often been considered a factor in the expansion of reading audiences. And because the rise of novel reading is also seen as a contributing factor, I intend to focus on Russian women largely in terms of their interest in fiction—often obtained (in extract or in serialized form) from the periodical press.[7]

As used here, the phrase "periodical press" denotes both journals and almanacs.[8] Fiction was found more often in journals, but almanacs carried it (albeit in extract, given their pocket-size dimensions). Thus much of the evidence here will refer to almanacs as well as journals. Moreover, because fiction often appeared in periodicals, references in memoirs to novel reading are sometimes tantamount to references to journal reading and will occasionally be discussed without direct mention of periodicals. An emphasis on this aspect of women's novel reading will reveal a body of previously neglected female readers during the Nicholaevan era; hence my title "A Larger Portion of the Public." A variation of this phrase occurs in a well-known essay on reading in Russia published in 1802 by Nikolai Karamzin.[9] My motive in adapting the phrase is to emphasize that even before the 1830s there appears to have been a larger public than we are often led to think. I also want to suggest, by linking the concept of female readers with readers of novels, that women may have constituted a larger portion of that public.[10]

Students of the history of readership in general will be aware of the difficulties presented by the paucity of primary data. The study of intellectual reading habits is least problematic: intellectuals tend to leave a host of memoirs and the like. But the middle levels of society leave fewer records. There are other sources of data, such as journal and newspaper subscriptions, library circulation records, and censorship lists, but these are often scarce for periods such as the early nineteenth century.[11] The difficulty becomes greater when the study involves women, for their traditional lack of visibility also applies to their reading. The problem is intensified when the study concerns a patriarchal society such as early-nineteenth-century Russia, in which women were not expected to follow intellectual pursuits.[12] However, some memoirs exist, including one or two by obscure women in straitened circumstances.[13] I also refer to belletristic literature, for although the use of literature as historical source material is considered risky by some, scholars such as A. V. Blium have advocated the judicious inclusion of this kind of evidence.[14]

My final resource is a group of twenty-two subscription lists (almost 12,000 subscriptions) discovered in a variety of Russian imprints covering the period from 1825 to 1846, and, in particular, a cluster of five within this group that were taken from almanacs.[15] The information in the lists is rich, often including full name, sex, title, profession, class, rank, and/or geographic provenance. The value of these data for readership history is clear; instead of a faceless group of 7,000 subscribers (associated with the record-breaking journal *Biblioteka dlia chteniia*), the individuals in these lists emerge as distinct readers, often with clearly marked roles in Russian society. Although the lists record subscribers, not readers, to estimate readership one need only point to a statement made in 1848 by Prince P. Viazemskii: "Sometimes a journal here has 4,000 to 5,000 subscribers, consequently up to 100,000 readers."[16]

Most of the lists were found in separately published editions, but five represent issues of almanacs published from 1825 to 1842.[17] The information they provide about women is important to the study of women readers. Although the yearly almanacs — with an average edition size of 1,200 copies — could not match the circulation figures of monthly journals (by which almanacs were supplanted in the late 1830s), they were more vital than journals in the early reign of Nicholas I. Besides the fact that their popularity paralleled a vogue for almanacs throughout Europe, there was a practical reason for their currency in Russia. Because the censorship apparatus regarded periodical literature as dangerous owing to its wide appeal and frequency of publication, publishers turned to the serial almanac, which allowed more time for the resolution of censorship difficulties.[18] Thus almanacs constituted a crucial element of the periodical literature available to readers in the second quarter of the century.

Fiction and the Periodical Press

In the early years of Nicholas I's reign, poetry, not prose fiction, constituted the major vehicle of Russian literature, and almanacs, not journals, largely conveyed this genre to the educated Russian public. Almanacs themselves were hardly numerous until the appearance of titles such as *Poliarnaia zvezda (Polar Star)* in 1823, *Mnemozina* in 1824, and *Severnye tsvety (Northern Flowers)* in 1825, and poetry was also published in separate editions.

Before this, Russians had been well supplied with fiction in the form of foreign novels, often published in translation, separately and in journals. During the reign of Alexander I, popular novelists had included August Lafontaine, August von Kotzebue, Stéphanie-Félicité de Genlis, and Ann Radcliffe. Their popularity continued well into the 1820s, although the years 1827–1829 are better known as marking the summit of Sir Walter Scott's popularity in Russia. The picture changes with the 1830s. In Matvei Ol'khin's bookstore catalog of 1846 (with coverage from 1831), translations of Scott have fallen to three entries and Radcliffe to only one, whereas Paul de Kock tops the list with thirty-six entries, followed by Eugène Sue, Alexandre Dumas, Honoré de Balzac, George Sand, and James Fenimore Cooper.[19]

As mentioned, novels were also published in journals, in extract or installments. In the late 1820s, three journals in particular published Western novels: Nikolai Grech's *Syn otechestva (Son of the Fatherland)*, Nikolai Polevoi's *Moskovskii telegraf (Moscow Telegraph)*, and Shalikov's *Damskii zhurnal (Ladies' Journal)*. *Syn otechestva* and *Moskovskii telegraf* published Samuel Richardson, Scott, Victor Hugo, and Balzac, and lesser lights such as Lafontaine, Radcliffe, and Genlis. *Damskii zhurnal* was largely filled with tales by French women writers, some little known but others, like Genlis, of widespread popularity. Of the three, *Syn otechestva* survived longest into the 1830s and was joined by others that included novels among their offerings. Senkovskii's *Biblioteka dlia chteniia*, established in 1834, was successful but controversial, not least because of Senkovskii's habit of rewriting the endings of novels (for example, Balzac's *Père Goriot*).[20] Mikhail Pogodin's *Moskovskii nabliudatel'*

(Moscow Observer) published George Sand's *Simon* in 1836, and Andrei Kraevskii's *Otechestvennye zapiski (Notes of the Fatherland)*, founded in 1839, published translations of Sand on a regular basis.[21]

With the publication of Pushkin's *Evgenii Onegin (Eugene Onegin)* beginning in 1825, Mikhail Lermontov's *Geroi nashego vremeni (Hero of Our Time)* in 1840, and Nikolai Gogol's *Mertvye dushi (Dead Souls)* in 1842, the period witnessed three first-rate works of Russian literature. Like foreign novels, the new Russian fiction often appeared in extract in journals and almanacs. Prior to its full edition of 1833, *Onegin* was included in extract in the almanac *Severnye tsvety* in 1827 and *Nevskii al'manakh (Neva Almanac)* in 1829, as well as in the journal *Moskovskii vestnik (Moscow Messenger)* in 1827 and 1828. Lermontov's *Geroi* also appeared in *Otechestvennye Zapiski*. No one would dispute the significance of these novels, but their prestige has reinforced the view that the reading public was a small, discriminating coterie of like-minded men. And the tendency in literary studies to focus on canonized novels has obscured the fact that many other works were also widely read.[22] Yet a full consideration of the contemporary public cannot ignore the cultural significance of such works or their readers.

The domestic novels of authors such as Faddei Bulgarin, Mikhail Zagoskin, and Ivan Lazhechnikov emerged in the late 1820s. Bulgarin's *Ivan Vyzhigin* was featured in 1825–1827 in his own journal, *Severnyi arkhiv (Northern Archive)*, before its best-selling edition of 1829, and extracts from his second novel, *Dmitrii Samozvanets*, appeared in *Nevskii al'manakh* (also in 1829). Zagoskin's second major work, *Roslavlev* (1831), was published in extract in N. I. Nadezhdin's journal *Teleskop (Telescope)*, and his short novel *Vecher na Khopre (Evening on the Hopyor)* was included in the journal *Biblioteka dlia chteniia* in 1834. Lazhechnikov's *Poslednii Novik (The Last Novik)* was issued serially in 1831, 1832, and 1833, and a chapter also appeared in the almanac *Sirotka (Orphan)* in 1831. His second major success, *Ledianoi dom (Ice Palace)*, was featured in the almanac *Dennitsa (Daybreak)* in 1834 and was also serialized in *Teleskop* in 1834 and 1835, before its appearance in a separate edition.[23] Thus, like journals, almanacs served as repositories for contemporary fiction. And some almanac editors, like some journal editors, catered specifically to the female audience: while P. N. Shalikov's *Damskii zhurnal* was appearing in Moscow from 1823 to 1833, S. N. Glinka issued a similar publication from 1826 to 1829 entitled *Moskovskii al'manakh dlia prekrasnogo pola (Moscow Almanac for the Fair Sex)*.

However, novel reading in general was widespread and increasing in the early years of Nicholas I's reign.[24] Analysis of the subscription list for Bulgarin's best-seller *Ivan Vyzhigin* reveals that of 410 subscribers, those solely identifiable as aristocrats or landowners account for only 14. A larger number (179) identify themselves as military officers or civil servants; 73 others are noblemen whose service sphere is unspecified. In addition, 11 subscribers can be identified as professionals, and 44 as merchants.[25] The number of subscriptions does not, of course, define the novel's audience. (The first edition of 1829, a total of 4,000 copies, apparently sold out in three weeks, and two more editions in 1830 brought the total to 7,000 copies sold.)[26] But the presence of 44 merchants (including, it is true, 16 booksellers) may already surprise those who have considered the reading public a small, homogeneous group.

If we then examine the subscribers according to their position in the Table of Ranks, and add the military, civil, and other nobles in the average-to-lower ranks (nine through fourteen) to the 44 merchants, the total is 123.[27] If this figure is added to those whose status is similar or unspecified, and therefore probably low, the result is a group of middle-rank readers approaching 206 of 410 subscribers. Since the list of subscribers to *Ivan Vyzhigin* appeared in the 1820s before the impact of such novels had truly been felt, this figure, though imprecise, already suggests an expanding audience. In the case of *Petr Ivanovich Vyzhigin* (1831), the number of merchant subscribers increased to 16.9 percent (versus 10.7 percent for *Ivan Vyzhigin*), or 121 of 716 subscribers.[28]

Female Readers

According to male memoirs, women read novels assiduously. Konstantin Batiushkov remembers the works of Mme. de Genlis as one of the "catechisms for young ladies." Pushkin in 1830 laments ironically: "Our ladies . . . do not read [the critics] . . . instead they read that coarse Walter Scott." Belinskii in 1836 portrays the reception of the journal *Biblioteka dlia chteniia* by the family of a provincial landowner and presents the daughter as drawn to the fiction of Zagoskin and Konstantin Masal'skii.[29] The male view in belles lettres is equally suggestive. In a scene set in St. Petersburg in 1827, a visiting landowner complains to a bookseller: "My purse is empty! If it weren't for my daughter . . . I wouldn't buy your novel for anything." In Bulgarin's *Ivan Vyzhigin,* images range from the country gentlewoman Mrs. Gologordovskii and her "affable" daughters reading romances, to the name day feast of a provincial lawyer's wife, who displays French journals, to the fifteen-year-old Grunia, who sits reading "La Nouvelle Héloise."[30] Thus we already have evidence of a female audience for novels, and indeed that male observers identified women with novels.

Evidence from women — often as condescending as the male portraits — makes it equally clear that novel reading was widespread. An Englishwoman in Russia in the late 1840s notes that well-born ladies were spending their leisure reading "silly French romances," and she adds, "the amusements of the country ladies in winter are very few — driving in sledges, practicing piano, and reading French novels."[31] The memoirs of Russian women are also sometimes dismissive of novels. Praskov'ia Tatlina, from a Moscow clerical family, first read fiction at about the age of ten, in 1818. She delights in Christian Heinrich Spiess and Radcliffe, but not the moralizing tales of Mme. de Genlis. Two years later she reads Voltaire, whose tone is so disturbing to her traditional upbringing that she is tempted to throw the book on the fire.[32]

This is exactly what another woman reader does. Nadezhda Sokhanskaia, an intense young gentlewoman from the Ukrainian steppe, is so frustrated by her reading material in the early 1840s that she begins to burn a trunk full of "brigand novels" *(razboinichie romany).* Her earlier reading had included journals such as *Vestnik Evropy (European Herald)* — begun by Karamzin in 1802 — and writers such as Pushkin and Zhukovskii. Later she read a story by Gogol, published in 1834 in the almanac *Novosel'e (Housewarming),* as well as authors such as Radcliffe, Bulgarin, and Zagoskin, whom she read, at age eight, around 1831. Her further reading included Polevoi, Lazhechnikov, Marlinskii, Masal'skii, and even François August René Chateaubriand.[33]

Sokhanskaia's autobiography is among the richest sources for female reading habits. Unmarried, with little to do after her return from school at Khar'kov Institute in 1840, she read avidly: "I was overwhelmed with energy for reading. Not before or during the institute had it so encircled all desires.... When I thought of books... I felt chills and fire, a genuine fever... I was ready not to eat and not to sleep for days on end, just give me books!"[34] Other women also indicate enthusiasm for novels. Anna Smirnova read extensively but was especially attracted to Walter Scott, whom she read both at court in St. Petersburg in the late 1820s and together with Karamzin's daughter, Sofiia (who was passionately fond of English novels).[35] Tat'iana Passek, with her cousin Aleksandr Herzen, read Johann Wolfgang von Goethe, Friedrich Schiller, and Jean Jacques Rousseau in Moscow in 1829, but later, while staying with her husband Vadim in Tver' in the winter of 1833–1834, she was clearly reading Lazhechnikov's *Poslednii Novik*—for she was delighted to meet the author himself at a ball in the Noblemen's Assembly Room.[36] Toward the late 1830s, the passion among women for George Sand is attested in the memoirs of Praskov'ia Tatlina. Her daughters, Nadezhda and Masha, read novels by Hugo, Balzac, and Sue, but it was their thirst for Sand that most alarmed and estranged their mother.[37]

These many images in literature and memoirs surely suggest widespread novel reading among women. But are the subscription lists equally persuasive? My pool of twenty-two lists is drawn from a variety of publications; the majority (just under 75 percent) fall in the area of literature, including poetry, plays, and fiction. Six of the lists represent novels; five, as noted, represent serial publications in the form of almanacs (of the literary variety, including poetry, tales, and extracts from novels).[38] The total number of novel subscribers amounts to 1,484. The two most popular novels, Bulgarin's *Ivan Vyzhigin* and *Petr Ivanovich Vyzhigin,* had 410 and 716 subscribers respectively. The other four novels had totals ranging from 65 to 135. Yet the number of female subscribers amounts to only 71, and this must be reduced to 69 (or 4.6 percent) because two women—Praskov'ia Davydova, wife of a military officer in Orel, and Anna Magaziner, wife of a civil servant in Kiev—subscribed to both of Bulgarin's novels. Most of the women appear on Bulgarin's two lists,

23 for *Ivan Vyzhigin,* and 36 for *Petr Ivanovich Vyzhigin.* There are no women at all on the Zotov list, and Shcheglov and Shteven number only 6 between them.[39]

Given that in the larger pool of twenty-two lists, the female showing is small again (393 subscriptions out of 11,898, or 387 if account is taken of duplicate subscribers, and in both cases, only just over 3 percent), does this mean that the evidence from the memoirs should be discounted? We may let these figures temper our reliance on memoirs, but there are compelling reasons why the extent of the subscription data for women need not be discouraging to historians of reading expansion. Despite a demonstrated interest in novels, women subscribed to four of the six novels in groups of only six or fewer, suggesting a reluctance to subscribe to certain titles, such as Shteven's story of gypsies or Zotov's of Napoleon. (Other nonfiction titles in the pool fared even less well: historical works were particularly lacking in female subscribers.)[40] Yet a total of 59 women appear on the two Bulgarin lists (23 for *Ivan Vyzhigin* and 36 for *Petr Ivanovich Vyzhigin*), and if subscribers to Radcliffe's novels were examined, the percentage of women would probably be higher. Thus female tastes may account to some extent for the low subscription rates by women, but they do not adequately explain the dearth of female subscribers. Sokhanskaia grew so discontented with literary journals that she focused on historical writing.[41] More telling is the fact that although she read both Vyzhigin novels, her name does not appear on either list. In other words, the lists do not record all readers. So the answer to the question of how women obtained their fiction, and why, may provide another possible explanation for the paucity of women subscribers.

First, however, we should note that the profile of women readers encountered so far has included younger and older women, single and married women, widows, and "old maids" — all from many different areas of Russia. There is indeed a tendency in literature (as well as memoirs) to present female novel reading as a provincial pastime. But the evidence from Passek, Smirnova, and especially Tatlina suggests that in the capitals, too, women were fond of novels. The preponderance of provincial women in the lists — like the overall paucity of women subscribers — may simply be attributable to problems of access, rather than to other factors.

Access to Novels

How, then, were Russian women obtaining novels? The data on novels published separately did not reveal large numbers of female subscribers. Because fiction was frequently published in almanacs, did women subscribe more heavily to these? The total number of subscribers to my five almanac issues was 993, ranging from 48 for *Nevskii al'manakh* (1830) to 375 for the 1842 issue of *Russkaia beseda (Russian Conversation)*. The corresponding figures for women subscribers were 3 for *Nevskii al'manakh* and 24 for *Russkaia beseda* (1842); women subscribers to all five issues numbered 76.

Thus women subscribers to the almanacs amounted to 7.7 percent — slightly higher than in the case of separately published novels. This tendency is confirmed in the larger group of twenty-two lists. The highest female showing is the 16.7 percent female contingent of subscribers to the almanac *Sirotka*, published in Moscow in aid of orphanages: of 162 subscribers, 27 are women. Women were perhaps more encouraged in this case by the almanac's purpose than by its form or content. However, it does contain an extract from Lazhechnikov's *Posledii Novik* (highly valued by Tat'iana Passek), and one of the subscribers to *Sirotka* was Praskov'ia Davydova of Orel, who also subscribed to Bulgarin's two novels.

Even so, the female subscription rate in the case of almanacs is hardly more impressive than in the case of separately published novels. But cultural development in Russia was such that access to reading materials for women was restricted. If we leave aside questions of illiteracy in the lowest social echelons and assume some education for noblewomen at the institutes (and occasionally at home), obstacles still remained. Of course, since my earlier remarks showed that many women succeeded in gaining access to almanacs and journals, this point should not be stressed unduly. But it seems evident that women did encounter difficulties in obtaining reading materials.

Perhaps the most severe involved the question of appropriate female behavior.[42] Praskov'ia Tatlina drew on books when attempting to broaden her daughters' education: "How else," she asks, "should one provide this but by reading?" Yet many were the social pressures she faced: "My relatives told me that I should not tear my children out of the milieu to which they belonged; that a girl being brought up at home, preparing to be a wife and mother, should occupy herself with needlework, sewing . . . in a word, with as little intellectual work . . . as possible."[43] In situations like this, women would have been deterred by their own fears, if not by others, from acting in so daring a manner as to become a subscriber.

There were exceptions, particularly among women from higher social levels. Anna Osipovna Smirnova, who spent the years 1826–1831 at court, records how she later subscribed to Pushkin's journal *Sovremennik (The Contemporary)*. Sokhanskaia recalls finding the same journal on the library shelves of a local landowner, Mariia Ivanovna.[44] Moreover, increasing numbers of works by women appeared in the journals of the late 1830s and early 1840s, including fiction by Nadezhda Durova and Elena Gan published in *Biblioteka dlia chteniia* and *Otechestvennye zapiski*. Sokhanskaia's first story, *Maior Smagin (Major Smagin)*, was published in *Syn otechestva* in 1844.

But despite successful contributions to fiction in journals by women both well-known and obscure, women as a group remained constrained by social prejudice—even as readers of literature. Elizaveta Vodovozova, from a poor gentry family, provides another example of the constraints: her elder sister was told by the local priest in the late 1840s that "educated women were only a laughing stock."[45] It seems likely, therefore, that many women would have encouraged their fathers or husbands to enter subscriptions for them.[46] Indeed, girls and unmarried women are often shown obtaining reading materials through men—either by using personal libraries or by borrowing purchased materials, frequently journals. Tatlina emerges from her strict religious upbringing by using her uncle's library. At the institute in Khar'kov in the mid-1830s, Sokhanskaia obtains an issue of *Biblioteka dlia chteniia* from a favorite teacher. Later still, while using the library of Mariia Ivanovna, Sokhanskaia meets the estate bailiff, who lends her a host of other journals, including *Otechestvennye zapiski, Moskvitianin (The Muscovite), Maiak (Lighthouse), Panteon, Repertuar,* and also *Syn otechestva*. Sokhanskaia's ecstasy on receiving this windfall makes it clear that she had not thought of placing her own subscriptions.[47]

It was not only girls and young women who relied on men for assistance. In an image taken from the memoirs of M. A. Dmitriev, the listeners are older women: "I remember the country reading of novels. . . . Someone would read, the others would listen, especially the ladies and old maids. What terror the celebrated Mrs. Radcliffe would disseminate. . . . What sympathy they felt for the . . . heroines of Mme. de Genlis!"[48] This brings up another method by which women gained access to print materials: the practice of reading aloud. Its precise extent is another uncharted facet of female reading — and the source of an indeterminate number of hidden "readers." But Sokhanskaia's delight in the journal issue received from her teacher was shared with many other girls (there were almost forty in the institute) on two successive nights (in or about 1836): the girls sat on their dormitory floor surrounded by candles and listened to Sokhanskaia recite Aleksei Timofeev's romantic tale "Konrad von Teifelburg."[49]

In other words, it is likely that women subscribers were few because they avoided subscribing in their own right. The question of money probably entered into it; Sokhanskaia and Tatlina were far from wealthy, and periodicals were not inexpensive.[50] But women in Russia, unlike their counterparts in Western Europe, were permitted to hold property in their own names, and it may be presumed that wellborn women had money at their disposal. Moreover, the fact that provincial women are prominent in the lists suggests that limited finances alone cannot explain the lack of subscription activity.[51] Provincial women would not have been wealthier than urban women, but they were undoubtedly more affected by book trade vagaries and may well have been impelled by this to brave social convention to obtain the materials they sought.

Social Groups/Estates & Female Readers

From which social groups did women readers come? Were access difficulties equally distributed? Here the evidence from subscriptions is helpful, confirming that access was not available to all. Of the 69 female novel subscribers, 9 (13 percent) belong to the aristocracy, and 15 (21.7 percent) to military and civil rankings; 26 (37.7 percent) also belong to the nobility (sphere unspecified).⁵² These account for 72.5 percent of the female group. Only one woman belongs to the merchant estate.

These percentages are close to those revealed if we divide all women in my database (387) into the same categories.⁵³ Those belonging to the aristocracy amount to 44 (11.4 percent), another 101 (26.1 percent) belong to military and civil rankings, and 138 (35.7 percent) are nobles whose service sphere is unspecified—altogether, 73.1 percent of women subscribers. Only 1.6 percent (6 women) are merchants. Moreover, both sets of data indicate that female subscribers were of high birth. Noblewomen in each case constitute more than 70 percent, and the percentage of women from the upper ranks within these groups is also high. Among women subscribers in general, 89.7 percent of noblewomen were at the eighth rank or above; among women subscribers to novels, 96 percent of noblewomen met this criterion.

It should be noted that both sets of data contain relatively large groups of women with category unspecified (just over 24 percent in each case), and these groups may include some lowborn women (since a woman of low birth was more likely to omit her category). But the emphasis on highborn female subscribers is confirmed if we analyze the 76 female subscribers to almanacs, 40 (52.6 percent) of whom are identifiable as noblewomen.⁵⁴ (Because 35 of the women almanac subscribers are listed without specification as to category, it is possible that the number of noblewomen is even greater.) Although the percentage of those identified as aristocratic is only 5.3 percent, again the percentage of women from the upper ranks (rank eight or above) within the group of noblewomen is high (87.5 percent). Although the percentage of women at the ninth rank or below is higher than before (12.5 percent, versus 4 percent for female novel subscribers), this is explained by the fact that the majority of this lower-status group appear as subscribers to *Russkaia beseda,* published in the 1840s and more likely to include low-ranked subscribers.

This larger percentage of women clearly belonging to the lower ranks in the almanac count is still small in actual terms (five subscribers), perhaps owing to the nature of the publications involved. Almanacs certainly evolved in the late 1820s from an emphasis on verse to an increasing number of prose offerings. *Mnemozina* (1824–1825) carried little in the way of prose fiction, whereas *Nev-*

skii al'manakh — a publication that received, incidentally, much less critical acclaim — carried somewhat more fiction in its various issues from 1825 to 1833; and *Russkaia beseda* (1841–1842) carried many examples of prose fiction. But while almanacs increasingly carried extracts from popular fiction, it appears that almanacs retained a certain class distinction as showpieces of the wealthy.

Be that as it may, analysis of female subscribers to separately published novels and almanacs reveals a predominance of highborn women. Women from lower social levels were not conspicuous as readers. For them, the difficulties regarding access via subscription would have been greater than those discussed earlier, when the concern was largely with educated women. In the merchant estate, education was far from prevalent. Even for women from the other low-status groups with a partial education, financial considerations would have been a greater concern. Thus merchant women had far to go in terms of developing a habit of reading, and even women in other low-status classes lagged behind their social superiors. Even so, there are several interesting examples of women from lower social levels in the larger pool of subscribers. Two were wives of merchants: Irina Grigor'evna Restsova from Kolomna, who subscribed to the novel *Petr Ivanovich Vyzhigin,* and Anna Fedorovna Shaposhnikova from Riga, who subscribed to Bulgarin's collected works of 1830. A third woman merchant, Agrafena Avchinnikova — an honorary commercial secretary in Odessa — was one of only ten female subscribers to Polevoi's *Istoriia russkogo naroda (History of the Russian People),* which began publication in 1829.[55] Finally, two other lower-middle-class women subscribed to Bulgarin's *Rossiia v istoricheskom, statisticheskom . . . otnosheniiakh (Russia: History, Statistics . . .),* published in 1837: A. A. Teriaeva, an actress, and L. D. Tikhaia, wife of a staff doctor in Novodvinsk. Thus, as indicated earlier, the low profile displayed by merchant and other low-status women does not signify a total lack of reading within these categories.[56]

Female Motives for Reading

What were the motives that led Russian women to read in increasingly large numbers, much as their European counterparts? It may be useful here to quote from a passage by Jane Austen: "To be a renter . . . of books! And to be having anyone's improvement in view in her choice! But . . . Susan had read nothing, and Fanny longed to give her a share in her own first pleasures."[57] This passage encapsulates a fundamental opposition regarding motivation: pleasure versus improvement. Of the eight potential motives noted hereafter, six fall within this opposition.

Reading for pleasure is generally thought to include at least four motives: enjoyment, companionship, escapism, and voyeurism.[58] The first two are clearly positive but differ in that one involves solitary reading, the other group interaction. The first also requires active involvement (since an individual reader, even when reading for pleasure, is required to make some effort), whereas the second involves a more passive approach. Among female readers under Nicholas I, examples abound of both types. Sokhanskaia frequently refers to the enjoyment she drew from reading, largely as a solitary pastime.[59] The delight she felt in a sudden gift of journal issues is reflected in a question to P. A. Pletnev, the addressee of her memoirs: "Do you understand what this meant for me? It seemed to me that I was . . . soaring in space under the stars. I forgot about the days and hours . . . and remembered one thing, reading."[60] Sokhanskaia always expresses herself with intensity, but this underscores the enjoyment she derived from reading. Elizaveta Popova differed in her reading practices. An elderly Moscow lady acquainted with the Slavophiles, Popova left a portrait of her daily habits dating from 1847. Lonely and melancholic, she seems to prefer the more passive approach of reading with a companion. She often visits her friend Katerina Sverbeeva and passes the evening with journals such as *Otechestvennye zapiski* and *Sovremennik*. On another occasion, she has the following to say: "I did not expect such pleasure from this day. That good, magnanimous Panov came to see me, spent some time sitting with me, and read to me from his [periodical *Moskovskii] Sbornik (Moscow Symposium)* extracts from Pavlova's novel *Dvoinaia zhizn' (Double Life)*."[61]

Women's reading for pleasure might also stem from escapism, usually considered a negative reason for reading, but not surprising given their limited opportunities for self-expression in Nicholaevan Russia. Yet one encounters such instances in a person who also reads for other reasons—complicating attempts to draw a rigid profile of differences among readers. Sokhanskaia refers to periods of intense boredom in the empty steppe, which she fills with books and especially journals. But unlike Nadezhda Durova, Sokhanskaia always preferred reading to other activities. The record of Durova's military service contains few references to reading: she once considers asking her captain for books but fears he will regard this desire as a weakness. Durova only returns to reading in the form of Mrs. Radcliffe—which she does in 1816 to escape the boredom of a four-month leave at home in Sarapul.[62] The conventional reaction to such reading is likely to be negative. The young Baron Korf, for example, urged Passek in 1826 to throw aside the "harmful kind of reading," "writings of secret castles," "tender and fatal passions." But it is worth noting Karamzin's view: "In very bad novels there is still a certain logic and rhetoric; [the person] who reads them will speak better and more coherently than the utter ignoramus who has never opened a book."[63]

Turning to the remaining four motives for reading, two fall under the rubric of reading for improvement.[64] One might be termed reading for the purpose of "cultivation"; the other, reading for advancement. The goal in the first instance seems to be cultivation of tasteful behavior or appropriate knowledge, but the underlying cause is apparently the dictates of class (in most cases the nobility). Sometimes this prescription is explicitly acknowledged. Sokhanskaia remembers that "there was a splendid attitude toward learning in our home. No one ever obliged us to study with brute force, but we constantly heard that it is impossible to live without learning—that one is only a nobleman if one is good and knows a lot, and that girls must certainly study so as to be clever."[65]

This may be one reason why the novels of Mme. de Genlis were so popular with Russian women, especially the provincial gentry. One may agree with Tatlina, who disliked their heavy-handed tone, but they also portray the satisfaction found in reform—images apparently persuasive to many. Among their lessons on female behavior, reading itself was included: in *Tales of the Castle* (1782), we witness the metamorphosis of the vapid Delphine into a sensible young lady. First comes a conversation between her and the saintly Henrietta: "'How do you know all this?' asked [Delphine]. . . . 'I!' said Henrietta . . . 'I have an earnest desire to learn, for which reason I love to read.' 'Love to read! How very strange,'" replies Delphine. Later, Delphine takes up a book: "[She] ran over the leaves at first with . . .

indifference. . . . As she read on, she began to take pleasure in what she read, and was surprised to find that reading could make time pass away more agreeably than most other amusements."[66]

Of course, Genlis's writings were not considered serious literature. But scholarly and literary texts were also typical of this type of reading—which was frequently "extensive" in nature.[67] As Viazemskii recalls of the Petersburg society figure Anna Smirnova: "Her knowledge was varied, her reading instructional and serious, though not to the detriment of novels and newspapers. Even theological questions and theological debates were appealing to her." Similarly with Elizaveta Popova in Moscow: although she enjoyed Pavlova's novel, her journal reading in company with Sverbeeva dealt with topics like Gogol's philosophical standing or Konstantin Kavelin's article on Novgorod. Sokhanskaia's landowning neighbor Mariia Ivanovna read Jean Racine, Jean-Francois Marmontel, Jean-Pierre Claris de Florian, and Chateaubriand; as Sokhanskaia noted, she was "an intolerable relic of that age which was brought up on French encyclopedists."[68]

The foregoing discussion of reading for "cultivation" has distinguished two subvarieties, which may be labeled "behavioral" and "intellectual." The implication is that a cultivated knowledge of certain works and issues would have been considered appropriate for Russian noblewomen at all levels, especially in, but not limited to, intellectual circles. But Popova would not have agreed with this assessment. She held a poor opinion of women and would have considered her reading an exception, rather than the norm. Thus reading by noblewomen for the purpose of cultivation apparently took place on a sliding scale. Sometimes its goal was merely appropriate social behavior, but sometimes it extended to the acquisition of knowledge. In the first instance, intellectual accomplishment was limited; in the second, a more sophisticated individual would emerge.

Instances of the other kind of reading for improvement, or advancement, are less often found. An obvious example, however, is Praskov'ia Tatlina. In providing music lessons, schooling, and reading materials, her goal for her eldest daughter, Natasha, was financial independence, not social accomplishment.[69] Tatlina sought, and the reason is clear: born to an old clerical family and married to an undistinguished military officer, her status was fairly low and her resources (after her husband's death) strained. But her relatives viewed her desire for "advancement" as an attempt to "tear [her daughters] out of the milieu to which they belonged." Another example of reading for improvement other than cultivation is Anna Smirnova, who reads *Zemledel'cheskaia gazeta (Agricultural Newspaper)* while settled on her estate in Moscow province in the summer of 1838.[70] For a woman, the acquisition of specialized agricultural knowledge would certainly represent advancement beyond traditional roles: instances of females in charge of estates are not uncommon, but there is usually a bailiff who is responsible for the technicalities of land management.

Finally, one can also distinguish at least two other motives for reading; both are related to a desire for self-affirmation. These include reading as a source of group solidarity and reading with a view to rebellion. On the eve of her arranged marriage in 1826, Tatlina noted: "Two weeks passed by in preparations . . . I read the novels of Radcliffe . . . I lived in a fantasy world."[71] If we view this as a search for group solidarity, not escapism, her motive appears more positive. Radcliffe's heroines were more steadfast than one might expect, and Tatlina would certainly have responded to the efforts of the heroine Emily in *The Mysteries of Udolpho* (1794) to withstand an unwanted marriage. Radcliffe's novels are also more levelheaded than her reputation suggests. She creates mysterious situations but usually deflates the reader's susceptibility by providing rational explanations.[72] Emily's fortitude would have represented a fine role model for Russian women faced with patriarchal restrictions. With the exception of Aleksandr Pushkin's Tat'iana (and a few other figures in writings by women), such heroines were little in evidence in Russian novels of the period—helping to explain Radcliffe's continuing popularity.[73]

Yet much as Tatlina exemplified awakening self-affirmation among Russian women by challenging educational expectations, she did not go as far as her daughters in rebelling against convention. Her daughters reached their teenage years as George Sand's popularity swept Russia in the late 1830s and 1840s. Their motive in reading Sand was rebellious in two respects. First, they defied authority in focusing on materials that their mother could not approve. As Tatlina notes: "George Sand seduced Natasha. She did not go further [in her reading], while the writings of that woman do not at all present a womanly ideal, but only one of the escape routes from her slavish, senseless situation. . . . I completely fell out with Natasha in my view of the vocation of a woman. I respected 'useful' love; while she was infected with so-called Sandian ideas."[74] But they not only read; they also emulated Sandian behavior by asserting their independence.[75] Their rebellion appears to be both a result of and a motive for reading.

Conclusion

This essay has sought to qualify the perception of homogeneity among Nicholaevan audiences by identifying female readers based principally on their reading of fiction in periodicals. The mere existence of a female audience disrupts the notion of homogeneity. And although it is true that female readers of novels—those that were published separately as well as in almanacs and journals—were largely from the higher nobility, the many images from memoirs and correspondence suggest that quantitatively as well as qualitatively, women readers represented a "larger portion" of the public than is usually acknowledged. Although most of the texts considered represent a limited range of noncanonical works that rarely appear to advantage in studies of Russian literature, what this study reveals is precisely the existence of a group of readers usually discounted for failing to meet established canons.

Other aims of this essay have been to probe the female contribution to the expansion of the reading public, and the role therein of fiction. As regards the first point, a positive conclusion based on subscription lists is problematic. The growing ranks of readers appear to have emerged from the middle levels of society (the gentry and the upper echelons of the merchantry). Because the women in the lists are heavily from the upper levels of the nobility, it is difficult to relate them to this development—and the memoirs are not precise enough in terms of identifying social ranking to affect the image in the lists. Yet if we accept that social conventions deterred women from subscribing, and note that women from lower levels would have been most likely to feel this restriction, it is possible to assert that they too constituted a growing audience. This suggestion is reinforced when we recall the increasing importance of fiction. As we have seen, women were clearly avid novel readers. So the conclusion is inescapable that women were a force in the growing popularity of fiction, and therefore also in the expansion of the public that it engendered.[76]

The role of almanacs and journals in developing the female audience for fiction was likewise substantial. Periodicals were judged to be as threatening as novels by the tsarist government precisely because of their tendency to include fiction—and the evidence presented here indicates that women eagerly sought them for that reason. Although almanacs reached the public less frequently and commanded smaller circulation figures than journals, as the medium of choice in the late 1820s, they were an important force not only in developing the Russian periodical press but also in expanding portions of the reading public. Moreover, the evidence from almanacs shows that here too, women played a role in supporting them.

However, it was the transition from almanac to journal in the 1830s—marked in 1833 by the larger-format almanac *Novosel'e* and by the appearance in 1834 of the first thick journal, *Biblioteka dlia chteniia*—that constituted a truly significant force in expanding the reading public in that decade.[77] In facilitating the parallel transition from verse to prose, journals ensured the increasing availability of fiction—a development in itself designed to assist the expansion of readership, especially its female component. To return to the characterization of the preform period cited at the beginning of this essay, it proves somewhat misleading to suggest that literature and journals "reflected . . . [a] generally male preserve." Under Nicholas I—and later, as the following essays reveal—women were clearly avid readers of journals, and, in small but increasing numbers, also contributors.

Notes

An earlier version of this essay was intended for my dissertation ("The Expansion of Russian Reading Audiences, 1828–1848," UC Berkeley, 1999), and I gratefully acknowledge comments received from Nicholas Riasanovsky, Hugh McLean, and Reginald Zelnik. The essay was then recast for this volume, and I also acknowledge the insightful comments offered by Jehanne Gheith and Barbara Norton.

1 Donald Fanger, "Gogol and His Reader," in *Literature and Society in Imperial Russia, 1800–1914*, ed. William Mills Todd III (Stanford, 1978), 67.

2   In discussing the Russian nobility *(dvorianstvo)*, historians usually choose between two terms, "nobility" and "gentry." Some, however, distinguish between "nobility," "gentry," and "aristocracy," reserving "aristocracy" for the nobility's higher levels and "gentry" for the lower. I use "gentry" to mean the lower levels of the nobility—both landed and landless—and do not visualize the wealthiest provincial landowners in this category.

3   Regarding the term "middle class," historians have viewed the concept in the Western sense as largely foreign to Russia—although recent scholarship is reevaluating the issue; see Edith W. Clowes, Samuel D. Kassow, and James L. West, eds., *Between Tsar and People: Educated Society and the Quest for Public Identity in Late Imperial Russia* (Princeton, 1991); and Harley D. Balzer, ed., *Russia's Missing Middle Class: The Professions in Russian History* (White Plains, N.Y., 1996). My use of the term refers to petty landowners, junior military officers and civil servants, emerging professionals, and upper-level (first and second guild) merchants. Many in the first four groups were technically nobles; to describe them as "middle-class" is to suggest that contemporary readers (especially males) were no longer merely "noble" in the Western sense.

4   Andre Meynieux, *Pouchkine, homme de lettres et de la littérature professionnelle en Russie* (Paris, 1966), 470–71; T. Grits, V. Trenin, and M. Nikitin, *Slovesnost' i kommertsiia: Knizhnaia lavka A. F. Smirdina* (Moscow, 1929), 240; V. G. Berezina, *Russkaia zhurnalistika vtoroi chetverti XIX veka (1826–1839 gody)* (Leningrad, 1965), 20. Discussing American fiction from 1835 to 1855, J. L. Machor notes that "many of the leading periodicals . . . achieved circulations of 5,000 . . . equivalent today to the . . . *New Yorker*" ("Historical Hermeneutics and Antebellum Fiction: Gender, Response Theory, and Interpretive Contexts," in *Readers in History: Nineteenth-Century American Literature and the Contexts of Response* [Baltimore, 1993], 83).

5   The literary historian S. P. Shevyrev suggested that "the thirst for reading is spreading . . . to the very limits of Russia" ("Slovesnost' i torgovlia," *Moskovskii nabliudatel'*, no. 1 [1835]: 20). Publishing statistics confirm the trend: the reference work *Entsiklopedicheskii leksikon*, initiated by Adol'f Pliushar in 1835, commanded 6,116 subscriptions.

6   Recent works that examine aspects of readership in Nicholaevan Russia include A. Dolinin, *Istoriia, odetaia v roman. Val'ter Skott i ego chitateli* (Moscow, 1988); V. P. Kozlov, *"Istoriia gosudarstva Rossiiskogo": N. M. Karamzina v otsenke sovremennikov* (Moscow, 1989); and A. I. Reitblat, "F. V. Bulgarin i ego chitateli," in *Chtenie v dorevoliutsionnoi Rossii: Sbornik nauchnykh trudov* (Moscow, 1992), 55–66.

7   Regarding women as contributing to the expansion of reading audiences, a good example is antebellum America (Machor, "Historical Hermeneutics," 64, 67). On the novel as a contributing factor, an obvious source is Ian Watt's *The Rise of the Novel: Studies in Defoe, Richardson, and Fielding* (Berkeley, 1957).

8   After a flurry of new titles just after 1800, journals yielded briefly in the 1820s to almanacs. The situation changed again in the 1830s, with the appearance of thick journals such as *BdCh* (1834) and *OZ* (1839). On almanacs in the 1820s, see N. P. Kashin, "Al'manakhi dvadtsatykh-sorokovykh godov," in *Kniga v Rossii*, ed. V. A. Adariukov, vol. 2, *Deviatnadtsatyi vek* (Moscow, 1925), 100–138; N. P. Smirnov-Sokol'skii, *Russkie literaturnye al'manakhi i sborniki XVIII–XIX vv.* (Moscow, 1965); and also my article "Russian Literary Almanacs of the 1820s and Their Legacy," *Publishing History* 17 (1985): 65–86. On journals under Nicholas I, see A. G. Dement'ev, *Ocherki po istorii russkoi zhurnalistiki, 1840–1850* (Moscow, 1951); and Berezina, *Russkaia zhurnalistika vtoroi chetverti XIX veka*.

9   Female readers are not the focus of Karamzin's essay, but novel reading is, and he emphasizes that the genre "undoubtedly captivates a large portion of the public" [bez somneniia plenitelen dlia bol'shoi chasti Publiki]. See Karamzin, "On the Book Trade and Love of Reading in Russia," in *Selected Prose*, trans. Henry Nebel (Evanston, 1969), 187.

10 There are only passing references to the female audience in prerevolutionary Russia (see Iu. D. Levin's remarks on female readers in "Prizhiznennaia slava Val'tera Skotta v Rossii," in *Epokha romantizma: Iz istorii mezhdunarodnykh sviazei russkoi literatury* [Leningrad, 1975], 14).

11 See A. V. Blium, "Massovoe chtenie v russkoi provintsii kontsa XVIII–pervoi chetverti XIX vv.," *Istoriia russkogo chitatelia* 1 (1973): 37.

12 On the position of women in imperial Russia, see especially Barbara Clements, Barbara Engel, and Christine Worobec, eds., *Russia's Women: Accommodation, Resistance, Transformation* (Berkeley, 1991).

13 I have found useful memoirs by P. N. Tatlina and N. S. Sokhanskaia, who hailed from the middle levels of society (clerical and gentry families in impecunious circumstances). Tatlina's memoirs have recently been translated in full, and Sokhanskaia's in part, in *Russia through Women's Eyes: Autobiographies from Tsarist Russia*, ed. Toby W. Clyman and Judith Vowles (New Haven, 1996). All references are to the Russian editions, and all translations are my own.

14 A. V. Blium, "Khudozhestvennaia literatura kak istoriko-knizhnyi istochnik," *Kniga: Issledovaniia i materialy* 42 (1986): 100–122.

15 The almanacs include *Mnemozina*, vol. 4 (Moscow, 1825); *Nevskii al'manakh 1830 goda* (St. Petersburg, 1830); *Sirotka: Literaturyi al'ma-

nakh na 1831 god (St. Petersburg, 1831); and two issues (1, 3) of *Russkaia beseda* (St. Petersburg, 1841, 1842). The first and last of these titles were multivolume "collections" *(sobraniia)* published serially. But both were viewed as almanacs and are treated as such in Smirnov-Sokol'skii's bibliography, *Russkie literaturnye al'manakhi i sborniki.*

16 M. I. Gillel's son, *P. A. Viazemskii: Zhizn' i tvorchestvo* (Leningrad, 1969), 324.

17 The pool contains no lists from journals, and an expanded version of this study would benefit from samples of this type. But, as noted, the serial almanacs became a repository for short fiction; thus, analysis of almanac subscribers usefully supplements evidence of journal reading in memoirs.

18 Beaven [Remnek], "Russian Literary Almanacs," 75. See also Kashin, "Al'manakhi dvadtsatykh-sorokovykh godov."

19 M. D. Ol'khin, *Sistematicheskii reestr russkim knigam . . .* (St. Petersburg, 1846).

20 V. G. Belinskii, *Polnoe sobranie sochinenii*, vol. 2 (Moscow, 1953–1959), 34.

21 L. S. Herrmann discusses the availability of George Sand's novels in Russia in "George Sand and the Nineteenth-Century Russian Novel" (Ph.D. diss., Columbia University, 1979).

22 Both William Todd *(Fiction and Society)* and Joe Andrew (*Women and Russian Literature, 1780–1863* [New York, 1988]), focus on the three canonized writers. For exceptions to this emphasis on male authors, see Catriona Kelly, *A History of Russian Women's Writing, 1820–1992* (Oxford, 1994); and Kelly, ed., *An Anthology of Russian Women's Writing, 1777–1992* (Oxford, 1994). Still other categories less worthy of esteem but nonetheless widely read include fiction by second-rate male authors (e.g., Bulgarin).

23 The sudden emergence of these domestic novels reflects the shift in the 1830s from poetry to prose as the preferred literary medium.

24 In 1834 the newspaper *Severnaia pchela* observed: "Now in Moscow novels are being published right and left for conveyance to the fairs and into the villages" (Grits et al., *Slovesnost' i kommertsiia*, 207).

25 The list appears in F. V. Bulgarin, *Ivan Vyzhigin*, vol. 4 (St. Petersburg, 1829), i–xxiv. Some subscribers may have belonged to more than one category. However, if only aristocratic/landowner, military, or civil titles were given, I assigned subscribers to those categories. If only an honorific title was given, that subscriber was placed in a "Nobles: Sphere Unclear" category. But if military/civil titles were given in addition to aristocratic or honorific titles, the military or civil categories were preferred—since those titles probably represented the subscriber's

primary sphere of activity. A "professional" category was used for subscribers such as engineers, teachers, lawyers, and doctors. More details on assignment to categories in my database appear in the introduction to my dissertation.

26 I. E. Barenbaum, *Knizhnyi Peterburg* (Moscow, 1980), 89; G. H. Alkire, "Gogol and Bulgarin's *Ivan Vyzhigin*," *Slavic Review* 28 (1969): 290.

27 The Table of Ranks with fourteen grades for service nobility was introduced by Peter the Great in 1722. There were three groups: military, civil, and court. Servitors entered at the fourteenth rank (sometimes higher) and rose through promotions to higher status. Rank twelve in the military conveyed hereditary nobility, rank eight in the civil service.

28 See F. V. Bulgarin, *Petr Ivanovich Vyzhigin*, vol. 4 (St. Petersburg, 1831), 295–340.

29 Sergei Gessen, *Knigoizdatel' Aleksandr Pushkin* (Leningrad, 1930), 15; Levin, "Prizhiznennaia slava Val'tera Slotta," 14; Belinskii, "Nichto o nichem," 20.

30 "Stsena v kniznoi lavke," *Moskovskii vestnik* 5, no. 20 (1827): 486; F. V. Bulgarin, *Ivan Vejeeghen, or Life in Russia*, vol. 1 (London, 1831), 19–20, 118.

31 *The Englishwoman in Russia: Impressions of the Society and Manners of the Russians at Home* (London, 1855), 34, 177.

32 P. N. Tatlina, "Vospominaniia (1812–1854)," *Russkii arkhiv* 3, no. 10 (1899): 194, 196.

33 N. S. Sokhanskaia, "Avtobiografiia," *Russkoe obozrenie* (1896), no. 8: 466; no. 6: 486; no. 7: 26–27; no. 10: 493; no. 8: 479.

34 Ibid., no. 8: 466.

35 Levin, "Prizhiznennaia slava Val'tera Skotta," 10.

36 Tat'iana Passek, *Iz dal'nikh let*, vol. 2 (Moscow, 1963), 23.

37 Tatlina, "Vospominaniia," 205–6, 220.

38 Bulgarin's *Ivan Vyzhigin* and its sequel *Petr Ivanovich Vyzhigin* (1831) were "best-sellers." Citations for the other four (with location of subscription list) are Fedor Shcheglov, *Ivan, bezzabotnaia golova, i kum Matvei*, vol. 2 (Moscow, 1829), [173–74, 177–79]; *Uchitel'skaia vnuchka, ili pochemu znat' chego ne znaesh?* vol. 4 (Moscow, 1836), [1–4]; Ivan Shteven, *Tsygan, ili uzhasnaia mest': Proisshestvie minuvshego stoletiia*, vol. 2 (St. Petersburg, 1838), [271–78]; Rafail Zotov, *Napoleon na ostrove Sv. Eleny*, vol. 4 (St. Petersburg, 1838), [217–20]. For the almanacs, see note 16.

39 In the two lists providing information on geographic provenance, the number of provincial women ranges from 57 percent *(Ivan Vyzhigin)* to 72 percent *(Petr Ivanovich Vyzhigin)*.

40 Polevoi's *Istoriia russkogo naroda*, vol. 2 (1830), had ten women among

555 subscribers; Bantysh-Kamenskii's *Biografii rossiiskikh generalissimusov* . . . (1841) lists only one woman out of 254 subscribers; and Benjamin Bergmann's *Istoriia Petra Velikogo*, translated from German and likewise published in 1841, contains one woman out of 343.

41 Sokhanskaia, "Avtobiografiia," *Russkoe obozrenie*, no. 10: 486.
42 Various scholars have discussed the problems faced by Russian women in trying to emerge from the rigid roles dictated to them by a patriarchal society; see note 2.
43 Tatlina, "Vospominaniia," 205. Tatlina appears to refer here to the mid- to late 1830s.
44 A. O. Smirnova, *Zapiski, dnevniki, vospominaniia, pis'ma* (Moscow, 1929), 57; Sokhanskaia, "Avtobiografiia," no. 10: 485.
45 Elizaveta Vodovozova, *A Russian Childhood* (London, 1960), 30.
46 This solution would not always have served: referring to a slightly later period, the merchant woman Anna Volkova records that her husband scorned her requests to purchase books (see the essay by Adele Lindenmeyr in this volume). The same constraints probably applied when women sought to obtain novels from circulating libraries, very much in their heyday in the reign of Nicholas I. While Tatlina's daughters borrowed the novels of Sand, Balzac, Sue, and Hugo from the Moscow bookstore 'Gautier,' as the result of a subscription placed by their mother (Tatlina, "Vospominaniia," 205–6), Tatlina was willing to fight convention, as already noted.
47 Tatlina, "Vospominaniia," 194; Sokhanskaia, "Avtobiografiia," no. 7: 22; no. 10: [479], 484–85.
48 M. A. Dmitriev, *Melochi iz zapasa moei pamiati*, 2d ed. (Moscow, 1869), 48.
49 Sokhanskaia, "Avtobiografiia," no. 7: 22.
50 Among almanacs, *Nevskii al'manakh* (1825–1833) cost 100 rubles, and *Severnye tsvety* (1825–1832) 10 to 12 rubles per year. Among journals, *Moskovskii telegraf* cost 35 rubles, *Moskovskii vestnik* 40 rubles, and *OZ* 30 rubles (Gessen, *Knigoizdatel' Aleksandr Pushkin*, 18–19).
51 Of the thirty-two women who subscribed to the three-volume almanac *Russkaia beseda* (1841–1842), and the nineteen women who subscribed to Bulgarin's *Rossiia v istoricheskom, statisticheskom . . . otnosheniiakh* (1837) — both relatively large contingents of women — the provincial percentage ranges from 47 percent for the almanac to as high as 73 percent for the reference work.
52 The novels in question are listed in note 39, and the categories explained in note 25. The designations "military," "civil," and so forth are not meant to imply that the women so counted actually served in these capacities (women such as Nadezhda Durova were a clear exception in

the military). But women subscribers usually included their husband's or father's rank, either explicitly or by means of a female variant, and these ranks defined their social status.

53 It will be recalled that the larger group of 387 women (393 including duplicates) is taken from the full database of twenty-two subscription lists (11,898 subscriptions).

54 Citations for these almanacs are given in note 15.

55 Another particularly striking example of literate merchantry is provided by Anna Volkova, born toward the end of the Nicholaevan era; see Adele Lindenmeyr's essay.

56 Moreover, every class of women included nonreaders, as noted by Tatlina ("Vospominaniia," 205).

57 Jane Austen, *Mansfield Park* (New York, 1964), 310–11.

58 According to Joe Andrew, voyeurism sometimes typified literary figures and readers in the Pushkin period (*Women in Russian Literature*, 66–67). But as no evidence of voyeurism springs to mind regarding women readers, this fourth motive will not be discussed here.

59 Sokhanskaia, "Avtobiografiia," 37.

60 Sokhanskaia, "Avtobiografiia," no. 8: 466; no. 10: [479].

61 Elizaveta Popova, *Dnevnik Elizavety Ivanovny Popovoi: 1847–1852* (St. Petersburg, 1911), 13, quotation on 45. An extract from Karolina Pavlova's novel *Dvoinaia zhizn'* appeared in 1847 in the short-lived periodical *Moskovskii uchenyi i literaturnyi sbornik*.

62 Sokhanskaia, "Avtobiografiia," no. 8: 465; Nadezhda Durova, *The Cavalry Maiden: Journals of a Female Cavalry Officer in the Napoleonic Wars*, trans. Mary Fleming Zirin (Bloomington, 1988), 53, 215.

63 Levin, "Prizhiznennaia slava Val'tera Skotta," 14–15; Karamzin, "On the Book Trade," 189.

64 I prefer the term "improvement" to "education"—as more suggestive of the informal study I visualize as characteristic of "cultivation," and also suggestive of the social mobility that will be touched on under reading for "advancement."

65 Sokhanskaia, "Avtobiografiia," no. 6: 485.

66 Stéphanie de Genlis, *Tales of the Castle,* trans. Thomas Holcroft, vol. 1 (Philadelphia, 1814), 24–25.

67 Rolf Engelsing's notion that Europeans read a few titles repeatedly ("intensively") before 1750 and read more broadly ("extensively") after 1750 is summarized in Robert Darnton, "Readers Respond to Rousseau," in *The Great Cat Massacre and Other Episodes in French Cultural History* (New York, 1984), 249.

68 P. A. Viazemskii, "Salon A. O. Smirnovoi-Rosset," in *Literaturnye salony i kruzhki: Pervaia polovina XIX veka,* ed. N. L. Brodskii (Moscow,

1930), 210; Popova, *Dnevnik,* 10, 13; Sokhanskaia, "Avtobiografiia," no. 10: [479], 481. Popova also obtains and reads a forbidden political text—and disagrees with its contents (*Dnevnik,* 83).
69 Tatlina, "Vospominaniia," 205.
70 Smirnova, *Zapiski,* 66. The example here concerns a newspaper, not a journal, but similar topics were covered in *BdCh*—a frequent candidate for female reading.
71 Tatlina, "Vospominaniia," 197–98.
72 Ann Radcliffe, *The Mysteries of Udolpho* (London, 1966), 79–80.
73 Russian interest in France was so acute that even critical readers felt attracted to a French view of the world. See B. Tomashevskii, "Pushkin i frantsuzskaia literatura," in *Pushkin i Frantsiia* (Leningrad, 1960), 62–64.
74 Tatlina, "Vospominaniia," 220.
75 Ibid., 220–21.
76 Women's continued predilection for fiction, noted in this volume by Barbara Norton in regard to the journalist Kuskova, shows that cultural practices attracting women to journals in the era of Nicholas I persisted in later years.
77 Journals had of course been published earlier, and almanacs continued into the 1840s. But in general terms, the notion of a "transition" holds true.

Redefining the Perceptible

The Journalism(s) of Evgeniia Tur

and Avdot'ia Panaeva

JEHANNE M GHEITH

The following statement, by an anonymous "N. V.," was made about Evgeniia Tur at the time of her death in 1892 but could equally well be applied to Avdot'ia Panaeva (and many other women literati):

> In evaluating literary figures, especially those who are female, one must take into account not only what they accomplished with their pens, with their writings, but also what they accomplished by means of their influence and their sensitivity . . . which, in imperceptible ways, act positively on those surrounding them and on literature. This influence is, for the most part, invisible — it is not obvious even to those who experience it — but there is no doubt that its effects are instructive. This side of the character of the deceased E[lizaveta] V[asil'evna] [Tur] will probably remain unelucidated for a long time — male biographers only rarely attach any significance to such things. But this influence of hers did exist and for this, too, she deserves [our] gratitude and to be remembered fondly as one who accomplished great good.[1]

Although N.V.'s unproblematic division of the world into male and female is no longer tenable or intellectually satisfying,[2] this statement is an important early recognition of why women have fallen so easily out of Russian (and other) histories. Such histories, as many scholars have argued, foreground certain areas of activity that come to be considered palpable and significant, while other areas become "imperceptible."[3] This essay explores the "imperceptible and invisible influence" of Evgeniia Tur (1815–1892) and Avdot'ia Panaeva (1819/20–1893), two Russian women journalists of the mid–nineteenth century, and asserts that examining women's role in Russian journalism demands redefining traditional conceptions of the journalistic field in Russia, both in terms of who made up and shaped the field and in terms of the significance of various kinds of periodicals and their readers.

Journalism in Russia has largely been conceptualized as a "man's world," and scholarship has dealt almost exclusively with male journalists and male models of journalistic involvement.[4] I argue that studying women's involvement in the journalistic field reveals new aspects of that field and indicates that journalism extends beyond the categories usually thought of as constitutive of the institution; for example, the mechanics of printing, the role of the government (censorship, financial support, legislation), or the work of publishers, editors, and authors. All of these are important, but there is also a web of other factors—interrelations, casual conversations, physical and emotional support—that make journalism possible, and these should be included in scholarly conceptualizations of the topic. In this essay, I aim to demonstrate that the study of journalism should be as much a study of intangibles as it is of the visible manifestations of journalism. By reaching for the "imperceptible" and unbounded aspects of journalism, I contend that the cultural processes that make journalism possible are as important as the bound volume.

The 1860s is usually seen as a time of ferocious polemics, and it was that. But there was also a large moderate circle that—with some notable exceptions—has generally been ignored in scholarly discussions of the period.[5] By focusing on the cultural processes of journalism, on mediating roles and social relations, I seek to make palpable this middle ground, a middle ground that made up much of Russian educated society of this period.[6] In doing so, I focus on the mediating roles that Tur and Panaeva played and argue that factors such as relationships and the mechanisms of support are much more important in the creation of Russian journalism than has usually been recognized. There is a potential danger in this move, as it may reinforce stereotypes about women: that is, that women are primarily suited (or limited) to the relational. It would, of course, be inaccurate to assume that the kind of activity I describe (e.g., facilitating relationships, providing physical and emotional support) is all women were capable of (or, conversely, that men are incapable of these forms of nurture). Rather, as many scholars have argued, when members of nondominant groups participate in a dominant culture's institutions, they do so in ways that often look different from the strategies the dominant group employs.[7] Women's participation in Russian journalism is one example of this process. My study of Tur and Panaeva delineates some of the specific workings of this process in Russia of the midcentury and suggests the costs of forgetting those who fall outside dominant cultural paradigms.

In the late 1970s, an article appeared claiming Tur as the first Russian woman journalist.[8] Given that women as prominent as Catherine the Great were involved in journalism, this error indicates the extent to which women's contributions to journalism have not been seriously considered in the Russian context. Tur—like Panaeva—was among the early female journalists in Russia, but she was certainly not the first. Examples of earlier or contemporary women journalists include Catherine the Great, who published the moralistic-satirical journal *Vsiakaia vsiachina* (*All Sorts*, 1769); Ekaterina Dashkova, who founded two scholarly periodicals, *Sobesednik liubitelei rossiiskogo slova . . .* (*Conversational Journal of Lovers of the Russian Word . . .*, 1783–1784) and *Novye ezhemesiachnye sochineniia* (*New Monthly Works*, 1786–1796); Mariia Vernadskaia, who, with her husband, coedited *Ekonomicheskii ukazatel'* (*Economic Index*, 1857–1860) and also produced many publicistic articles;[9] and female reporters such as Aleksandra Sokolova and Aleksandra Toliverova.[10]

Panaeva, Tur, and Vernadskaia all entered the journalistic field in the middle of the nineteenth century. At this time, journalism in Russia was coming into its own as a powerful cultural force,[11] and editors and publishers in the 1850s and 1860s could potentially exercise a much more extensive influence in formulating public opinion than could earlier journalists or individual female reporters. Therefore, this time period is a particularly intriguing site at which to begin an investigation of women's journalism. And Panaeva and Tur provide a nice counterpoint to each other: they were approximately the same age (Tur, b. 1815; Panaeva, b. 1819 or 1820), they knew many of the same people, both wrote fiction, and both were deeply involved in journalism for many years, Tur in Moscow and Panaeva in St. Petersburg. But their paths into the field were very different, and so they provide two divergent examples, two possible models of how women could be journalists in nineteenth-century Russia.

Due to the dearth of information on Russian women journalists, it is difficult to place Panaeva's and Tur's journalistic achievements in context. How unusual was it, for example, for a woman in Russia to edit and publish a journal as did Tur, or to be an active member of an editorial staff as was Panaeva? Judging by the major reference works on prerevolutionary journalism (e.g., Lisovskii, Dement'ev, and Masanov), it was extremely rare indeed. But it is clear that these sources are incomplete: Panaeva, an active member of the editorial staff of the journal *Sovremennik (The Contemporary),* is not listed as a journalist in any of these sources. And although Vernadskaia coedited *Ekonomicheskii ukazatel'* with her husband, Ivan Vernadskii, only he is listed as editor in Dement'ev and Lisovskii.[12] It is particularly difficult to know, then, how many women were involved in journalism, because it is highly likely that other women also coedited publications with male relatives or friends and are similarly not listed in reference works.

Panaeva, born Brianskaia (the daughter of noted actors), is today a better-known figure than Tur, largely due to Kornei Chukovskii's reeditions of her fictionalized memoirs, *Semeistvo Tal'nikovykh (The Tal'nikov Family,* 1848), in the 1920s and the several republications of her *Vospominaniia (Memoirs)* since 1889.[13] Panaeva is usually discussed either as the author of memoirs or as the common-law wife of Nikolai Nekrasov. Yet she was a well-known author of fiction in her own right, writing under the pseudonym of N. Stanitskii; she contributed a great deal to *Sovremennik,* and she hosted a Petersburg salon that Belinskii, Chernyshevskii, Dostoevskii, Ivan Turgenev,[14] and others regularly frequented. This, as we shall see, is not only a social or literary but also a journalistic fact.

Evgeniia Tur, pseudonym of the Countess Salias de Turnemir, was born into the Sukhovo-Kobylin family and lived most of her life in the upper circles of aristocratic Moscow society (thus her social background was very different from Panaeva's). Several years after Tur's French-born husband was exiled to France (1844), she began publishing fiction (1849) to support herself and her children; financial need continued to be an important factor in her involvement in the Russian literary world. Tur quickly became a noted author of fiction; from 1849 to 1865, she was widely regarded as Russia's foremost woman author.[15] Panaeva and Nekrasov, in fact, were so enthusiastic about Tur's work that they postponed the publication of their novel *Mertvoe ozero (The Dead Sea)* in order to publish the first part of her novel, *Plemiannitsa (The Niece)*, in *Sovremennik*.[16] In the late 1850s and 1860s, Tur turned her attention to literary criticism (apparently an unusual activity for a woman in this period)[17] and wrote articles that were highly praised both by her contemporaries and by later scholars.[18] Throughout the 1840s and sporadically in the 1850s, she hosted a salon frequented by many of the most prominent figures of literary and intellectual Russia, including Timofei Granovskii, Nikolai Ogarev, and Turgenev.[19] In 1861 she founded a periodical, *Russkaia rech' (Russian Speech)*, which lasted for one year and one issue (January 1861–January 1862).[20]

As is clear from the foregoing descriptions, neither Tur nor Panaeva was exclusively or perhaps even primarily a journalist (at least by today's standards). This was not unusual for the period (the 1850s and 1860s), which witnessed the early stages of journalism as a profession in Russia.[21] For most of those who ran journals throughout the nineteenth century, this activity was only one aspect of a (usually literary or scholarly) career (cf. Dostoevskii, Katkov, Nekrasov, Panaev).[22] In this way, then, Panaeva and Tur followed the usual (male) journalistic script.

Panaeva's contributions to *Sovremennik* were significant, although they have been underestimated partly because much of her involvement in the journal was indirect or "imperceptible" in the way described by the anonymous author of the quotation with which this essay begins. According to Panaeva's memoirs, it was she who thought of the scheme by which Panaev and Nekrasov could buy the journal.[23] The main obstacle was a lack of funds, a seemingly insurmountable problem that Panaeva solved by suggesting that her husband sell some property so that he and Nekrasov could buy the rights to *Sovremennik*; Panaev followed this advice.[24] Thus Panaeva, through her practical vision, made possible the (re)birth of *Sovremennik*, which, under the editorship of Nekrasov, became the most popular journal of its day.[25]

Having a wide circulation was obviously important for the continuance of *Sovremennik*. And Panaeva's novel and novellas helped sell the journal. She wrote fiction regularly for *Sovremennik*, including two novels coauthored with Nekrasov (*Tri strany sveta [Three Sides of the World]* and *Mertvoe ozero*).[26] Her fiction was widely read, as evidenced both by the reviews of the day and by the fact that many of her works (both those she wrote by herself and those written with

Nekrasov) were reissued as separate volumes soon after they appeared in *Sovremennik*.[27] In addition, Panaeva claimed that Turgenev was one of her most enthusiastic readers.[28] A backhanded indication that her works were widely known and influential is that the renowned critic Dmitrii Pisarev complained that her fiction had too great an impact on Russian society.[29]

While later commentators have largely ignored her role in the running of *Sovremennik*, Panaeva saw herself as an integral part of the editorial staff of the journal. She performed many editorial duties, including reading manuscripts and proofs and reviewing books.[30] Also, at her suggestion, a section on fashion was added to *Sovremennik*, for which she then regularly wrote articles. These fashion pages may have contributed to the popularity of *Sovremennik*; in the West—and apparently in Russia—the inclusion of similar features helped increase the circulation of various publications.[31]

The few extant letters of Panaeva to Nekrasov also indicate the extent of her involvement with the journal. These letters are full of news about *Sovremennik*. In 1855 she wrote to Nekrasov saying: "And here's more good literary news for you. We and Kraevskii have been granted a political section, i.e., what we tried so hard to get last year. . . . Officially we are not supposed to know this yet, which is why we didn't print it in the announcement."[32] Panaeva says "we" worked to get a political section and "we" got one. Her use of language stands in striking contrast to that of Martsishevskaia, who edited these letters: in explaining the struggle for the political section, Martsishevskaia notes only the roles played by Ivan Panaev and Nekrasov without even hinting that Panaeva may have been involved.[33] It is exactly this kind of reportage that has resulted in Panaeva's becoming and remaining in- (or now perhaps we could say, barely) visible. Martsishevskaia also gives the lie to one point made by my epigraph writer: it is not only male scholars who fail to take "intangible" influences into account.

Panaeva was also instrumental in the "discovery" of some of those who contributed regularly to *Sovremennik*, most notably the critic Nikolai Dobroliubov. Ivan Panaev, after reading a manuscript by Dobroliubov, sent him away without offering him any hope of working with the journal. But Panaeva interceded and gave the manuscript to Nekrasov, who then met with Dobroliubov. Thus Dobroliubov's fruitful collaboration with *Sovremennik* was made possible through her influence.[34] Of course, Dobroliubov might have joined the staff of *Sovremennik* eventually, but given his premature death in 1861 (only four years after he began his association with the journal), Panaeva's timely intercession should not be underestimated.

Panaeva played a similarly instrumental role in the case of several collaborators for *Sovremennik,* including the author Fedor Reshetnikov.[35] When Reshetnikov first visited the offices of the journal, Nekrasov did not have time to meet with him and requested that Panaeva read Reshetnikov's manuscript, *Podlipovtsy (The People of Podlipnoe,* published in 1864), to determine whether the work was worth Nekrasov's time. She read and recommended the manuscript, and Nekrasov published it; Reshetnikov became a talented writer who published regularly in *Sovremennik* until his untimely death in 1871.[36]

In these relationships, Panaeva served as a mediator, a timeworn role for females and one that describes much of her involvement with *Sovremennik*. She helped with the business of running the journal by regularly negotiating with creditors and contributors[37] and, as Ledkovsky puts it, "through her diplomacy would provide indispensable sums to pay impatient contributors."[38] And Panaeva often facilitated relationships between literati who were otherwise at odds. An incident Panaev describes was apparently typical: several days after Belinskii had published a bitingly critical article on Vladimir Sollogub's society tale *Tarantas (The Traveling Cart),* Sollogub appeared at the Panaevs' while the critic was visiting. Belinskii wanted to leave, but Panaeva convinced him to stay and thereby was the agency by which a reconciliation between the two was effected.[39] This kind of mediation is exactly the kind of "invisible influence" that we must begin to document if we are to understand women's role in Russian history and literature. The network of relationships *(znakomstvo)* was of vital importance for literati: one's acquaintances often determined where one published one's works. Thus Panaeva's effect on these webs of relationships is a significant journalistic fact.

It is similarly difficult (and similarly necessary) to consider the role Panaeva's salon played in the running of *Sovremennik*. Ledkovsky notes that the aims of journalism were an important topic of discussion at Panaeva's salon.[40] Surely such discussion facilitated the publication of the journal in ways that are difficult to document but are no less real or significant for that. It is also clear that for both Panaeva and Tur, there was an intimate relationship between their salons and the journals in which they participated: many of the *raznochintsy* (nonnoble intellectuals) who attended Panaeva's "Mondays" collaborated on *Sovremennik*, and the liberal nobility who frequented Tur's salon were the future contributors to *Russkaia rech'*.

Panaeva helped to establish and run *Sovremennik*, but she was not primarily responsible for the journal. Tur, who founded, edited, and published *Russkaia rech'*, provides a different image of the Russian woman journalist in the nineteenth century. And *Russkaia rech'*, a small liberal paper that lasted for only one year, was a very different venture from *Sovremennik*, a so-called thick journal whose first editor was Pushkin and that, after Nekrasov and Panaev took over in 1847, became and remained for many years one of the most widely read and later widely studied journals of the nineteenth century. Panaeva, then, was a member of the staff of one of the most influential Russian journals of the nineteenth century, whereas Tur ran a publication that had no established tradition behind it, nor was it successful in material terms.

Tur began her work in journalism early; from the age of eighteen, she regularly helped Nikolai Nadezhdin with various editorial duties for *Teleskop (Telescope)*. Just as Panaeva did for *Sovremennik*, Tur read proofs and corrected them; she also translated several works for *Teleskop*.[41] Tur was intimately involved with Nadezhdin (they nearly eloped in 1836), and as she records in her diaries (1834–1836), he shared with her the details and frustrations of editing a journal. These experiences may have encouraged her later to found her own periodical, and they must have helped her to understand the practical side of journal publishing.[42]

From 1856 to 1860, Tur edited the belles lettres section of Mikhail Katkov's newly founded *Russkii vestnik (Russian Herald)*.[43] Her duties were extensive; she reviewed, evaluated, and corrected texts sent in for publication to the journal,[44] and several sources concur that Tur did an excellent job editing the section.[45] Many noteworthy works were published in *Russkii vestnik* during the time that she was in charge of the literature department; these included fiction by Saltykov-Shchedrin *(Gubernskie ocherki)*, Goncharov *(Ot Kronshtadta do mysa Lizarda: Iz putevykh zapisok)*, and Sergei Aksakov (parts of *Semeinaia khronika*).[46] Tur, like Panaeva, also had an eye for new talent, and she published works by unknown authors as well: an anonymous obituary writer (the author of the epigraph) credits Tur with the important discovery of Nadezhda Sokhanskaia.[47]

In fact, many works by women authors were published during Tur's tenure at *Russkii vestnik*. These included works by Russian writers (e.g., "E. Narskaia," Iuliia Zhadovskaia, and Tur herself) and by non-Russian writers (e.g., Elizabeth Gaskell's *North and South*, George Sand's *La Daniella,* and Harriet Beecher Stowe's *Uncle Tom's Cabin*). Also, the Ukrainian/Russian writer Marko Vovchok's (Vilinskaia) *Narodnye Ukrainskie rasskazy* were published in *Russkii vestnik* in Vovchok's Russian translation beginning in July 1858, eight months before Turgenev's translation appeared (March 1859).[48] Given Tur's emphasis elsewhere on improving the position of women (and particularly women authors), the fact that so many female writers were published in *Russkii vestnik* in this period suggests that she wanted to promote and encourage women writers and help them succeed.[49]

Tur left *Russkii vestnik* in April or May 1860, and the first issue of her own publication, *Russkaia rech'*, came out in January 1861. The basic tendency of Tur's journal was centrist, as she announced in her program statement:

Our publication will not admit any harsh extremes, nor any kind of doctrinairism . . . but instead will never betray one great principle: it will not forget that the main foundation of true freedom of opinion is respect for the right . . . of each person . . . to think independently. . . . It seems to us that the idea of unifying those literary forces, capable of serving the worthy goal of the gradual and peaceful progress of Russian society answers, as nothing else could, our needs today.[50]

Tur thus took up a mediating stance in the very form of her journal.[51] She also played the role of mediator (and nurturer) in other ways in her journalistic venture: like Panaeva, Tur facilitated the careers of others. Nikolai Leskov, Aleksandr Levitov, and Vasilii Sleptsov all published some of their first works in *Russkaia rech'* and later went on to become better known than their mentor.[52] And Aleksei Suvorin began what became an illustrious (and sometimes infamous) career as a journalist with *Russkaia rech'*; when he was still an unknown, Tur spotted his talent and insisted that he move to Moscow to work on her journal.[53] This is an example of Tur's "imperceptible influence"; like Panaeva's, this influence is not obvious given the way that histories have usually been constructed, and like Panaeva's, its effects were far-reaching.

Despite the differences in the forms of journalism in which they engaged, then, both women played mediating roles. And this focus on mediation is one of the reasons they have been (nearly) lost to history: the links, the mediators, have been less obvious than the extreme positions that the two women tried to reconcile.

Another similarity in the journalistic approaches of Tur and Panaeva is that both focused on women and both wanted to attract female readers, a growing audience in mid-nineteenth-century Russia. Panaeva demonstrated this by including a fashion section in *Sovremennik* and by concentrating on women's experiences in her fiction. The titles of her works bear witness to this, for example, *Zhenskaia dolia (Women's Lot), Stepnaia baryshnia (Lady of the Steppes),* and *Bezobraznyi muzh (The Ugly Husband)*.[54] Panaeva's concentration on women's concerns elicited a biting response from Dmitrii Pisarev, who, in a review of *Zhenskaia dolia,* took her to task for (among other things) misunderstanding "women's emancipation."[55] Tur included many works by women authors in *Russkaia rech',* just as she had when she edited the belles lettres section of *Russkii vestnik.* She also often published literary criticism of works by women, writing many of these articles herself. Heroines figure prominently in much of the fiction published in Tur's journal, and articles that discuss topics like education and labor usually take into account the views of, and effects on, women.

It is not surprising that Tur focused on such issues, for she expected that women would make up the main readership of *Russkaia rech'*.[56] Run by a woman, focusing on women's concerns, directed at women, was *Russkaia rech',* then, a "woman's journal"? This deceptively simple term may be misleading, for it is used to refer both to publications edited by women and to periodicals such as *Damskii zhurnal (Ladies' Journal,* 1823–1833) and *Rassvet (Daybreak,* 1859–1862), which were edited by men and catered to "women's tastes." Tur's journal fits into neither category, for though she ran it herself, her program was closer to that of the thick journals than to those of the other (known) periodicals run by women, such as *Russkaia khoziaika (Russian Housewife)* or *Moda (Fashion).* Little is known about these periodicals: *Russkaia khoziaika* was founded in 1861, had an all-female editorial staff, and focused on household matters (*domovodstvo*), and *Moda*, which centered on fashion, had four women publishers between 1851 to 1861.[57] One has only to glance at the subtitle of *Russkaia rech'* to see that the focus of Tur's journal was broader than those of *Moda* and *Russkaia khoziaika*. *Russkaia rech'* was to be a "Survey of Literature, History, Art, and Public Life in the West and Russia" [Obozrenie literatury, istorii, iskusstva i obshchestvennoi zhizni na zapade i v Rossii]. And politics was later added to this list.[58] Tur's paper, then, was anomalous, in the contexts of both the usual Russian thick journals and publications edited by women.[59] In terms of the range of topics covered, she published the kind of periodical usually associated with men, yet *Russkaia rech'* often focused on issues of concern specifically to women.

While Tur made few direct comments on the effect of gender on her literary activities and their reception, her correspondence indicates that she was aware that her decision to edit a journal was an unusual choice for a woman. Further, her experience demonstrates the kinds of gender-based difficulties that women encountered when they entered the journalistic world. It was not so much — or not only — that there was overt discrimination against women, but that such discrimination existed in less tangible (though no less real) ways (again the words of N.V. are applicable, though here differently nuanced). In a letter to her sister, Tur noted that being female was a disadvantage in publishing a journal: "The idea of starting a journal is impracticable in war time. . . . [Furthermore] I am a woman, which is an obstacle" [L'idée d'avoir un Journal est impraticable pendant la guerre. . . . je suis femme, cela empêche].[60]

Tur does not go on to explain why her gender would make it more difficult to launch a journalistic enterprise, assuming, perhaps, that the reasons are obvious. And in part, they are: women (in contrast to men) could not participate in civil or military service (roughly, the "public" realm), nor did they have access to university education until the late 1860s.[61] Without such education, it was difficult to obtain the qualifications necessary to work on a journal. In addition, many of the friendships that later led to journalistic collaboration were formed or cemented at the university (cf. Herzen and Ogarev, Katkov).

Such subtle formative societal influences posed enormous barriers to women's participation in the public realm, including journalism. Educated society did not approve of women taking public leadership roles, considering such positions improper for ladies. These attitudes made it difficult both for women to conceive of themselves as leaders and for society to accept women in certain highly visible or semiofficial capacities. Given the importance of the written word in Russia, editing a periodical was a powerful public role, for as noted in the introduction to this volume, it was one of the major ways of influencing opinion.[62]

Because it was difficult for women to establish the kinds of contacts necessary to be effective journalists, it is particularly important to make explicit how Tur and Panaeva gained access to journalistic circles. Panaeva's entrée was first through her legal husband, and later through Nekrasov. Although Tur's journalistic venture was much more independent of male influence than was Panaeva's, it was in her early work with Nadezhdin that Tur met people who later helped to facilitate her entrance into the literary world.[63] And as editor of the belles lettres section of *Russkii vestnik,* she had the opportunity to make many professional contacts with those who later agreed to contribute to her journal.

But Panaeva's and Tur's involvement in journalism was not merely a matter of having the right connections or opportunities. Many women would not have thought of working in journalism; for others, even if they had had the desire, it would not have been possible. Panaeva's and Tur's experiences indicate that being a woman posed specific difficulties for working as journalists: the two women were able to engage in this work partly because, in them, desire, talent, and opportunity coincided. Their persistence and imagination must also be taken into account. As far as we know, they had few models for the kind of journalistic work in which they engaged. It took a creative intelligence to envision the role for themselves; carrying it out demanded courage and a strong will.

Avdot'ia Panaeva was in large part responsible for the success of *Sovremennik,* though histories of the journal, even when they mention her, do not say so. Evgeniia Tur published and edited *Russkaia rech'* for a year. True, she failed to make it a popular publication with a long life; but given the obstacles with which she had to contend, it is remarkable that *Russkaia rech'* was published at all.[64]

It is, as N. V. warned, difficult to gauge the influence of these women on Russian society. And it is unclear whether later Russian women journalists consciously looked to Tur and Panaeva as models. But these two may be considered precursors for the later journalists, for in their insistent foregrounding of issues concerning women, Tur and Panaeva helped to establish women as a palpable presence in "public" discourse.[65] Further, by being involved in journalism, Tur and Panaeva were among those who made the concept of a Russian woman journalist a reality, thus making it easier for other women to imagine themselves in this role and to take it on.

My reading of Panaeva's and Tur's involvement in journalism shows that these women palpably contributed to the development of journalism. By implication, this analysis suggests that many other women were also contributing to the journalistic field in a variety of ways. And further, that if one shifts one's angle of vision, not only are women's contributions visible but the field of journalism also looks different: journalism is not simply, or even mainly, about economic processes or the activities of a few influential (male) journalists, nor is it adequately represented by studies that focus on the easily tangible—the published works. The cultural processes that engender journalism extend far beyond publication, both to the various kinds of work that make publication possible and to the effects of printed works on individual readers and social groups.

As noted in the introduction to this volume, scholarship on women's involvement in Russian journalism is in its early stages. Given the lack of a broader context, then, it is difficult to draw definitive conclusions about issues such as the specific influences of Tur's and Panaeva's journalisms or their readerships. It is clear, though, that both women directed their journalistic work to female readers. Yet the shape and significance of the interaction between readers and journals edited by women is largely unknown, for the composition, tastes, and influence of this group has been little studied (the preceding essay by Miranda Remnek is the first work to address the issue of female readership in any depth).[66] As Remnek's and other essays in this collection demonstrate, further research on this (or these) female reading public(s) and its (their) relationship to "women's journalism" will lead to a radical shift in understanding the role of journalism in Russian culture.

Notes

I am grateful to Beth Holmgren and Barbara Norton for insightful readings and very helpful comments on earlier drafts of this essay.

1 N. V., "Grafinia E. V. Sal'ias (Evgeniia Tur)," *Nizhegorodskie gubernskie vedomosti,* 25 March 1892. Hereafter I will refer to the anonymous author of this article as "N. V."

2 There are many cogent critiques of this and other kinds of essentialism (and of antiessentialism), as feminist critics work out ways to (partially) retain the category "woman," yet not restrict women to stereotypical paradigms. For various aspects of these debates, see note 7 in the introduction to this volume and Kathy Ferguson, *The Man Question: Visions of Subjectivity in Feminist Theory* (Berkeley, 1993); Diana Fuss, *Essentially Speaking: Feminism, Nature, and Difference* (New York, 1989); Elizabeth V. Spelman, *Inessential Woman: Problems of Exclusion in Feminist Thought* (Boston, 1988); Gayatri Chakravorty Spivak, *In Other Worlds: Essays in Cultural Politics* (New York, 1987).

3 See, for example, Henry Louis Gates Jr., *Loose Canons: Notes on the Culture Wars* (New York, 1992); Sandra M. Gilbert and Susan Gubar, *The Madwoman in the Attic: The Woman Writer and the Nineteenth-Century Literary Imagination* (New Haven, 1984); Robert von Hallberg, ed., *Canons* (Chicago, 1983–1984); Lillian S. Robinson, "Canon Fathers and Myth Universe," *New Literary History* 19 (1987): 23–35; Barbara Herrnstein Smith, "Contingencies of Value," *Critical Inquiry* 10 (September 1983): 1–35.

4 Virtually all the major histories and analyses assume that journalism was a male province. See, for example, note 5 in the introduction.

5 Exceptions to this include *Russia's Missing Middle Class: The Professions in Russian History,* ed. Harley Barzer (Armonk, N.Y., 1996); and *Between Tsar and People: Educated Society and the Quest for Public Identity in Late Imperial Russia,* ed. Edith W. Clowes et al. (Princeton, 1991).

6 For a fuller discussion of the critical middle ground in the 1860s, see my *(Not) Writing like a Russian Girl: Evgeniia Tur, V. Krestovskii, and Nineteenth-Century Women's Prose* (forthcoming, Northwestern University Press).

7 On this topic, see, for example, Gloria Anzaldúa, *Borderlands/La Frontera: The New Mestiza* (San Francisco, 1987); Henry Louis Gates Jr., *The Signifying Monkey: A Theory of African-American Literary Criticism* (New York, 1988); *Scattered Hegemonies: Postmodernity and Transnational Feminist Practice,* ed. Inderpal Grewal and Caren Kaplan (Minneapolis, 1994); Dorothy E. Smith, *The Everyday World as Prob-*

lematic: A Feminist Sociology (Boston, 1987); and Patricia Williams, *The Alchemy of Race and Rights: Diary of a Law Professor* (Cambridge, Mass., 1991).

8   See Valentin Dmitriev, "Pervaia russkaia zhurnalistka," *Literaturnaia Rossiia,* 17 July 1977, 24.

9   Vernadskaia (1831–1860), the first woman in Russia known to have written about political economy, contributed a number of articles on the position of women to *Ekonomicheskii ukazatel'*. See M. N. Vernadskaia, *Sobranie sochineniia pokoinoi Marii Nikolaevnoi Vernadskoi, urozhd: Shigaevoi* (St. Petersburg, 1862). *Ekonomicheskii ukazatel'* (with some title variations) was published until 1861. (Vernadskaia died 12 October 1860.)

10 Louise McReynolds details the activities of these (and other) reporters in "Female Journalists in Prerevolutionary Russia," *Journalism History* 14, no. 4 (1987): 104–10.

11 William Mills Todd III, "Periodicals in Literary Life of the Early Nineteenth Century," in *Literary Journals in Imperial Russia,* ed. Deborah A. Martinsen (Cambridge, 1997), 37–38, 60.

12 See *Russkaia periodicheskaia pechat' (1702–1894): Spravochnik,* ed. A. G. Dement'ev, A. V. Zapadov, and M. S. Cherepakhov (Moscow, 1959); *Russkaia periodicheskaia pechat' 1703–1900 gg.,* comp. N. M. Lisovskii (Petrograd, 1915); *Ukazateli soderzhaniia russkikh zhurnalov i prodolzhaiushchikhsia izdanii, 1755–1970 gg.,* ed. Iu. I. Masanov, N. V. Nitkina, and Z. D. Titova (1975; Newtonville, Mass., 1979). In the thirteen-page article on *Sovremennik* in *Russkaia periodicheskaia pechat' (1702–1894)* (article by S. G. Rudich), Panaeva is mentioned only once and then not directly in connection with *Sovremennik,* but rather at the end of the article as a contributor to *Illiustrirovannyi zhurnal.* Her editorial work is not noted; neither are her contributions (fiction) to *Sovremennik,* which were far more numerous than those she made to *Illiustrirovannyi zhurnal. Russkaia periodicheskaia pechat' 1703–1900 gg.* does not mention either Panaeva or Vernadskaia; Masanov does not mention Panaeva, Tur, Vernadskii, or Vernadskaia.

13 *Semeistvo Tal'nikovykh* was first published in 1848, and Panaeva's *Vospominaniia* first appeared in 1889 in *Istoricheskii vestnik.* Kornei Chukovskii edited and published her memoirs in 1927; this edition has been republished several times since then (1933, 1948, 1956, 1972). Chukovskii and G. V. Krasnov, who wrote the notes for some of these editions, frequently question Panaeva's accuracy, sometimes in biting terms. I suggest that Panaeva's forms of "inaccuracy" were neither as pervasive nor as problematic as Chukovskii and Krasnov indicate. See below, notes 24 and 36, for examples.

14 Throughout, whenever I refer to Turgenev, it will be to Ivan Sergeevich Turgenev and not to the other notable literati or intellectuals of the same surname (e.g., Aleksandr Ivanovich).

15 See, for example, A. N. Ostrovskii, *"Oshibka," Polnoe sobranie sochinenii,* vol. 10 (Moscow, 1978), 7–17 (originally published in *Moskvitianin* in 1849); I. S. Turgenev, *Polnoe sobranie sochinenii i pisem,* vol. 4 (Moscow, 1980), 473–90 (originally published in *Sovremennik* [January 1852]); Knizhnik (Golitsyn), *Slovar' russkikh pisatel'nits, Russkii arkhiv,* nos. 11–12 (1865): 1205; and the anonymous articles "*Povesti i rasskazy* E. Tur," *Damskii vestnik* (July 1860), and "*Povesti i rasskazy* Evgenii Tur," *Svetoch,* book 4 (St. Petersburg, 1860): 45–61.

16 B. V. Mel'gunov, *Nekrasov-zhurnalist (maloizuchennye aspekty problemy)* (Leningrad, 1989), 186.

17 Women who practiced literary criticism in mid-nineteenth-century Russia include Natal'ia Grot and Mariia Vernadskaia. In the 1850s, Grot's works appeared mainly in educational journals *(Zhurnal dlia vospitaniia);* throughout the 1860s, she published literary criticism. Vernadskaia produced publicistic articles and essays on political economy from the mid-1850s until her death in 1860. Mariia Tsebrikova (1835–1917), primarily a literary critic, published articles and fiction from 1860 to 1911. On Tsebrikova, see *Dictionary of Russian Women Writers,* ed. Marina Ledkovsky, Charlotte Rosenthal, and Mary Zirin (Westport, Conn., 1994), 659–62. On female critics, see also Catriona Kelly, "Missing Links: Russian Women Writers as Critics of Women Writers," in *Russian Writers on Russian Writers,* ed. Faith Wigzell (Oxford, 1994), 67–79.

18 "*Povesti i rasskazy* E. Tur," 99; D. D. Iazykov, "Literaturnaia deiatel'nost' Evgenii Tur," *IV* (May 1892): 489; A. S. Dolinin, introduction to *Gody blizosti s Dostoevskim,* by A. P. Suslova (Moscow, 1928), 171.

19 One significant difference between Panaeva's and Tur's salons is that the *raznochintsy* intellectuals did not visit Tur's salon regularly (even when they were in Moscow). *Raznochintsy* literally means "different ranks." The term applied to those who were intellectuals not of noble birth, a group that entered Russian urban society in the nineteenth century and became particularly important at the midcentury.

20 Because the format of Tur's journal was somewhere between that of a journal and a newspaper, I follow the practice of her contemporaries and refer to it as both. This slippage of terms was fairly common in the nineteenth century.

21 I am using the term "profession" loosely and following William Todd's description of the "professionalization" of Russian letters in his *Fiction*

and Society in the Age of Pushkin: Ideology, Institutions, and Narrative (Cambridge, Mass., 1986), especially 45–105.

22 There were exceptions: A. A. Kraevskii and A. S. Suvorin were primarily journalists.

23 A. Ia. Panaeva, *Vospominaniia* (Moscow, 1972), 153. Subsequent references will be to this edition. There are, of course, difficulties in citing Panaeva's memoirs as the main source on her journalistic activities, given the questions raised about their reliability (see notes 13, 24, and 36). In light of the importance of the project of (re)integrating Russian women's journalism into the history of Russian letters, and given the dearth of information available on this aspect of Panaeva's life, it is important to use all possible sources — recognizing, of course, that each presents only a partial perspective.

24 Krasnov, who compiled the notes for the 1972 edition of Panaeva's *Vospominaniia*, points out that Nekrasov does not mention her participation in this discussion. See Panaeva, *Vospominaniia*, 420 n. 3. There are many possible ways to interpret this fact; Krasnov intimates that Panaeva is wrong, though there is no compelling reason to trust Nekrasov's account over hers.

25 Pushkin was the original editor in 1836; P. A. Pletnev ran *Sovremennik* from Pushkin's death in 1837 until 1847, when Nekrasov and Panaev bought the rights to the journal.

26 *Tri strany sveta* was first published in *Sovremennik* from 1848–1849; parts of this work were republished in other journals, and it was reissued three times in the mid- to late nineteenth century (in 1848 and 1849, in 1851, and in 1872). *Mertvoe ozero* was first published in *Sovremennik* in 1851 and came out as a separate edition in 1852.

27 See, for example, Panaeva ("N. Stanitskii"), *Neobdumannyi shag (An Ill-Considered Step)*, *Sovremennik* (1850); *Zhenskaia dolia (Women's Lot)*, *Sovremennik* (March, April, May 1862, and as a separate edition in 1864); *Roman v Peterburgskom polusvete (A Romance in the Petersburg Demi-monde)*, *Sovremennik* 3–4 (March–April 1860, and separately in 1863).

28 R. V. Bykov, *Siluety dalekogo proshlogo* (Moscow-Leningrad, 1930), 84.

29 D. I. Pisarev, "Kukol'naia tragediia s buketom grazhdanskoi skorbi," *Sochineniia D. I. Pisareva v shesti tomakh*, vol. 4 (St. Petersburg, 1901), 151. Originally published in *RSlovo*, no. 8 (1864).

30 Kornei Chukovskii, introduction to Panaeva's *Semeistvo Tal'nikovykh* (Leningrad, 1928), 35.

31 Marzolf, *Up from the Footnote*, 12, 19, 20–21. Christine Ruane's and Carolyn Marks's essays in this volume detail the great interest in fash-

ion, which suggests that fashion pages increased the circulation of Russian periodicals. In 1859 *Sovremennik* first published its subscription figures (and it was the first journal to do so). There were 5,500 subscribers, which was the broadest readership of any journal of its time. See V. Evgen'ev-Maksimov, *"Sovremennik" pri Chernyshevskom i Dobroliubove* (Leningrad, 1936), 467.

32 K. Martsishevskaia, ed., "Tri pis'ma Panaevoi k Nekrasovu," *Literaturnoe nasledstvo* 53–54 (1949): 118.
33 Ibid., 117–30.
34 Panaeva, *Vospominaniia*, 254–55.
35 The fiction of Fedor Mikhailovich Reshetnikov (1841–1871) focused on nonaristocratic characters (e.g., peasants turned industrial workers, miners, strikers).
36 Panaeva, *Vospominaniia*, 349–51. Krasnov casts doubt on Panaeva's story, saying: "Such a conversation couldn't possibly have occurred" [takogo dialoga byt' ne moglo]. Panaeva, *Vospominaniia*, 459 n. 1. Even if Panaeva's chronology is off, however, Krasnov's statement is too strong; a similar conversation could have taken place at a different time.
37 Panaeva, *Vospominaniia*, 293–94.
38 Marina Ledkovsky, "Avdotya Panaeva: Her Salon and Her Life," *Russian Literature Triquarterly* 9 (Spring 1974): 429.
39 I. I. Panaev, *Literaturnye vospominaniia* (Moscow, 1988), 343.
40 Ledkovsky, "Avdotya Panaeva," 426.
41 See the diaries of E. V. Sukhovo-Kobylina, Institut russkoi literatury (IRLI) 25.495, *tetrad'* 1.1.38, entry of 19 September [1834]. Throughout, I use brackets to indicate that I have extrapolated the date from the material in the document.

   In a recent article, Lina Bernstein notes that A. P. Elagina engaged in similar work for the journal *Vestnik Evropy* from 1808 to 1809. See Bernstein, "Women on the Verge of a New Language: Russian Salon Hostesses in the First Half of the Nineteenth Century," in *Russia, Women, Culture,* ed. Helena Goscilo and Beth Holmgren (Bloomington, 1996), 216.
42 Tur's diaries also are essential reading for understanding the history of *Teleskop*. See, for example, her gloss on Petr Chaadaev's "Philosophical Letter" and aftermath, IRLI, 25.495, *tetrad'* 1, 1.38, entry of 19 September [1834].
43 In the twenty-odd years between her involvement with *Teleskop* and her work on *Russkii vestnik,* Tur married, had three children, separated from her husband, and became a well-known author.
44 Iazykov, "Literaturnaia deiatel'nost'," 489.
45 Ibid., and N. V., "Grafinia E. V. Sal'ias."

46 The English titles of these works are, respectively, *Provincial Sketches, from Kronstadt to Lizard Point: Travel Notes* and *Family Chronicle*.
47 Kokhanovskaia was the pseudonym of Nadezhda Stepanovna Sokhanskaia (1823/25–1884), a well-known writer in the 1850s and early 1860s.
48 Tur's association with Vovchok continued as the latter regularly attended Tur's salon in Paris in 1862. See *Literaturnoe nasledstvo. Iz Parizhskogo arkhiva I. S. Turgeneva. Kniga vtoraia iz neizdannoi perepiski* (Moscow, 1964), 197, 302. See also Tur to Vovchok, IRLI, 9524.lvib44, ll. 1–4.
49 "E. Narskaia" was the pseudonym of Katkov's sister-in-law, Natal'ia Petrovna Shalikova (1815–1878), who published fiction mainly in the 1850s. Iuliia Valerianovna Zhadovskaia (1824–1883) was primarily known as a poet but also wrote prose.
50 "Ob izdanii g-zhi Evgenii Tur v 1861 godu gazety *Russkaia rech'*," *Moskovskie vedomosti*, 27 November 1860, 2052.
51 It should be noted that many contributors to the journal were well-known academics of the Westernizer tendency, including the folklorist Aleksandr Afanas'ev, the historians Konstantin Bestuzhev-Riumin, Aleksei Galakhov, and Sergei Solov'ev, and the literary scholars Fedor Buslaev and Petr Bartenev. Bartenev published his well-known monograph "Pushkin v Iuzhnoi Rossii" in *Russkaia rech'*, beginning in no. 85 (22 October 1861): 509–12. Bartenev was the publisher of *Russkaia starina*, and Buslaev, a linguist and folklorist, was a professor at Moscow University.
52 N. S. Leskov (1831–1895) became one of Russia's best-known authors of short fiction, A. I. Levitov (1835–1877) became one of the foremost populist writers *(pisateli-narodniki)*, and V. A. Sleptsov (1836–1878) won a reputation both in literature and as a political activist (he organized lectures for women in St. Petersburg and founded the Znamenskaia Commune in 1863).
53 Suvorin went on to become a journalist of note, which raises the interesting question as to what influence women journalists had through male journalists (or male authors, as in the case of Sleptsov, Leskov, and Levitov). Although this topic is too large to address effectively here, the following facts are suggestive: Louise McReynolds notes that Sokolova's son, V. M. Doroshevich, became a more famous journalist than his mother (McReynolds, *News under Russia's Old Regime: The Development of a Mass-Circulation Press* [Princeton, 1991], see index). Tur's only son, E. A. Salias, became a writer of fiction and a journalist; he is also better known than his mother, as is attested by the recent republication of his collected works: E. A. Salias, *Sochineniia*, 2 vols. (Mos-

cow, 1991); see also Daniil Mordovtsev, *Avantiuristy,* and E. A. Salias, *Kudesnik* (Moscow, 1993). By contrast, only two of Tur's shorter works (*Dolg* and a translation of Bulwer-Lytton, *Poslednie dni Pompei*) have been republished in Russia since 1917. In addition, a work of Tur's has recently appeared in English: *Antonina,* trans. Michael Katz (Evanston, Ill., 1996).

54 *Bezobraznyi muzh* was published in *Sovremennik* (April 1848); *Stepnaia baryshnia* in *Sovremennik* (July 1855). The latter work has been reissued in V. Uchenova, ed., *Dacha na Petergofskoi doroge: Proza russkikh pisatel'nits pervoi poloviny XIX veka* (Moscow, 1986), 343–414; it has recently appeared in translation in *Russian Women's Shorter Fiction, 1835–1860,* ed. and trans. Joe Andrew (Oxford, 1996), 319–97.

55 Pisarev, "Kukol'naia tragediia," 152–56.

56 Tur to E. V. Petrovo-Solovovo, Rossiiskaia gosudarstvennaia biblioteka (RGB), MS Division, f. 223, l. 120 [letter of April–May 1855]. In this letter, Tur discusses the possibility of starting a periodical (perhaps with Leont'ev and Katkov), and she notes what she could contribute to such an enterprise: "I count on my name which is popular in the provinces. So many women would want to have a journal in which my novels and novellas were printed *exclusively.*"

Tur's emphasis on the importance of female readers throughout her correspondence provides one counterexample to Louise McReynold's assertion that "unlike England in the eighteenth century and, to a lesser extent, America, the female reader in Russia played a negligible role in bringing women into the writing profession" (McReynolds, "Female Journalists," 105).

57 See Christine Ruane's analysis of *Moda* in this volume.

58 To convince the censorship to allow her to include a section on politics, Tur merged the paper with *Moskovskii vestnik* and named Evgenii Feoktistov, the future censor, as editor. She claimed that this was a semantic change only and that she was still running the journal. See Tur to A. S. Suvorin, Rossiiskii gosudarstvennyi arkhiv literatury i iskusstva (RGALI), f. 459, o. 1, d. 3763, l. 27, letter of 8 July 1861. See also her letter to N. I. Subbotin, *Russkii vestnik* 10 (1903): 491. This strategy, of course, raises the possibility that there were female editors behind other ostensibly male-run publications as well.

59 In the 1880s, this kind of periodical was more common, as Carolyn Marks indicates.

60 Tur to E. V. Petrovo-Solovovo, RGB, MS Division, f. 223, l. 119 [letter of spring 1855].

61 It should be noted that there were exceptions; occasionally, women did appear prominently in the "public realm" (e.g., Ekaterina Dashkova

and Nadezhda Durova). Sources differ on the exact date on which Russian institutes of higher learning were opened to women. Partly this depends on what kind of education is meant, because although female auditors were sporadically allowed to attend university lectures at some Russian institutions throughout the 1860s, special courses for women were not opened until 1869, and some degree programs were established in the 1870s. See Ruth Dudgeon, "Women and Higher Education in Russia, 1855–1905" (Ph.D. diss., George Washington University, 1975); Christine Johanson, *Women's Struggle for Higher Education in Russia, 1855–1900* (Kingston, 1987), 28–50, 59–76; and Richard Stites, *The Women's Liberation Movement in Russia: Feminism, Nihilism, and Bolshevism, 1860–1930* (Princeton, 1990), 75–88.

62 In this sense, Panaeva's position was more socially acceptable than was Tur's, for Panaeva played a behind-the-scenes role in running *Sovremennik*. In fact, she frequently diminishes her accomplishments in her memoirs. (See, e.g., her *Vospominaniia,* 153). Such self-deprecation both reflects and contributes to the social construction of gender as an "other" and lesser category; Panaeva has too often been taken at her own self-valuation, and scholars have not further examined her accomplishments and influence.

63 Feoktistov, *Vospominaniia E. M. Feoktistova: Za kulisami politiki i literatury 1848–1896,* ed. Iu. G. Oksman (Leningrad, 1929), 366.

64 See chapter 4 of my dissertation, "In Her Own Voice: Evgeniia Tur, Author, Critic, Journalist" (Stanford, 1992), for a fuller treatment of the reasons for the failure of *Russkaia rech'*.

65 Although men have usually been considered to be the primary framers of the discourse around the woman question in Russia, many women participated in this dialogue. See Jane Costlow, "Love, Work, and the Woman Question in Nineteenth-Century Women's Writing," in *Women in Russian Literature,* ed. Toby W. Clyman and Diana Greene (Westport, Conn., 1994), 61–75; and Arja Rosenholm, "The 'Woman Question' of the 1860s, and the Ambiguity of the 'Learned Woman,'" in *Gender and Russian Literature,* ed. Rosalind Marsh (Cambridge, 1996), 112–28.

66 Jeffrey Brooks, in an important study, briefly discusses female readers of a later period. See Brooks, *When Russia Learned to Read: Literacy and Popular Literature, 1861–1917* (Princeton, 1985), especially 159–60.

The Development of a Fashion Press in Late Imperial Russia

Moda: Zhurnal dlia svetskikh liudei

CHRISTINE RUANE

Women's fashion magazines, with their focus on the latest clothing styles, beauty tips, and gossip, have traditionally been viewed as "fluff" journalism and were largely ignored by scholars until recently. Seemingly unconcerned with politics or other "weighty" affairs of state, fashion magazines have celebrated the beautiful, the contingent, the fleeting nature of women's modes of dress. Because the buying and wearing of fashionable clothes were increasingly defined as "women's work" in nineteenth-century Russia, these magazines quickly became the quintessential exemplar of the women's press.[1] Yet despite its supposedly frivolous nature, the fashion press was instrumental not only in changing the ways Russians thought about clothing but also, and more importantly, in providing a forum for a serious cultural debate about the place of Russians in the modern world. Were Russians merely going to ape the modes and manners of the French, the arbiters of good taste among the Great Powers, or were they going to try to express a "Russian sensibility" in their cultural preferences? The answer to this question was by no means obvious to the readers of the Russian fashion press. The discussions about which path Russia should choose found in fashion magazines reveal the deeper cultural forces at work in the late imperial period.

If the fashion press provided a forum for cultural debate, it also played a vital role in creating a place for women in Russian journalism. The enormous success of the "marginalized" fashion magazines frequently allowed women journalists and publishers to move into other more "serious" areas of journalism dominated by men. Thus fashion magazines served as an important stepping stone for both women journalists and the women's press. This essay seeks to explore the relationship between fashion journalism and the women's press, as well as to highlight the deeper cultural forces at work in late imperial Russia, by analyzing the development of one fashion periodical, *Moda: Zhurnal dlia svetskikh liudei (Fashion: A Magazine for Society People)*, published in St. Petersburg between 1851 and 1861.[2]

The history of the Russian fashion press can be divided into two distinct periods. Between 1830 and 1870 men and women publishers tried to create a distinctly Russian fashion magazine that would appeal to the elite by reporting the fashion news in both Paris and Petersburg. The success of these magazines then encouraged publishers to expand the market to include the provincial nobility who wanted to ape the dress and mores of their Petersburg cousins. The second period (1870–1917) marked the rise of the modern fashion magazine. Now the market extended beyond the nobility to include individuals from the middle and sometimes even the lower strata of Russian society. Most magazines in this period dropped any coverage of Russian fashion news and reported only on what was à la mode in Paris. In so doing, publishers helped to include Russian women in the world of high fashion, making them feel that they were on equal footing with their Western European counterparts.[3]

Moda was just one of many fashion magazines published in Russia by the mid–nineteenth century. Its history is typical of other magazines as they tried to create and sustain in Russian women an interest in fashionable dress. But more was discussed on *Moda*'s pages than what hat to wear. *Moda* served as a training ground for Russian women to participate not just in journalism but also in the commercial and political life of the empire. The magazine's fashion reporting reflected the cultural and economic forces shaping Russian life at midcentury, belying the notion of the fashion press as "fluff" journalism. Because what Russian women put on each morning affected not just themselves but also how others perceived Russia, *Moda*'s reporters, arbiters of fashionable dress in Russia, served as vital participants in the debate to define social and national roles.

The publication of any magazine represents years of hard work. In the case of imperial Russia, the complex process of creating and funding a new magazine was compounded by government red tape.

All printed material had to be approved by the government's Main Administration for Censorship Affairs before it could appear in print, as Carolyn Marks details in the following essay. This cumbersome process ensured that the government would have a direct influence not only on what was printed in the periodicals but also on the publishing business itself.

Moda's publication history represents a typical example of how this complex process of government censorship and entrepreneurial spirit worked in imperial Russia. The magazine was the brainchild of Elizaveta Frantsova Safonova, the wife of a government official. In 1836 she received permission to publish *Zhurnal noveishego shit'ia (Magazine of New Sewing)*. The magazine was a success, and in 1838 the government permitted her to move her publishing venture from Moscow to St. Petersburg under the new title *Sanktpeterburgskii zhurnal raznogo roda shit'ia i vyshivan'ia (Magazine of Various Kinds of Sewing and Embroidery)*.[4] At the same time, recognizing the growing market for fashion magazines, Safonova petitioned the Censorship Administration to begin a new periodical called *Listki dlia svetskikh liudei: Zhurnal parizhskikh mod (Pages for High Society: A Magazine of Paris Fashions)*. Rather than limit itself simply to reproducing pictures and descriptions of foreign fashions, *Listki* would also provide "light, enjoyable reading" that would highlight the activities of the *belle monde* both at home and abroad.[5] Safonova hoped that a fashion magazine detailing the comings and goings of high society would have wide appeal. In 1846 she successfully petitioned the government to change the name of this new periodical to simply *Zhurnal parizhskikh mod (Magazine of Paris Fashions)*.[6] Unfortunately, this new name caused problems. Booksellers and subscribers confused Safonova's magazine with another called *Parizhskie mody (Paris Fashions)*, published in Moscow. To prevent the loss of any more subscribers to this rival, in 1850 Safonova again petitioned to change the name of her magazine to *Moda: Zhurnal dlia svetskikh liudei*.[7] The first issue appeared on 1 January 1851.

Moda's successful start did not put an end to changes at the magazine. Apparently hoping to make her publishing ventures into a family business, Safonova soon asked the government for permission to allow her daughter, Sofiia Lund, to publish *Moda*.[8] Just one year later, for unspecified reasons, Lund relinquished control of the magazine to Olimpiada Grigorevna Riumina, who became its publisher.[9]

The choice of Riumina is an interesting one, for she was the wife of an officer in the Imperial Guards who also served as an assistant to the inspector at the Konstantinskii School for Cadets. Her husband's position placed Riumina near court circles, which would have enhanced her ability to report on the court's social and sartorial activities. In 1854 Riumina's husband, Vladimir Nikolaevich, assumed the position of publisher.[10] He had big plans for the magazine, and in 1855 he petitioned the government to change the name and format of *Moda*. Riumin wanted to call his new publication *Peterburgskii vestnik* (Petersburg Herald). It would provide readers with advice on household management and light reading with little emphasis on fashion.

This time, the Censorship Administration refused permission to publish the new periodical because Riumin was trying to steer the magazine away from fashion into literature. His plans thwarted, Riumin gave the position of publisher back to his wife. Just a few months later, Riumina gained approval to add belles lettres and information about the fashion industry to *Moda* while still maintaining an emphasis on fashion.[11] In 1859 Nadezhda Vladimirovna Utilova, the widow of a government official, petitioned the Censorship Administration to allow her to take over as editor and publisher of *Moda*, for Riumina had recently died. In the following year, Utilova asked permission to allow Fedor Alekseevich Zinov'ev, a former lieutenant in the Volyninskii regiment and editor of a rival magazine, *Severnyi tsvetok (Northern Flower)*, to serve as managing editor and copublisher of *Moda*. In so doing, Zinov'ev merged the two magazines and also assumed some of *Moda*'s financial debts.[12]

All these changes in publishers indicate the fast pace and volatility of journalism in the mid–nineteenth century. Although many individuals were interested in starting magazines, few possessed the kind of business acumen and, perhaps more important, the financial resources to keep their publishing ventures afloat. These difficulties were compounded by capricious government censors who could and did scuttle the plans of ambitious publishers. Nevertheless *Moda*'s history also shows the significant role women played during the early years of fashion journalism. It was women like Safonova, Riumina, and Utilova and their female subscribers whose interest in fashions and fashionable people made *Moda* into a viable journalistic venture.

Moda's publishers and editorial staff had a clear agenda for their magazine. Disappointed with French fashion magazines, which only discussed events in France, *Moda*'s creators wanted a periodical that would express the interests of "our own fashionable set, with its own interests." According to the "Publication Program," which appeared in the first issue,

> Therefore we all feel the need for a fashionable publication that quickly and truthfully advises the public on all the fascinating appearances among the fashion elite, following not only the changes in toilette, but all changes that are of interest to high society in the area of fine arts and in various objects subject to changing fashions. . . . The publisher will use all possible means in order to bring literary as well as artistic attitudes to the attention of the public.[13]

The purpose of the bimonthly fashion magazine was to define the tastes and interests of Petersburg high society, which were supposed to be different from those of Western European, and in particular, Parisian, trendsetters. As we will see, the attempt to separate Russian from French interests proved to be more complicated than this simple declaration of independence would suggest.

Before analyzing the content of *Moda,* a few words are necessary about readership. Accurate numbers of subscribers to individual periodicals in Russia are difficult to find.[14] I have been unable to locate any such figures for *Moda*. However, a few hypotheses can be made based on available information. The cost of a subscription was eight rubles. This amount was rather high and probably meant that only wealthy noble families could afford to subscribe to the magazine. Furthermore, the whole focus of the periodical was on Petersburg high society. Each issue contained detailed discussions of the balls, parties, and other social events at which the elite gathered.

Moda appealed to more than Petersburg society, however. It also provided the provincial nobility with valuable information about the social life in the capital, which allowed them to feel themselves a part of the social whirl, if only vicariously. Many of the advertisements had a separate set of instructions for Petersburg residents and for individuals who ordered goods through the mail. Indeed, it was duly noted in 1856 that six copies of *Moda* were mailed to Omsk.[15] For those who were members of the fashionable elite as well as those who aspired to become a part of that world, *Moda* was required reading.

To entice readers to subscribe to *Moda,* the magazine offered a number of services to its readers. First and foremost, each issue appeared with a colored fashion plate of the latest fashion direct from Paris. Produced by French illustrators, half of the plates bore French descriptions of the clothes, and the others provided a Russian translation. For eighteen rubles more, subscribers could receive colored plates of both male and female fashions. In 1854 the magazine offered to send to its subscribers at a special discounted price the tissue paper used in making dress patterns.[16] In 1857 *Moda* tried another marketing strategy by offering the complete patterns of the outfits that appeared on its pages. More than five hundred subscribers requested back issues of the magazine to obtain the patterns.[17] These patterns could then be taken to a dressmaker or a tailor to facilitate the design of a new outfit. The magazine also provided from time to time a selection of books on embroidery and knitting.[18] All of these services helped to encourage subscriptions, particularly from women readers.

In addition to the readers' services, *Moda*'s advice columns and advertisements lured subscribers, and it is here that the gendered message of the magazine emerges most clearly. The advice columns complemented the advertisements that appeared in the magazine. And both the advice and the advertisements were aimed at women consumers. Advice about cosmetics would frequently run in the same issue with an advertisement for a new cosmetics store in St. Petersburg. The needlework column appeared simultaneously as the magazine was offering books on the subject. Thus the advice columns drew women subscribers not only to the magazine but also to the merchandise of the shops that advertised in its pages, thereby helping to promote the development of a fashion industry in Russia.

Initially, the advertisements in the magazine were rather small: just a few lines announcing the name and address of the store and the goods sold. However, they quickly grew in size, offering more information about the goods displayed. Finally, in 1858, the last page of each issue carried a full-page advertisement entitled "The Best Petersburg Stores" [Luchshie peterburgskie magaziny]. The advertisement contained recommendations for the best store in a variety of categories: fabrics, dresses, flowers, cosmetics, shoes, and lingerie. Most of the stores mentioned in the recommendations were regular advertisers in the magazine or were frequently mentioned in the fashion columns.[19] Like all other kinds of media, the Russian fashion press developed a mutually beneficial system of rewards for subscribers, advertisers, and publishers. And just as important, the consumers of both the goods and magazines were women.

Having established for itself a substantial number of readers, *Moda*'s chief mission was to advise women of the latest fashions in Paris and Petersburg. Women were seen as too capricious to make such decisions on their own. That was why they needed fashion "experts" to tell them what to wear. The writers for the magazine attempted to define what the styles for each season were and, more importantly, what they were not. To do this, *Moda* had to convince its readers that its writers really did know what the latest styles were. Only one year after its inauguration, the magazine recorded the most shocking change in women's fashions, the introduction of bloomers. The columnist reported that "the new invention of the transatlantic Mistress Bloomer could be seen everywhere where fashion reigns."[20] Two issues later, the same columnist reported a sighting on *Nevskii Prospekt* of two young women from wealthy society families promenading in bloomers. The columnist described their outfits in detail but reported that they presented "an original, but slightly strange picture." Petersburg women were advised that few Parisian women actually wore bloomers, and therefore neither should anyone else.[21]

This discussion of bloomers reveals some interesting things about *Moda* and its readers. Bloomers were quite a shock to high society in both Europe and America. The early 1850s were the period of high Victorianism, with rigid gender roles and dress. The idea of women wearing trousers shocked most proper society men and women, and Amelia Bloomer was roundly criticized for her attempt at "dress reform" that so clearly attacked gender norms. However, *Moda*'s fashion expert appeared to be unaware of this controversy and only saw bloomers as the latest fashion statement. It is not surprising, then, that the two young women might have been confused about the appropriateness of wearing bloomers. Having committed an error in its reporting on fashion, the magazine quickly tried to correct its mistake by informing these young women of their social gaffe. Although the magazine was attempting to be an arbiter of Petersburg fashions, this incident demonstrates the lack of sophistication of the Russian fashion industry at that time and the gullibility of some of the magazine's readers who would wear anything the magazine decreed as high fashion.

Throughout its years of publication, each issue of *Moda* began with a column called "Fashionable Society" [Modnyi svet], which discussed the social whirl in St. Petersburg as well as the news from Western Europe.[22] Articles described the "in" cultural events, who attended them, and what was worn. Another regular column was named "Telegraph" [Telegraf]. (This anonymous piece described in precise detail the latest styles for the coming season. To further substantiate the authenticity of *Moda*'s advice, the clothing described was identical to the clothes in the fashion plates. In the April 1852 issue, the "Fashionable Society" column changed format. On the first of the month, Olimpiada Riumina, who had just begun her tenure as publisher of *Moda,* discussed Paris fashions, and on the fifteenth, Baronessa von B-l-r wrote about Petersburg fashions.

The division of the column into two parts revealed the fundamental problem that faced the magazine: how could it report on French fashions when the stated purpose of the periodical was to provide a vehicle for Russian styles and tastes? The magazine's writers could not forbid a discussion of French fashion because the elite wore nothing else, and these individuals set the tone for the rest of society. Moreover, in the 1850s, the Russian fashion industry was still in its infancy and could not really compete with Paris fashions. This dilemma proved a difficult one for the magazine, for its very survival depended on creating a niche for itself as a *Russian* fashion periodical. To solve this problem, the magazine tried to come to terms with these issues in a variety of ways.

One way in which *Moda* tried to deal with the problem of competing French fashions was to suggest that Russian women knew more about French fashion than the French, the ability to imitate marking an important step in the integration of French fashion ideas into Russia. In 1854 an article entitled "The Russian Invasion" [Invasions russes], written by the magazine's Parisian correspondent, Countess Renneville, appeared first in a Parisian journal and then in *Moda*. According to the article, Countess Renneville met a Russian woman in Paris. The two went shopping together to find a wedding present for a mutual friend. Much to Renneville's surprise, the Russian woman knew all the best shops in Paris, as well as the perfect goods to buy. Renneville concluded, "The Russian woman displayed such taste in her choices, her knowledge of the intricacies of etiquette and practical knowledge of fashion, that I, a talented chronicler of fashion, say with complete honesty, that I felt like a pupil before her."[23]

Just a few months later, there was more good news from the fashion capital. During the winter months of 1853 and 1854, Russian fashions had appeared on the streets of Paris. According to Baronessa von B-l-r, a cloak named the Muscovite mantle had become all the rage among Parisian women, and in Brussels, the exclusive tailoring shops were advertising a man's coat called a Toulska.[24] According to the baronessa, this indicated that Russian fashions were beginning to have an influence on French designers.[25]

Russian influence on French fashions was one indicator of the development of an indigenous fashion industry within the Russian empire. Another was the appearance of the first Russian lithograph in *Moda* in 1855. Although the goods advertised were French and the lithograph was clearly of an inferior quality when compared with the French ones, it signaled an attempt to prove that Russia was developing the necessary infrastructure to create and sustain a fashion industry of its own.

Thus the editors of *Moda* clearly saw that part of their task was to promote the Russian fashion industry. During the 1850s, Russian stores selling Russian-made products competed with the many French, English, and German boutiques in the Russian capital. These Russian entrepreneurs and their manufactured goods were greeted with considerable fanfare on the pages of *Moda*. After several years of touting the wonders of the Petersburg outlets of the French stores DeLisle and Au Bon Ton, the magazine's writers began to highlight Russian-made fabrics and stores. In March 1854 the fashion advice column reported on the abundance of goods in a store that was described as "completely Russian, founded and run by a Russian man" named Riabkov.[26] A year later, an article about the same store featured the work of the store's designer, Arkadii Zhdanov. The columnist described Zhdanov's work: "Not limited by a simple imitation of foreign designs, Zhdanov himself invents and creates new designs, trying to adapt them to the conditions of our climate and the needs of society."[27]

The problem of the suitability of Paris fashions to the Russian climate was a constant refrain found in the magazine and was used to justify wearing Russian designs instead. To give one example, in 1851 the Petersburg correspondent commented: "When at the beginning of the winter there appeared for the first time hats [that left a woman's head open to the cold air], many were surprised that this design could appear among us in Russia at such a time of year when the severe frosts compel even men to wrap themselves up in fur coats and closed hats." The conclusion of the writer was that no matter what the fashion in Paris, Petersburg women needed to wear warm hats for winter, preferably hats made from Russian furs.[28]

The real problem for Russian women was not the disparity in climates. With the outbreak of the Crimean War in 1854, France and Russia became enemies. Therefore many Russian women felt that it was unpatriotic to continue to buy French fashions during the war. To demonstrate their patriotism, some Russian society women took to wearing Russian dress to their balls and soirees. Society women appeared in long Russian jumpers called sarafans and traditional Russian headdresses to dance the polonaise and the waltz. This state of affairs shocked many Russians. Wearing traditional Russian clothing to Western European–style social gatherings presented a clash of cultures that could not be permitted to continue even in the name of patriotism.

In July 1856 an article appeared in *Moda* entitled "Russian and General European Dress" [Kostium russkii i obshcheevropeiskii]. According to the author of this anonymous article, "Native dress reflects the nature and education of its people, both in the past and in the present." The reporter went on to criticize the misplaced patriotism of many Russian women and compared them to children who dress in ridiculous costumes to fight their imaginary enemies. If Russian women insisted on wearing traditional dress, then they needed to return to their Muscovite ancestors' style of living. To support these claims, the author quoted from N. I. Grech, a well-known Russian conservative, who complained, "Jumping around during a polka or waltzing in the style of dress of the empress Natal'ia Kirilovna [Peter the Great's mother, who lived during the seventeenth century] is absurd and funny." Grech begged the women of Russia to dress "like all the other well-bred women and girls in Europe. Wear sarafans and ribbons only when they suit you and to please your husbands. But don't think that patriotism consists of this: that a beautiful hat interferes with healthy thoughts and a French corset stifles a Russian heart."[29] Echoing Grech, the very idea that patriotism could find expression in clothing was absurd, according to *Moda*'s expert on fashion. The expert's advice was "that the dress of women from educated society should be tasteful, conforming to the habits and customs of the modern [*sovremmenoi*] epoch."[30]

This piece of fashion advice provides an interesting perspective on cultural transmission. Before the fashion woes caused by the Crimean War, there had been a divisive intellectual controversy centered on Russia's place in world civilization. According to the Westernizers, Russia had remained outside the confines of European civilization until Peter the Great had forcibly dragged his subjects into the European family of nations. By the early 1840s, the Westernizers believed that Russia was or should be a full participant in European life and culture. An opposing view was taken by the Slavophiles. They believed that all that was good and unique had been destroyed in Russia's cultural encounter with Europe, with a few notable exceptions.[31] A third view was put forth by the Russian government, which supported traditional modes of life for the lower classes but firmly believed that the ruling class must be thoroughly Europeanized to govern properly.[32] Thus for Russians the place of their country in European culture was a hotly contested issue. The debate about the nature of fashion in Russia was central to the larger concerns educated Russians had about national identity.

Moda's columnist offers a solution to this debate, one that attempts to resolve this divide in Russian culture between Slavophiles and Westernizers. Rather than simply saying that since the conclusion of war with France, Russian women could again wear French fashions without guilt, the author advances a more far-reaching proposal. *Moda*'s fashion critic begins by arguing that Muscovite and European cultures are separate entities; elements of one cannot be used with the other. This is why wearing Russian dress to dance the waltz is so offensive. If Russians insist on wearing national costume, then, it is necessary for them to adopt the entire lifestyle of their Muscovite ancestors, according to the author.[33] They must abandon their European palaces, furnishings, and food and return to a seventeenth-century style of living.

Returning to the old Muscovite ways was not something that most members of Russian high society wanted to do. They considered their European lifestyle a vast improvement over the dark, overcrowded palaces of their Muscovite ancestors. Elite women, especially, had a lot to lose if this approach were adopted, for it would mean returning to separate living quarters and a more restricted way of life. Moreover, the very separateness of Muscovite culture meant that Russians could never become members of the European community. This position was anathema both to members of the Russian government and to elite society. Nor was the adoption of Muscovite culture favored by the publishers of *Moda*, for there were no fashion magazines in old Muscovy. Thus another approach to the problem of what clothes to wear needed to be found.

Consequently, *Moda*'s fashion critic talks about "modern" rather than "European" culture, thus taking the potential sting for Russian patriots out of wearing French clothes. In this usage, "modern" is a more neutral word because it does not refer to a specific nation or geographic area. Modern clothing could be worn both by individuals who felt themselves to be Europeans and by Russians who wanted to serve the autocracy but identified themselves as Russians rather than as Europeans. This distinction was particularly important for conservatives because the autocracy remained committed to European dress as the style of dress for all government functions. To substantiate this claim for modernity, *Moda*'s expert invokes Peter the Great's solution to the problem of Western dress. The author claims that Peter understood that Russians could give up their old clothing because it was superfluous to their inner being. Russians could participate in modern life and cultural forms by wearing modern clothing because the art of fashion was superficial and did not violate their inner sense of national identity. Furthermore, the author appears to be arguing that culture in the mid–nineteenth century was no longer "European" but "modern." Therefore Russians could participate in the creation of modern culture and yet remain true patriots. Because modernity was not confined to any geographic area, it allowed for cultural contributions from Russia and the United States that lay outside the traditional parameters of Western European culture.

At the same time, this debate over what women should wear during the Crimean War belies the very claims of *Moda*'s fashion critic. If fashion was superfluous to an individual's national identity, then why did it matter what women chose to wear? In fact, this debate clearly demonstrates that modes of dress remained a disputed issue in nineteenth-century Russia, with state interests playing an important role in the debate. While the fashion industry was attempting to erase national costume in favor of "modern" fashion, there were moments when the state demanded patriotism in dress. The Crimean War was just such a moment. Men donned Russian army uniforms, and women were expected to display their patriotic fervor through their dress as well. In both cases, the appropriate uniforms and dresses were influenced by European modes of dress; nevertheless, to the supporters of the Russian war effort, these clothes became visible markers of positive national traits that reflected the true character of Russian men and women. Thus the debates about modern fashion versus national costume continued to play an important role in the evolution of Russian imperial culture.[34]

Moda's cultural significance was overshadowed by some serious problems that the magazine faced. The most serious of these was competition from other fashion magazines vying for the same market. During the 1850s, magazines such as *Lastochka (The Swallow)*, *Buket (Bouquet)*, and *Merkurii mod (Fashion Messenger)* all competed for the fashion market, but the one magazine that presented the greatest challenge to *Moda* was *Severnyi tsvetok (Northern Flower)*.[35] To lure readers, the publishers of *Severnyi tsvetok* decided on a bold move. Rather than publish once a month, they would publish every week. This publication schedule also meant that a fashion plate would appear on a weekly basis as well. By printing plates from *Moniteur de la Mode*, the best Parisian fashion magazine, and charging a mere ten rubles for an annual subscription, the publishers hoped to attract a significant portion of the fashion market in Russia.[36] Because *Moda* continued to publish only semimonthly, it did indeed find itself competing with *Severnyi tsvetok*.

However, *Severnyi tsvetok* began to experience financial difficulties with its weekly production schedule. The publishers could not keep the subscription rate at ten rubles because the production costs had skyrocketed in the years following the Crimean War.[37] Something needed to be done for both *Severnyi tsvetok* and *Moda*. The solution to these problems came in 1861 with the merger of the two magazines as *Severnyi tsvetok: Modnyi zhurnal dlia svetskikh liudei (Northern Flower: A Fashion Magazine for High Society)*. The new editor and copublisher was Fedor Zinov'ev, who had previously edited *Severnyi tsvetok*. Along with the merger came a new statement of purpose for the magazine. In ten short years, it was no longer necessary to decry Russian dependence on foreign fashion magazines or to justify the creation of a Russian fashion periodical. Instead, the new editor proclaimed: "In short, our magazine must be a handbook, a constant guide of the Russian woman, her enjoyable companion, adviser, and friend, attentive and useful."[38] The new publication would be divided into five sections: literature, fine arts, home economics, fashion, and miscellaneous, with particular attention paid to articles about education. No longer focusing exclusively on the comings and goings of the elite, *Severnyi tsvetok* tried to appeal to larger numbers of women readers beyond the elite. Fashion was only one component of the new magazine. Now there would also be extensive discussions of women's domestic concerns. Thus the entire format and tone of the periodical changed with the merger. Despite these noble intentions, however, *Severnyi tsvetok* quickly ran into trouble. The individuals who had been contracted to mail the issues to subscribers failed to send out the magazine. They pocketed the money instead.[39] This catastrophic event proved insurmountable for the publishers, and the magazine ceased publication in 1861.

The demise of *Moda* after its merger with *Severnyi tsvetok* occurred for several important and interrelated reasons. The problem with the mailing service was only a symptom of other more serious concerns. Indeed, a number of other periodicals failed at the same time as *Moda*, revealing deeper questions about the future role of the Russian nobility. The Crimean War debacle had ushered in the era of the Great Reforms. These reforms were intended to transform Russia into a modern industrial nation, but the changes posed a serious threat to the aristocratic way of life. The days of parties, balls, and visits to the dacha were now threatened by the very real concerns about how the elite were going to sustain themselves economically without serf labor. It is likely that the nobility curtailed some expenditures while they tried to figure out how the reforms were going to affect their standard of living. One easy way to retrench was for these noble men and women to cancel their magazine subscriptions, which many of them did. Thus *Moda*'s failure represents the anxieties many members of the Russian elite felt as their world began to change.

Moreover, the merger of *Moda* and *Severnyi tsvetok* brought about a change in the magazine itself. *Moda* had celebrated the fashions and court life of Petersburg high society, but the new magazine defined itself as "a handbook, a constant guide of the Russian woman." Fashion was to be only one component in *Severnyi tsvetok*, which would also include articles on home economics and domestic life. *Severnyi tsvetok* transformed itself into a completely different magazine from *Moda*. This dramatic shift resulted in large part from the important debates that were raging in Russian society over the woman question. Critical of the superficial life of most noblewomen, who were being trained to be "fashionable dolls," many members of Russian society called for a new emphasis on motherhood and domesticity to give greater meaning to Russian women's lives.[40] This call represented an attempt to give elite women a greater role in Russian social life. The de-emphasis on the aristocratic life of leisure and a renewed interest in family life had even become part of the ideology of court life in the nineteenth century.[41] Although some radicals in Russia went a step further and advocated full equality for women, most members of Russian educated society agreed that women should focus more on domestic concerns than on fashion.

The switch in editorial policy that echoed these larger social debates created problems for the magazine's publisher. The individuals who subscribed to the magazine did so because they were fascinated by fashion and court life. However, the shift to domestic concerns meant that these women would have to look elsewhere for their fashion news. Thus the editorial policies helped to undercut the fashion market that the magazine had worked so hard to create in the first place. Although unethical business practices played a major role in its demise, it is likely that these editorial changes would also have affected the magazine's future marketability.

Thus *Moda*'s demise was one indicator of the end of the golden era of the nobility, a lesson that was not lost on the publishers of other fashion magazines. The marketing strategies developed by *Moda*'s publishers would be applied elsewhere by those hoping to capture a wider female audience. During the second half of the nineteenth century, new fashion journals expanded the market for fashion not by focusing exclusively on women of the elite but by including information and readers' services of interest to women of many social groups. In their attempts to create a mass market for fashion, these magazines developed a whole new set of marketing strategies.[42] To give one example, *Modnyi svet (Fashionable Society)*, published between 1868 and 1905, appeared weekly. It was inexpensive and contained cheaper-quality reproductions of Paris fashions than had *Moda*. Nevertheless it provided extensive coverage of the latest styles. There were no longer detailed discussions of elite social functions, but advice columns on every subject from cosmetics to cooking. There were also short stories and poems that focused on women's lives all across the social spectrum. And occasionally there were news items dealing with women's issues, such as women's quest for higher education in Russia. Finally, because the mass market for women's magazines was growing in the 1870s and 1880s, as Carolyn Marks has pointed out, there was no need for dramatic changes in editorial policy as had happened in the case of *Moda* and *Severnyi tsvetok* a decade earlier.

Moda's contribution to the fashion press was an important one. It helped to define the relationship of a fashion industry to Russian cultural life. By integrating on its pages both foreign and domestic fashions, it helped to legitimate the new Russian fashion industry. Rather than continue the artificial divide that separated clothing into French or Russian, the magazine suggested that Russians view themselves as part of the modern world that they were helping to shape in their own special way. Following this line of reasoning, Russians could wear French fashions and not betray their national identity. In other words, they could be modern and Russian at the same time.

Having resolved this cultural conundrum, at least temporarily, the fashion media wanted to spread this gospel of modernity beyond the confines of the elite to the vast untapped Russian domestic market. In the long run, *Moda* could not meet this challenge because it catered to the interests of the elite. But what it was able to do was to develop marketing strategies that used elite Russian women's desire for fashionable clothing as a means of selling more magazines. Noblewomen were drawn to *Moda* because it offered not just fashion news but also ways of obtaining beautiful clothing through advertisements and special offerings of books, patterns, and fashion plates. These marketing strategies were later used by other magazines to reach a wider audience. Thus the twofold strategy of *Moda*'s founders was successful in accomplishing their joint goals of establishing a Russian fashion magazine and furthering the development of the

Russian fashion industry. *Moda*'s ability to combine fashion and publishing served as a significant moment in the development of a modern women's press. Finally, the magazine's attempts to arbitrate fashion trends reveal how the fashion press addresses the weighty issues of nationalism, gender roles, and cultural adaptation not just in imperial Russia but in all countries.

Notes

1 For an analysis of the gendering of clothes shopping in Russia, see Christine Ruane, "Clothes Shopping in Imperial Russia: The Development of a Consumer Culture," *Journal of Social History* 28, no. 4 (Summer 1995): 765–82. For an analysis of the gendering of the French fashion press, see Jennifer Michelle Jones, "'The Taste for Fashion and Frivolity': Gender, Clothing, and the Commercial Culture of the Old Regime" (Ph.D. diss., Princeton University, 1991), 212–58.
2 I have chosen to translate *zhurnal* as "magazine" because of *Moda*'s format. *Moda* was richly illustrated and contained a wide range of articles on happenings at the court, cultural events, and advice columns. This placed it in sharp contrast with the thick journals of the time, which were not illustrated and tended to publish "weightier" discussions of Russian social, economic, and cultural life. However, some of the most popular thick journals from the first half of the nineteenth century, such as *Moskvitianin* and *Severnyi vestnik*, had fashion columns as a regular feature to attract more women readers to periodicals intended for a male and female audience.
3 The development of a Russian fashion industry and its attempt to define a national identity will be discussed in greater detail in my forthcoming book on the history of the Russian fashion industry from 1700 to 1917.
4 Rossiiskii gosudarstvennyi istoricheskii arkhiv (RGIA), f. 772, op. 1, d. 1024, l. 3 and d. 1741, l. 1. I am indebted to Carolyn Marks for helping me locate the archival materials pertaining to *Moda*.
5 RGIA, f. 777, op. 1, d. 1408, ll. 6–9.
6 RGIA, f. 777, op. 1, d. 1408, l. 39.
7 RGIA, f. 772, op. 1, d. 2070, l. 6.
8 RGIA, f. 772, op. 1, d. 2632, l. 1.
9 RGIA, f. 772, op. 1, d. 2632, ll. 4–9.
10 RGIA, f. 772, op. 1, d. 2632, ll. 10–15.
11 RGIA, f. 777, op. 1, d. 1408, ll. 108–22.
12 RGIA, f. 777, op. 1, d. 1408, ll. 155–65.

13 "Programma izdaniia na 1851 god," *Moda: Zhurnal dlia svetskikh liudei,* no. 1 (1 January 1851): n.p. Hereafter cited as *Moda.*
14 See the articles by Carolyn Marks and Miranda Remnek in this volume for further commentary on this important issue.
15 "Zametka," *Moda,* no. 16 (15 August 1856): 136. Omsk is a city located in western Siberia. To the elite of Petersburg, it would have been considered a frontier town. Perhaps Dodge City, Kansas, would be a nineteenth-century American equivalent.
16 "Rukovodstvo k sostavleniiu vykroek po risunkam zhurnala Mody," *Moda,* no. 2 (15 February 1854): 1–2. For a history of paper patterns, see Claudia Kidwell, *Cutting a Fashionable Fit: Dressmakers' Drafting Systems in the United States* (Washington, D.C., 1978).
17 "Otvety na mnogochislennye pros'by," *Moda,* no. 1 (1 January 1857): 26.
18 *Moda,* no. 16 (15 August 1856): 137.
19 An example can be found in *Moda,* no. 2 (15 January 1858): 45.
20 "Modnyi svet," *Moda,* no. 1 (1 January 1852): 3.
21 "Modnyi svet," *Moda,* no. 3 (1 February 1852): 18–19.
22 The first French correspondent was named Countess Renneville. She was replaced by Victoria Mon-Magu in May 1856. The column was renamed "Modnaia letopis'" in 1852.
23 "Modnaia letopis' (Pis'mo v redaktsiiu iz Parizha)," *Moda,* no. 1 (1 January 1854): 6.
24 The name *Toulska* suggests a coat commemorating the Russian city of Tula, which was famous for its guns and samovars.
25 "Modnaia letopis'," *Moda,* no. 7 (1 April 1854): 53.
26 "Modnaia letopis'," *Moda,* no. 6 (15 March 1856): 47.
27 "Magazin Riabkova i modnye fantaziia," *Moda,* no. 6 (15 March 1855): 47.
28 "Modnyi svet," *Moda,* no. 2 (15 January 1851): 10–11.
29 "Kostium russkii i obshcheevropeiskii," *Moda,* no. 14 (15 July 1856): 114. According to the author, some of the ideas for this article were taken from another article entitled "Nariady i mody," in *Zhivopisnoi Russkoi biblioteki.*
30 "Kostium russkii," 115.
31 An introduction to this controversy can be found in Andrzej Walicki, *The Slavophile Controversy: History of a Conservative Utopia in Nineteenth-Century Russian Thought,* trans. Hilda Andrews-Rusiecka (Notre Dame, 1989).
32 Richard S. Wortman, *Scenarios of Power: Myth and Ceremony in Russian Monarchy,* vol. 1 (Princeton, 1995).
33 "Kostium russkii," 114.

34 This debate ignores the whole question of what happens when Ukrainians, Armenians, Poles, and members of other ethnic groups put on "Russian" clothing. As an imperial power, Russians were reluctant to think about the implications of this reasoning for non-Russians who served in the army or lived within the borders of the empire.

35 The publisher of *Severnyi tsvetok* was a woman by the name of M. Staniukovich. N. I. Lisovskii, *Russkaia periodicheskaia pechat', 1703–1900 gg.* (Petrograd, 1915), 34.

36 "Ot redaktsii," *Severnyi tsvetok*, no. 44 (29 October 1860): 273–75.

37 Ibid.

38 "Ob"iavlenie," *Severnyi tsvetok: Modnyi zhurnal dlia svetskikh liudei*, no. 3 (1 February 1861): 94.

39 F. Zinov'ev, "Ot redaktsii," *Severnyi tsvetok: Modnyi zhurnal dlia svetskikh liudei*, no. 12 (15 July 1861): 384.

40 A good introduction to these debates can be found in Richard Stites, *The Women's Liberation Movement in Russia: Feminism, Nihilism, and Bolshevism, 1860–1930* (Princeton, 1991), 29–63.

41 Richard Wortman, "The Russian Empress as Mother," in *The Family in Imperial Russia: New Lines of Historical Research*, ed. David L. Ransel (Urbana, 1978), 60–74; and Wortman, *Scenarios of Power*, especially 247–54.

42 See Carolyn Marks's essay in this volume for more information on these strategies. For a history of the mass-circulation newspapers and their marketing strategies in the period following the emancipation of the serfs, see Louise McReynolds, *The News under Russia's Old Regime: The Development of a Mass-Circulation Press* (Princeton, 1991), 30–51.

"Provid[ing] Amusement for the Ladies"

The Rise of the Russian Women's Magazine

in the 1880s

CAROLYN R. MARKS

The rise of the women's magazine in Russia during the 1880s is a symbol of change both in Russian women's lives and in the activities and expectations of Russia's middle estates.[1] As the preceding essay by Christine Ruane reveals, this change was already in the making two decades earlier. The present essay examines the commercialization of the women's magazine and what its growing popularity demonstrates about Russian urban society and culture in the 1880s.

Russia in the 1880s, rocked by Alexander II's death in 1881, does not seem a likely incubator for a women's press. Historians and critics often describe the decade as one of counterreform and growing repression following the accession of Alexander III on March 1, 1881.[2] Yet social and cultural trends outside of government control, such as the rise of women's literacy and demand for lighter reading fare among women within the growing middle estates,[3] profoundly affected Russia during this period as well.[4] While this confluence of forces ultimately brought about the closure of many women's periodicals during the early 1880s, it also set the scene for a highly competitive, consumer-oriented professional women's press[5] to emerge by the end of the decade.[6] Following a brief overview of women's publishing before the reform period, the present essay will focus on the careers of four publishers of women's periodicals, two women and two men, during the 1880s. The aim is not only to provide insight into their experiences but to explore how a variety of variables — market conditions, new technologies, censorship, social change, and personal identity — defined these individuals' paths within the profession and, ultimately, the women's press itself.

One of the conclusions that elements of this essay may seem to support is that women were excluded from the public sphere with the onset of capitalism.[7] If one focuses, for example, on government policy with respect to gender roles (in this case, censorship and women's education), then women's opportunities would seem only to be narrowing. However, such observations must serve as only a first step in clarifying the complex changes taking place in Russian society that were not only reshaping gender roles in the 1880s but even eroding the broader set of values once shared by government and society. Although the women's magazines of the early eighties did seem to promise only increasingly narrow gender roles for women, by the end of the decade, these publications offered evidence of ever broader possibilities and encouraged female readers to consider such examples.

The earliest Russian women's periodical did not debut with such images. Nikolai Novikov introduced *Modnoe ezhemesiachnoe izdanie, ili Biblioteka dlia damskogo tualeta (Fashion Monthly, or Reading for Ladies Couture)* in 1779. The first of its kind in Russia, it was dedicated to elite women, read mostly by the nobility of St. Petersburg and Moscow, and meant to provide them amusement in the form of light reading to fill spare moments. That publication disappeared at the end of its first year, but others followed, eventually introducing fashions from the West and providing needlework patterns.[8] In the 1830s, Elizaveta Safonova and Mariia Koshelevskaia became the first women to establish their own publications for female reading. Their serials, *Vaza (The Vase,* 1836–1884) and *Vestnik parizhskikh mod (Paris Fashion Herald,* 1836–1850), were published for forty-eight and twenty-five years respectively.[9]

The appearance of *Rassvet (Daybreak)* in 1859, however, heralded a new type of women's periodical "devoted to the formation of women's opinions."[10] Previous women's publications had professed to entertain their readers or simply to provide them with clothing patterns, but midcentury Russian society's interest in reform and the controversial woman question prompted the creation of journals with the specific purpose of encouraging education (a trend that mirrored not only the changes taking place in Russia but also the existence of such journals in the West). As a result, two strains of women's popular periodicals coexisted from the 1860s: the "magazine" offering fashions and light reading, and the "journal" seeking to guide women's moral and intellectual development and advocating the reforms that would make such growth possible.[11]

Zhenskii vestnik (*Women's Herald*, 1866–1868) was the epitome of the latter type. Produced in the format of the thick journal, it focused on social, cultural, and women's issues. Others such as *Modnyi magazin (Fashion Magazine)* tried to combine the feminine distractions of fashion and high society gossip with more edifying pieces.[12] Although it cannot be said that *Zhenskii vestnik* was the publishing success that *Modnyi magazin* first was, its controversial articles provoked the ire of the censors, attracted public attention, and raised debate, which was probably its aim. *Modnyi magazin,* for its part, reflected on the question of women's role in reformist Russia and urged readers to be responsible, critical, and intelligent. Despite their differences, both journals engaged serious issues and elicited responses from both readers and the Russian press.

Following the early to mid-1860s, the impetus behind women's journals ebbed. Government tolerance for critical journalism, while never unlimited, had diminished by the 1870s. The Temporary Press Laws of 1882 — a reaction to Alexander II's assassination, and Alexander III's hostility to his father's reforms — further limited coverage of controversial issues and provided censors with broader powers to punish and close down publications.[13] If a publisher or editor chose to address such topics, she or he would have to dilute their substance and might still face penalties from a cautious censor. Advances in print technology adopted by some well-to-do publishers during the 1870s and 1880s also undermined women's journals, which characteristically could not afford, for example, the newer high-speed printing presses.[14] Unable to keep up with their competition, the less-polished publications lost subscribers. As the makeup of the urban population changed, so did the readership of women's periodicals. In contrast to the primarily educated, elite women who subscribed to the journals of the 1860s, the readers of the 1880s sought the lighter fare of the new illustrated literary-fashion magazines, which were easier to read and, in some cases, did not even necessitate a literate audience to be appreciated.

Circulation figures demonstrate the growing popularity of the women's magazine. *Modnyi svet* (*Fashion World*, 1867–1905) in 1883 distributed 15,000 copies of each issue, far ahead of other women's magazines and comparable to *Novosti (The News)* and *Syn otechestva (Son of the Fatherland)*, but far behind that of the best-loved publication, *Niva (Cornfield)*, which printed 100,000 copies. As an emerging competitor to *Modnyi svet*, Nikolai Alovert distributed 5,000 copies of the first issue of *Vestnik mody (Fashion Herald*, 1885–1917) in 1885, but the rest of the women's press lagged behind that figure.[15]

The procedure for establishing a periodical in St. Petersburg began with a petition to the Main Administration for Censorship Affairs requesting authorization from the Ministry of Internal Affairs for the publication. The petitioner proposed a program, subscription prices, frequency of publication, the identity of, and documentation for, the publisher(s) and editor(s) of the new periodical, and the name of the printer. Inquiries followed by the Censorship Administration to the Department of Police to determine the petitioner's political sympathies and ensure her or his reliability. If the individual posed no threat to the government, the Censorship Administration would recommend approval. At this stage, the petitioner would be required to sign a separate agreement not to transfer publishing rights to anyone else without the approval of the Censorship Administration. If the petitioner agreed, she or he received the desired authorization (often during the next few days), including the license needed for printing the new periodical, which would be retained by the printing firm indicated in the petition. If the publisher or editor wanted to modify the publication in any manner subsequently, she or he would again have to apply to the Censorship Administration for approval. A petition process begun in Moscow or any other city would first go through that city's Censorship Administration, which would come to a preliminary decision and then request approval from the Main Administration of Censorship Affairs in St. Petersburg.

During the 1880s, a total of twelve women's periodicals existed, some for only a year and others for the entire period.[16] Of these twelve, seven dated from the 1870s or earlier. Only five were launched during the eighties (fewer than in previous decades), and six folded during this time (ten had discontinued during the 1860s and six during the 1870s), so that by 1885 only four women's periodicals remained, although that number rose again to six in 1889. Although these figures for the eighties as a whole indicate only a slight decrease in the overall number of total periodicals, a year-by-year examination reveals further that either opportunity or interest diminished after 1883, a year after the new censorship regulations.

Another set of patterns is visible in the typology of the women's press. Compared to women's publications before and after the 1880s, the content of women's periodicals in this period achieved a greater, though nowhere near equal, balance between fashion features (accounting for more than 60 percent of periodicals' content) and other articles (38 percent), the foci of which include foreign countries (18 percent), society (8 percent), homemaking (6 percent), literature (2.5 percent), culture (2 percent), women's issues (.5 percent), and other items (1 percent).[17] Eleven of the twelve women's publications of the eighties were issued in St. Petersburg and break down according to genre as follows: three were strictly fashion publications (including needlework);[18] seven combined fashions with literature, illustrations from contemporary life, household tips, beauty and hygiene, foreign and domestic news, and correspondence;[19] and one was a specialized pedagogical publication for women pursuing education.[20] The single Moscow serial, *Drug zhenshchin*, shunned fashion, however, offering instead a program of literature, biographies, women's issues, household tips, data on women's work, the law as it related to women, and a special concentration on raising and educating children, especially girls. Clearly, St. Petersburg served as the center of the women's press and Russia's fashion hub. The Moscow journal, which was the only women's periodical that Moscow produced between 1862 and 1903, seems to have been a rejection of the fashions that figured so prominently in the Petersburg magazines.

Effective commercial financing determined the longevity of women's periodicals during this decade. All the St. Petersburg periodicals, with the single exception of the government-subsidized *Zhenskoe obrazovanie* (*Women's Education*, 1876–1891), covered their costs through subscriptions and advertisements or relied on the personal resources of the publisher or editor.[21] Subscription rates for these publications ranged from four to twenty-eight rubles, with most costing between six and ten rubles.[22] Competitive pricing at the time was becoming a more important tool for success. *Modnyi svet* drew record numbers of subscribers not only because of its content but because until 1885 it also boasted the lowest price: its least-expensive edition, without delivery, was five rubles per year. Because it also came out weekly, unlike others that appeared biweekly or monthly, this pricing was the more significant. Advertising was also vital to the financing of a women's periodical. On average, the number of advertisements per women's publication in 1883 had more than doubled over that of 1876 and was ten times that of 1867.[23] Notices for books, cosmetics and toiletries, household wares, medications, and other periodicals predominated. The cost of these announcements (*ob"iavleniia*) usually ran at twenty kopecks per line, with one publication charging thirty kopecks per line, thirteen rubles for a half page, and twenty-five rubles for the entire page. As many serials of this period contained from two to five pages of ads, this source of funding could be substantial, especially for a weekly publication.

An affordable periodical, after all, attracted subscribers. If the publisher could maintain low prices, however, that meant she or he was probably producing a publication with a large circulation and, therefore, a steady and significant source of revenue. A very low price indicated a serious campaign to win subscribers over to a new publication. Personal financing was another option. A few of these publishers and editors found themselves, at some point, forced to fund a publication from their own resources. For Nikolai Alovert, it was a means of ensuring quick success when he began his magazine, *Vestnik mody*, because that way he was able to underprice already established publications and provide readers with the latest costly fashion illustrations.[24] But Sofiia Mei's recourse to personal funds signaled the start of *Modnyi magazin*'s decline; having exhausted her money in 1882, she was forced to sell.[25] *Drug zhenshchin*, which required both its publisher and editor to finance it from start to finish, closed down in its third year, never having been able to generate its own resources.[26]

Financial success depended on consumer appeal, which in turn rested on the business decisions made by publishers and editors. The components that made up the identities of these individuals (gender, social origins or status, age, education or training, geographic location, and ethnicity) had some bearing on how each one chose the type of periodical to be published. Social status, education, and technical skill, for example, determined both the level and sort of resources available and served as indicators of the experience a publisher or editor already had in the field. All these characteristics thus influenced the success or failure of a publication. What follows is a review of the available personal data on the editors and publishers of women's periodicals of the eighties, which will serve as background for a closer look at four of these individuals.

Of the seventeen publishers and editors of women's publications in the 1880s, eight were men, and nine were women. All eight men served as publishers, five of them simultaneously as the editors of their periodicals. Of the nine women, two were publishers, two were editors, and five acted in both capacities. In terms of socioeconomic status, twelve of these individuals, six women and six men, came from the middle estates. Three (two women and one man) were of the nobility. Data for the remaining two (one woman, one man) are unavailable. Ten out of the seventeen (59 percent) were Russian, and an additional three bearing foreign surnames were likely to have been born in Russia of families that had immigrated to Russia at some earlier time.[27] One, Herman Goppe, had come from the German region of Westphalia and settled in St. Petersburg in the 1860s. For the remaining three, data are not available.

Variables of age, education, and geographic origins are more difficult to determine. We may assume that each individual was born between 1820 and 1850 (data available on five place them into that range). With regard to education, all these individuals had to be literate and thus had some degree of formal education; data exist for six of them, two of whom had extensive experience in publishing before starting a women's periodical. Of the eight whose geographic origins are traceable, four were from the provinces and had moved into St. Petersburg; two were natives of Moscow (the same two women who ran the single Moscow publication); and two more (one woman and one man) had been born in St. Petersburg.[28]

Several conclusions may be drawn from this information. First, although entry into publishing and editing was open to women as well as men, when gender is correlated with length of publication, men outnumber women among periodicals lasting more than five years (four out of the eight men versus three out of nine women).[29] Socioeconomic data show that members of the middle estates accounted for 70 percent of this group and, it turns out, predominated among the longest-running publications. In fact, the two most successful publishers, both men, came from the middle estates. These two individuals also had training and/or lengthy prior experience in the publishing industry. Neither was a native of St. Petersburg.

The remainder of this essay explores case studies of four publishers to demonstrate how elements of identity interacted with socioeconomic changes to affect women's periodicals. These individuals were Sofiia Mei, publisher and editor of *Modnyi magazin,* Herman Goppe, publisher and editor of *Modnyi svet,* Anna Volkova, editor of *Drug zhenshchin,* and Nikolai Alovert, publisher and editor of *Vestnik mody.*

The earliest, chronologically, was Sofiia Grigor'evna Mei, publisher and editor of *Modnyi magazin.* Mei was born in 1821 into the Polianskaia family of St. Petersburg (probably nobility). In the late 1850s or early 1860s, she hosted one of St. Petersburg's popular salons, where well-known literary figures such as Nikolai Nekrasov, Aleksei Pisemskii, Fedor Berg, and Vsevolod Krestovskii gathered, many of whom would later contribute to her journal.[30] Sources also note that in her youth, she had access to the best circles of St. Petersburg, although her connections to the literary world, which would make her salon popular, were strengthened by her marriage to the poet Lev Mei in 1852.[31]

When *Modnyi magazin* debuted in 1862, Sofiia Mei was forty-one years old and in need of a way of earning money. Lev Mei's literary career had hardly earned them enough to live on, so she turned to publishing. At the time, only two periodicals in St. Petersburg targeted a female audience: *Rassvet,* primarily meant for younger women, and the long-lived fashion and literary journal *Vaza.* Mei's *Modnyi magazin* thus established its niche among educated women.[32] The journal's format and style combined sophisticated, witty reviews of Russia's past, future, and the role of its citizens, characteristic of Russian thick journals, with lighter discussions about fashion, high society, and homemaking typical of imported women's publications. The format of the first year's issues was that of a thick journal, not the folio size that was useful for illustrated fashion journals; in fact, *Modnyi magazin* rarely used illustrations in its first year. The colorful language of the journal reflected the hopes and energies of the early 1860s: "revolutions" occurred in fashion; women were to use their "freedom" to act with "reason" both in the way they dressed and in how they comported themselves. In writing the fashion column, Mei once added the disclaimer that, as a professional, she was obliged to cover the latest in Paris fashions, but that did not necessarily mean she endorsed them![33] This statement reflects the widespread perception that fashions were a trivial matter, certainly not a subject on which an intelligent woman would waste time.

Between these first years of lively debate and the 1880s, however, the journal lost its edge. This decline was due to a series of external personal and political events. A second marriage (not long after her first husband died in 1862) brought Mei relative wealth, ending her dependence on income from the journal.[34] Censorship controls tightened again in the mid- to late 1860s as the tsar and his government decided the intelligentsia had played out its role in preparing the country for reform and now needed to be reined in. The return of stricter censorship meant that Mei could not continue to invoke revolution and emancipation to fire the imagination of readers.[35] Even more damaging to the journal's ability to compete was that although Mei had modernized it to an extent, she, like many who came after her, either could not or chose not to invest the resources required to revamp the journal so that it could command a popularity equal to the magazines.

In the years since Mei had begun *Modnyi magazin*, the subjects that made a journal popular had changed. In the journal's early years, the sixties, she had been able to draw on the period's intellectual debates through the creative personalities and contributions of her salon; such connections had given the publication prestige and authority. By the late sixties, however, the decline of the salon and growing government suspicion of critical discourse had forced periodicals like Mei's to soften their approach. Correspondingly, what had been considered a useful connection to the business of publishing, in this case Mei's literary friends, no longer gave her an edge. Neither did she have access to the type of professional and technical resources that were now required to create an eye-catching product. Unable to keep up with changing market demands, *Modnyi magazin* lost money. Mei sold it in the early 1880s, and in 1884 it was finally absorbed into one of Goppe's commercial publications.[36]

By the 1880s, women's publications routinely reported events in Europe and the United States, from fashion in Paris and Berlin and women's education throughout Europe and the United States to sensational news items meant to titillate the reader.[37] Except for literature, information came in increasingly short clips: for example, the miscellany (*smes'*) section of women's serials began to provide the social, cultural, and sometimes political overview that the feuilleton earlier covered. Periodicals with introspective discussions and instructional or critical reviews reminiscent of past times were overtaken by colorful Russian versions of the latest and most stylish of European fashion publications and were produced by large publishing firms such as Goppe's.

Herman Dmitrievich Goppe had come to St. Petersburg in 1861. Born in Westphalia, Goppe arrived with several years' experience in the publishing trade in Belgium, England, and Germany. His introduction to the Russian publishing industry was as an order clerk in the Wol'f and Diufur bookstores, where he worked until establishing his own publishing company in 1866.[38] His first work on a women's publication was with the journal *Mody i novosti* (*Fashion and News,* 1866–1867), a Russian translation of the French fashion journal *La Saison*.[39] In late 1867 he started his own publication: *Modnyi svet.* The new periodical combined engravings of Paris fashions with Russian-language descriptions; literature, both translated and originals in Russian; and a feuilleton that covered society news both in Russia's two capitals and abroad.

Goppe's success in this venture did not stem from the novelty of the magazine's program, which differed little from that of its stiffest competition, *Novyi russkii bazar* (*New Russian Bazaar,* 1867–1898). He did emphasize quality, but what most set Goppe apart was his marketing strategy to attract readers of his own community, the St. Petersburg merchantry.[40] This growing socioeconomic group had the money to afford leisure publications, and its women looked forward to ever greater time in which to read them.[41] Goppe perceived these changes and marketed accordingly. Middle-estate women, he proposed, deserved high-quality content and format at a reasonable price: "Guided by a single goal—to provide amusement [udovol'stvie] for the ladies [dam]—I neither spared expenses nor sought profits; rather, I have priced my journal so that every budget-minded homemaker can afford to buy it and discover not only the broadest variety of fashion, but also interesting reading to fill her moments of leisure."[42] Goppe's publication was received with enthusiasm. During the first year, its circulation figures of 5,000 to 6,000 were equal to that of *Modnyi magazin,* then in its heyday; only about 1,000 less than *Novyi russkii bazar;* and far ahead of *Vaza*'s meager 600 to 700 copies.[43]

The publication's strong entrance into the market was due to the expanded pool of readers that it had targeted, but its long-term growth would depend on Goppe's ability to continue finding ways to enlarge the social spectrum of his audience. In 1868, for example, *Modnyi svet* had introduced two editions (at different prices) to Russian women. Each edition of *Modnyi svet* differed *only* in the number of color fashion prints from Paris that came as the magazine's supplement. Fifteen years later, the magazine was issuing three such editions and had tripled its circulation to 15,000. Thus, with this one innovation, Goppe had arrived at a means of profitably luring wealthier subscribers away from the more expensive publications, that is, by supplying them with more of the most elegant and expensive content.[44] Another example: in 1868, one of the main features of *Modnyi svet* was a feuilleton (a typical feature at the time), which provided commentary on issues such as foreign and domestic culture, the woman question and women's education, foreign news, and the Russian press. By the 1880s, the miscellany had displaced the feuilleton. Its entries might move abruptly from one topic to the next with little in common or could be grouped according to subject matter under one or more headings in various parts of the publication. Such pieces were easy to write (or translate, if borrowed from a foreign publication), could cover the same breadth of material as the feuilleton, and required no commentary from the editor. Consequently Goppe cut down on production time and costs, despite the magazine's ever-increasing editions and circulation figures, and bypassed the censorship restrictions that discouraged publications from discussing the items they printed.[45] The audience, for its part, found quick and easy reading in these often amusing clips on fashion, beauty, society, culture, and, especially, women's interest stories from the West and Russia. In short, the miscellany was ideal for light entertainment and could make serious points without suffering censorship.

Low cast, increasing numbers of editions, and a sensitivity to readers' interests stood behind Goppe's most significant contribution to women's periodicals: consumerism. His advertisements reinforced readers' expectations of amusement and novelty with fanfares that introduced new sections, reminders of the magazine's popularity, and spotlights on the coming year's attractions. Just as important, he earned their loyalty by delivering on his generous promises. Advertisements for *Modnyi svet* emphasized the reliability of the publication: "Every issue of *Modnyi svet* provided by the editors to the St. Petersburg Newspaper Expedition [for delivery] *is always accurate and comes with all of its supplements.*"[46] Elsewhere he reminded subscribers that "*Modnyi svet* has more subscribers than all other fashion journals in Russia together — the best proof of its worth."[47] Next to such claims sat guarantees of thousands of fashion illustrations and hundreds of clothing patterns in addition to engravings of fashions and scenes from daily life, literature, music, features on etiquette, beauty, and health, plus each edition's supplements.

Finally, Goppe had the training, resources, and ties to those with know-how. He himself had pioneered some technological changes, particularly in the areas of wood engraving *(ksilografiia)* and polytype, and his publishing house had invested in the latest machines, which enabled the production of large numbers and better quality in shorter periods of time.[48]

Goppe's successes in the sixties, however, not only did not deter amateurs but seemed rather to inspire ever greater efforts. From the 1860s into the early 1880s, the number of women's popular periodicals doubled, on average, from four per year to nine, all in St. Petersburg. After 1883 until the turn of the century, the average slumped again to five per year. While this sharp drop reflected more stringent censorship after Alexander II's death, it was also a tribute to Goppe's business ability, for the serials that survived past the mid-eighties were either Goppe publications or those that operated on the same level.

The growing popularity among urban women of commercial women's magazines, however, generated concern in some quarters. From Moscow, one group of women tried to reverse the rise of the magazine and the changes it signified for women. Their journal, *Drug zhenshchin*, was first established in 1882 by Mariia Boguslavskaia (1840–?) to provide spiritual guidance in order to repulse the "extremely materialistic tendencies" of Russian women "of the middle estates" and of mothers unable to give their children adequate moral training.[49] The first half year of publication, however, elicited little positive public response, forcing Boguslavskaia to search for additional means of financing the journal. In August 1882 she petitioned the Ministry of Internal Affairs to subsidize the publication for seven months to give the journal time to establish a following.

Her request betrays the skepticism that the journal had met: "Everyone likes the name of the journal *Drug zhenshchin;* they also like that it is a women's journal, but everyone is surprised at its religious tendency and view it as a defect. . . . I am very ashamed to turn to you with this request, but I was driven to it because it would be too depressing to have to admit that they were right, that a journal with religious content would never work out."[50] The ministry declined the request, as it came from a private publication.[51] Thus, to save *Drug zhenshchin,* Boguslavskaia passed effective control of the journal to one of its contributors, Anna Volkova. Boguslavskaia remained nominal publisher and editor, since transferring her publishing or editing rights would have required approval from the Censorship Administration.[52]

Anna Ivanovna Volkova (1847–1910) was a member of the Moscow merchantry. Born into the wealthy Vishniakov family, she had been educated with governesses and at a series of boarding schools in Moscow. Disappointed that her marriage in 1863 to the merchant banker Volkov brought her neither new experiences nor companionship, she sought stimulation in reading what was available at home, as well as subscribing to journals such as the radical *Zhenskii vestnik* and *Zhenskoe obrazovanie.* Like other women of the time, she had also read John Stuart Mill's *On the Subjection of Woman.* Her interest in the woman question and education led her into the intelligentsia circles of the Moscow merchantry, where she found a likeminded community that supported and encouraged her intellectual development. These personal experiences, combined with increasing restrictions placed on women's higher learning in Russia, convinced her that middle-estate women must fight for educational rights and equality or be confined to the home. In that spirit, she began submitting her articles and translations for publication in *Drug zhenshchin* in 1882. When the journal faltered under Boguslavskaia, Volkova stepped forward with the needed financing and reshaped the journal into a tool for advancing her own cause.[53]

According to Volkova's correspondence, however, *Drug zhenshchin* had already exhausted itself (and the interests of its readers) when she took over in late 1882. Nevertheless Volkova kept the publication going for eighteen months, which, given the circumstances, was remarkable. Dropping the religious emphasis, she added two new sections: a bibliography concerning women's issues and a discussion of legal decisions bearing on women. Her correspondence, however, attests to the difficulties of gathering publishable materials, attracting writers with recognized names, and gaining notoriety.[54] One contemporary wrote, "I always saw her busy at work compiling the needed materials and contributing not only her time, but also, to the extent it was possible, the money to keep the journal afloat . . . it is unfortunate, though, that *Drug zhenshchin* never received much sympathy from society."[55] It was even hard, according to one reader, to find copies of the journal in St. Petersburg libraries. Similar reports came from other cities.[56] In August 1884 Volkova closed the journal, no longer able to cover its losses.[57]

The journal closed because the issues it raised were not problematic to enough women readers; had its content addressed what was perceived as a more widespread need among the growing middle-estate readership, it would have succeeded better in attracting subscribers and continuing publication. In other words, *Drug zhenshchin* was not satisfying the consumer demands of the eighties. Nor was it serving the interests of any other influential individual or institution that recognized that service and, in return, financed it (aside from Volkova herself and a few other sympathetic people). The notion of creating a commercial publication at minimum cost and for maximum appeal, like Goppe's, was the farthest thing from Volkova's mind. *Drug zhenshchin,* rather, had been resurrected to serve as a podium from which Volkova could educate readers and prepare them to resist the limits the government was placing on opportunities outside the home for middle-estate women. She had no sympathy or understanding for ladies filling their spare moments with "trivia" such as fashion, beauty, and light reading. She had rejected the enforced leisure that wealth conferred on Moscow's merchant women, only to see commercial fashion magazines start to glamorize it during the next two decades, reaching an ever larger audience as individual wealth grew. Simultaneously, as the government narrowed access to education for Russian women, it became more difficult for women to obtain the training necessary to maintain socially acceptable public roles. In reaction, *Drug zhenshchin* featured articles about women's legal rights, emphasized the importance of educating oneself, and related examples of women in other countries.[58] Yet Volkova had to cover these subjects in a style that had censorship approval and that would not seem threatening to the political status quo.

That only one periodical at the time served to represent the cause is not a surprise, nor is it hard to believe that Volkova championed such views. The ideals of the prereform and reform periods—equality, opportunity, and moral obligation—were part of her identity. She had educated herself from the books and journals of that period in an effort to avoid the isolated existence of the merchant wife.[59] Having rejected the woman's role prescribed by her estate, she now had to defend her choice, both morally, which would explain her righteous tone (especially present in her diary), and legally, to protect the lifestyle she had chosen. But Volkova was not trying to escape her socioeconomic background. Rather, the strong pride she voiced about the accomplishments of the Moscow merchantry was inflected with impatience at their continued backwardness.[60] The journal was her tool to raise the moral and intellectual level of the merchantry—the same audience at which the fashion magazine was directed—and to broaden roles for women within that community.

Shaping the different experiences of Goppe and Volkova were the elements of gender, ethnicity, and location. For a woman without technical training, in this case in the publishing industry, there would be no place in a competitive market until Russian society could accept the role of the competitive woman entrepreneur. Authority derived from success in the marketplace was replacing the moral authority that, in the past, had accompanied the journalist as society's educator and critic. Goppe, with his training, won credibility as a reward for his publishing achievements, whereas Volkova saw morality and service to the public good as the legitimate foundations of authority. Ethnicity may have reinforced these different viewpoints. As a Russian, Volkova inherited the cultural tradition that valued journalism's role in promoting the social good. Goppe, a German who had arrived in the 1860s to establish a successful business, was unencumbered by the Russian past.

Location, too, played its part. St. Petersburg was strongly influenced by Western contacts and values, unlike Moscow. Since the reforms of Alexander II, Petersburg had become practically the only source of women's periodicals in Russia. That these publications resembled their Western counterparts was a result of changing (i.e.,

Westernized) values in the capital. Meanwhile, Moscow had retained many of the values and institutions of 1860s Russia; this was reflected in the fact that moralism and emphasis on serving the public still had a strong voice in *Drug zhenshchin*.

If Goppe's earlier successes in the marketplace had encouraged a string of would-be competitors, his virtual monopoly on women's periodicals by the end of 1884 seems to have provoked the appearance of an equal. In 1883 Goppe had acquired the rights to Mei's former serial *Modnyi magazin*, which was then absorbed into his existing publication to form *Modnyi svet i modnyi magazin*. In the following year, he swallowed up the only other viable competition, *Novyi russkii bazar*. The remaining women's popular periodical, *Vaza*, closed down by the end of the year.[61]

Noticing this trend in mid-1884, Nikolai Pavlovich Alovert (birthdate unknown) moved to fill the void. Originally from Voronezh, Alovert was a member of the *meshchanstvo*, an old urban estate that included artisans and small traders. He had already established himself in St. Petersburg as the editor of several technical journals, including *Konek (Hobbyhorse)*, *Zapiski imperatorskogo russkogo tekhnicheskogo obshchestva (Notes of the Imperial Russian Technical Society)*, *Fotograf (Photographer)*, *Elektrichestvo (Electricity)*, and *Mezhdunarodnoe delo (International Affairs)*, when he petitioned the Censorship Administration in August 1884 for permission to publish and edit a new women's magazine of fashion, literature, beauty, homemaking, and news. He received approval on the familiar condition that he not transfer the publication to another editor or publisher without consulting the Censorship Administration.[62]

Alovert used two strategies to break Goppe's monopoly. Coopting Goppe's tactics from the start, Alovert presented readers with three editions of *Vestnik mody* at a lower price than Goppe offered.[63] Then he raised the issue of nationality, his own and Goppe's, in a way meant to cause subscribers to question the authenticity of the latter's publications. In the first issue of *Vestnik mody*, Alovert suggested that other women's magazines were not what they seemed to be. By not delivering the latest, most popular fashions direct from Paris, the publishers and editors of such magazines were deceiving readers. Instead they obtained their illustrations via Berlin and were thus offering Paris fashions adjusted to German tastes. Being Russian himself, however, Alovert "understood" that Russian women wanted only the latest, straight from Paris: "[But], it has so happened that that's not what they've got. Every single Russian fashion journal to the present, these 'messengers of fashion' [*vestniki mody*], have been nothing more than German fashion publications *(Modenwelt, Bazar)* with Russian text."[64] *Vestnik mody* would rectify the situation. Henceforth, he intimated, women would have a publication they could count on to meet their needs. Reinforcing this trust was the magazine's "Russianness": the symbolic usage of old Slavic print for the title, framed by a banner of traditional Russian lace. Alovert thus invoked the negative feelings of his Russian audience toward Germany to undermine the competition. He then reassured them that his publication would be more reliable and familiar, in short, the real thing.

During the course of 1885, Alovert introduced into the publication a rapid series of changes to broaden its popularity. In fact, even before the first issue of *Vestnik mody* had appeared, he had petitioned the Censorship Administration for approval of changes to the program that would add the features "Shopping Review" (Obozrenie magazinov) and "Correspondence" (Pochtovyi iashchik), as well as further lower the price of the second edition.[65] When these requests were denied (for not even one issue of the journal had been published), he countered by releasing the first two issues for 1885 early, in December 1884, including the unauthorized "Shopping Review."[66] After an appeal in late December, the censors permitted Alovert to introduce a set of prices for three-month subscriptions but still rejected the additional sections. Undaunted, by June 1885 he added a fourth edition and an optional supplement of patterns; in August another supplement, a set of books and brochures on beauty and personal hygiene, was permitted, as was a high-priced fifth edition.[67]

The Goppe publishing house's response reflected *Vestnik mody*'s gradually growing success. At first, Alovert's nationalistic claims drew no reaction from Goppe, who saw no threat to his magazine's reputation from an upstart. However, in late spring 1885, the firm was rocked by Goppe's death. Alovert's subsequent inroads into the market finally provoked an appeal to the Censorship Administration from the widow Adel' Goppe in late 1885. The immediate cause was an advertisement in *Pravitel'stvennyi vestnik (Government Herald)* in which Alovert claimed to publish "*the only Parisian* fashion journal in Russia."[68] Adel' Goppe claimed false advertising and requested that the censors prohibit such claims.[69] The censors, however, declined to become involved: "Any praise some publisher prints about his journal could seem unfair or offensive to the competition and result in endless such claims."[70] Thus the Censorship Administration declined to get involved in what it perceived as an economic issue.

Simple claims of superiority, however, do not explain why from 1884 until the turn of the century every women's popular magazine was produced either by the publishing firm Goppe or by Alovert.[71] In quality and quantity of content, both indeed met the needs of the growing numbers of urban, literate women of moderate means. Following the lead of Goppe and inspired by women's publications in the West, Alovert loaded *Vestnik mody* with features meant not only to update readers on high society fashions but also to guide them in the development of proper manners. An etiquette column called "Life in Society and at Home" (Zhizn' v svete i doma) imparted the rules of decorum from the dacha to the dress ball, reinforced the rules of behavior for men versus women, and held up as examples the most elite members of Russian society, the nobility. The magazine frowned on any behavior smacking of poor upbringing: "Among all of high society's customs and practices, ignorance of proper dress is a clear sign of vulgarity and lack of tact";[72] and "in the family just as in society, tact and good manners are essential . . . and are acquired through proper training."[73] These columns served a dual purpose. On one level, they provided a set of rules needed by the upwardly mobile. But for the majority who could only dream of high society, the columns gave them a glimpse into a world not their own, fed their fantasies, and thus captivated them.

Vestnik mody also featured a series of articles that good-humoredly questioned popular perceptions of women's inferiority. In the magazine's first issue, the column "Woman in the Judgment of Man" (Zhenshchina pered sudom muzhchiny) promised to place gender in its historical context "so that the reader could judge the nonsense that has been invented on the subject."[74] It first noted that virtually all versions on the creation of women placed them in a subordinate position, and then asked, "Is it really not clear that all these tales are the inventions of men and are the same everywhere? That in every country men are profoundly egotistical and unjust toward women?"[75] But, the magazine assured its readers, these misconceptions would soon disappear: "For the longest time, lacking education and opportunity, women were not able to fight their accusers. Only a couple of centuries ago did a few women take up the pen; already they have succeeded in disproving many of th[ose] allegations . . . of which soon no traces will be left."[76]

In February the magazine again turned to the image of women bringing about change, this time in recognition of their achievements in the field of medicine. "The successes of women-doctors have been so brilliant that to speak now of their activities does not require one to conclude in defense of their existence."[77] A series of examples followed. This style would continue to be characteristic of the magazine.

By reintroducing into the women's magazine these popularized versions of the woman question, *Vestnik mody* widened its circle of female readers. Rather than offering the didactic, dry articles of *Drug zhenshchin,* Alovert's style aimed to entertain, enliven, and provoke. Anecdotes pointed out the absurdities of contemporary society, miscellaneous clips recorded the professional achievements of women everywhere, and quotations from the famous reinforced women's gifts and abilities in a humorous, lighthearted way. This style was appealing because it did not require of the reader anything other than amusement, while *Drug zhenshchin*'s insistent style had demanded a response, action if possible. *Vestnik mody* never would, for its main purpose was simply to attract and keep a readership; the breadth of Alovert's magazine's content was the most effective way of attracting and maintaining the widest audience possible.

The commercial success of the women's magazines *Modnyi svet* and *Vestnik mody* testifies to the expanding business activities carried out by members of the middle estates in Russia's cities and points to the significant changes taking place in Russia's economy and social structure. These activities, enabled largely by the reforms begun in the 1860s and related technological progress, created a small—although growing—relatively independent economic sphere. For publisher-cum-entrepreneurs such as Goppe and Alovert, this new space suffered relatively little from government control via censorship. As the foregoing examples indicate, professional skill and aggressiveness became the most important characteristics of the effective publisher and editor. The marketplace rewarded the competent and the risk takers. Thus, as long as their access to professional training was limited, women would be excluded from this domain.

On the other hand, the new rules of success must have played a part in inspiring ever greater numbers of young women to pursue a professional education, since the knowledge they would need to compete derived from experience and training. With few exceptions, both government and society had confined access to that training to men. Beginning only in the late eighteenth century, a few women managed to acquire the relevant skills, and still, society continued to frown on those who stepped outside accepted female roles.[78] Some women, like Mei, had found ways during this period to stretch these boundaries through semipublic activities such as publishing and hosting salons. But these experiences had been limited to the elite and had not provided the sort of background that would be valued in the marketplace.

The exception of Adel' Goppe in this study strengthens the point. As the wife of Herman Goppe, she seems to have gained experience in her husband's publishing business, acquiring useful skills through her involvement.[79] Following his death, she ran the Goppe publishing house for ten years until her own death, even expanding the operation by introducing other women's publications.[80] Only because of her husband's death, however, was she able to test her skills on her own, albeit inherited, business.

This gender gap in knowledge and experience seems to have had broader consequences for women publishers and editors in the 1880s than the period just before or following it. Use of new technologies and men's contributions toward technological improvement increased circulation and quality far beyond what amateur publicists could offer. At the same time, magazines were opening up a new kind of domestic world for their female audience. Readers had access to glamorous fashions, and the issues of homemaking and mothering became the subject of expert advice. Now turned into a sort of science, homemaking gained prestige.

The laws of competition eventually led to a broadening of subject matter as a vehicle for expanding readership. By the end of the eighties, women's magazines had turned to the still unsolved problems of women's education, professionalism, and gender relations (without, of course, abandoning fashion and the domestic scene). In the process, they supplied readers with a new range of images; the appearance of the female student and the woman doctor, for instance, implied that these ideas were gaining social acceptance. The magazines thus helped to legitimize a pro-education, pro-equality agenda. Rather than insist on the need for legal reform to allow for these new roles, however, they instead challenged women to enter the marketplace by spotlighting women professionals, their activities, and their achievements.[81]

The rules of commercial business promoted individualism through economic competition and thus undermined government paternalism, at least for as long as the market remained unregulated. These new ideals, though, were not an unqualified blessing. The race for profit had justified otherwise intolerable behavior, such as Alovert's false advertising campaign that played on anti-German feeling to undermine the Goppe publishing firm. In Russia's case, then as in more recent times, it proved impossible to replace the government's role in controlling individual and social behavior with a ready-made and widely accepted set of internalized rules governing conduct, that is, values that would unify Russian society and provide a fundamental vision for the country's future. Yet this imperfect transformation was a dynamic process with the potential to go in different directions. By the late 1880s, women's magazines were providing their audiences an ever broader set of roles from which to choose, in both the home and the professional world.

Notes

I would like to thank E. Willis Brooks, Ksenia Menshova, and the editors of this volume, Barbara Norton and Jehanne Gheith, for their valuable suggestions.

1. The middle estates included merchants, the petty bourgeoisie (*meshchanstvo*), honorary citizens, government officials, and military officers. Women belonged to the estates of their fathers or, if married, their husbands.
2. B. I. Esin, *Russkaia zhurnalistika 70-ich–80-ich godov XIX veka* (Moscow, 1963), 10; *Russkaia dorevoliutsionnaia gazeta* (Moscow, 1971), 46; Vl. Rozenberg, "V mire sluchainostei," in *Russkaia pechat' i tsenzura v proshlom i nastoiashchem*, ed. Vl. Rozenberg and V. Iakushkina (Moscow, 1905), 135.
3. As Miranda Remnek's essay in this volume suggests, women's maga-

zines became viable only in the second half of the nineteenth century with the growth in literacy among women of the middle estates and the increase in wealth outside of Russia's elite.

4 Louise McReynolds, *The News under Russia's Old Regime: The Development of a Mass-Circulation Press* (Princeton, 1991), 122; B. I. Esin, *Istoriia Russkoi zhurnalistiki XIX v.* (Moscow, 1989), 196; K. K. Arsen'ev, *Zakonodatel'stvo o pechati* (St. Petersburg, 1903), 152.

5 The women's press often indicated its target audience in the title or subtitle, such as *Drug zhenshchin* (1882–1884) or *Rassvet* (1859–1862), which was subtitled "Journal of Science, Art, and Literature for Girls from Fourteen Years of Age"; alternatively, it focused on an activity or interest that was at the time gender specific: *Modnyi magazin* (1862–1883), for example.

6 The quest for profit through publishing for a female audience raises an interesting question about women as a market during the 1880s. The present study will not address directly the extent to which women had access to spending money, although the growth in circulation figures for women's periodicals during the period, which this study does trace, seems to indicate that women had more money to spend.

7 Louise A. Tilly and Joan W. Scott, *Women, Work, and Family* (New York, 1978); and more recently, Gerda Lerner, *The Creation of Feminist Consciousness: From the Middle Ages to Eighteen-Seventy* (New York, 1993).

8 I have been able to identify nine such publications: *Magazin angliiskikh, frantsuzskikh i nemetskikh noveishikh mod* (1791), *Damskii zhurnal* (1806), *Modnyi vestnik* or *Vseobshchii modnyi zhurnal* (1816–1817), *Dlia schast'ia zhenshchin* (1823–1833), *Vaza* (1836–1884), *Vestnik parizhskikh mod* (1836–1850), *Magazin damskikh i muzhskikh mod* (1843), *Girlianda* (1846–1860), and *Magazin zhenskogo rukodeliia* (1847–1849).

9 *Vaza* was originally called *Zhurnal noveishego shit'ia*, changing its name in 1838 to *Sanktpeterburgskii zhurnal raznogo roda shit'ia vyshivan'ia* and in 1847 to *Vaza*. It closed in 1884.

10 Richard Stites, *The Women's Liberation Movement in Russia: Feminism, Nihilism, and Bolshevism, 1860–1930* (Princeton, 1978), 37.

11 This typology, which distinguishes women's magazines from women's journals, is a modern one. According to Webster's, a magazine is "a periodical containing miscellaneous pieces (as articles, stories, poems) often illustrated." It defines a journal as "a periodical dealing esp[ecially] with matters of current interest" (*Webster's Ninth New Collegiate Dictionary* [1983], s.v. "magazine" and "journal"). Oxford provides the following definition for a journal: "newspaper or periodical, esp[ecially] one

that is serious and deals with a specialized subject" (*Oxford Advanced Learner's Dictionary of Current English*, 4th ed., s.v. "journal").

As the titles of nineteenth-century women's periodicals reveal, Russian usage did not employ this typology. Thus the standard dictionary of the period defines "journal" simply as "a periodical publication, appearing on a weekly, monthly, or other regular schedule" (Vladimir Dal', *Tolkovyi slovar' zhivogo velikorusskogo iazyka v chetyrekh tomakh*, vol. 1 [Moscow, 1995], s.v. "zhurnal").

12 Its publisher and editor was Sofia Mei-Rekhnevskaia; the journal was produced in St. Petersburg.

13 Esin, *Russkaia zhurnalistika*, 10; *Russkaia dorevoliutsionnaia gazeta*, 46. The press laws are found in *Polnoe sobranie zakonov Rossiiskoi imperii*, 3d collection (St. Petersburg, 1886), 2:390–91.

14 Esin, *Istoriia russkoi zhurnalistiki*, 196.

15 The figure for *MS* is from "G. D. Goppe i ego izdatel'skaia deiatel'nost'," in *Pamiati Germana Dmitrievicha Goppe, 1836–1885* (St. Petersburg, 1885); others are listed in A. A. Bakhtiarov, *Istoriia knigi na Rusi* (St. Petersburg, 1890), 272; the first-issue circulation of *MS*'s competitor, *VM*, is listed in Rossiiskii gosudarstvennyi istoricheskii arkhiv (RGIA), f. 777, op. 3, 1884, d. 82, l. 3 (24 November 1884).

16 Women's periodicals comprised a small number of total available serial publications: in 1881 there were 153 serials of general interest. Rozenberg, "V mire sluchainostei," 135. Women's periodicals also had to compete with such popular journals as *Niva*, that covered women's interests too.

17 Data are based on a representative sampling of twenty women's periodicals between 1867 and 1917. Content was broken down into 123 subcategories divided into thirteen general areas: culture, economy, fashion, foreign topics, homemaking, legal questions, literature, politics, religion, society, women's issues, advertisements, and other.

18 *Mody i rukodel'ia* (1874–1880), *Modistka* (1889–1898), and *Vestnik mody dlia modistok* (1889–1896). Note that none of these was published between 1881 and 1888.

19 *Vaza*, *MM*, *NRB* (1867–1898), *MS*, *Modnye vykroiki* (1872–1883), *Zhenskii trud* (1880–1883), and *VM*. Seven was an increase in the number of such publications (there had been five in the seventies, four of which continued into the eighties) and signaled the beginning of their predominance among women's publications through the end of the empire and into the early Soviet years.

20 *ZhO* (1876–1891).

21 The exception may have been justified by contemporaries because the journal had intially been published as a service to the St. Petersburg

Women's Gymnasia; RGIA, f. 776, op. 5, 1872, d. 103, 1.4 (22 May 1872) and ll. 78–79 (28 November 1891).

22 *ZhO*, however, could price itself from two rubles fifty kopecks to three rubles fifty kopecks with delivery because of government subsidies.

23 The relative frequency of advertising usage was based on a sampling of twenty women's periodical publications for the years 1867, 1876, 1883, 1896, 1905, 1912, and 1917 and was calculated by dividing the average number of ads found in the publications each year (total number of ads by number of publications sampled in that year) with the total average number of ads in these publications for the entire period (total number of ads by total number of publications). This method allows for comparison by factoring out the disparities in the numbers of periodicals sampled per year.

24 "Ot izdatelia," *VM* 1 (1 January 1885): 1.

25 "Smes'," *IV* 4 (1889): 253.

26 Ch. Vetrinskii [V. E. Cheshikhin], "Anna Ivanovna Volkova: Biograficheskii ocherk," in *Vospominaniia, dnevnik i stat'i,* ed. Ch. Vetrinskii (Nizhnii Novgorod, 1913), xxi.

27 The three names were Alovert, Gettse, and Volkenshtein.

28 Published personal data on editors and publishers come from the following sources. For Herman Goppe: *Bol'shaia entsiklopediia* (St. Petersburg, 1902), s.v. "Goppe, German Dmitrievich"; "Smes'," *IV* 20 (May 1885): 494–95; *Novyi entsiklopedicheskii slovar'* (St. Petersburg, n.d.), s.v. "Goppe, German Dmitrievich"; *Entsiklopedicheskii slovar'* (St. Petersburg, 1893), s.v. "Goppe (German Dmitrievich, 1836–1885)"; and *Pamiati Germana Dmitrievicha Goppe*. For Sofiia Mei: *Russkii biograficheskii slovar'* (Tipografiia I. N. Skorokhodova, n.d.), s.v. "Rekhnevskaia, Sofiia Grigor'evna"; and "Smes'," *IV* 4 (1889): 253. Further information on other individuals was gathered from the Russian State Historical Archives, fondy 776 and 777, where the petitions for permission to publish periodicals are kept.

29 Also noteworthy is that two of the long-running periodicals directed by women dated from the previous two decades and folded, owing to financial troubles, in the early eighties.

30 *Russkii biograficheskii slovar'*, s.v. "Rekhnevskaia, Sofiia Grigor'evna."

31 "Smes'," 253.

32 *Russkii biograficheskii slovar'*.

33 V. K-ii, "Gde chto delaetsia (fel'eton)," *MM* 1 (1862): 529. Mei's remark might also be read as a nationalist sentiment. As is clear from Christine Ruane's essay in this volume, and as will be seen further in my essay, fashion does contain a nationalistic component, which seems to emerge especially during periods of political and ethnic tension.

34 "Smes'," 253.
35 RGIA, f. 776, op. 11, 1871, d. 154 part 1, l. 209 ob.
36 RGIA, f. 777, op. 3, 1882, d. 91, and f. 776, op. 4, d. 98.
37 One example is a story featured in *MS* 12 (23 March 1883): 127–28, about abnormal hair growth on women: "Smes'."
38 "Smes'," *IV* 20 (1885): 494–95.
39 Advertisement, *Mody i novosti* 34 (8 November 1867): 265. Apparently, *La Saison* also appeared in London under the title *The Young Ladies' Journal*, in Berlin as *Die Modenwelt*, and in translation under other names in Turin and Florence, Madrid, The Hague, Copenhagen, Budapest, and Warsaw.
40 Compare this development with Miranda Remnek's study of readership in the period of Nicholas I, which reveals that periodical audiences were mostly elite. Clearly by the 1860s this had begun to change.
41 On the growing merchant class and its aspirations toward high society, see James H. Bater, "Between Old and New: St. Petersburg in the Late Imperial Era," in *The City in Late Imperial Russia*, ed. Michael F. Hamm (Bloomington, 1986), 65–66.
42 "O podpiske 1869 g.," *MS* 1 (8 December 1868).
43 RGIA, f. 777, op. 2, 1869, d. 28, 1. 5 ob. The circulation figures for both *NRB* and *MM* would decline further by 1871 (5,350 to 6,000 and 3,500 to 4,300 respectively), while that of *MS* would rise further to 6,200 to 7,000; RGIA, f. 776, op. 11, 1871, d. 154 part 1, ll. 193–95. Also compare to the circulations in 1869 for *SPVed*, at 8,500, and *Golos*, at 7,000; Bakhtiarov, *Istoriia knigi na Rusi*, 271.
44 *Pamiati Germana Dmitrievicha Goppe*. A breakdown of how many readers subscribed has not been discovered.
45 In 1882, for example, the censor limited the journal *DZh* to printing judicial decisions concerning women "without discussions of those decisions," RGIA, f. 776, op. 8, 1881, d. 44, ll. 22–24 (22–27 November 1882).
46 Emphasis in original; "Ot glavnoi kontory redaktsii," *MS* 8 (23 February 1883): 1.
47 "O podpiske na 1883 god na 'Modnyi svet,'" *MS* 2 (8 January 1883): 1.
48 *Bol'shaia entsiklopediia*, s.v. "Goppe."
49 The first quoted phrase is found in Boguslavskaia's petition to establish the journal, RGIA, f. 776, op. 8, 1881, d. 44, ll. 1–12 (17 October 1881); her statement that the journal was directed at middle-estate women is found in a later petition for financial aid, RGIA, f. 776, op. 8, 1881, d. 44, l. 19 (18 August 1882).
50 Ibid., l. 20.
51 Ibid., l. 21 (2 September 1882). As noted, however, *ZhO*, a contempo-

rary publication, did receive regular financing from the government of 1,000 rubles per year, increased to 2,500 rubles in 1891 with the journal's expansion.

52 RGIA, f. 776, op. 8, 1881, d. 44, ll. 9–10 (n.d.) and l. 17 (23 December 1881). This obligation was required in both petitions to which this study has access for the 1880s, reflecting an increase in the obstacles the Censorship Committee set up in the 1880s (see below) and was not only a result of the unusual (i.e., nonfashion) content of the journal itself. On censorship in the 1880s, see Esin, *Istoriia russkoi zhurnalistiki*, 126, and "Russkaia legal'naia pressa kontsa XIX-nachala XX veka," in his *Iz istorii russkoi zhurnalistiki kontsa XIX-nachala XX v.* (Moscow, 1973), 5; and Rozenberg, "V mire sluchainostei," 135.

53 For biographical information, see Adele Lindenmeyr's discussion of Volkova in this volume, and Vetrinskii, "Anna Ivanovna Volkova," i–xvii.

54 RGALI, f. 1035, op. 1, d. 2, ll. 1 ob.–3 ob., 13–13 ob. (January–April 1883), 16–17 (24 February 1884); and Vetrinskii, "Anna Ivanovna Volkova," xx–xxi.

55 Vetrinskii, "Anna Ivanovna Volkova," xxii–xxiii (the quotation is from a letter by A. N. Filippov about Volkova).

56 Ibid., xx–xxi.

57 For suggestions as to why the journal closed, see RGALI, f. 1035, op. 1, d. 2, ll. 9–10 (13 October 1883).

58 Vetrinskii, "Anna Ivanovna Volkova," xix; Volkova, *Vospominaniia*, 69; and Stites, *Women's Liberation Movement*, 168.

59 Adele Lindenmeyr suggests that Volkova's education was probably better than Volkova was willing to admit.

60 Vetrinskii, "Anna Ivanovna Volkova," xxii–xxiii; and Volkova, *Vospominaniia*, 53, 175.

61 The only other journal directed at women was a pedagogical publication, *ZhO*.

62 RGIA, f. 776, op. 8, 1884, d. 284, ll. 1–2 (2 August 1884).

63 Alovert implied in his journal that he was subsidizing these rates; "Ot izdatelia," *VM* 1 (1 January 1885): 1.

64 Ibid.

65 RGIA, f. 776, op. 8, 1884, d. 284, l. 15 (20 December 1884).

66 Ibid., l. 20 (15 January 1885).

67 Ibid., ll. 1–32.

68 Italics in original; RGIA, f. 777, op. 3, 1884, d. 82, l. 16 (20 January 1886).

69 In fact, *Novyi russkii bazar* had originally been based, as its name indicates, on the German journal *Bazar*. However, by the 1880s, it drew

most of its fashions from the Parisian publication *Les Modes de Paris;* see *NRB* 1 (1 January 1883): 1. *MS* claimed that its illustrations were Parisian. The artist's name on the journal's 1883 prints, however, was German; *MS* 1 (1 January 1883): supplement. Ironically, *VM* itself advertised that its fashions came from not only the French *Moniteur de la Mode* but also the German magazine *Bazar;* RGIA, f. 777, op. 3, 1884, d. 82, l. 11 (n.d.).

70 RGIA, f. 777, op. 3, 1884, d. 82, ll. 15–15 ob. (20 January 1886).
71 In fact, with the death of Adel Goppe in 1895, the Goppe journals were run until 1901 by the Goppe daughters, at which time the last Goppe fashion publications, *Parizhskaia moda* and *Modistka*, ceased. The Goppe publishing house rights at that time were transferred to M. A. Meller. Alovert's publications, however, continued to run until 1917; RGIA, f. 776, op. 8, d. 532, ll. 11–16.
72 "Zhizn' v svete i doma," *VM* 30 (27 July 1885): 338.
73 *VM* 34 (24 August 1885): 377.
74 "Zhenshchina pered sudom muzhchiny," *VM* 1 (1 January 1885): 15.
75 Ibid.
76 Ibid., 15–16.
77 "Obo vsem," *VM* 6 (5 February 1885): 82.
78 Perhaps best known is the example of Nadezhda Durova, who disguised the fact that she was a woman in order to escape the limits society and government placed on women's activities. See Nadezhda Durova, *The Cavalry Maiden: Journals of a Russian Officer in the Napoleonic Wars*, trans. Mary Fleming Zirin (Bloomington, 1988).
79 The opportunities available to middle-estate women, the wives and daughters of artisans and traders, for gaining similar exposure in the process of increasing the family earnings, were probably greater than for women of the upper estates. This observation has been demonstrated for other societies and obviously deserves more attention in the Russian case.
80 See, for instance, *Modistka*.
81 However, with the restrictions on women's institutions of higher learning, one wonders to what extent these visions were realistic.

Anna Volkova

From Merchant Wife to Feminist Journalist

ADELE LINDENMEYR

Reading the other essays in this volume, one might conclude that noble birth and a cosmopolitan upbringing were practically prerequisites for women's involvement in journalism in imperial Russia. Although women from nonnoble backgrounds did occasionally make their way into print, the merchant estate, notorious in the eyes of the intelligentsia for its social and cultural backwardness, was usually dismissed as inhospitable terrain for the production of writers or intellectuals, especially of the female sex. As a daughter of this estate, Anna Ivanovna Volkova, born in 1847 to one of Moscow's most conservative, patriarchal merchant families, seemed destined for social invisibility. Instead, she overcame a scanty formal education and an early, intellectually stifling marriage to edit a pioneering feminist periodical and to write prolifically for numerous others on issues concerning women, children, education, charity, and social reform. Although Volkova was not the only merchant daughter to surmount the conservative traditions of her estate and create an independent life for herself, her long career in journalism represented an unusual achievement.

Volkova's voluminous literary output, along with her editorship of a journal for women, would seem to ensure her a prominent place in the history of Russian journalism. Unlike other women profiled in this volume, however, Volkova neither contributed to the production of a major periodical nor produced original literary work, as did Avdot'ia Panaeva and Evgeniia Tur. Unlike women such as Ekaterina Kuskova and Ariadna Tyrkova, Volkova played no visible role in the sphere of politics or culture. The walls of her Moscow home, rather than Balkan battlefields, defined the boundaries of her journalistic work. More striking for their quantity than for their quality, her writings consisted primarily of short, factual pieces for a variety of highly specialized journals such as *Detskaia pomoshch'* (*Children's Aid*), *Remeslennaia gazeta* (*Artisans' Gazette*), and *Tekhnicheskoe obrazovanie* (*Technical Education*), unfamiliar probably to most contemporaries as well as to scholars today. If Volkova's escape from the stereotype of Moscow merchant women was exceptional, her writings were not.

The ordinary work of this unusual woman is the subject of this essay. An examination of her work sheds light on two little-known aspects of Russian journalism: the world of small-circulation specialized publications devoted to promoting progress in Russian economic life, education, social welfare, and the status of women; and the production of that staple of nineteenth-century journals, the reports of Russian and foreign news. More important, Volkova's life provides a rare opportunity to examine how one woman journalist in late-nineteenth-century Russia understood her experiences as a woman and a journalist. Her written legacy, which includes an extremely personal memoir of her childhood and a diary she kept for twenty years (published after her death at her request),[1] makes it possible to explore the relationship between her journalism, on the one hand, and her private concerns and personal experiences on the other.

The main focus of this essay is on how Volkova identified and represented herself. Without question, the most important factor shaping her life was her sex. As this essay will show, Volkova was extremely sensitive to the social prejudices and discrimination she believed women in general and she in particular encountered. Although the term "feminist" was not introduced into the Russian language until late in Volkova's life, her passionate advocacy of education, autonomy, and equal rights for women justifies the designation of Volkova as an early advocate of equal-rights feminism in Russia.[2] Influenced by the works of J. S. Mill (his *Subjection of Women* had a profound impact on her views)[3] and by others, and the progress of women's rights movements abroad, she also drew heavily on her personal experiences as a girl and woman to shape her position on the woman question.

Volkova was also highly conscious of her identity as both a writer and a reader. In addition to examining how and what she wrote, this essay explores why she wrote, what reading and writing meant to her, and her views on the role of the journalist in Russia. Her approach to the written word was heavily influenced by a third aspect of her identity, her generation. Volkova belonged to the "generation of the 1860s," and that era's idealism and faith in progress deeply colored her own beliefs and work. When she began writing in the 1880s, however, that era had passed; and the conflict between optimism and pessimism about Russia's future discernible in her writing reflected the larger plight of Russian liberalism in the late nineteenth century.

Volkova's early life, especially as she represented it in her published memoir and diary, is crucial to understanding both her writing career and her views in adulthood. She regarded many aspects of her upbringing as reflecting practices and values typical of the patriarchal Russian merchantry in particular, and characteristic of elite attitudes toward girls in general. She belonged to one of the oldest merchant families of Moscow; the Vishniakov family firm, headed by her domineering grandfather, manufactured braid and gold lace.[4] Though materially comfortable, her childhood, as she tells it, was marked by severe emotional deprivation and loneliness. Even her physical surroundings—her grandfather's huge, dark house walled off from the surrounding city and protected by dogs, and the low, narrow, and dark nursery she shared with her brother—reflected the absence of light and warmth she perceived in her upbringing.[5] Her parents were both strict disciplinarians, who in Volkova's view clearly favored her younger brother and denied their daughter the affection she craved. "I do not remember any affectionate words, tenderness, from mother or father."[6] Instead, both parents whipped the girl (and much less often, her brother) to punish childish pranks.

Volkova's parents were distinguished by neither their education nor their cultural interests. After receiving a limited and practical education at home, typical of that provided to the sons of old-fashioned merchant families in the early nineteenth century, her father, Ivan Petrovich Vishniakov, entered the family business at an early age.[7] Her mother, also from a Moscow merchant family, had received the more refined but unsystematic and impractical upbringing commonly provided to the daughters of well-to-do merchant and noble families at this time.[8] She dressed with elegance and taste, Volkova recollected, played the piano, and read voraciously, especially French magazines, but even classics like Voltaire.[9] Stricken with cancer in her early twenties, she died at age twenty-nine, when

Volkova was nine; her long wasting illness and terrible suffering darkened Anna's childhood. Within six months after her mother's death, her father remarried.

Young Anna's own education was, in her estimation, extremely poor. After a sequence of indifferent or nasty governesses, she was sent to two private schools in Moscow to finish her education. Volkova was particularly critical of the strict, punitive pedagogical methods used by both her mother and governesses: "I, as usual, grew capricious and studied poorly when they ordered me, and immediately learned everything at the slightest affectionate look or gentle tone of my governess's voice."[10] Books and the writing of autobiographical sketches, or "poems in prose," Volkova later recalled, offered the only refuge in her unhappiness.[11] The image of reading and writing as a source of comfort and an outlet for self-expression continued to shape Volkova's representation of herself as a reader and writer in adulthood; frequent comments in her diary suggest that she viewed her writing as a psychological outlet or at least a diversion from her depression and the stresses of her family life.[12]

Her formal education at an end, in 1863 Volkova married at age sixteen the merchant banker Gavril Gavrilovich Volkov, ten years her senior. The selection of her suitor by her parents, her young age, and the disparity in age and experience between bride and groom conformed in every respect to the arranged marriage typical for the daughters of Russian merchant families in the nineteenth century.[13] Nevertheless, Volkova entered marriage with the expectation of finding in her new husband the intellectual companion she had longed for as a girl. Only her isolation, loneliness, and desire to escape her father's and stepmother's beatings and insults can explain such naive, unrealistic hopes for this match.[14] These hopes were bitterly disappointed:

I began to speak with my husband about books, about a library, about the desire to read, imagining that he too, my ideal, thought the same as I, and aspired to the same things. And suddenly, disillusionment! My husband called me a fool, which greatly astonished me. He wouldn't give me money for books, but ordered me to buy a pillow and embroider it for him for his name day. I obeyed, though I could not possibly understand why it was permissible to embroider a pillow, but not to read.[15]

The marriage, though a long one (Volkov died in 1905), was contentious and unhappy; in her diary, Volkova frequently if obliquely refers to family upsets, quarrels, and scenes.[16]

Thus the self-portrait Volkova paints is of an ill-educated, emotionally starved, lonely child and young woman who yearned for intellectual stimulation and companionship but found herself imprisoned by expectations and limitations imposed by her gender and social estate—the conservative, stifling milieu of the Moscow merchantry. Her memoir of her childhood repeatedly emphasizes the cruelty and humiliation she experienced at the hands of parents and teachers, and their denial of love or gentleness. One begins to wonder how such an embittered child and psychologically crippled woman, whose unhappiness with her life pours out of virtually every page of her published memoir and diary, could ever have found sufficient strength and confidence in herself to become an editor and writer.

The answer lies in part in certain features of her biography that suggest a counterpoint to the main themes just outlined. For example, Volkova never really explains what she considered so "inconsistent" or inadequate about the content of her education, which appears to have been fairly typical for Russian upper-class girls generally, and probably significantly better than that given to girls in the majority of merchant families. Her mother taught her to read and write in French as well as Russian at the age of five or six, for example, and Volkova clearly felt comfortable in the former language.[17] But Volkova yearned for more education. She devoted much attention in her writing to the topic of higher education for women, and she may have felt considerable bitterness that it became possible for young women to gain a higher education in Russia only in the late 1860s and 1870s, when Volkova, married and with a growing family, was unable to take advantage of it.

Nevertheless her diary and published articles reveal a well-read, well-informed, and intellectually curious woman who stayed abreast of cultural developments and current events in Russia and the West. She habitually read several Russian daily newspapers and monthly thick journals such as *Russkaia mysl' (Russian Thought), Russkoe bogatstvo (Russian Wealth),* and *Vestnik Evropy (European Herald).* She enjoyed the friendship and respect of a circle of Moscow intellectuals and writers who appear to have assembled regularly at her home. Several times acquaintances urged her to take a leadership position in congresses or associations, though modesty, shyness, or lack of self-confidence prevented her from assuming a more visible role in intellectual life or in charity, the women's movement, or other civic causes with which she sympathized.[18] Moreover, she was not the only woman from the merchantry to participate actively in Moscow intellectual and civic life. By the 1880s, other women of her generation, most notably the textile magnate Varvara Morozova, were also holding salons, publishing journals, and supporting the arts, education, and philanthropy.[19]

Finally, the personality of the girl Volkova depicts in her memoir of her childhood supplies a key to the question of how the isolated, unhappy merchant wife became an editor and prolific writer. "According to the stories of my elders," she wrote, "I was very capricious, playful in early childhood and stubborn."[20] Rarely allowed to play with other girls, she often amused herself in the large house she shared with her parents and uncles by playing tricks on the grown-ups or leading her brother in mischief. Forced by her grandmother to learn knitting, for example, the young Anna kept breaking the needles and tossing them out the window.[21] Her response to the frequent birchings and scoldings, her mother's favoritism toward her brother, and the absence of affection was to fight back, to become more willful, mischievous, and spirited, rather than to submit to what she perceived as unfair or cruel treatment. In fact, this deeply felt sense of the injustice of the treatment she received at the hands of parents, governesses, and later her husband—the counterproductive teaching methods, the withholding of affection toward an unhappy child, the senseless prohibition against reading—may have impelled Volkova to write, especially about subjects close to her own experiences as a child and a woman.

Volkova's first tentative venture into print, marking her move from the private sphere of marriage and family into public activity, supports the supposition that writing was not only an outlet for her personal disappointments and views but also a way for her to develop alternate scripts for her own life. Her first publication, appearing in 1880, was an anonymous translation of a melodramatic novel by the prolific but now completely forgotten French writer Ernest Daudet (1837–1921). *La Baronne Miroël* (1877) is a melodrama about the disastrous consequences of arranged marriages. Only after her wedding does the innocent, virtuous baroness learn of her husband's debauched habits, mistresses, debts, and other misdeeds. Although her hopes for happiness are broken, she nobly endures his betrayal until a final confrontation, when she fatally stabs him while defending herself against his attempt to force her into sexual relations. Recognizing her virtue, a French court acquits her of murder.[22] Volkova's decision to translate this novel, with its theme of marital betrayal, hardly seems accidental. It may very well have echoed some of her own marital experiences, and its happy ending (the baroness finds true love in a worthy young officer) expressed her hope that female virtue would be rewarded.[23]

After publishing her translation, Volkova contributed a few signed articles to the journal *Drug zhenshchin (Women's Friend)* during its first year in 1882.[24] Financial problems at the journal and the government's denial of a subsidy convinced its editor to ask Volkova, who was a relatively wealthy woman, to become editor and, presumably, chief financial supporter as well.[25] When she assumed control of *Drug zhenshchin,* Volkova evidently regarded herself as a lonely pioneer; writing in 1883, she counted herself among only twelve female editors in all of Russia.[26] As Rhonda Clark's recent research has revealed, however, by the 1880s a considerable number of women, including ones from the merchantry, participated actively in producing Russian newspapers and journals (Clark counts at least fifty-three female editors and publishers in Moscow and St. Petersburg in that decade).[27]

Volkova's misperception of the extent of women's participation in editing and publishing reflected a complex but consistent pattern in her self-representation. In embarking on the path of writer and editor, Volkova sought to portray herself as unique. At the same time, she understood her experiences in journalism, like her childhood and marriage, to be broadly typical of the plight of women in her society. Her reaction to an encounter with a "fairly educated and intelligent" man, related in her diary in 1886 (two years after the demise of *Drug zhenshchin*), illustrates this dual perception. Hearing from someone that Volkova had once edited a journal, the man had reacted with amazement and quizzed her intently about how she had become interested in such a pursuit, and whether she had really found editing a journal interesting and engaging.[28] Volkova was clearly wounded by this man's surprised and slightly skeptical reaction toward her journalistic undertakings. With characteristic self-deprecation, she first attributed his reaction to the unique circumstances of her education and social background: "I don't know," she wrote, "in my view, one should be much more surprised by the fact that I didn't 'stick to my own affairs' with my inconsistent education, and not by the fact that I could become interested in journalism."[29] But she went on to find the real reason not in herself but in society's construction of gender roles:

A woman is supposed to be interested in fashion, pies, pickles, jams, and other things, with embroidery, if you will, and nothing else. . . . if she takes it into her head to become interested in something else, then that's the end, she's dead; offensive gibes, little smiles flavored with sarcasm, that's the helping hand from society. . . . women themselves are more merciless than men in this case. Having become stupefied in their femininity, feminine women, as it is accepted to call women who are occupied with fashion and cooking, become spiteful against those martyrs who carry, stumbling, the heavy banner of the woman question.[30]

Volkova clearly saw herself as one such martyr.

Such discouraging reactions,[31] along with her own modesty and lack of self-confidence, help to explain why, after the demise of *Drug zhenshchin,* Volkova tried her hand at editing a journal only once more, in 1899. As she relates in her diary in late 1901, it was "out of consideration and courtesy toward the people who asked me to take part in this work" that she allowed herself to be persuaded to become an editor as well as contributor to the journal *Drug zhivotnikh (Animals' Friend).* Her diary also reveals that she never felt wholly committed to this endeavor; however sympathetic the cause of animal protection might be, in her view, it was "premature" for Russia, where human beings were still being flogged. Even more tragic and compelling than the plight of animals was the plight of Russia's children—apprentices, factory workers, orphans, abandoned children. The cause of child welfare, along with women's emancipation, was much closer to her heart than animal protection, she explained.[32]

Although her editing experience was limited, Volkova's other involvement in journalism was extensive and long-lived. From her entry into print in the early 1880s to her death in 1910, she produced hundreds of articles published in thirty-two different newspapers and journals.[33] Between 1885 and 1895, her most prolific period, she annually wrote dozens of articles for several different journals.[34] After 1895, the volume of Volkova's output began to diminish; in the mid-1890s, Gavril Volkov became paralyzed, and his wife, her own health deteriorating, became the head of both her household and the family banking business.[35] Yet between 1898 and 1904 she still published between forty and sixty articles annually in as many as twelve different periodicals.

An exact count of Volkova's published articles is difficult to obtain, in fact.[36] Although she published some signed, full-length pieces, she tended to specialize in writing the usually anonymous "current events" columns that were monthly features of many Russian journals. Volkova began writing these columns as editor of *Drug zhenshchin*. From 1885 to 1895, most of her effort went into columns that appeared regularly in other specialized periodicals. They included reports of recent Russian developments in charity or education for the charity journal *Detskaia pomoshch'*, the vocational education monthly *Remeslennaia gazeta*, and the major education journal *Vestnik vospitaniia (Education Herald)*, as well as surveys of recent publications for *Bibliograficheskii kruzhok (Bibliographic Circle)* and *Etnograficheskoe obozrenie (Ethnographic Review)* (in 1893 and 1894 she wrote regular monthly columns for all five).

Although Volkova occasionally published an article in the major daily newspaper *Russkie vedomosti (Russian News)*, the vast majority of her writings appeared in what one contemporary called "little tiny journals [malen'kikh zhurnal'chikov] of an ideological orientation, published without capital, in an amateur way [kustarnym sposobom]."[37] These specialized "little journals" concentrated on education, vocational training, women's emancipation, charity, or temperance. Few of the journals in which she published could have had more than a few hundred subscribers.[38] Volkova's lack of self-confidence may explain in part why she chose relatively obscure outlets to express her views. At the same time, the concerns of these journals were close to her. Their specialized focus allowed her to find an already interested and committed audience for the ideas and information she wished to communicate. An article on the successes of coeducation in America, for example, would arguably have a more concentrated impact on public opinion when published in *Vestnik vospitaniia* (1895, no. 6), than if it were published in the mass-circulation daily *Russkie vedomosti*.

Volkova's choice of this kind of journal for her work also accorded with her belief that being a writer entailed certain moral obligations. In her view, the world of Russian journalism was sharply divided into two opposing camps: the liberal press, dedicated to the cause of progress and enlightenment, and reactionary publications such as *Moskovskie vedomosti (Moscow News)* and *Grazhdanin (Citizen)*, which she detested.[39] A journalist, she believed, should write only for periodicals whose orientation matched his or her own convictions. In her diary in 1894, at the height of her own writing career, Volkova praised another female journalist of her acquaintance. But this woman had one strange, incomprehensible characteristic, Volkova found: she did not discriminate among periodicals but would work for any that published her writings and paid her. Volkova tried to find an explanation for such behavior:

Perhaps it is caused by lack of funds, yes, very likely, it is explained by that alone. She acknowledges this and says that organs of the press that are out of sympathy with her spirit and views serve only as a way to obtain the means of existence. There, in those organs, she is a worker [*remeslennitsa*], and translator from languages seldom found in Russia, like, for example, Italian. In organs sympathetic to her she is a different, true, enthusiastic, sympathetic creature [*natural*]![40]

Volkova recognized that her comfortable material circumstances allowed her to write only for "sympathetic" periodicals. But her views also betray the influence of the liberal ethos of her generation of the 1860s, according to which the primary purpose of the written word was to promote moral education and progress.

Writing for these small-circulation specialized journals also complemented her involvement in charities and other civic causes, as both a participant and financial supporter. According to the editor of Volkova's memoir and diary, she lived modestly for someone of her wealth but spent "many thousands" of rubles a year, a "significant part" of which was charitable donations.[41] The journal *Detskaia pomoshch'*, for example, to which Volkova contributed regularly throughout its ten-year existence, was published by the Society for the Care of Indigent Children (Obshchestvo popecheniia o neiumushchikh detiakh), founded in Moscow in 1883. Volkova, who was passionately committed to the cause of child welfare, belonged to this society. Finally, she may have received a measure of the respect, appreciation, and intellectual companionship she longed for from these "little journals." Operated on a shoestring, they no doubt valued her collaboration: her regular columns on recent developments in education or charity made up an important part of their content, and in addition, Volkova never accepted any fee or honorarium.[42]

At first glance, it is easy to dismiss Volkova's journalistic writings as derivative. Most of her articles were relatively short—a few paragraphs, a few pages—and seldom developed a sustained idea or theme (although her reports on women's education in *Drug zhenshchin* were occasionally quite lengthy).[43] In general, she concentrated on relaying information, not interpreting it.

Volkova was no investigative reporter roaming Moscow streets, notebook in hand, interviewing sources. She obtained most of her information second- or thirdhand. For her chronicles of events in Russia, for example, she relied primarily on her extensive reading of newspapers and journals. Sometimes the information originated in a relatively obscure provincial periodical, from which it would be reported in a major Moscow newspaper or journal; reading it in the latter, Volkova would recycle the information or report into one of the specialized publications for which she wrote.[44] When it came to Moscow news, her connection was more direct; at least her involvement with many Moscow associations, and her conversations with the acquaintances who attended the weekly salon at her home, kept her abreast of developments in Moscow education, charity, and intellectual politics. All the same, her writing drew heavily on her reading.

This was especially true in the case of the chronicles of foreign developments that formed such a significant part of her journalistic output. For these, Volkova relied almost exclusively on reports first published in foreign periodicals, especially specialized ones from France such as *Revue pédagogique* or *Le Foyer domestique*. Her articles on foreign topics seem to have been mostly faithful translations of the originals.[45] Seldom did she draw any explicit connection to Russian reality or needs. A brief article on London's famous settlement house Toynbee Hall may serve as an example. Published in *Detskaia pomoshch'* in 1892, the article cites as its original source an article in *Revue pédagogique* the same year. Volkova's version provides no direct clue as to why she chose to introduce this subject to a Russian audience. After recounting the origins of Toynbee Hall and describing its operations and activities, the article concludes with a positive assessment of the institution and the "sincerity and complete sympathy" of the residents who served the needy there. There is no discussion of any relevance Toynbee Hall might have for Russia.

Volkova was occasionally less diffident about offering her own analysis and opinions when she wrote about Russia. The chronicles about developments in female education in Russia she wrote as editor of *Drug zhenshchin,* for example, combined a large amount of information with judgments on numerous matters: the injustice of excluding women scholars from scientific conferences, for example, or the slow progress in providing enough places in secondary schools for all the girls seeking to attend. As editor of this journal, Volkova may have felt more confident in conveying her judgment in those cases when she felt she could claim some knowledge and expertise, as with women's education in Russia.

Like many other Russian journalists, Volkova frequently did not sign her articles or used an abbreviated form of her name (such as "An. V."). The mainstay of her journalistic output, the columns on current events, were almost never signed. She usually attached her entire name or an abbreviated form of it to articles she wrote on a single topic, however. Although it is difficult to draw any firm conclusion from her use of anonymity, Volkova may have believed that most of her work, by conveying information, did not warrant her signature; only the occasional piece that went into more depth needed attribution.

Appearing objective, impersonal, and derivative on the surface, on a deeper level Volkova's published writings are permeated with her personal experiences and beliefs. Most of her work dealt with subjects closest to her heart: education and vocational training, the position of women, the upbringing of children, innovations in charity and social reform. In her treatment of these subjects, she often described or prescribed approaches that were the diametric opposite of her own experiences as a child or woman.

Volkova used her writing to script alternatives to the personal and social realities she experienced as a girl and a woman. Her columns on current developments in Russia and abroad describe women's and children's lives rich in opportunity, intellectual stimulation, and mutual support. Russia's first female medical students, whom she followed avidly in *Drug zhenshchin,* for example, successfully overcome the many obstacles placed before them, and contributions and support for women's medical and higher education pour in from sympathetic local governments and individual citizens. Women in Belgium enter professional schools, and women meeting in Germany discuss military training and service for girls. French schoolchildren go on field trips, and American children enjoy free borrowing privileges at specially designed, bright, and cheerful children's libraries.[46] In the world she describes in her journalistic writing, parents do not use the corporal punishment she suffered to discipline their children. Girls are not handed over to ill-educated governesses but enter well-organized secondary or vocational schools. Young women are not forced into marriage when they are sixteen years old but can look forward to further education and satisfying lives serving the public good.

In the same way, her articles depict a political world that in many respects was the antithesis of Russia as she perceived and described it in her diary. Commenting on current events in her diary, Volkova frequently expressed irritation and disgust at the ubiquitous, meddlesome, and ignorant intrusions of the tsarist police and censorship.[47] She deplored the actions of a suspicious, reactionary, autocratic government to whittle away the Great Reforms of the 1860s and to thwart laudable initiatives in popular education or welfare undertaken by enlightened local governments or concerned citizens.[48] In general, Volkova subscribed to the late imperial liberal scenario of a progressive intelligentsia locked in a struggle over Russia's future with an abusive, repressive, and backward-looking government.

In the progressive, optimistic world depicted in her journalistic writings, however, different values prevailed. That ideal alternative world was almost always to be found in the West, where Volkova saw few obstacles to progress and enlightenment. Her chronicles of modern Western charity, for example, described numerous initiatives undertaken by an enlightened public that attended compassionately to the needs of its children and poor. Reporting on the women's movement abroad, Volkova was similarly upbeat. The cause of women's suffrage in England is rapidly gaining supporters with each passing year, she announced; American women are far ahead of their sisters in the Old World in their political rights.[49] In the West the progress of women's rights, the broad public support for free and universal education, rapid advancements in technical training and vocational education for men and women, and more humane and enlightened methods of parenting all bespoke a society that treasured its children, valued education, advanced the rights of its women, and marched forward.

The worldview pervading Volkova's journalistic writings also presents a striking contrast to the tone of her more intimate writings. The implicitly if not explicitly optimistic message behind her reports about female education in Russia, Danish vocational schools, French teacher education, the prevention of tuberculosis in Belgium, special institutes for the blind or deaf in the United States, or the countless other innovations she chronicles was unambiguous: all problems in human society could be addressed and significantly ameliorated, if not eliminated, by the efforts of well-intentioned, right-thinking people.

By contrast, in her diary she expressed an extremely bleak view of human nature that contradicted such optimism about progress. Frequently referring to human stupidity or vanity, Volkova revealed herself to be quite a misanthrope. Particularly striking is her interpretation of the motives behind the good deeds she chronicles in such detail in her journalistic writings: "Oh people, people! Wishing to get ahead, they use as a cover the striving for social good, but in essence the thirst for fame guides them and nothing else."[50] People may seem to desire good, but their "humane speeches" and their "concern for people" recede before the stronger forces of egoism and vanity (154). As one grows up, she commented, one begins to learn the great contradiction between one's elders' lofty words and their actual deeds, and one loses "faith in the moral ideal" (153).

This daughter and wife of the Moscow merchantry also shared the Russian intelligentsia's hostility toward money, profit, and capitalism. Driven by greed and self-interest, people lie and cheat in pursuit of money—the god, the "golden calf" of the nineteenth century, she wrote in 1885 (52). After lamenting the recurrence of famine in the Russian countryside in 1898, the deaths and suffering, and the insufficient relief donations, Volkova continued:

Money, money! Its power over people is omnipotent. How many abominations, indignities, even crimes of all kinds are committed in the world because of it. But these crimes are not always in the open, sometimes they happen in secret, unforeseen by the law. The spider spins its web, slowly, solidly and carefully and attains its goals, catches flies and feeds on them. People do the same thing, but the nets cast by them are more dangerous. And victims die. . . . Time passes, civilization grows, progress moves forward, but spider-people live and multiply, only their actions take on a different hue, more subtle, less noticeable to the eye of outsiders. The spiders put on the cloak of virtue, propagandize themselves with charitable deeds, and so on, and so on. (163–64)

Deeply pessimistic about Russia's political future, Volkova also shared the view of many members of the intelligentsia about the direction of economic development. In Russia the "yoke of capitalism," she wrote in 1898, has replaced the yoke of serfdom. Once the nobility lived parasitically off of the peasantry; now the "bourgeoisie" exploits peasants and workers. The latter, like peasants before them, are increasingly conscious of their oppression, and "our Russia has begun to imitate the West in the organization of strikes" (165). Yet unlike other Russian critics of capitalism, such as Fedor Dostoevskii or the populists, Volkova's distaste for it does not seem to have dimmed her admiration for Western Europe or the United States. Nor did it prevent her from wholeheartedly supporting the improvement of technical and vocational education in Russia. She gave considerable financial and moral assistance to her cousin Aleksei Semenovich Vishniakov, for example, to promote modern business education in Russia.[51]

In summary, Volkova's writings reveal a sharp contrast between the anguished pessimism about both Russia and human nature that colored her diary, on the one hand, and the confident tone and message of progress found in her published articles, especially those about the West, on the other. Censorship may have played a certain part in keeping Volkova from expressing her more negative opinions more openly or forcefully and probably also deterred her from making in print some of the bleaker, more pessimistic judgments one finds in her diary. As her diary shows and her experience at *Drug zhenshchin* must have taught her, she was well aware of the powers the Russian government had to muzzle the press.[52]

But this duality also originated in Volkova's hypersenstive yet idealistic personality, to which disappointment and disillusionment came as easily as unrealistically high expectations.[53] Prone to intense self-examination, she was plagued by feelings of intellectual inadequacy and isolation throughout her life. Her self-doubts and loneliness, traits that she attributed to features of her social origin, childhood, and upbringing, were continually reinforced, in her view, by society's treatment of women in general.

Writing and editing provided more than a psychological outlet for this lonely and unhappy woman. Journalism gave her the means to counter the pessimism and despair she felt about her world, a way to construct an alternative realm of progress and enlightenment. The foundation on which Volkova constructed this alternative world derived in part from her own life experiences, especially her somber childhood and difficult marriage, and her sense of the double burden she bore as a woman and a product of a stifling merchant milieu. Yet the concerns and the hopes she expressed in her writings transcended the biographical and personal to embrace the prevailing Russian liberal vision of the world. Like her fellow liberals in the late imperial period, Volkova searched the experience of the West for guidance and hope to counter the grim conditions and prospects she perceived in her native land. After coming of age in the era of the Great Reforms, and imbibing its faith in progress, Volkova did not manage to enter public life until the 1880s. This era of increased censorship, reaction, and counterreforms in Russian politics left her, like others of her generation, profoundly discouraged. By creating a heroic narrative of human progress based on Western development, Volkova and other reform-era liberals constructed through their journalism a kind of life raft for themselves and a vision of a happier future for their troubled country.

Notes

1 Anna Ivanovna Volkova (née Vishniakova), *Vospominaniia, dnevnik i stat'i*, ed. Ch. Vetrinskii [V. E. Cheshikhin] (Nizhnii Novgorod, 1913), "Predislovie," vi.
2 Originating in France, the word "feminism" was not used widely until the end of the nineteenth century; on this and "equal rights feminism" as one of several types of feminism, see Karen Offen, "Defining Feminism: A Comparative History Approach," *Signs: Journal of Women in Culture and Society* 14, no. 1 (1988): 119–57. "Feminizm" does not appear in the leading nineteenth-century Russian dictionary, Vladimir Dal's

Tolkovyi slovar' zhivogo Velikorusskogo iazyka (1882). Two decades later, the word does appear in the major encyclopedia of the late imperial period, but the entry advises the reader to "see Emancipation of women" (*Entsiklopediia Brokgauz-Efron*, vol. 69, 1902). The entry on the emancipation of women in the same encyclopedia (vol. 80, 1904) uses the term *feministka* (in addition to "feminist movement" and "feminist unions"), which it defines for readers as "adherents of women's emancipation"; the latter is defined as the movement to "equalize the rights of both sexes." See also Richard Stites, *The Women's Liberation Movement in Russia: Feminism, Nihilism, and Bolshevism, 1860–1930* (Princeton, 1978 and 1990), chaps. 3 and 7.

3 Ch. Vetrinskii, "Anna Ivanovna Volkova: Biograficheskii ocherk," in Volkova, *Vospominaniia*, xiv.

4 Information on the Vishniakov family may be found in Volkova, "Vospominaniia detstva," in *Vospominaniia*, 3; Vetrinskii, "Anna Ivanovna Volkova," vii; and P. A. Buryshkin, *Moskva kupecheskaia* (Moscow, 1991), 183–84. Volkova's uncle wrote a family history: N. P. Vishniakov, *Svedeniia o kupecheskom rode Vishniakovykh (1762–1847)*, 3 vols. (Moscow, 1903–1911).

5 Volkova, "Vospominaniia detstva," 3–4.

6 Ibid., 7.

7 Vetrinskii, "Anna Ivanovna Volkova," vii–viii.

8 See Muriel Joffe and Adele Lindenmeyr, "Daughters, Wives, and Partners: Women of the Moscow Merchant Elite," in *Merchant Moscow: Images of Russia's Vanished Bourgeoisie*, ed. James L. West and Iurii A. Petrov (Princeton, 1998), 95–108. See also Catriona Kelly, "Teacups and Coffins: The Culture of Russian Merchant Women, 1850–1917," in *Women in Russia and Ukraine*, ed. Rosalind Marsh (Cambridge, 1996), 55–77.

9 Volkova, "Vospominaniia detstva," 4; Vetrinskii, "Anna Ivanovna Volkova," ix.

10 Volkova, "Vospominaniia detstva," 18.

11 Vetrinskii, "Anna Ivanovna Volkova," x–xi.

12 For example, her diary entries of 24 February, 25 February, and 23 March 1889; Volkova, "Zametki i vpechatleniia," in *Vospominaniia*, 96–98.

13 See Joffe and Lindenmeyr, "Daughters, Wives, and Partners."

14 Vetrinskii, "Anna Ivanovna Volkova," xi–xii. The young Anna's romantic dreams may also have been raised by the love that developed between one of her young uncles and her governess; faced with opposition from Volkova's parents to such an unsuitable match, the couple eloped. Volkova, "Vospominaniia detstva," 26.

15 Quoted in Vetrinskii, "Anna Ivanovna Volkova," xii.
16 For example, she wrote on 5 May 1888: "The winter of the past year has been rather hard for me: family troubles have completely worn me out. Every day scandals, scenes, senseless screams, swearing, and then again a lull, and so without end" (Volkova, "Zametki i vpechatleniia," 90). Volkova also occasionally referred to her disappointment in her marriage; for example, the entry of 30 May 1894 (142).
17 Volkova, "Vospominaniia detstva," 16. French periodicals served as the major sources for many of her articles.
18 Vetrinskii, "Anna Ivanovna Volkova," xxii–xxiv. In the 1890s, for example, acquaintances from the feminist movement tried to convince Volkova to take a prominent part in the women's peace movement, which, they felt, her journalistic work for and about women had earned her. And in 1894 she was invited to become the secretary of a congress on technical education; "I, of course, refused out of fear of my inability [neumenie] and so on, and so on. . . . I am very glad, I am ready to do all that I can, but fear of my clumsiness [neumelost'] drives me crazy" (Volkova, "Zametki i vpechatleniia," 127).
19 See Joffe and Lindenmeyr, "Daughters, Wives, and Partners"; and Natal'ia Dumova, *Moskovskie metsenaty* (Moscow, 1992), especially 64–76.
20 Volkova, "Vospominaniia detstva," 7.
21 Ibid., 6.
22 *La Baronne Miroël* is a good example of the extremely popular French melodrama that Fedor Dostoevskii found so ridiculous in the last chapter of his *Winter Notes on Summer Impressions*. I am grateful to Jehanne Gheith for information about Russian attitudes toward French novels.
23 The editor of Volkova's memoir and diary asserts that her choice of this "weak" novel for translation was "characteristic" because she too had been married "by force" to a man who fell far short of the ideal (Vetrinskii, "Anna Ivanovna Volkova," xvi).
24 Volkova, *Vospominaniia*, prilozhenie 2, 271.
25 Vetrinskii, "Anna Ivanovna Volkova," xx. On *DZh* see also the essay by Carolyn Marks in this volume.
26 *DZh*, no. 3 (1883): 174.
27 See Rhonda Lebedev Clark, "Claiming Voice, Profession, Livelihood: Women Periodical Publishers and Editors of Moscow and St. Petersburg, 1860–1905," paper presented at the summer workshop on Slavic women, University of Illinois at Urbana-Champaign, 21 June 1995.
28 Volkova, "Zametki i vpechatleniia," 49.
29 Ibid. The expression Volkova uses, "ne v svoi sani sela," translated here as "I didn't stick to my own affairs," undoubtedly is a reference to a play

by Aleksandr Ostrovskii, *Ne v svoi sani ne sadit'sia*. The play relates the misfortunes encountered by a merchant's social-climbing daughter who seeks to marry into the nobility.

30 Ibid.

31 Although only this negative reaction is mentioned in her published diary, she received the warm support of several men from the Moscow intelligentsia for her efforts at *DZh* (Vetrinskii, "Anna Ivanovna Volkova," xxii–xxiii).

32 Volkova, "Zametki i vpechatleniia," 185–86.

33 Volkova, *Vospominaniia*, 271. For the list, see the appendix to the present volume.

34 For a bibliography of Volkova's published works see *Vospominaniia*, 271–93. It lists only three works not published in a periodical, but as separate brochures: *Prizrenie pokinutykh detei* (1894), *Zhenskoe dvizhenie v raznykh stranakh* (1900), and *Kommercheskoe obrazovanie v Danii, Shvetsii i Norvegii* (1902). The latter two were published to benefit particular philanthropies.

35 E. I. Shchepkina, "Vospominaniia i dnevniki russkikh zhenshchin," *IV* 137 (1914): 554.

36 According to Shchepkina, Volkova published 486 articles and "little articles" *(stateiki)*, if one counts as a single article (instead of up to twelve) the columns appearing regularly in sequential issues of a journal. The bibliography appended to her published memoir and diary (see note 34) lists the recurring columns as a single article.

37 Shchepkina, "Vospominaniia," 554.

38 For example, 598 copies of *Detskaia pomoshch'* were "distributed" during 1886, its second year of publication, and it ended the year with a deficit of 162 rubles; see *Detskaia pomoshch'* 5, no. 1 (15 January 1887), 1. For some circulation figures of other journals at this time, see the preceding essay by Carolyn Marks.

39 Volkova, "Zametki i vpechatleniia," 153–56. Russian journalism was experiencing other profound changes in the 1880s that Volkova could hardly have welcomed. Commercially oriented publications, without a particular political stripe, now competed with the older, ideologically oriented thick journals, which had served as the arbiters of opinion for the generation of the 1860s, and with which Volkova identified more closely. On these changes see Louise McReynolds, *The News under Russia's Old Regime: The Development of a Mass Circulation Press* (Princeton, 1991), chap. 5.

40 Volkova, "Zametki i vpechatleniia," 125–26.

41 Vetrinskii, "Anna Ivanovna Volkova," xxvii.

42 Ibid., xxi. She probably also supported these little journals financially, as she had *DZh.*

43 Ibid.

44 This was how she obtained much of the information for her writings for *DZh,* for example, although she also drew on other materials, such as letters to the journal.

45 A comparison of Volkova's 1899 article "Shkol'nye assotsiatsii dlia sodeistviia narodnomu obrazovaniiu v Soed. Shtatakh i Italii," *Russkii narodnyi uchitel',* no. 3 (1899), reprinted in Volkova, *Vospominaniia,* 254–57, with its source (an article by Paola Lombroso on "Les Cooperatives scolaires," published in *La Revue des Revues,* no. 18 [1898]: 596–99) reveals Volkova's to be a faithful translation. She made few changes beyond shortening the original slightly, and reordering the sections on the United States and Italy. She did not translate the final paragraph that expressed the original author's opinions, nor did she add anything indicating her own evaluation of the initiatives described in the article.

46 Articles on these and other topics, forming a sample of her entire published work, are included in Volkova, *Vospominaniia,* prilozhenie 1.

47 See, for example, her bitter criticism of the police and government repression in diary entries for 12 May and 1 August 1893, and her denunciation of penalties leveled by the censorship against *RVed* in an entry for 25 April 1898, in Volkova, "Zametki i vpechatleniia," 109–11, 163.

48 Several diary entries during 1887 deplore government restrictions on access to education and report threats to local self-government institutions and the judicial reforms of 1864; ibid., 64–70, 72, 75, 79.

49 "Raznye izvestiia," *DZh,* no. 3 (1883): 184–85.

50 Volkova, "Zametki i vpechatleniia," 118. Further quotations from this diary will be cited in the text.

51 Buryshkin, *Moskva kupecheskaia,* 183–84. Volkova bequeathed her large library to Moscow's Commercial Institute; proceeds from the sale of her published memoir and diary went to benefit her cousin Aleksei Vishniakov's Moscow Society for the Promotion of Business Education (Vetrinskii, "Anna Ivanovna Volkova," xxiv).

52 Volkova, "Zametki i vpechatleniia," 82, 119, and 163. On the experience of women journalists with censorship, see the introduction to this volume and the essays by Carolyn Marks and Barbara Norton.

53 See Vetrinskii, "Anna Ivanovna Volkova," for his comments on her personality, based apparently on information from people close to her.

Meeting the Challenge

Russian Women Reporters and the Balkan Crises

of the Late 1870s

MARY F. ZIRIN

As the essays in this volume demonstrate, Russian women had to be tough and tenacious to make their way into journalistic careers in general, and the masculine camaraderie of newspaper editorial offices created special challenges for them that were compounded by common perceptions of the limitations of their sex. Restricted in their access to higher education and public space, women in Russia in the middle decades of the nineteenth century, like their counterparts in Western Europe and America, were limited in the fields they could discuss with authority; and society was quick to confound dearth of information and experience with lack of capability.[1] Women contended against the prevailing perceptions of their sex as "intuitive," "emotional," and "sensitive"—in a word, feminine—that made it difficult for them to gain credibility writing in such "masculine" fields as history, economics, politics, and the sciences, all of which were central to the journalistic enterprise. This essay deals with an offshoot of Russian journalism that was particularly slow to admit women as colleagues—writing for newspapers—and with the remarkable ways in which three early reporters, Ol'ga Alekseevna Novikova (1840–1925), Anastasiia Vasil'evna Kairova (1845–1888), and Varvara Nikolaevna Mak-Gakhan (1850–1904), were catapulted into extended, prolific careers as international correspondents by the upheavals of the Serbian campaign of 1876 and the Russo-Turkish War of 1877–1878.

The development of newspaper reporting as a profession for women depended on the existence of papers for which to report. It was only in the mid-1860s that the Russian government made the operation of private mass-circulation newspapers in Moscow and

Petersburg viable by replacing mandatory prepublication censorship with a system of postpublication penalties that included suspension of the right to publish advertisements, revocation of the privilege of selling copies on the street, and the dread "third warning" that meant suspension of publication altogether for weeks or even months.[2] Among the so-called political papers (those that modeled themselves after journals and for which coverage of foreign affairs was a major concern), the most prominent were, in Petersburg, *Golos* (*Voice*, founded by Andrei Kraevskii in 1863 and edited by him until its demise twenty years later) and *Novoe vremia* (*New Times*, founded in 1867, edited and published by Aleksei Suvorin and Vladimir Likhachev from 1876 to 1878 and by Suvorin alone thereafter); and in Moscow, *Russkie vedomosti* (*Russian News*, sometimes called the "professors' paper," founded in 1863 and run by editor-publisher Nikolai Skvortsov from 1866 until his death in 1882 and then by a collective of intellectuals). From 1863 to 1887 Mikhail Katkov published the semiofficial *Moskovskie vedomosti* (*Moscow News*) under lease from the government. During their careers, Novikova wrote for *Moskovskie vedomosti* and *Novoe vremia*, Kairova for *Novoe vremia* and *Golos*, and Mak-Gakhan for *Golos*, *Russkie vedomosti*, and *Novoe vremia*.[3]

Surveying the development of newspapers in Russia from the 1860s to the 1917 Russian Revolution, Louise McReynolds writes, "Few trades offered comparable opportunities for those who had to substitute ambition for traditional qualifications, and the conventional barriers of gender, ethnicity, and social estate dissolved in the face of tremendous demand."[4] For the early years at least, the operative word for women is "dissolved," with its implication of a gradual process. McReynolds's impressionistic article "Female Journalists in Prerevolutionary Russia," mentions only two women active before the 1890s. "Lialia" (A. E. Golubkova) appeared in print once with an exposé of women's employment firms in 1864, which suggests that she was more interested in unmasking unscrupulous practices than pursuing a reportorial career. From the late 1860s, Aleksandra Sokolova eked out a living as a journalist specializing in coverage of cultural and musical events for various newspapers.[5] Although there were more female reporters in Russia than McReynolds indicates, there was certainly no phenomenon in Russia to match the reporters Varvara Mak-Gakhan met in America in the early 1880s:

In the field of journalism American women feel completely equal with men; they occupy the posts of colleagues and editors of newspapers in every city and town in the United States; many of them are ordinary reporters, while others, the highest paid, are specially sent out to frequent good society, visit the theater, opera, and private balls, attend receptions and dinners, and furnish a timely account of all these amusements to the newspaper offices.[6]

Her summary suggests that even in America, women reporters' most secure domain was society and celebrity journalism.[7] The early Russian newspapers had no concept of running special features of this type to attract a female audience, and in the prerevolutionary and Soviet periods, official censorship and puritanical codes of public discourse restricted the development of anything resembling the gossip-mongering Western press, although the cheap "boulevard" papers had a piquant character all their own.

In the years between 1863 and the Balkan crisis, the Petersburg or Moscow newsroom was apparently an indifferent or even hostile milieu for women. Many were undoubtedly present as translators, compilers, clerks, and bookkeepers, but they have left virtually no trace in the published annals of newspapers or the memoirs of individual reporters. From the standard biographical and bibliographical sources, one woman, Aleksandra Vasil'evna Zhandr (d. 1883), emerges as an authentic reporter. Her obituary in *Moskovskie vedomosti* reads: "For a long time she was our correspondent in Vienna and then, after moving to Moscow, compiled with a discriminating and experienced hand a review of contemporary social phenomena under the heading 'Kaleidoscope.' "[8] There is no further information as to what "a long time" means in this context or when she occupied those posts. Reporting was deliberately anonymous, and women who may have covered events from the provinces for major newspapers may be identified now only through a search of extant ledgers and other internal documents.[9]

Two of the political papers, *Russkie vedomosti* and *Golos*, did publish lists of contributors from which we can draw rough estimates of women's participation. The second section of a jubilee volume put out by *Russkie vedomosti* is a listing, with varying amounts of biographical or autobiographical information, of approximately 920 reporters, feature writers, and editors.[10] From this list, we can conclude that the editors of that "professors' paper," who boasted being the proud inheritors of Nikolai Chernyshevskii's legacy, had neither the time nor the inclination to mentor a woman like Vera Pavlovna (the heroine of Chernyshevskii's influential programmatic novel *Chto delat'? [What Is to Be Done?]*, 1863), who acquired two self-sacrificing males to interpret her vatic dreams and oversee the progress of her career.[11] Some seventy of the entries, or about 7 percent, are for women; other sources yield another six female contributors. More than half, or approximately forty, of those women published fewer than five pieces in *Russkie vedomosti* during its first fifty years. It appears that only a handful of women contributed to the newspaper at all before 1880.[12]

The picture is only slightly brighter for women's contributions to *Golos*. In the volume that came in 1878 to celebrate the first fifteen years of the newspaper, two women, one of them Kairova, are named as regular contributors *(sotrudniki)*. Ten other women are listed in the category of "occasional" *(sluchainye)* contributors.[13] Overall, despite the activism of the few enterprising women we can trace, reporting in the early years of the political press remained a masculine confraternity. The emergence of three women as international journalists in the mid-1870s can therefore be attributed to an increased demand for foreign news arising out of Russia's conflict with the Turks.

The Balkan crisis originated in revolts that broke out in Bosnia and Herzegovina in 1875 as Muslim landholders sweated Christian peasant labor in order to pay draconian taxes imposed by the Ottoman Empire.[14] Serbia and Montenegro seized upon the unrest as an opportunity to throw off Turkish suzerainty. In Moscow and Petersburg, organs of the Pan-Slavic movement called Slavic Benevolent Committees began whipping up agitation by reporting publicly on the oppression of Orthodox Slavs in Turkish dominions and collecting monies to equip and dispatch a cadre of volunteer officers to organize the Serbians' nascent army.[15] Tsar Alexander II was reluctant to involve Russia directly in the Balkans, but enthusiasm for the enterprise spread throughout literate Russian society and, seemingly by osmosis, into the peasantry. It took the volunteers until the spring of 1876 to raise the necessary funds and move. The Serbian-Turkish War, declared in late June 1876, was a series of defeats for the Serbs and ended in an armistice on 1 November, during which six European powers met with the Porte in Constantinople to try to establish a permanent peace. The conference failed, and in April 1877 Russia declared war against the Ottoman Empire.

The contrast to the Crimean War, when Nicholas I kept news of the campaign under tight control, is striking: the Russo-Turkish War was the first in modern Russian history to be largely driven by popular opinion. It gave women unprecedented opportunities to display their organizational abilities. Caught up in the fervor, women, including several of the first Russian women doctors, were involved in setting up hospitals and reception points and serving as nurses along the northern periphery of the front, particularly in Romania and the Caucasus. A number of them wrote personal accounts of their service, published either at the time or retrospectively.[16]

Women reported sporadically from the front. Elena Likhacheva, the wife of *Novoe vremia*'s copublisher, visited Serbia and published two articles about her experiences in the journal *Otechestvennye zapiski (Notes of the Fatherland)*: "From Serbia," warning of growing tensions between the local population and Russian soldiers, and "English and Russian Charities in Serbia."[17] In 1877 and 1878, a writer named Iuliia Karaffa-Korbut ("Iu. Vladimirova" or "Iu. Vladimirtseva," 1831–1911) filed occasional dispatches for *Golos* from Giurgiu, a Romanian town on the Danube that was a strategic point in all Russia's involvements in the Balkans. Other women wrote about the war from the home front. Aleksandra Veselovskaia (1840–1910) contributed two summaries of foreign opinion on the "eastern" question — the crisis looming in the western reaches of the Ottoman Empire — to *Russkie vedomosti* in 1876 and 1877.[18] During the Balkan crisis, the historian Ekaterina Novosil'tseva ("T. Tolycheva") published two articles in *Moskovskie vedomosti*: "A Tale Told by Two Bulgarian Nuns," which is a contribution to the literature of mistreatment of Christian Slavs by the Turks, and "Our Attitudes toward Prisoners (1812, 1854, 1857)," which furnished historical background to controversy over Russian peasants' tendency to treat prisoners of war as fellow sufferers rather than enemies.[19] Women's heightened activism in the first Russian war to be covered extensively by the press undoubtedly facilitated the decisions Novikova, Kairova, and Mak-Gakhan made to become journalists. In the biographical sketches below I treat them in the order in which they began their careers: Novikova and Kairova in late autumn 1876, and Mak-Gakhan only after she was widowed in 1878.

Ol'ga Novikova was one of a dying breed of salon diplomats, a noblewoman who under ordinary circumstances might have remained content to display her verve and wit privately in her Petersburg and London drawing rooms. Instead, stung by the death of her brother, the first fatality among the Russian volunteers in Serbia in 1876, Novikova took to print as a tireless advocate for Russia in England.[20] The pro-Turkish Tory Benjamin Disraeli (prime minister from 1874 to 1880) dubbed the woman the English came to know as Mme. Olga Novikoff the "M.P. [Member of Parliament] for Russia." That dismissive appellation became a badge of honor: in 1909 the prominent journalist and editor W. T. Stead used it as the title of a two-volume collection of Novikova's reminiscences and correspondence with important men. Thanks to Stead's encompassing first-person commentaries, the book is a major biographical source.[21]

Novikova and her brothers, Aleksandr (1833–1910) and Nikolai Kireev (1841–1876), had a privileged childhood in a family of loyal Muscovites. Tsar Nicholas I was godfather to all three, and they in turn remained faithful all their lives to the ideals of "autocracy, orthodoxy, and nationality" promulgated during his reign.[22] In 1860 Ol'ga married Ivan Novikov, who until his death in 1890 was by turns an officer of the General Staff, a general on the staff of Grand Duke Nicholas, and curator of St. Petersburg University. The couple had one son, Aleksandr (1861–1913). Evidently inspired by her mother, a famous salon hostess, Novikova began collecting intellectual lions as a girl and during the early years of her marriage hosted her own evenings in Petersburg. After the Vatican Council's declaration of papal infallibility in 1870, Novikova followed her brother Aleksandr into what became for both a lifelong campaign to create a Christian bloc of Orthodox churches, Old Catholics, and Anglicans to counter Roman Catholic apostasy.[23] By the 1870s she had begun spending several winter months each year in England, and in January 1873 the Russian ambassador introduced her to William Gladstone, leader of the Liberal Party (Whigs) and four times prime minister of England. Common interest in ecclesiastical issues made Gladstone and his wife frequent visitors to Novikova's salon.

From Novikova's Slavophile background and interest in religious politics, it was a short step to commitment to the Pan-Slavic crusade to liberate Orthodox Slavs in the Balkans. In July 1876 Novikova was shocked to learn that her brother Nikolai had been killed in battle.[24] She deluged her English friends with letters of which the refrain was that she owed her brother's death to England's support of the Turkish cause. Novikova became the liberals' ally in the campaign to thwart Disraeli's drive toward intervention by furnishing Gladstone with a stream of information designed to refute rumors of Russian atrocities in Central Asia and expansionist aims in the Balkans.

Novikova also began writing impassioned articles on the strained relations between Russia and England. She formed a long-lasting journalistic alliance with Stead, who opened the pages of his Liberal paper, *Northern Echo,* to her from 1876. Late that same year she began contributing pieces, most of them under the rubric "News from England," to Katkov's conservative *Moskovskie vedomosti.* Throughout the crisis in the Balkans, Novikova arranged to translate and circulate in England Ivan Aksakov's fiery speeches to the Moscow Slavic Benevolent Committee. Since he stressed Russia's humanitarian duty to protect Orthodox Slavs from their Turkish overlords and downplayed geopolitical ambitions, his speeches were ideal propaganda for the détente between England and Russia that had become Novikova's goal.[25] When Aksakov was permitted to establish the weekly newspaper *Rus' (Russia)* in 1880, Novikova became an irregular but enthusiastic contributor.[26] From 1884 to 1891, Stead's *Pall Mall Gazette* gave her an equally hospitable forum in England. She published occasional articles and letters to the editor in a number of other newspapers and journals in both countries and languages, as well as in French and Belgian periodicals.[27]

At first Novikova published her articles under the initials of her maiden name, O. K., but the identity of the author soon became an open secret in England, and her later works were usually signed by the compound "O. K. (Mme. Olga Novikoff)." In March 1882 Aksakov unmasked her in Russia in a note appended to the first of a triad of articles, "Crisis in Serbia" (translated and abridged from originals in the English *Contemporary Review*). They were written, he noted, by "O. A. Novikova, who has long been familiar to our reading public under the signature O. K. and enjoys widespread fame in Europe, particularly in England." In her English articles, she "steadily, boldly, and not without benefit, fights for her country against the hostile prejudices toward Russia that have become so deeply rooted in Europe."[28]

Novikova quickly established a pattern of reprinting important articles as pamphlets and collections. Her early pieces in English were combined, first as *Is Russia Wrong?* in 1877 and then expanded as *Russia and England from 1876 to 1880: A Protest and an Appeal* (3d ed., London, 1880). Her last pamphlets, containing articles by herself and others, appeared in Russia in 1914 and 1915.[29] Topics she addressed included antiliquor campaigns in Finland and Gladstone's writings on sobriety; memorial articles about her brother Aleksandr; Christianity versus Judaism; England's role as Russia's ally in the First World War, then under way; and suggestions for Russian spas that could replace those in Europe made inaccessible by the war.

By 1878 she was identifying herself as a journalist. A more accurate label would be publicist or propagandist. Her articles in Russian and English over the forty years of her career display the wide range of subjects and personalities that captured her interest, her role as mediator between cultures, and her fierce adherence to the ideals of her youth. She followed ongoing developments in the Balkans and protested Austro-Hungarian policies "in 1879 when she satirized Lord Salisbury's Austrian Evangel; in 1881 when the Slavs rose against the enforcement of the conscription; in 1882, when she published her memorable manifesto-book, *Skobeleff and the Slavonic Cause*; in 1888, when she denounced Austria's supposed designs upon Salonica; and again in 1908, when she was the first to lift up her voice of protest in the *Times* against the lawless [Austrian] annexation of Bosnia and the Herzegovina."[30] In 1885, reporting on English rumors that the Russians were planning a campaign to capture Herat (Afghanistan), she attributed a denial of the story to "one who is of the highest authority on all matters relating to the foreign policy of our empire."[31] In 1904 she presented the Russian point of view on the Japanese war.[32]

On the issue of Russia's treatment of its Jews, Novikova parted company not only with Russians of goodwill, but with Gladstone, Stead, and the Liberals who were her English allies. Since the pogroms in the Pale of Settlement in the early 1880s, the subject had become a matter of contention in both Russia and abroad. In 1890 she published a series of "letters" upholding Russia's right to deal with Jews as it pleased: "I maintain that every nation has the full right to promulgate laws against foreigners, be they Jews, Chinese or some other."[33] An intelligent woman and a skilled polemicist, Novikova remained stubbornly impervious to new ideas and influences. In 1917, as the Russian monarchy collapsed, she reaffirmed her ideals in the terms of Nicholas I's reign: "What are the tenets of Panslavism? Religion, autocracy, and nationality. . . . In fact we are the opposite pole to the Nihilists, who hate every idea of God, who detest autocracy and despise nationality."[34] By the time of the revolution, Novikova had outlived her entire family, and her last years witnessed the destruction of the society she had been so eloquent in defending.[35]

One prominent editor recalled that in the early days of the Russian mass-circulation press, readership, particularly among the young, "went up only when there was a war, major trials, or terrorist attacks."[36] Anastasiia Kairova made news in two of those ways: she was the defendant in a widely publicized criminal trial and shortly afterward began reporting for Russian newspapers as a foreign correspondent from Central Europe and the Balkans during the Serbian crisis and the Russo-Turkish War. The third factor entered into her life with the assassination of Alexander II in 1881, which undoubtedly played a role in ending her career as foreign correspondent.

Kairova grew up in Petersburg in a dispossessed household that had to scrabble to survive. Her only formal education was a year and a half as a student at an institute for noble girls. Only recently has it been established that from the early 1860s she was the mistress of Fedor Koni (1809–1879), an amiable editor of theatrical journals and author of one-act comedies.[37] The chaos of Kairova's childhood suggests that this liaison with a man thirty-six years older might have represented an escape from her dysfunctional family. The couple had two daughters. As events were to show, Koni remained avuncularly devoted to Kairova, but in late 1874, the restless woman embarked on a career as an actor and an affair with the married manager of the provincial theater that hired her. On 8 July 1875, at a dacha near Petersburg, Kairova attacked her lover's wife with a razor, inflicting wounds to her neck and face. The incident was sordid and straightforward, but the one-day trial in late April 1876 became a notorious test case for the newly instituted jury system.

Since Kairova never denied committing the crime, the question before the jury was that of her sanity, and five psychiatrists testified at the trial. Her mother did her best to exonerate her by furnishing details of hereditary instability in the family and Kairova's "unbalanced" behavior in childhood. A brief account of a quarrel Kairova had with "a certain gentleman" was the only suggestion of Koni's role in her life: although the psychiatric evidence included the fact that she had borne children, a process that might "cause psychic derangement even in a physically healthy woman," nothing was said about their paternity.[38] Nobody was quite sure why Kairova was acquitted. There was speculation that the jury felt she had suffered enough. The wife, also an actor, was able to return to the stage six weeks after the attack, while Kairova had spent nearly ten months awaiting trial in prison and psychiatric ward.

In a bizarre twist of circumstances, by late fall 1876, some six months after the trial, Kairova was reporting from Serbia as a correspondent for *Novoe vremia*. Judging from the enthusiasm and enterprise she brought to the job, it was a lifesaver, the emotional and intellectual outlet she had sought so feverishly and foolishly elsewhere. The newspaper's editor, Alexei Suvorin, had himself been at the front from June to August 1876. Before her abortive acting career, Kairova had served as secretary of *Birzhevye vedomosti (Stock Market News)*, but the idea that this experience qualified her to replace him as correspondent in Serbia is too fantastic not to have been her own.[39] Koni's popularity in Petersburg literary circles undoubtedly helped her realize the goal as well. In the three years between the trial and Koni's death, his supportive letters demonstrate his continuing role in Kairova's life.[40]

As the Balkan crisis proceeded, there were not enough "qualified journalists . . . [to] keep pace with the demands of the many publications that needed reporters; even Kraevskii and Suvorin shared the services of at least one prominent reporter, N. S. Kairov."[41] Kairova did report for both *Novoe vremia* and *Golos* for a few months, but in late December 1876, Kraevskii hired her to report on the peace conference in Constantinople as a full-time "special correspondent." She remained in the Ottoman capital until the Russians declared war on Turkey in April 1877, moved on to Athens until July, and began reporting from Vienna and occasionally from Budapest later that summer. Since Austria-Hungary was Russia's major rival for influence in the South Slavic area, it was a key post. Kairova's last identifiable dispatch from Vienna appeared in mid-May 1880.

In an undated fragment of a letter Koni wrote to Kairova in late 1876, he complained that he had seen no dispatches from her for two weeks: "Strike while the iron is hot. I myself have witnessed the streetseller peddling *Novoe vremia* by saying, 'There's an article by A. K. today.'" By the time she began reporting for *Golos* from Constantinople, she had replaced her own transparent initials (A. K.) with the undecipherable pseudonym N. S. She changed her signature again to the initials of her first name and patronymic (A. V.) during her brief time in Athens, perhaps because she found it inadvisable to advertise herself as the person who had just been investigating the Greek community in the Ottoman capital. The Athens dispatches, however, refer to incidents Kairova had reported on in Constantinople and leave no doubt that she was N. S., and in Vienna she reverted to that signature once and for all.[42]

In April 1877 Koni reported rumors spreading in Petersburg that *Golos*'s N. S. was female. We would expect to find mention of a Russian woman reporter somewhere in the memoirs and papers of government officials, diplomats, church prelates, fellow reporters, and other public figures of many nationalities whom she interviewed, but it would take a long search through many works in many languages to find them. No matter how Kairova appeared in person, in print she was a verbal transvestite who used for herself the grammatical forms that identify masculine gender in Russian. The world she reports on is almost entirely male, and most of the time her masculine voice interacting with it is convincing. Close reading reveals an occasional sly hint at her disguised identity: it is surely with tongue in cheek that she speculates that the adjutant who hesitates to usher her into the presence of the Russian commissioner in Bulgaria must take her for a "non-com in mufti" [pereodetyi unterofitser].[43] In addition to referring to a soldier out of uniform, *pereodetyi* (literally, cross-dressed, a term that has only recently come into English usage and in both languages is a participle formed from the Latin verb *transvestire*), also refers to a person in disguise or dressed for a masquerade.

Although Kairova never again matched the number of articles she filed from Constantinople (forty-nine appeared in *Golos* in the 105 days between 28 December 1876 and 17 April 1877), a conservative estimate is that during the three and a half years that she wrote for

Golos, the newspaper printed between one and two of her "letters" per week, for a total of close to three hundred altogether. Others that she wrote never saw print. Russian newspaper publishers were always threatened by postpublication penalties that could—and in Andrei Kraevskii's case eventually did—bankrupt them. When the censor chose to chastise Kraevskii for some infraction, Kairova's articles reached only yearly subscribers or failed to appear altogether. "The public and editors alike are happy with your articles and they are read avidly. Many complain that *Golos* is now forbidden street sales [v raznosku]," Koni told her in his letter of 1 February 1877. While she was in Athens, *Golos* was suspended for one and a half months for publishing, on the day that the tsar declared war, an editorial suggesting that intervention might be a bad idea.[44] Koni assured her that her articles would be printed in the short-lived newspaper *Nash vek (Our Century)*, which subscribers were receiving instead of *Golos*, but on 19 June he wrote that only one had actually appeared.

The figures for Kairova's dispatches are for what she conceived of as her "letters." She also filed immediate short telegrams whenever news was breaking (from *Golos*'s "special correspondent" without further identification). Koni's letter of 27 April 1877 reported that a telegram sent by Kairova had scooped the tsar:

First of all, I will tell you what a commotion you aroused with the telegram about the opening of [the Turkish] parliament and the sultan's speech. Just imagine, the War Minister [Dmitrii Miliutin] made his report to the emperor at nine A.M. that day and introduced those subjects. The emperor asked where [Miliutin] had gathered the information, since he hadn't yet received an official telegram. The minister indicated that it was from *Golos*. They immediately sent for the issue, and the fun began. The embassy report arrived only at four [P.M.]. Since then *Golos* is in the emperor's study by eight [A.M.]. But that isn't all.

Kraevskii also ran a private service, the International Telegraph Agency, to which other Russian newspapers subscribed. Koni went on to write that the editors of those papers had demanded to know why they had not received the telegram about the sultan's speech, and it had to be explained to them "that *Golos* has its own correspondent independent of the agency, that it pays his fee and does not share his telegrams unless (1) it has his permission, and (2) they make payment to him as well. The mention of money doused them with cold water."

For the modern reader, there is a curious rhythm to Kairova's telegrams and the follow-up articles that traveled overland. The telegraph was a relatively recent innovation, and after receiving the up-to-the-minute information it offered, her readers had to wait well over a week to read her chatty elucidation: in those "letters," she gave details, commented on the significance of previously reported events, and added local color. Kairova's telegrams and letters alike generally appeared on pages 3 to 5 of *Golos* under the rubric "Foreign News." Her coverage of the Congress of Berlin (eight articles between 16 June and 5 July 1878), twenty-two articles entitled "The East after the War" (published between 16 June and 4 October 1879), and a few other pieces appeared on the front pages as feuilletons *(fel'etony)*, feature articles that were printed across the bottom six inches of all six columns of the first and usually the second page, occasionally running onto page 3. The articles titled "The East after the War" report Kairova's impressions of the Balkan situation; they were filed from various points of an extended tour she made of the region.[45]

Kairova never pretended to omniscience but reported in first-person singular the opinions of a loyal but outspoken Russian. (When she used "we," she always meant "we Russians.") At first she assumed that her reports actually were letters to the editors of *Golos* and would be revised before publication. For instance, on 30 January 1877, describing a pamphlet circulating in Constantinople that contained purloined Russian dispatches to and from Vienna, she wrote, and *Golos* printed: "I am sending you the pamphlet at the same time as this letter. Make whatever use of it you find necessary and possible." Since the letters appeared just as she wrote them, the effect was to suggest a running relationship with the reader, and Kairova soon learned to exploit it. She was quick to emend her dispatches: "I sent you today by telegraph the news that at the emergency council [of the Turkish government] called on Saturday, January 6, . . . it was decided to reply to all European demands with a decisive and unconditional refusal. Afterward I learned that that was not quite correct."[46]

The quality of her letters is as striking as the quantity. She had the modern reporter's skills of being able to develop personal sources among Russian diplomats and local officials, rapidly combing newspapers in the major Western languages, and transmitting the quiddities of the scene. She also knew how to grab readers' attention. The first words of her first dispatch from the Constantinople conference (28 December 1876) indicated that the position was not what she had expected: "Now [the Russian ambassador] Ignat'ev is a Turcophile, and [the head of the English delegation] Salisbury is a hater of the Turks and aims to trip up their policy. That's the first news I heard after my arrival in Constantinople. 'Salisbury is spineless' say the English; 'Salisbury is a traitor' cry the Turks."[47] She summed up the early days of the conference cogently, explicating the Turks' stratagems for deflecting European demands. In a report with the dateline of 14 January (*Golos*, 13/25 January), Kairova reports on the unfounded optimism of 11 January, a sunny day on which the Turkish stock market rose and the Russian embassy was full of "animation and assurance." The rosy outlook was deceptive. With a "phalanx" of other reporters, she witnessed the Turks abruptly quitting the conference hall and, making the rounds of embassies, found out that the Turks were categorically refusing all forms of Western oversight.

While Novikova floated in the geopolitical empyrean, grandly deciding the fate of countries she never visited, Kairova slogged along on the ground. Convinced, as she wrote repeatedly, that understanding internal politics was basic to mastering a country's international policies, during her years in Vienna and Budapest, Kairova dealt extensively with the complexities of the mixed nationalities, religions, and political trends of Central Europe and the Balkans. She repeatedly criticized as shortsighted the Russian policy of concentrating on protection of the Orthodox Slavs, pointing to the importance of Greeks and Catholic Slavs as factors in the balance of power among Russia, Austria-Hungary, and the deteriorating Ottoman Empire. Twenty years earlier, Austria and Hungary had been divided into two monarchies with a single ruler and unified major ministries, and Kairova often reported on tensions between the central government and the trend toward federalism.[48]

Perhaps her most valuable insights were into local conditions. She learned the terrain well enough to point out when arbitrarily redrawn borders cut peasants off from fields they had traditionally cultivated and to complain about such unfeeling disruptions of human lives. The boundaries drawn at the Congress of Berlin, she wrote in disgust, rewarded both Serbia and Bulgaria "with a good measure of completely unneeded hostile elements" (3 July 1878). Although Kairova did not express open anti-Semitism, she tended to portray the Jewish population of Constantinople and the Balkans as mercantile exploiters and was not above suggesting that a disproportionate number of Western newsmen were Jewish.[49] She liked to use anecdotes to illustrate changes in the popular mood. In her letter of 19 March 1877, she reported from Constantinople: "Yesterday there was an aurora borealis—a very rare phenomenon here. The Turks were terribly frightened . . . but explained the phenomenon in a rather original and unexpected fashion: they maintain that it is a reflection of the bivouac fires of a huge Russian army situated on the Prut and are greatly disheartened by it."

I can only speculate as to why Kairova stopped reporting for *Golos* in mid-May 1880 and apparently never wrote for a newspaper again. The Russo-Turkish War ended in January 1878, after the Russians took Plevna and were within a few days of occupying Constantinople. The following summer, the Congress of Berlin ended the threat of renewed conflict, and as the army returned home and a rising tide of domestic terrorism led to the assassination of Alexander II in February 1881, the Russian public's attention turned inward. Kraevskii may have felt that he could no longer afford a full-time correspondent in Vienna. Kairova's reporting had already begun to shift northward, as we can see her last feuilletons for *Golos*, "Poles on Germany and the Germans" (26 and 28 April 1880). In 1881 she began contributing to major Russian journals. From May to the end of the year, she published regular articles from Berlin in the prestigious *Vestnik Evropy (European Herald)*. For *Russkaia mysl' (Russian Thought)* in 1882 she produced a series, "Russian and German Policy in Connection with the Slavic Problem." Gradually Kairova took on historical topics, publishing "George Sand on the French Revolution of 1848 and Public Figures in It" in 1883 in *Russkaia mysl'* and two articles on the partition of Poland in *Vestnik Evropy* that same year. Her article "Religious War in the Sudan" was printed in *Delo (Cause)* in 1884. Just after the Serbian-Bulgarian War of 1885 and during the escalation of an internal crisis in Bulgaria, Kairova published in June 1886, in that same radical journal, long passages that Kraevskii had chosen to excise from her 1879 feuilletons ("The East after the War"), in which she sketched rising tensions between the remaining Russian troops and the Bulgarians. For *Delo* she added a fierce preface about the Russian "fear of the truth" *(pravdoboiazn')* that she felt had led to the mistakes in Russia's Balkan policy:

Had that [excised] information reached those on whom the choice of personnel and the direction of events depends, who knows! — perhaps some of it would have or at least might have been foreseen and eased. . . . In practice truth often remains an "editorial secret," in no way less strict and, of course, just as constructive, as the notorious ancient "secrets of the chancellery." Who is at fault? The editors? No — *everyone*. Everyone: those who write and those who control the writers and those who read. Fear of the truth is a trait we all share.[50]

The obituary in *Istoricheskii vestnik (Historical Herald)* indicates that in her last years, Kairova translated documents for a publication of the Imperial Russian Historical Society. She died of angina pectoris on 23 February 1888 and received a modulated compliment from her peers: "The deceased possessed unquestionable literary talent and remarkable energy *for a woman*. As a correspondent, she fulfilled the multiple onerous [mnogotrudnye] obligations so honorably and with such talent that she was in no way inferior to the best *male* correspondents" (italics mine).[51]

Varvara Mak-Gakhan married into the newspaper profession when she chose a nomadic life with an American reporter, Januarius Aloysius MacGahan (1844–1878; I use the Russian transliteration of Varvara's name to distinguish her from her husband).[52] This was a bold departure for a woman from the proud Elagin clan, but she was a child of the Chernyshevskii era, in rebellion against her older sister's determination to see her make a conventional marriage.[53] Jan MacGahan was an intrepid young reporter for the *New York Herald* who first came to Europe in January 1871 to cover the Franco-Prussian War and the Paris Commune. He and Varvara met that November when he was assigned to write about the Russian royal family's winter retreat near Yalta. Over the next months, their paths crossed again in Odessa and Petersburg, where Varvara had taken a post as teacher in a private girl's boarding school and, in her own words, was in effect "disinherited and banished from the family" for the initiative.[54] By spring 1872 the couple was engaged, and when Jan's extended stay in Western Europe threatened to disrupt their relationship, Varvara took the bold step of joining him in Paris that October. They married in January 1873. For the next five years, Varvara adapted her life to the demands of Jan's nomadic career. In 1874 she moved to Biarritz while MacGahan covered the Carlist campaign in Spain, and their son Paul was born there. During that campaign and again during the years of Jan's involvements in the Balkans, Varvara positioned herself to receive, rewrite into Russian, and expeditiously transmit his dispatches to Kraevskii's *Golos* and his telegraph agency.

Just as the Russian volunteer expedition reached Serbia, the underground Bulgarian Revolutionary Committee instigated a revolt in southern Bulgaria on 20 April/2 May 1876, which was brutally suppressed by the Turks.[55] Reports of the annihilation of entire villages and the deaths of tens of thousands of men, women, and children trickled abroad. In England, Disraeli dismissed these stories as "coffee-house babble," and the *Daily News,* stung by the slur on its reporting, hired MacGahan to investigate. His dispatches from Bulgaria that summer painted a horrifying picture of the devastated area and created an international uproar.[56] MacGahan went on to cover the Serbian-Turkish War of 1876 and the ensuing Russo-Turkish War. Varvara Mak-Gakhan, as always positioning herself nearby, spent most of the campaign in Bucharest. After the Treaty of San Stefano was signed in March 1878, Jan wrote her to join him in Constantinople, where he died of typhoid on 9 June.

Varvara Mak-Gakhan took up her pen independently after Mac-Gahan's death. Kraevskii offered her "a permanent staff position," and passing through London, she also made arrangements to report from Petersburg for the *New York Herald* and the *Sydney Herald*. In 1880 *Golos* commissioned her to cover the American election and what turned out to be the tragically short presidency of James Garfield; her last article reported the execution of his assassin. She chose to remain in the United States and, after *Golos* folded, became a long-term American correspondent (1883–1898) for *Russkie vedomosti,* at first sending "Letters from America" signed by initials and then writing articles datelined New York or Washington under her name.[57] She also wrote for a number of journals, most often *Vestnik Evropy* between 1882 and 1891 and *Severnyi vestnik (Northern*

Herald) from 1889 to 1894. In autumn 1894 she made a trip to Russia to report for a consortium of eight American newspapers, including the *New York Times,* on the illness and death of Alexander III and the accession of Nicholas II.

For Russian periodicals, Mak-Gakhan wrote about America as an intelligent but not unprejudiced outside observer. Much of her reporting concentrated on distinctive features of American women's lives. Her first contributions to *Vestnik Evropy* in 1882 were typical. The opening article of a set of four under the rubric "Americans at Home" summarized the recent national elections and, in particular, the role of moneyed interests in determining the outcome. The other three articles were devoted to women, and especially to the enfranchisement that American women had been stubbornly pursuing since the 1840s.[58] Because federalism was foreign to imperial Russia, Mak-Gakhan was struck by a shift in the suffrage movement's strategy: after the post–Civil War initiative to gain the vote by amendment to the U.S. Constitution failed, women switched to obtaining it state by state. Over the years, she wrote repeatedly about businessmen, farmer's associations, the financing of public schools, journalism and American reading habits, resorts, poverty, and orphanages, as well as such major events like elections and the Chicago Exposition. Mak-Gakhan also examined her two countries in fiction: under the pseudonym Pavel Kashirin, she published a "satirical novella" about American life, "Something New over an Old Lining," in *Vestnik Evropy* and under her own name a novel in English, *Xenia Repnina: A Story of Russia Today.*[59]

Her career came to a stuttering halt in January 1897 after the appearance of an article by E. N. Matrosov (whom nobody in Petersburg seemed to know) in the right-wing *Istoricheskii vestnik.* Matrosov attacked Russians who reported from America, among them a "Madame Y," whom he identified as bearing her late husband's Anglo-Irish surname. Madame Y was accused of knowing nothing of American life and being uninterested in learning, "sitting in her room in the quiet of her working nook" and composing articles in which she "remains silent about some major phenomena of government and political life, tries deliberately every way she can to distort others, and, finally, heaps lies and slander on still others." (The implication, of course, is that Matrosov could do better.) He also charged that in the *New York Sun,* Mak-Gakhan had passed off word-for-word translations of recent Russian books as her own articles.[60]

Mak-Gakhan struck back in a sarcastic article published in the equally conservative *Russkoe obozrenie (Russian Review)*.[61] She also demanded that the Russian Writers' Union for Mutual Aid (Soiuz vzaimopomoshchi russkikh pisatelei) convene a Court of Honor (the union's newly created mediation service for Russian writers) to consider the charge of plagiarism. In 1899 the court found Matrosov's accusation groundless.[62] Formal exoneration failed to restore Mak-Gakhan's career, however, perhaps in part because her reply to Matrosov had included intemperate remarks about the Jewish immigration in New York. Whatever the cause, V. D. Rak points out that even after the court exonerated her, "liberal organs refused the services of M. G. . . . and in her last years she contributed only to *Moskovskie vedomosti* (from 1899), *Novoe vremia*, and *Nabliudatel'* [*Observer*] (1901–03)."[63] After a last visit to Russia in early 1903, Varvara Mak-Gakhan died of cancer in New York on 15 February 1904. It is lamentable that a journalistic squall cast a lasting cloud over her constructive contributions to Russia's knowledge of American life.

Although the Balkan crisis and the Russo-Turkish War offered all three unprecedented opportunity, these Russian gentry women pursued their careers in very different ways. International reporting was a field in which they could exploit the skill that was a prerequisite of the rudimentary education most gentry girls received: fluency in French, English, and/or German. Novikova and Mak-Gakhan served as mediators between Russia and Anglophone cultures by writing for both Russian and English-language newspapers and journals; insofar as we know, Kairova confined herself to reporting on European affairs in Russian periodicals. All three wrote unabashedly as Russians and, despite their disparate backgrounds, shared common national prejudices. They tended to the conservative side of the political spectrum and gave no indication of being aware that they might be setting a path for other women to follow. Mak-Gakhan, the widow of a legendary reporter, and Novikova, the sister of a Pan-Slavic martyr and the confidante of great men, had identities to exploit. Kairova became a journalist bearing the burden of a past to conceal. While there was speculation about the sex and identity of the reliable reporter for *Golos* in the Balkans, whatever sensation her real name might have caused was buried in brief obituaries.

Mak-Gakhan, who from time to time reminded readers of her status as a widow with a son to raise, was the only one who addressed women readers, writing extensively about aspects of female life in the United States. She was careful, however, never to suggest that American women's aspirations might be applicable to Russia. Novikova maintained anonymity for the first few years but then saw the advantages of representing liberated Russian womanhood to the West and let it be known publicly that O. K. and Ol'ga Novikova were the same person. Focused as she was on influencing English policies toward Russia, Novikova had no interest in reporting on women's issues in either country. Kairova used a male print persona and, moving exclusively in the masculine spheres of diplomacy, politics, and journalism, rarely wrote about women. At most, it might be argued that her impatience with male posturing betrays a feminine element in her reportage.

Writing for newspapers and journals was a profession for Mak-Gakhan and Kairova; taking to public print became a cause for the financially independent Novikova. She was naively convinced of the influence her polemical articles exercised and never realized that she had become a pawn in the political contest between Liberals and Conservatives in England and, to a lesser degree, in international maneuvers between England and Russia. Long after the destruction of the world her mordant articles sought to preserve, Novikova remains a fascinating figure on the fringes of the history of Anglo-Russian relations. Mak-Gakhan carved out a modest place for herself in the Russian press by reporting on America, a country removed by oceans from direct political conflict with Russia and exoticized as a frontier culture. Her articles still offer insights into an intelligent Russian's view of American life in the late nineteenth century. Any modern reporter of the international scene would instantly recognize Kairova as a colleague for the fervor and ingenuity with which she covered fast-breaking events. Resurgence in the 1980s of conflicts among the peoples of the Balkans gave her down-to-earth articles renewed immediacy.

The careers of Ol'ga Novikova, Anastasiia Kairova, and Varvara Mak-Gakhan together form an absorbing episode in the history of

Russian women's struggle to storm the bastions of masculine privilege. How much their example influenced later women reporters remains open to investigation, but they made an undoubted contribution by convincing the innumerable powerful men with whom they dealt — the gatekeepers to women's advancement — that they were up to the challenges of international journalism.

Notes

Much of the research for this essay took place at the Summer Laboratory sponsored by the Russian and East European Center of the University of Illinois at Urbana-Champaign, and I wish to thank in particular the staff of the UIUC Slavic Library. I am indebted to Avrora Alekseevna and Elvina Arkad'evna Kononovy for research in St. Petersburg. Thanks to Jehanne Gheith and Barbara Norton for tireless and tactful editing.

1 On education, see Christine Johanson, *Women's Struggle for Higher Education in Russia, 1855–1900* (Kingston and Montreal, 1987). On women's position in society, see William G. Wagner, *Marriage, Property, and Law in Late Imperial Russia* (New York, 1994).

2 The rules for the provincial press were different. For the censorship regulations of 1865, see Charles Ruud, *Fighting Words: Imperial Censorship and the Russian Press, 1804–1906* (Toronto, 1982), 137–49. Appendix 1 (237–52) gives the text of these regulations in translation.

3 For the evolution of Russian newspapers, see Effie Ambler, *Russian Journalism and Politics, 1861–1881: The Career of Aleksei S. Suvorin* (Detroit, 1972), 13–35; and Louise McReynolds, *The News under Russia's Old Regime: The Development of a Mass-Circulation Press* (Princeton, 1991). What "mass circulation" meant in Russia at that time, when only a small fraction of the population was literate, is indicated by the fact that *Golos*'s print run in 1865 was just under 5,000; in 1877 more than 22,000 copies came off the press (*Piatnadtsatiletie gazety "Golos": 1863–1877*, comp. V. O. Mikhnevich, ed. A. A. Kraevskii [St. Petersburg, 1878], 50). By contrast, in the 1860s and 1870s, the *London Times* had a circulation close to 60,000, and its popular rivals, *Daily Telegraph* and *Daily News*, more than twice that (Oliver Ward and James Bishop, *The Story of "The Times"* [London, 1983], 89–90). In addition to the "political," Ambler categorizes the newspapers of the time as "informational" (the financial paper *Birzhevye vedomosti* and "boulevard," or popular press, which, to the horror of the intelligentsia, sprang up like weeds in the 1880s (Ambler, *Russian Journalism*, 28–30). On the last

category, see Jeffrey Brooks, *When Russia Learned to Read: Literacy and Popular Literature, 1861–1917* (Princeton, 1985), 117–41.

4   McReynolds, *News*, 148–49.
5   Louise McReynolds, "Female Journalists in Prerevolutionary Russia," *Journalism History* 14, no. 4 (winter 1987): 104–10. The other women in McReynolds's sample are Varvara Tsekhovskaia-"Ol'nem" (1872–1941) and Ariadna Tyrkova-Williams (1869–1962).
6   "Amerikantsy—doma: Ocherki amerikanskoi zhizni," *VE*, no. 11 (1882): 137.
7   It was only in the mid-1880s that the first notorious American newswoman, "Nellie Bly" (Elizabeth Cochrane Seaman, 1865–1922), began a career that combined spectacular stunts and serious investigative journalism.
8   *MVed*, 30 April 1883, 3. For the standard sources of information about Russian women writers, see June Pachuta Farris's bibliographic essay in this volume.
9   "The surnames and addresses of correspondents were then a great secret among the editors, since revealing the name of a person who decided to write about the deprivations of local life, and especially to unmask irregularities, threatened that audacious soul with innumerable unpleasantnesses" (A. S. Posnikov, "Iz moikh vospominanii," in *Russkie vedomosti, 1863–1913*, vol. 1, *Sbornik statei* [Moscow, 1913], 65).
10 *Russkie vedomosti, 1863–1913*, vol. 2, *Sotrudniki "Russkikh vedomostei," 1863–1913* (Moscow, 1913).
11 A major thesis of *Chto delat'?* was that Russian men had a responsibility to remove the handicaps their female compatriots labored under in the patriarchal order by overseeing their psychological and social integration into society.
12 The compilers themselves point out that the list is far from complete, and the figures I give are supplemented by fragmentary information from other bibliographic sources. For instance, why Sokolova is not included as a contributor is inexplicable: by her own account, for five years in the early 1870s, she was in charge of the *RVed*'s coverage of theaters, and by the time the jubilee volume appeared, she had published reminiscences of those days (Aleksandra Sokolova, "Vstrechi i znakomstva," *IV*, nos. 6–10 [1911] and no. 3 [1913]). See Jehanne Gheith's essay in this volume for discussion of the omissions of Russian women's writings from major reference sources.
13 *Piatnadtsatiletie gazety "Golos,"* 3–11. Sokolova states that for a time she wrote a regular column (feuilleton) of news from Moscow for that Petersburg newspaper, but once again her name is not in the compilation.
14 For the political and military situation in the 1870s, see Barbara Jela-

vich, *Russia's Balkan Entanglements, 1806–1914* (Cambridge, 1991), 170–78.

15 Jelavich defines Pan-Slavism for that period "as a program calling for the removal of the Orthodox Slavs from foreign control, their organization into separate states, and the establishment of a federation under Russian leadership" (157).

16 For autobiographical works, see *Istoriia dorevoliutsionnoi Rossii v dnevnikakh i vospominaniiakh: Annotirovannyi ukazatel' knig i publikatsii v zhurnalakh*, ed. P. A. Zaionchkovskii et al., vol. 3.2 (Moscow, 1980), 190–244.

17 "Iz Serbii," *OZ*, no. 10 (1876): sec. 2, pp. 182–89; and "Angliiskaia i russkaia blagotvoritel'nost' v Serbii," no. 2 (1877): sec. 2, 275–85. Likhacheva is best known for her history of female education in Russia, *Materialy dlia istorii zhenskogo obrazovaniia v Rossii*, 4 vols. (St. Petersburg, 1890–1901).

18 *Russkie vedomosti, 1863–1913*, vol. 2, *Sotrudniki*, 39.

19 "Rasskaz dvukh bolgarskikh monakhin," *MVed*, 19 January 1878; and "Nashi otnosheniia k plennym (1812, 1854, 1857)," 11 August 1877.

20 English sources frequently compare Novikova's influence to that exercised by Dorothea Lieven (née Benkendorf, 1784/5–1857), wife of the Russian ambassador to England from 1812 to 1834, who served as an important liaison between the British government and the Russian court. See N. A. Belozerskaia, "Kniaginia Dar'ia Khristoforovna Liven," *IV*, no. 3 (1898): 875–904.

21 W. T. Stead, ed., *The M.P. for Russia: Reminiscences and Correspondence of Mme. Olga Novikoff*, 2 vols. (London, 1909). A. M. Belov's "Zarubezhnaia publitsistika," *IV*, no. 5 (1909): 547–68, is a précis of Stead's book.

22 For those ideals, see Nicholas Riasanovsky, *Nicholas I and Official Nationality in Russia, 1825–1855* (Berkeley, 1967).

23 In 1873 Novikova translated for publication a pamphlet Aleksandr wrote on the proposed alliance and published anonymously in English her own brochure, *Christ or Moses — Which?*, a comparison of Jewish "materialism" and Christian "idealism." A revised edition of Novikova's brochure appeared in 1895. For Kireev, see *Modern Encyclopedia of Russian and Soviet History*, ed. Joseph L. Wieczynski, vol. 17 (Gulf Breeze, Fla., 1980), s.v. "Kireev, Aleksandr Alekseevich"; and *Russkie pisateli: 1800–1917. Biograficheskii slovar'*, ed. P. A. Nikolaev, vol. 2 (Moscow, 1994), s.v. "Kireev, Aleksandr Alekseevich." An article on Novikova appears in vol. 4 of *Russkie pisateli* (Moscow, 1999).

24 Nikolai Kireev, like the rest of the Russian volunteers, was ostensibly in Serbia to train the army rather than lead it into battle. For his involve-

ment in the campaign, see *Voennaia entsiklopediia*, vol. 12 (St. Petersburg, 1913), s.v. "Kireev, Nikolai Alekseevich."

25 For Aksakov's career in the 1870s, see N. I. Tsimbaev, *I. S. Aksakov v obshchestvennoi zhizni poreformennoi Rossii* (Moscow, 1978), 232–46.

26 The run of *Rus'* preserved at the Institute d'Etudes slaves in Paris includes the following articles by Novikova: "O. K.," "Irlandskoe zatrudnenie," 3 January 1881; "Preniia o Kandagare," 24 January 1881; "Neskol'ko slov o Karleile," 7 February 1881; "Ne vse to zoloto shto blestit," 28 February 1881; *"Angliiskii opium,"* 16 May 1881; "Konstitutsionnye okovy," 6 June 1881; *"Daily News,"* 4 July 1881; "Konets evreiskoi agitatsii v Anglii," 20 February 1882; O. Novikova, "Krizis v Serbii," 13 March 1882, 20 March 1882, and 27 March 1882; "Skhodstvo i razlichie," 10 April 1882; "Ral'f V. Emerson," 8 May 1882; "Tomas Karleil," 5 June 1882 (and two subsequent issues); "Iz Anglii," 15 December 1884; "Dnevnik Gordona," 17 August 1885; and "Dva slova iz Londona," 30 November 1885. Aksakov died in 1886, and the newspaper with him.

27 Stead summarized Novikova's career in journalism as follows: "Madame Novikoff, as I have always been proud to repeat, began her contributions to the Press in the *Northern Echo*. I was her first editor. She has contributed since then to the *Pall Mall Gazette* . . . , the *Daily News*, the *Daily Chronicle*, the *Times*, the *Observer*, and the *Daily Mail*. Articles by her have been published by the *Nineteenth Century*, the *Contemporary Review*, the *Fortnightly Review*, the *Review of Reviews*, the *New Review*, *Fraser's Magazine*, and at least one of the quarterlies. On the Continent she has contributed to the *Nouvelle Revue*, the *Flandre Libérale*, and other papers. In Russia her contributions have appeared in the *Moscow Gazette*, the *Novoe Vremya*, the *Russ*, the *Contemporary News*, and the *Svet*" (*M.P. for Russia*, vol. 2, 438). In the 1890s she wrote articles for *Russkoe obozrenie* as well.

28 "Krizis v Serbii," *Rus'*, 13 March 1882, 11.

29 The pamphlets appeared under the common title, *Neskol'ko slov*, 3 nos. (Petrograd, 1914–1915).

30 Stead, *M.P. for Russia*, vol. 1, 504.

31 "The Truth about the Russian Advance," *Pall Mall Gazette*, 24/25 February 1885.

32 "Is Russia Right?: The Other Point of View," *Daily Mail*, 13 January 1904.

33 The articles were reprinted in a pamphlet, *The Philo-Jewish Meeting at the Guildhall: Some Letters by Olga Novikoff (O.K.)* (London, 1890). In 1917 Novikova stated her prejudice even more brutally: "The Jew is

the Cuckoo of Russia; he is forcing the aborigines out of their own nest" (*Russian Memories*, with an introduction by Stephen Graham [London, 1917], 114).

34 Novikoff, *Russian Memories*, 202.
35 There is a massive archive of Novikova's papers in Rossiiskii gosudarstvennyi arkhiv literatury i iskusstva in Moscow. Stead's letters to Novikova are in the Bodleian Library, Oxford.
36 D. N. Anuchin, "Iz vospominanii," in *Russkie vedomosti, 1863–1913*, vol. 1, *Sbornik statei*, 71.
37 The Koni-Kairova connection became public only in 1977 when Evgenii Sviiasov published three letters Koni had written to Kairova a hundred years earlier: "F. A. Koni. Pis'ma," in *Ezhegodnik rukopisnogo otdela Pushkinskogo doma na 1875 god* (Leningrad, 1977), 123, 133–41.
38 These details are drawn from *Golos*'s account of the trial published on 29–30 April and 2–3 May 1876. Dostoevskii also discussed it at length in *Dnevnik pisatelia* (F. M. Dostoevskii, *Polnoe sobranie sochinenii*, vol. 23 [Leningrad, 1981], 5–20). For press reaction to the verdict, see the endnote on p. 355. In a scene near the end of *The Brothers Karamazov*, a townsman compares the outcome of Dmitrii Karamazov's trial for patricide to Kairova's case: "'After all, during Lent they acquitted an actress who cut the throat of her lover's legal wife.' 'But she didn't finish the job,'" someone else retorts.
39 On Kairova's post at *BVed*, see A. M. Skabichevskii, "Pervoe 25-letie moikh literaturnykh mytarstv," *IV*, no. 4 (1910): 29–31.
40 Koni's relationship to Kairova should be kept in mind in assessing the letters; despite his obvious bias, however, they are a unique source for the reception of her reporting in Petersburg. There are seven letters from Koni to Kairova in the Institut russkoi literatury (IRLI) archive (r. 1, op. 12, ed. khr. no. 345) written between late 1876 and 3 December 1877. The ones that Sviiasov published (see note 37) are dated 27 April, 28 September, and 3 December.
41 McReynolds, *News*, 87. McReynolds conflates Kairova's longtime signature, N. S., and the masculine variant of her name.
42 Other special correspondents for *Golos* abroad were also identified only by initials or brief pseudonyms.
43 *Golos*, 14 July 1879, 1.
44 *Golos*, no. 102, appeared on 14 April 1877, and no. 103 on 25 May.
45 Identifying themselves as Westerners, the Russians called the Ottoman Empire the "East" or "Orient" [Vostok] despite the fact that Constantinople (Istanbul, 28.57° E) and its holdings in South-Central Europe and the Balkans lie west of St. Petersburg (30.25° E).

46 The issue of *Golos* in which the letter appears is 6 January 1877 by the Julian calendar, 18 January by the Gregorian. *Golos* identified its issues both ways; Kairova's letters bear the local dateline.

47 As this quotation indicates, one of Kairova's reportorial ploys was invented dialogue, which makes her an early practitioner of "faction" or dramatized presentation of actual events.

48 For instance, Kairova's letter of 2 November 1878 outlines the maneuvers of Slavic Croats, Czechs, and Galician Poles for an autonomy within the empire similar to that the Hungarians enjoyed under the Crown of St. Stephen.

49 That Jews were becoming too prominent in the newspaper business seems to have been a common perception at the time. In her memoirs, Aleksandra Sokolova states baldly that the petty press in Russia from the 1880s "fell entirely to the disposal of Yids and bears the character more of a Jewish kahal [assembly of elders] than a Russian editorial office" ("Vstrechi i znakomstva," *IV*, no. 3 [1911]: 863).

50 "Vospominaniia gazetnogo korrespondenta o Bolgarii (Pis'mo k izdateliu)," *Delo* 2 (June 1886): sec. 2, 1–54, quotation from page 2.

51 *IV*, no. 4 (1888): 237. Kairova's archive in the Gosudarstvennaia publichnaia biblioteka (GPB) (f. 327) awaits a biographer.

52 See *Russkie pisateli*, vol. 3, s.v. "Mak-Gakhan, Varvara Nikolaevna." Dale L. Walker's *Januarius MacGahan: The Life and Campaigns of an American War Correspondent* (Athens, Ohio, 1988) cites extensively from Mak-Gakhan's papers in a family archive in the United States.

53 On the women of the sixties, see Arja Rosenholm's monumental *Gendering Awakening* (Helsinki: Ki Kimora Publications, 1999).

54 Walker, *Januarius MacGahan,* 53.

55 See Barbara Jelavich, "Russia and the April Uprising," *Southeastern Europe/L'Europe du sud-est* 4, no. 2 (1977): 217–32.

56 Iono Mitev, "MacGahan and the April, 1876 Uprising," *Southeastern Europe/L'Europe du sud-est* 4, no. 2 (1977): 268. MacGahan's reports appeared in book form later that year: *The Turkish Atrocities in Bulgaria: Letters of the Special Commissioner of the Daily News J. A. MacGahan* (London, 1876).

57 *Russkie vedomosti, 1863–1913*, vol. 2, *Sotrudniki*, 111.

58 "Amerikantsy-doma," *VE*, nos. 7, 10–12 (1882).

59 "Novoe na staroi podkladke," *VE*, nos. 1–4 (1888); *Xenia Repnina: A Story of Russia Today,* with an introduction by Vas. Verestchagin (New York, [1890]).

60 E. N. Matrosov, "Zaokeanskaia Rus': Sotsiologichesko-opisatel'nyi ocherk," *IV*, no. 1 (1897): 245–46.

61 "Vozrazhenie g. Matrosovu (Graf Leliva tozh')," *Russkoe obozrenie*, no. 6 (1897): 956–61. The parenthesis evidently refers to a pen name used by Matrosov.
62 "Sud chesti pri Soiuz vzaimopomoshchi russkikh pisatelei: Zasedania 26-go ianvaria i 4-go fevralia 1899 g.," *IV*, no. 3 (1899): 1109–12.
63 *Russkie pisateli,* s.v. "Mak-Gakhan, Varvara."

Writing for Their Rights

Four Feminist Journalists: Mariia Chekhova, Liubov' Gurevich, Mariia Pokrovskaia, and Ariadna Tyrkova

ROCHELLE GOLDBERG RUTHCHILD

Russian women writers are finally getting serious and sustained scholarly attention from Western scholars.[1] Journalism, often at the intersection of literature and politics, has been less studied. The world of Russian journalism continues to be perceived as a man's world, sprinkled with a few exceptional females. Indeed, the most recent book on Russian newspapers claims that Russian women "did not develop a specific 'women's journalism' that stemmed from a gender-based consciousness" save for some sporadic signs before the First World War.[2] As the essays in this volume demonstrate, "gender-based consciousness" could be found in the thick journals dating back at least to the 1850s, and not only in those literary and political journals but also in a wide range of publications appealing primarily to women.

In Russia, the causes of social reform and women's rights were especially intimately intertwined. Ann Hibner Koblitz notes that the "confluence of science, feminism, and social activism" particularly marked the Russian intelligentsia in the 1860s and 1870s.[3] Russian women had been prominent in their country's radical movements, fought for the right to equal education and access to the professions, and outnumbered other women at European universities where women were accepted as students. Chafing against the rigid gender roles decreed by social custom and tsarist law, educated Russian women were equal to men in their lack of many basic civil rights.[4] Because universal suffrage did not become a possibility until 1905, Russia's women's suffrage movement emerged much later than those of Western Europe and North America. In Russia, the right to vote at all, for women or men, except for a small group of landowners (including women through male proxies), was not granted until Nicholas II was forced to do so by the revolution of 1905. By granting men but not women the right to vote, the tsar and his advisers brought Russia to parity with almost every other country in which citizens voted.[5]

1905 was a watershed. Few expected the tsar to champion women's rights, but the opposition of the chief leaders of the liberation movement to women's suffrage was different. The retreat from the commitment to women's equality that had marked earlier democratic generations reverberated through the small educated elite from which most social activists came, provided the impetus for the emergence of a women's suffrage movement, and marked a new stage in women's participation in Russian journalism. The founding of women's rights organizations, and the emergence of a larger pool of potential supporters and readers, created the conditions for the establishment of an explicitly feminist press and feminist writing.[6]

In this essay I will examine the lives and careers of four feminist journalists, Mariia Chekhova, Liubov' Gurevich, Mariia Pokrovskaia, and Ariadna Tyrkova. Of the four, most have fallen into obscurity, are known only for their literary work, or are mentioned only briefly in monographs. Although each took a different path in her advocacy of women's rights, and some resisted the appellation "feminist," their lives and work indicate the ways in which women could be journalists and feminists in early-twentieth-century Russia, often bridging the literary and political worlds.

The lives of these women before 1905 were not dissimilar from others of their class. All were from relatively privileged backgrounds, all experienced sex discrimination as a barrier to their full achievement in life, all benefited from earlier feminist battles for higher education and access to the professions, and all at some point challenged traditional roles for women. What impelled them to specifically feminist activity? In many ways, their early lives resemble those of Russian women from privileged families who became revolutionaries. Some historians, examining the comparatively large number of memoirs by women revolutionaries, have concluded that intelligentsia women who stayed politically active moved "from feminism to radicalism."[7] The activism of Chekhova, Gurevich,

Tyrkova, and Pokrovskaia shows that women's choices were more complex and varied. Instead of abandoning the specific quest for women's rights, they fought to include feminism in any understanding of Russian social change.

Of the four women, three were fully of the noble estate. The fourth, Liubov' Gurevich, was of mixed social background; her mother was from the nobility, and her father, a Jewish convert to Russian Orthodoxy, was not. Three of the four were literally "children of the sixties." Ariadna Tyrkova was born in 1869; Gurevich and Mariia Chekhova, both from families of professional educators, were born in 1866. They were of the first generation in which women could choose teaching, as opposed to domestic tutoring, as a recognized profession.[8]

Liubov' Gurevich grew up in a progressive urban intellectual household. Her father, Iakov Gurevich, was a lecturer in history at St. Petersburg University and the Bestuzhev courses[9] and later editor of the liberal Russian pedagogical journal *Russkaia shkola (Russian School)*. Gurevich no doubt learned something about editing and publishing a journal from him. Gurevich's mother, Liubov' Ivanovna Il'ina, sister of the writer Ekaterina Tsekina-Zhukovskaia, supported and encouraged her daughter's interest in literature. Although she remembered fondly her relationships with her parents, Gurevich presented herself later as someone who chafed against the restrictions of her sex.[10]

Mariia Pokrovskaia was older, born in 1852 in remote Penza province. From 1873 she worked as a teacher at a girls' primary school in Tambov province, until admitted in 1876 to the women's medical courses, first opened in 1873. She graduated five years later, and from 1882 to 1888 worked as a Zemstvo doctor in Pskov province before settling in St. Petersburg as one of twenty-four Duma doctors, physicians paid by the city to give aid to the poor.[11] Pokrovskaia's activism was driven by a deep social concern for the poor and a strong identification with, and advocacy for, women. Unlike Liubov' Gurevich and many other educated women who felt stifled by the sex-segregated education of their youth, Pokrovskaia seems to have found comfort and recognition in same-sex settings. Years after her three-year stint as a schoolteacher, Teminkov locals remembered her as a charismatic figure who drew girls to her and was a positive influence on the "self-perfection" *(samousovershenstvovanie)* and development of her female students. In contrast, Mariia Chekhova, sent to a boarding school *(pansion)* filled with young noblewomen, "little angels" *(angelochki)* learning ballroom dancing, spurned a job offer there as antithetical to her ideals. "This is not pedagogical activity, this is not service for enlightenment. Did I really train to keep dance time for a bunch of 'little angels'?"[12]

The youngest of the four, Ariadna Tyrkova, born in St. Petersburg seventeen years after Pokrovskaia, has left the fullest biographical information. In the ten years before her death at age ninety-two in 1962, she wrote memoirs of her childhood and adult years; her son added another book of reminiscences based on her writings.[13] Tyrkova was one of seven children of a minor government official and his Polish–Baltic German wife. Her father was a military officer and a traditionalist; her mother, a "convinced woman of the sixties."[14] Tyrkova's older brother Arkadii was arrested for revolutionary activity in connection with the assassination of Alexander II. As a result, she was expelled from the Obolenskii *gimnazium* in St. Petersburg as a troublemaker; her serious and quiet friend Nadezhda Krupskaia, later Lenin's wife, finished her course without incident and continued teaching at the gimnazium for several years.[15]

All four women benefited directly from the activism of earlier feminists who had successfully battled to make higher and professional education in Russia available to women. Chekhova, Gurevich, and Tyrkova attended the Bestuzhev courses.[16] Ariadna Tyrkova originally wanted to be a doctor, but the government ordered the medical and higher courses for women closed the year she graduated from her gimnazium. The medical and natural science courses were still closed when she finally enrolled in the Bestuzhev mathematics faculty in 1889. At the Bestuzhev courses, Tyrkova again caught the eye of the authorities; called in by the director twice, she was warned to stay away from funerals and political demonstrations, often one and the same in that period.[17] Tyrkova was not alone; Gurevich's outspoken advocacy of women's rights and critique of traditional morality almost resulted in her expulsion.[18]

Each of the four women responded differently to the traditional expectations that they marry and have a family. Pokrovskaia remained single and childless. Gurevich had a daughter, Elena Nikolaevna Gurevich, but never married.[19] Chekhova, née Argamakova, had on the surface the most traditional relationship, a monogamous marriage to Nikolai Chekhov that produced six offspring, four daughters and two sons.[20] However, their marriage was certainly not traditional in the sense of the "unlimited obedience" to patriarchal authority written into the tsarist law code.[21] Of the four, Chekhova achieved the closest to the ideal of the companionate marriage cherished among the democratic intelligentsia. Together with her husband, she founded a pioneering Zemstvo school in Tver' province. In 1903 Chekhova opened a Sunday school in Tver' and, with her husband, later taught at Moscow's Prechistenskie courses, the first Russian "Workers University."[22]

Ariadna Tyrkova also sought a companionate relationship. Dropping out of the Bestuzhev courses after a year, she married Alfred Borman, an engineer, in 1890. But Tyrkova's marriage was neither supportive nor a lifetime partnership of like-minded activists, like the Chekhovs. Tyrkova felt stifled, and after seven years the couple separated.[23] The act of leaving the marriage liberated Tyrkova but also brought new material difficulties to a woman used to dressing in the latest Paris fashions. The twin sanctions of tsarist law and social custom made breaking up a marriage especially difficult and traumatic. Divorces were rare and extremely difficult to obtain. Aside from the social sanctions, women faced severe economic pressures. Tyrkova does not seem to have gotten a divorce; the marital separation left her with two children and the need to earn a living on her own. She was aided immeasurably by her mother, who provided essential child care and moral support, but little money.[24]

Tyrkova had no way to earn a living, no "profession." Teaching was closed to married women; other professions required long and arduous training; some, like the law, were not open to women. Tyrkova chose journalism, which required no professional license or extensive training.[25] But even as a journalist and writer, she faced a major obstacle. Women authors had more difficulty than men in getting their work published. To establish herself and earn some desperately needed money, Tyrkova turned to using a male pseudonym, Vergezhkii, derived from the name of her family estate. She was first published in 1897.[26]

In her autobiography *Na putiakh k svobode (On the Road to Freedom)*, Tyrkova describes in detail the difficulties of her life as a single mother, trying to support herself as a theater critic and with any other writing assignments she could obtain, living in St. Petersburg and supporting a family. When her marriage broke up, Tyrkova felt lost; her personal experience showed her "how difficult it is especially for women to establish a balance between the personal and the societal."[27] Political and personal events blended; as she wrote later, "the quickening of the revolutionary rhythm coincided with a sharp change in my personal life."[28] At the end of the nineteenth century, Russian society sought its road to freedom; so did Tyrkova. It was bumpy for both.

Tyrkova was thirty-six, Chekhova and Gurevich thirty-nine, and Pokrovskaia fifty-three in 1905. All four women had established careers; all had challenged the system before entering into feminist political activity. Gurevich and Pokrovskaia were sufficiently accomplished to merit entries in the 1901–1904 edition of the Brokgauz-Efron encyclopedia.[29] Gurevich published her first article while still a student at the Bestuzhev courses.[30] Of the four, Gurevich was the most involved and best known in the literary world. With the poet Akim Volynskii, she edited and published the journal *Severnyi vestnik (Northern Herald),* beginning in 1891. Although Gurevich was but twenty-five years old and recently graduated from the Bestuzhev courses, she was the driving force behind *Severnyi vestnik.* She borrowed money from her family to buy the journal in 1891, and she managed its affairs throughout. Her stewardship of the journal was marked by the publication of such modernist writers as Zinaida Gippius, Dmitrii Merezhkovskii, Mirra Lokhvitskaia, and Fedor Sologub, and a large number of works by women writers and poets such as Annie Besant, Sofia Kovalevskaia, Lou Andreas-Salome, Zinaida Vengerova, and Ol'ga Shapir.[31] Many articles about women's status in society and the work of populist economists such as Aleksandra Efimenko filled the pages of the journal. In 1899, when *Severnyi vestnik* ceased publication, Gurevich was left with a mass of debts. The stress took its toll; Gurevich later described this time as the "most difficult period of my life," and she appears to have had a nervous breakdown.[32]

In contrast to Gurevich, Pokrovskaia was a prolific writer, seemingly indestructible and imperturbable. She began to write not because of economic necessity or literary aspirations but in response to the appalling conditions she saw in her medical practice. She authored numerous articles on medicine, nutrition, and public health published in various thick journals such as *Vrach' (Doctor), Vest-*

nik Evropy (European Herald), Russkaia mysl' (Russian Thought), in newspapers, and in publications of the Russian Society for the Preservation of Public Health (Russkoe obshchestvo okhraneniia narodnogo zdraviia). Dedicated to making public health information available to the poor, she also created her own series of advice pamphlets. From her experiences as a doctor, she vividly described the living conditions of the poor peasant and proletarian, writing about the effects of living in chimneyless huts on the development of eye diseases and breathing problems, the effects of water quality on illness and death rates, and the relationship between crowded urban housing and public health. Convinced that disease prevention consisted primarily in changing unhealthy behavior, she concerned herself not only with living conditions but with living habits. She wrote guides to picking the right apartment, keeping a clean house and popular hygiene, directed primarily at women.[33]

Pokrovskaia's awareness of discrimination against her sex was heightened by her experiences as a Zemstvo and Duma doctor. In a short, barely disguised autobiographical essay entitled *Kak ia byla gorodskim vrachom dlia bednykh (How I Was a Doctor for the City Poor),* she wrote, "'I was not only a doctor, but also a pioneer for women. I had to serve the people and also prove to society that women could in practice be as good doctors as men.'"[34] Her experiences dovetailed with those of other female physicians whose memoirs were published in various thick journals at the turn of the century.[35] Throughout her career, Pokrovskaia called herself "Woman-Doctor" [Zhenshchina-vrach']. To Pokrovskaia, nothing symbolized the debased status of women in Russian society more than prostitution, which was regulated by the government through a system of registration and medical inspection. In pamphlets, articles, and speeches, Pokrovskaia protested fiercely against legalized prostitution as enslavement of women. That she had once been accosted and propositioned when walking alone at night no doubt spurred her anger.[36]

Pokrovskaia's attempts to win support for her views within the Russian Society for the Preservation of Public Health and other organizations met with mixed results.[37] Perhaps feeling stymied by her battles in the Public Health Society, perhaps seeking to develop more of a constituency for her battles for her causes, perhaps anticipating the revolutionary upheavals of 1905, she founded *Zhenskii vestnik*

(Women's Herald) in 1904. Pokrovskaia did not state her immediate motivation for starting the journal. Whatever her reasons, the peripatetic physician's timing was excellent. *Zhenskii vestnik*, the longest lived of any Russian feminist journal, in the thirteen years of its existence provided a forum for Pokrovskaia's views on an eclectic range of issues and events concerning women. Only the Bolshevik revolution silenced the journal.[38]

While Pokrovskaia's experience as a physician led her to feminist journalism, Ariadna Tyrkova's political work led her to feminism. Tyrkova was already politically active and was one of the four women (another was Ekaterina Kuskova) who were frequent contributors to the liberal journal *Osvobozhdenie (Liberation)*, edited by the former Marxist Petr Struve.[39] Arrested in 1903 for attempting to smuggle copies of *Osvobozhdenie* from Finland to Russia, Tyrkova left her children and fled abroad to escape prison. She joined Struve's circle in Paris. At that point, in Tyrkova's experience, there was no need for a separate feminist struggle; every progressive Russian supported women's rights: "I myself had never thought about women's equality. In our circle in Paris that question was never raised. . . . At that moment I believed so in my equality with men that it never occurred to me to prove it."[40]

Tyrkova did not return to Russia until the height of revolutionary activity in 1905, and after much of the bitter debate among the liberals who formed the Constitutional Democratic (Kadet) Party about support for women's suffrage. She missed the first party congress held in October, at which Anna Miliukova and her husband, Kadet leader Pavel Miliukov, fought an open and heated battle over inclusion of a women's suffrage plank in the party platform.[41] Tyrkova was so aroused by the hypocrisy of the Kadet men opposed to women's rights that she made her first political speech before a large audience at the January 1906 Kadet congress. Responding to Miliukov and others who opposed a mandatory women's suffrage plank, she demanded: "How can you ignore half the population and still speak of universal suffrage and democratic beginnings?"[42]

Ironically, Tyrkova's feminism helped her advance within the Kadet Party. Her verbal jousting with Miliukov, along with her writing and work as an assistant to the Kadet deputies, led to an invitation from the influential party leader and State Duma deputy Prince Dmitrii Shakhovskoi in April 1906 to join the Kadet Central Committee.[43] Tyrkova became the token woman on the Central Committee of the Kadet Party from 1906 until 1917; Anna Miliukova's public arguments with her husband were not similarly rewarded.[44]

For Tyrkova, the connection between social change and women's rights had been severed by leaders of the liberation movement; this awakened her gender consciousness. Liubov' Gurevich, age thirty-nine in 1905, found similar attitudes among parties that nominally supported equal rights and women's suffrage. Drawn to the Social Democrats (her sister, Anna Gurevich, was a Bolshevik), her first impressions were negative. Both the Bolsheviks and Mensheviks supported women's rights on paper; in practice, mention of the issue drew "inappropriate half-smiles and grins" from Social Democratic men. Gurevich protested, calling for "a close tie between the woman question and the revolutionary movement." Referring to the more sympathetic position of the German socialist leader August Bebel, she argued that "Bebel did not fear the woman question as do the Russian Social Democrats."[45]

Stung by the sexism of liberal and left men, Liubov' Gurevich joined the Women's Equal Rights Union (Soiuz ravnopraviia zhenshchin) established in 1905, attended the organization's first and subsequent delegate congresses, spoke at meetings, and wrote women's rights pamphlets such as *Pochemu nuzhno dat' zhenshchinam vse prava i svobody (Why It Is Necessary to Give Women All Rights and Freedoms)* and *Zhenskoe dvizhenie poslednykh dnei (The Present-Day Women's Movement)*, among others. She also volunteered her publishing and distribution experience in the service of the union, writing Chekhova that she was "working all the time for the cause of women's equal rights," noting that there was "nothing about women's rights in any of the St. Petersburg bookstores," and offering to distribute feminist pamphlets in the capital and to Trudovik Party Duma representatives.[46] Gurevich was also one of four women who worked with the committee on equal rights of the first Duma on the ultimately stillborn task of laying the legal groundwork for women's equality.[47]

By the end of 1905, then, each of the four women was moved to feminist writing and other political activity. Although there are similarities in their feminist awakenings, their activity indicates the diversity within a movement so often painted as monolithic and "bourgeois." Gurevich and Chekhova allied themselves with the left wing of the liberation movement; Tyrkova, with the liberal Kadets; and

Pokrovskaia, with women as a separate oppressed group, as Linda Edmondson discusses in the following essay. Tyrkova found her feistiness rewarded within the liberal establishment; Gurevich was spurned by the Social Democrats; Chekhova found acceptance from the Socialist Revolutionaries and their Duma allies the Trudoviki;[48] Pokrovskaia rejected male political parties.

All four women wrote for the feminist journals; Gurevich, Tyrkova, and Pokrovskaia penned pamphlets and articles for thick journals. In addition, Mariia Pokrovskaia and Mariia Chekhova served as editors of two of the chief feminist publications to appear between 1904 and 1917. Pokrovskaia and Chekhova represented the two major feminist factions; their ideological battles were fought out in part in the pages of their journals. Pokrovskaia argued for the centrality of women's issues; Chekhova believed that feminist success was inextricably linked with the success of the liberation movement as a whole.

Pokrovskaia began *Zhenskii vestnik* in September 1904, with a statement of purpose explaining why she had launched the journal and outlining the key elements of her feminist politics. There was, she wrote, no journal in Russia exclusively dedicated to discussing the woman question; she sought to fill a void by opening up a forum for discussion of the woman question. *Zhenskii vestnik* was dedicated to "improving [women's] situation and their active participation in the progress of our society"; no other journal had this goal. Arguing for a solidarity between women that crossed class lines, Pokrovskaia saw her goal as bridging the gap between the *intelligentki,* or educated women, and poor women, to end the "constant war between the sexes," and to create "full equality between women and men in the family and in society." She urged her readers to start a dialogue with her, to serve as a source of information about women's status in other parts of the country. In return, she promised news about the women's movement in Russia and abroad, and to pay special attention to "questions of social, domestic and personal hygiene." The thirty-seven-page first issue also contained a translation of a story by Olive Schreiner, historical notes about the existence of matriarchy in early Europe, an article about women's participation in war as soldiers (the early Slavs), and as nurses and doctors, and women's "peaceful propensities." In line with Pokrovskaia's interests, there was also a health section, including an invitation to all educated women *(intelligentnye zhenshchiny)* to join a newly formed Women's Sanitary Society in St. Petersburg (Zhenskoe sanitarnoe obshchestvo).[49]

Like *Soiuz zhenshchin (Union of Women),* Mariia Pokrovskaia's *Zhenskii vestnik* decried the extremes of poverty and wealth so endemic to Russian society. The journal consistently devoted space to the condition of the downtrodden factory workers, servants, and peasants. Like Chekhova, Pokrovskaia believed that feminists "cannot place their hopes in the bourgeoisie and the aristocracy," but on "the working people [who] have experienced and experience now the full weight of lack of rights — these are the ones we can count on now."[50]

Unlike the Equal Rights Union, many of whose members participated in the Moscow uprising in 1905, Pokrovskaia deplored revolutionary violence, charging that men fighting for freedom were insensitive to the price paid by women and children. At the time of the uprising, she wrote: "Women know that it is not through violence and slaughter that we can recreate life, but only through peaceful reform."[51] She objected to strikes because of their consequences for women, advocating that men stay home and women join the picket lines: "We ask: Who bears the chief burden of the strike? The wife and mother. And under these circumstances men accuse women of conservatism, when the latter seek to dissuade men from participation in strikes. Let the men stay home with the children during strikes and let the women be free to leave the hungry cries!"[52]

Pokrovskaia, more separatist than Equal Rights Union members, sought not to revive but to reshape the progressive Russian intelligentsia's commitment to both women's rights and social change through her journal and the first Russian women's political party. To her, sex discrimination overshadowed all other injustice; men deprived women of political rights and made them economically dependent. Women could gain freedom only by their own efforts. Pokrovskaia had worked with the Union of Women, but by the late fall of 1905, she was convinced that feminists needed more than a union and more than the newly emerging legal political parties. No male-dominated party, argued Pokrovskaia, could really champion the interests of women. If they wanted to learn necessary political and organizational skills free from male intimidation, women should form their own, separate political party. Reversing traditional arguments used against female political participation, she claimed that her sex would ennoble the business of governing, since women represented the highest ideals of humankind. Like many Western feminists, Pokrovskaia believed that politics suited women better than men, but in actually founding a political party, she moved one step further. The Women's Progressive Party (Zhenskaia Progressivnaia Partiia) joined the Women's Equal Rights Union as the second women's rights organization to appear in Russia in 1905 and one of the first women's political parties in the world. It was born in conflict. In December 1905, thirty-three women attended the organizational meeting; those favoring a strict equal-rights emphasis lost out to those, including Pokrovskaia, favoring a more comprehensive analysis of the causes of, and cures for, women's oppression.[53]

Zhenskii vestnik became the forum for the Women's Progressive Party, beginning in January 1906 by publishing its platform, a mix of feminism, pacifism, and socialism. The program contained demands common to left and liberal parties for suffrage for women and men, and for equal rights on the land, in education, and in employment. Reflecting Pokrovskaia's major concerns, it called for the "elimination of the unfair distribution of wealth and the just payment of labor," improved public health measures, and an end to the registration of prostitutes. There was a strong pacifist call for the "destruction of militarism," the replacement of armies by citizen militias, and the "unification of all the peoples of Russia in the name of humanitarian ideas." All this was to be accomplished by harnessing the Romanovs to the framework of a constitutional monarchy.[54] Pokrovskaia's criticism of labor militance and her advocacy of a constitutional monarchy did not endear her to other women activists, both inside and outside the autonomous women's movement. Aleksandra Kollontai labeled Pokrovskaia and her followers "right feminists" and charged that their ostensible concern for the poor belied their true class interests. And Chekhova dismissed the Women's Progressive Party as "vague Christian utopianism."[55]

The Women's Progressive Party attracted no more than a handful of members. With neither money nor membership, the party could act like a political party, but its activism was limited. Despite Pokrovskaia's injunctions against male-dominated parties, she and her party could do little but support the efforts of larger and better-funded women's groups and various male politicians to enact equal-rights legislation. News of the Women's Progressive Party soon faded from the pages of *Zhenskii vestnik;* remaining loyalists formed the Club of the Women's Progressive Party. As Linda Edmondson points out, this gave Pokrovskaia a legal women's rights organization (the Women's Union was not legal) and enabled her and her allies to continue to operate in the period of reaction after 1906.[56]

The topics covered in the pages of *Zhenskii vestnik* ranged far beyond women's suffrage; many seem quite modern. Free love, domestic violence, women's self-defense, reproductive rights, child care, marriage, divorce, women's health, suicides, women in the workplace, discrimination, and sexual harassment were all discussed in the journal, as was sexuality. Reflecting the predominant mores, articles about sex presumed heterosexuality; celibacy was presented as the only alternative. Pokrovskaia was not antisex; she wrote positively about the "liberation of the body," and women's sexual pleasure. Overall, the breadth of topics covered was unique for the period.[57]

In contrast to Pokrovskaia, who had published widely before launching *Zhenskii vestnik,* Mariia Chekhova had the least journalistic experience of the four women discussed here. Chekhova was among the group of thirty who gathered in Moscow in late February 1905 to form the Women's Equal Rights Union. We do not know what specifically moved her to feminist activity, but she shared much of it with her husband. The Chekhovs served together on the boards of the Teachers Union (Vserossiiskii soiuz uchitelei) and the Women's Equal Rights Union in 1905. Chekhov was the only man on the governing council of the Equal Rights Union and contributed articles to the journal edited by his wife.[58]

Chekhova edited *Soiuz zhenshchin* for the entire two and a half years of its existence, from June 1907 to December 1909. Like *Zhenskii vestnik,* the journal had a troubled history. Though authorized by the Union of Women's Third Delegate Congress in May 1906, the first issue did not appear until June 1907.[59] By then the Union of Women was already falling apart, the victim of internal strife, lack of resources, hostility on the left, and police repression. Although Chekhova seems to have been key in making *Soiuz zhenshchin* a reality, the contributors' list for the first and subsequent issues reads like a Who's Who of the feminist intelligentsia and their supporters.[60]

Once launched, *Soiuz zhenshchin* staked out its ground within the women's movement and within the larger genre of women's journals. It had no fashion advertising, only advertising for other publications such as *Dlia narodnogo uchitelia (For the People's Teacher)*, the *Teosoficheskoe obozrenie (Theosophical Review)*, and the *Vestnik kurortov i lechebnykh uchrezhdenii (Sanitoria and Health Resorts Herald)*, reflecting the profession and predilections of many of the journal's readers. *Soiuz zhenshchin* cost fifteen kopeks an issue, or 1.5 rubles a year; women workers averaged about 3 rubles a week. The first issue appeared in June 1907; the journal was published monthly until December 1909. Issues ranged between sixteen and forty pages in length; the press run was one thousand per issue.[61]

Several themes stood out in *Soiuz zhenshchin*. First was that voting rights were key to women's liberation. As stated in the journal's masthead: "This journal will be dedicated to questions connected with equal rights for women and primarily for their voting rights which is the first necessary step on the path to their liberation."[62] Second, women themselves had to fight for their rights. Bitter experience with liberals and socialists made this clear: "The political liberation of women must be only in the hands of women."[63] Third, the fight for women's rights had to be connected with the liberation movement as a whole, thus distinguishing the Women's Equal Rights Union from "narrow feminism." There was no mention of the word "feminism" in the masthead. Indeed the only mention of feminism in the journal was in a negative context. An unsigned editorial in the second issue, probably written by Chekhova, stated: "We are far from that naive and nearsighted feminism which dreams about resolving the woman question outside of ties with general political and social questions, equalizing women's rights with men independent of general rights and social equality."[64] For Chekhova, the full liberation of women was possible "only when all exploitation of one person by another is ended, that is, under socialism."[65]

Tyrkova, Chekhova, and Gurevich, despite their different political propensities, found common ground in writing about, and lobbying for, women's rights in this period. Typical of Tyrkova's writing was "Pobeda zhenshchiny" ("Women's Victory"), liberally quoted by Chekhova in the October 1907 issue of *Soiuz zhenshchin*. Tyrkova decried "the legacy of serfdom," the "blind negation of individual personality," and the "dangerous separation of women's interests from the interests of the entire country."⁶⁶ Gurevich's *Soiuz zhenshchin* articles focused on her experiences and those of others lobbying for women's rights in the Duma and with left and liberal political parties.

Articles in *Soiuz zhenshchin* emphasized the economic aspects of women's exploitation; *Zhenskii vestnik* underlined the primacy of gender-based oppression. Chekhova in particular regarded Pokrovskaia as a threat, attacking her and her Women's Progressive Party in the pages of *Soiuz zhenshchin* for "vague Christian utopianism."⁶⁷ Pokrovskaia in return criticized the Union of Women and its journal for failing to take sufficiently into account deep-rooted sexual prejudice. Critiquing an article by Tyrkova arguing that women's low wages were the principal cause of prostitution, Pokrovskaia countered that prostitution existed under different economic systems and that the "worst slavery for women is sexual slavery." These kinds of views brought the wrath of Chekhova, who accused Pokrovskaia of having "unfounded dreams and idealistic airy sentences." Chekhova had her own dream of restoring the ties between the liberation of women and the ideals of socialism.⁶⁸

Both *Soiuz zhenshchin* and *Zhenskii vestnik* suffered throughout their existence from lack of funds. If socialist publications were still able to count on some wealthy patrons for funds, the feminists were not so fortunate. Appealing primarily to a small group of educated Russian women who, if they had jobs, were underpaid and overworked, the journals were unable to find patrons or matrons to sustain them. *Soiuz zhenshchin* owed its survival to the volunteer labor of its staff and to small monthly contributions of five rubles apiece from twenty women who resolved to help support the journal. By the third year, there were only eight financial backers.⁶⁹

From the beginning, *Zhenskii vestnik*'s existence was a tenuous one. Among the intelligentsia, its most likely subscribers, few responded to the call of the "herald." In part this was due to male hostility—some subscribers' husbands had gone so far as to fling copies into the fire.⁷⁰ But mostly women were indifferent to, or disapproved of, Pokrovskaia and her journal. Some criticized its modest size and its subscription price of three rubles a year, others its "ideological side."⁷¹ Though disheartened by the lack of response, Pokrovskaia persisted. From the beginning, she wrote, she knew that *Zhenskii vestnik* would not be as thick or as attractive as other journals, but all her efforts to raise more money had failed. She hoped, in launching her venture, that it would soon attract wide female support and that this would allow for improvements. Every year there was a deficit. More than once she had been ready to quit, but stopped. "I was always held back," she wrote, "by the thought that there would be no other organ in defense of women's rights."[72] All the same, it was the apathy of women that was the hardest to take: "They begrudge giving three rubles for propaganda urging the betterment of their own situation!" And she looked forward to the day when this would no longer be true: "When the consciousness of women is awakened, then they will spend much greater sums on propaganda, then they will not begrudge the money, and even jail will not be frightening."[73]

Mariia Chekhova also wrote about the lack of a strong base of support for her journal, *Soiuz zhenshchin*. For her, its history mirrored the history of the Women's Equal Rights Union: "Its members outgrew those ideas which had made it possible for them to unite around the journal despite some differences in their political perspective and in their views on the women's movement. Three years of working on the basic questions of the women's movement gave each of them a more defined point of view. They went their separate ways and some dropped out of general work altogether."[74] Chekhova had already gone her separate way, but still within the feminist movement. In January 1909, she became president of a new organization, the League of Women's Equality (Liga ravnopraviia zhenshchin), in St. Petersburg. For the last year of her editorship of *Soiuz zhenshchin*, Chekhova was involved in building a new organization; for her, the union model had outlived its usefulness. The League, legally registered, became the chief feminist organization from 1909 to 1917.

The arrests of many activists and the demoralization of others in the wake of government repression, the limited resources of female backers, and the drifting away of subscribers were all strong political and economic factors that led to the decision to suspend publication of *Soiuz zhenshchin*. But there were also personal factors that to some signaled the real reason for the demise of the journal. At the beginning of 1910, Mariia Chekhova moved to Moscow to follow her husband, whose work had taken him there. This move, according to feminist activist M. V. Orlovskaia, was the key factor in the decision to stop publishing *Soiuz zhenshchin*.[75] Whether this was indeed true or a convenient excuse used by Chekhova to break her last official connection with the union cannot be known on the basis of current evidence. True or not, there was not sufficient energy left in the Union of Women to find a successor or successors to Chekhova, or to finance continued publication of the journal.

The demise of *Soiuz zhenshchin* left but one feminist publication in Russia — Pokrovskaia's *Zhenskii vestnik*, and its circulation was low. Other journals with a feminist slant did appear between 1908 and 1917, but they generally did not last. Chief among them were *Zhenskaia mysl'* *(Woman's Thought)*, published in Kiev from 1909 to 1910; *Mir zhenshchin (Women's World)*, issued in Moscow from 1912 to 1916; and *Zhenskaia zhizn'* *(Woman's Life)*, from 1914 to 1916. Journals devoted solely to literature and feminist politics could not capture sufficient readership or revenue. The most successful publication that devoted substantial space to feminist issues was a hybrid. *Zhenskoe delo (Woman's Cause)* combined the approach of a more traditional woman's magazine with politics. Articles such as "Chto takoe feminizm?" ("What Is Feminism?") coexisted with fashion news, recipes, and ads for such products as Kubaka, carbonated springwater "from radioactive sources."[76] *Zhenskoe delo* appeared from 1910 until the Bolshevik revolution.

Feminist and capitalist publishers were not the only ones to direct their attention to women. In 1914 the Bolsheviks and Mensheviks, concerned about the appeal of feminism to women workers, began publishing their own women's magazines, both coinciding with the second celebration of the socialist women's holiday, International Woman's Day. The Menshevik effort, *Golos rabotnitsy (Voice of the Woman Worker)*, lasted two issues. *Rabotnitsa (Woman Worker)*, though addressed to women, took pains to deny any links to feminism. The linkages between class and gender, between an idealized socialism and a demonized feminism, were not to be easily addressed or resolved in *Rabotnitsa* or later Bolshevik efforts.

Of the four feminist journalists, only Mariia Pokrovskaia remained consistently involved in feminist press activity from 1905 to 1917. After the demise of *Soiuz zhenshchin*, Chekhova centered her activity in the Women's Equal Rights League. Tyrkova continued to write about feminist issues, reporting on the First All-Russian Congress of Women (Pervyi vserossiiskii zhenskii s"ezd) in 1908 (she,

Chekhova, Gurevich, and Pokrovskaia were all delegates), and describing a 1909 speaking tour for women's rights in the provinces.[77] But she also tried her hand at mainstream journalism, becoming the editor in 1911 of the Petersburg daily newspaper *Russkaia molva (Russian Talk)*, which had the second highest circulation in the capital. There she worked with her old friend Petr Struve as economics editor and with Aleksandr Blok as literary editor.[78]

Political setbacks such as the demise of the Union of Women could also magnify individual problems. Discouraged by the feminists' lack of success and her growing indebtedness, Liubov' Gurevich confessed to Mariia Chekhova in 1908 that she would have to drop out of political activity to support herself and her daughter. "I have," she wrote, "spent too much of my energy all my life trying to resolve in practice the 'woman question,' fighting my way with a child in my arms and without any help."[79] Gurevich wrote two articles for *Soiuz zhenshchin* in 1907 and then announced the resumption of her literary writing in 1908, most notably as a critic.[80] She devoted more of her time to work with the dramatist Konstantin Stanislavskii, as the first editor of his theoretical works and an enthusiastic supporter of the Moscow Art Theater.[81]

The First World War brought choices between pacifism and patriotism. Tyrkova, who in 1909 had written a passionate antiwar article for one of the last issues of *Soiuz zhenshchin*, now supported the war.[82] So did Pokrovskaia, who applauded the government ban on the sale of hard liquor and filled the pages of *Zhenskii vestnik* with articles describing women's discovery that, in the words of one contributor, they "can be as smart, [and] as hard workers as their husbands, fathers, brothers."[83] And in March 1916, with the economic situation steadily worsening, Pokrovskaia became one of the directors of a Women's Economic Union (Zhenskii ekonomicheskii soiuz), with the goal of "improving the economic and moral situation of women."[84]

The events of 1905 sparked the creation of the first feminist political organizations in Russia; the 1917 February revolution reinvigorated the feminists and gave the movement its biggest victory. Chekhova, Gurevich, Pokrovskaia, and Tyrkova all supported the revolution and lobbied the Provisional Government to grant women suffrage and the right to hold elective office. To pressure the government, the feminists organized the largest women's rights demonstration in Russian history. Gurevich described the "endless orderly column, with red banners unfurled and placards," an estimated 35,000 women, with the venerable radical Vera Figner at the head.[85] Tyrkova was part of the delegation that met with government leaders after the march and heard them agree to grant women's right to vote. Thus suffrage, the chief goal of feminist movements everywhere, was won by Russian feminists in twelve years, earlier than in the United States, Great Britain, France, and Germany, with their more established women's movements.[86]

Ariadna Tyrkova pushed the boundaries of women's rights further than suffrage. Capitalizing on the new right of women to hold political office, in the summer of 1917, she won election to the Petrograd (formerly St. Petersburg) city soviet. Her legislative role proved short-lived. She was on the lists of candidates for the Constituent Assembly but was defeated by leftist candidates, among them Lev Trotskii. Soon after, she fled the country.[87] Tyrkova became quite active in Russian émigré circles, voicing in her writing her strong opposition to the Bolshevik revolution and its aftermath, as in her memoir *From Liberty to Brest-Litovsk*.[88] But in her three volumes of memoirs and the reminiscences of her son, Tyrkova's feminist activity receives short shrift, adding up to just a few pages.

Chekhova, Gurevich, and Pokrovskaia stayed in Russia after 1917. *Zhenskii vestnik* ceased publication after the Bolshevik revolution; Pokrovskaia's fate is not certain, although she is thought to have died in 1921 in Petrograd, at the age of sixty-nine. Chekhova and her husband enthusiastically embraced the revolution. She died in 1934. Gurevich continued to write and publish as a literary and theater critic. She is best known for her writing about Stanislavskii. Maintaining friendships with Chekhova and Praskov'ia Ariian, editor of *Pervyi zhenskii kalendar' (First Women's Calendar)*, she did not continue to advocate for women's rights in print. She died in 1940, at the age of seventy-four.[89]

The feminist journalists discussed in this essay all exhibited extraordinary determination, energy, and independence in challenging the social and political norms of their day. Their feminist journalism came into its own in connection with the events of 1905 and served as a significant forum for women's rights news and analysis at a time of organizational flux, revolution, and repression. For Mariia Chekhova, Liubov' Gurevich, Mariia Pokrovskaia, and Ariadna Tyrkova, writing meant different things. Chekhova used the journal *Soiuz zhenshchin* as a way to continue to publicize women's rights issues and keep sympathizers informed at a time when the Union of Women organization was disintegrating. For Pokrovskaia, writing and publishing a feminist journal was a way to alert women to the need to organize by themselves and fight against the myriad forms of their oppression. For Tyrkova and Gurevich, feminist political writing was a way to use their skills to contribute to the movement for women's rights and perhaps earn some money in the process.

The successful striving of these women is remarkable in light of the social and cultural barriers to women's activity outside the home. Despite the Russian intelligentsia's traditional support for women's equality, feminist autonomy and outspokenness had their price. The four women often confronted public apathy and hostility as they advanced their feminist agendas. Feminist activism meant women demanding political rights for themselves. This flew in the face of the long tradition of female self-sacrifice honored and glorified by Russian revolutionary and religious tradition. It may help explain the particularly fierce hostility to feminism displayed in 1905 and afterward by many male and female radicals, liberals, and conservatives, as well as the apathy of many educated women.[90]

In addition to pressures outside the home, the lives and achievements of Chekhova, Gurevich, Pokrovskaia, and Tyrkova reflect the complex interrelationships between the public and private spheres. For example, marital status, affirmed by society and critiqued by many feminists, affected each woman differently. For Mariia Chekhova and Nikolai Chekhov, a supportive relationship encouraged and nourished political work. But even here, balancing the demands of family and feminist activity could be problematic, as Chekhova's move to Moscow to be with her husband was blamed for the demise of *Soiuz zhenshchin*. On the other hand, a broken marriage could also, as with Tyrkova, create the possibility of a career in journalism, if for no other reason than pure survival. No marriage at all, as with Gurevich, created the kind of intense economic and psychological pressures that could push a woman out of the public arena. Or for Pokrovskaia, no marriage apparently freed her to devote all her energies to her career, writing, and feminist activity.

A study of these feminist journalists offers insight into the different paths taken by educated women in Russia at the turn of the century, shows the diversity within a feminist movement too often portrayed as monolithically bourgeois, and makes more visible the ways in which the linkage of overall social change with the woman question that characterized the Russian intelligentsia in the second half of the nineteenth century changed in the early twentieth century. These feminist journalists, in their words and the way they lived their lives, provide rich source material for a fuller study of changing social consciousness in turn-of-the-century Russia and demonstrate that Russian women had indeed developed a "specific 'women's journalism' that stemmed from a gender-based consciousness."

Notes

    Research for this essay was supported by a grant from IREX, with funds provided by the U.S. Department of State (Title VIII) and the NEH, by Faculty Development Grants and an independent study leave from Norwich University, by the 1995 University of Illinois Summer Research Laboratory, and by the Davis Center for Russian Studies at Harvard University. The assistance of Valerii Klokov, Elena Korkina, Boris Egorov, Natasha Rogova, Zina Nikitina, Gregory, Anna Tamarchenko, Vicki Gabriner, and Rafael Ruthchild was invaluable for my research in Russia. Esther Kingston-Mann, Brenda Meehan, and Elizabeth Wood gave very helpful comments on earlier versions of this essay.

1 See, for example, works cited by Jehanne Gheith in the introduction, note 16.
2 Louise McReynolds, *The News under Russia's Old Regime* (Princeton, 1991), 151.
3 See Ann Hibner Koblitz, "Spreading the Gospel of Science: Journalism and the *Shestidesiatnitsy*," in *Science, Women, and Revolution in Russia* (London, forthcoming).
4 For a comprehensive discussion of the chief laws affecting women in tsarist Russia, see William G. Wagner, *Marriage, Property, and Law in Late Imperial Russia* (Oxford, 1995).
5 Ironically, at the same time, acceding to pressure from a unified nationalist movement in an adjacent part of his empire, the tsar granted women in Finland the right to vote and run for office, a first for Europe. On women's suffrage in various countries, see Robin Morgan, ed., *Sisterhood Is Global* (Garden City, N.Y., 1984). On civil rights in Russia,

see Olga Crisp and Linda Edmondson, eds., *Civil Rights in Imperial Russia* (Oxford, 1989). On Finland, see N. Mirovich, "Pobeda zhenskogo dvizheniia v Finlandii," *Russkaia mysl'* 7 (1907): pt. 2, 164–71.

6 By feminism I mean advocacy of political, social, and economic equality between the sexes. Two major published sources in English about the Russian feminists provide basic information about the feminist press. See Linda Harriet Edmondson, *Feminism in Russia, 1900–1917* (Stanford, 1984); and Richard Stites, *The Women's Liberation Movement* (Princeton, 1978, 1991).

7 See Barbara Alpern Engel, *Mothers and Daughters: Women of the Intelligentsia in Nineteenth-Century Russia* (Cambridge, 1983), 109–26; and Margaret Maxwell, *Narodniki Women: Russian Women Who Sacrificed Themselves for the Dream of Freedom* (New York, 1990).

8 See Engel, *Mother and Daughter,* and Maxwell, *Narodniki Women.* For an excellent discussion of women and the teaching profession in this period, see Christine Ruane, *Gender, Class, and the Professionalization of Russian City Teachers, 1860–1914* (Pittsburgh, 1994).

9 The Bestuzhev courses were established in St. Petersburg in 1878. The courses had wide support in educated circles and inspired similar efforts in Moscow, Kiev, and Kazan. They were the only women's courses to remain in existence through the reign of the reactionary Alexander III, surviving a prohibition on new admissions in 1886 and government suspicions of women students' radicalism. Christine Johanson, *Women's Struggle for Higher Education in Russia, 1855–1900* (Kingston and Montreal, 1987), and Ruth Arlene Fluck Dudgeon, "Women and Higher Education in Russia, 1855–1905" (Ph.D. diss., George Washington University, 1975), are the best sources in English on the struggle for women's higher education in Russia.

10 "Liubov' Iakovlevna Gurevich," in *Pervye literaturnye shagi: Avtobiografii sovremennykh russkikh pisatelei,* ed. F. F. Fidler (Moscow, 1911), 181–98, quotation on 190. Mariia Chekhova expressed similar feelings in her memoirs. Tsentral'nyi gosudarstvennyi istoricheskii arkhiv gorod Moskvy (TSGIA), f. 2251, Mariia Aleksandrovna Chekhova, o. 3, d. 4, ll. 2–3. On Gurevich, see *Novyi entsiklopedicheskii slovar' Brokgauz Efron,* vol. 15 (St. Petersburg, 1913), s.v. "Gurevich, Liubov' Iakovlevna"; *Modern Encyclopedia of Russian and Soviet Literatures,* ed. George J. Gutsche, vol. 9 (Gulf Breeze, Fla., 1989), s.v. "Gurevich, Liubov Yakovlevna": *Russkaia literatura XX veka (1890–1910),* ed. S. A. Vengerov, vol. 1 (Moscow, 1914), s.v. "Gurevich, L. Ia"; "Vospominaniia L. Ia. Gurevich," in *O Stanislavskom* (Moscow, 1948), 117–76; and *Dictionary of Russian Women Writers,* ed. Marina Ledkovsky, Charlotte Rosenthal, and Mary Zirin (Westport, Conn., 1994), s.v.

"Gurevich, Liubov' Iakovlevna." Gurevich's perception that her gender restricted her was not unique. Inessa Armand as a teenager reacted strongly to negative gender stereotypes. R. C. Elwood, *Inessa Armand, Revolutionary and Feminist* (Cambridge, 1992), 17.

11 For sources on Pokrovskaia's life, see "Mariia Ivanovna Pokrovskaia," *PZhK na 1905 god,* 394–96. See also *Entsiklopedicheskii slovar' Brokgauz-Efron,* vol. 24 (St. Petersburg, 1903), s.v. "Pokrovskaia (Mariia Ivanovna)." On Pokrovskaia's work as a Duma doctor, see E. Ia. Belitskaia, "Poliklinicheskaia pomoshch' v dorevoliutsionnom Peterburge i uchastie v nei zhenshchin vrachei," *Sovetskoe zdravookhranenie* 10 (1972): 64–68. M. I. Pokrovskaia, *Kak ia byla gorodskom vrachom dlia bednykh: Iz vospominanii zhenshchiny vracha* (St. Petersburg, 1903), is a fictionalized account of the life of a woman Duma doctor but clearly reflects the author's personal experience.

12 "Pokrovskaia," *PZhK,* 395. Chekhova material in TSGIA, f. 2251, o. 3, d. 4, ll. 2–3.

13 Ariadna V. Tyrkova-Williams, *To, chego bol'she ne budet* (Paris, 1954), describes Tyrkova's childhood and adolescence. *Na putiakh k svobode* (New York, 1952) continues the story beyond the 1905 revolution; *From Liberty to Brest-Litovsk* (London, 1919, and Westport, Conn., 1977) covers the 1917 revolutions and their aftermath. Tyrkova's son Arkadii Borman added further reminiscences in *A. V. Tyrkova-Vil'iams po ee pis'mam i vospominaniiam syna* (Louvain and Washington, 1964).

14 Tyrkova, *Na putiakh,* 7–8.

15 *Revoliutsionnoe narodnichestvo 70-x godov XIX veka: Sbornik dokumentov i materialov,* ed. S. S. Volk, 2 vols. (Moscow-Leningrad, 1965), vol. 2, 383.

16 The Bestuzhev courses, the largest of the Russian women's higher education courses, graduated 2,229 women between 1882 and 1903. Including graduates of other women's courses and medical courses, graduates of foreign universities, and dropouts, the total, approximately 8,000, is tiny compared to the total female population of 63 million listed in the 1897 census. See V. R. Leikina-Svirskaia, *Intelligentsiia v Rossii vo vtoroi polovine XIX veka* (Moscow, 1971), 151–52, for the Bestuzhev figures. See Norton Dodge, *Women in the Soviet Economy* (Baltimore, 251), for the census figures.

17 *Vysshie zhenskie (Bestuzhevskie) kursy: Bibliograficheskii ukazatel'* (Moscow, 1966), 86–90, 147; Johanson, *Women's Struggle,* 90. On Tyrkova's experience, see Tyrkova, *To, chego,* 252, 259–65.

18 *Dictionary,* s.v. "Gurevich."

19 On Liubov', see *Dictionary,* s.v. "Gurevich." Gurevich wrote a number of autobiographical pieces, but she never mentioned her daughter, who

may have been fathered by the writer Nikolai Molostvov (Stanley Rabinowitz, conversation with author, June 1995).
20 TSGIA, f. 2251, o. 3, descriptions of *dela* (files) 1–4, 11–14, 17.
21 *Svod zakonov Rossiiskoi Imperii*, vol. 10 (St. Petersburg, 1887), pt. 1, 30.
22 On Chekhova, Chekhov, and the Prechistenskie course, see *K 25-letiiu Prechistenskikh rabochikh kursov, 1897–1922* (Moscow, 1922), and *Prechistenskie rabochie kursy. Pervyi rabochii universitet v Moskve. Sbornik statei i vospominanii k 50-letiiu kursov, 1897–1947* (Moscow, 1948), 47. On Chekhova in general, see "M. A. Chekhova," *PZhK na 1912 god*, 8–11.
23 Tyrkova, *Na putiakh*, 25.
24 Women political activists of different stripes faced the same dilemmas as Tyrkova. On the ways in which mothers often aided their daughters in seeking independence and in radical political activity, see Engel, *Mothers and Daughters*.
25 The most extensive discussion of the restrictions against married women is on the marriage ban for schoolteachers. See Christine Ruane, "The Vestal Virgins of St. Petersburg: Schoolteachers and the 1897 Marriage Ban," *Russian Review* 50 (April 1991): 163–82. For Tyrkova's decision to become a writer, see *Na putiakh*, 13. This decision was not unique; revolutionary activist Alexandra Kollontai made a similar one, declaring: "I hate marriage. It is an idiotic and meaningless life. I will become a writer." Quoted in Barbara Evans Clements, *Bolshevik Feminist: The Life of Aleksandra Kollontai* (Bloomington, 1979), 16.
26 *Dictionary*, s.v. "Tyrkova, Ariadna Vladimirovna."
27 Tyrkova, *Na putiakh*, 24.
28 Ibid., 13.
29 *Entsiklopedicheskii slovar' Brokgauz-Efron*, 41 vols. (St. Petersburg, 1901–1904). Gurevich's entry is in vol. 9; Pokrovskaia's entry is in vol. 24.
30 Deeply moved by the diary of Mariia Bashkirtseva (1858–1884), a Russian artist who died at the age of twenty-six, Gurevich traveled to Paris in 1886 to see Bashkirtseva's studio and talk with her mother. Gurevich's article, a biographical and psychological study, appeared in the journal *Russkoe bogatsvo* in 1888, and she also translated Bashkirtseva's diaries from French into Russian. "Liubov' Iakovlevna Gurevich," 188; *Dictionary*, s.v. "Gurevich," 236. Stanley J. Rabinowitz, author of the *Dictionary* entry, has made an important contribution chronicling Gurevich's budding feminist consciousness and early literary activities, especially in connection with Bashkirtseva's diary and

SevV. See his "No Room of Her Own: The Early Life and Career of Liubov' Gurevich," *Russian Review* 57 (April 1998): 236–52.

31 On the gifted mathematician and writer Sofia Kovalevskaia, see Ann Hibner Koblitz, *A Convergence of Lives: Sofia Kovalevskaia, Scientist, Writer, Revolutionary,* 2d ed. (New Brunswick, N.J., 1993). Olga Shapir was a *shestidesiatnitsa,* a well-known and prolific writer and feminist activist whose works touched on most of the burning social issues of the day, especially the woman question. Zinaida Vengerova was a prominent literary critic, literary historian, and translator who "played a central role in promoting literary modernism in Russia."

32 V. V. Stasov, *Nadezhda Vasil'evna Stasova: Vospominaniia i ocherki* (St. Petersburg, 1899), 440–41. "Liubov' Iakovlevna Gurevich," 188–97; *Dictionary,* s.v. "Gurevich." For a description of Gurevich's mood after the closing of *SevV,* see "Liubov' Iakovlevna Gurevich," 194–96. For a comprehensive history of *SevV* and an appreciation of Gurevich's key editorial and managerial role and her collaboration with Volynskii, see Stanley J. Rabinowitz, "*Northern Herald:* From Traditional Thick Journal to Forerunner of the Avant-Garde," in *Literary Journals in Imperial Russia,* ed. Deborah A. Martinsen (Cambridge, 1997), 207–27, especially 214–25.

33 "Pokrovskaia," *PZhK na 1905,* 394–96; Belitskaia, "Poliklinicheskaia pomosch'," 64–68; and M. I. Pokrovskaia, *Po podvalam, cherdakam, i uglovnym kvartiram Peterburga* (St. Petersburg, 1903), 52.

34 Belitskaia, "Poliklinicheskaia pomosch'," 67.

35 See Toby Clyman, "Women Physicians' Autobiography in the Nineteenth Century," in *Women Writers in Russian Literature,* ed. Toby W. Clyman and Diana Greene (Westport, Conn., 1994), 111–25.

36 "Pokrovskaia," *PZhK na 1905 god,* 395.

37 Ibid., 396.

38 It is not clear if Pokrovskaia deliberately named her journal after the earlier *ZhV* (1866–1868).

39 Tyrkova, *Na putiakh,* 216–17.

40 Ibid. It is hard to believe that someone who attended the Bestuzhev courses had never thought about women's equality before, but this statement does show a common characteristic of a number of memoirs of Russian feminists. Most omit or discount their feminist activity.

41 Women's suffrage, argued Miliukov, was "unrealistic," would offend peasant men and give the vote to "backward" peasant women, and took time away from more important "questions of principle," such as whether to have a republic or a monarchy. See I. V. Gessen, "V dvukh vekakh: Zhiznennyi otchet," *Arkhiv russkoi revoliutsii* 22 (1937): 204;

and Pavel Miliukov, *Vospominaniia*, 2 vols. (New York, 1955), vol. 1, 308. Anna Miliukova does not seem to have written her version of these events.
42 Tyrkova, *Na putiakh*, 69.
43 Ibid., 293.
44 Tyrkova died in Washington, D.C., at the age of ninety-two. The epitaph for her in the *Russian Review* does not mention her feminist activity, citing only her biography of Anna Filosofova, but without context. See Anita Norman, "Ariadna Tyrkova-Williams," *Russian Review* 21, no. 3 (July 1962): 277–81.
45 *Ravnopravie zhenshchin: Tret'ii s" ezd soiuza ravnopravnosti zhenshchin, otchety i protokoly* (St. Petersburg, 1906), 17.
46 TSGIA, f. 2251, d. 1, no. 163, Gurevich letter to Chekhova, 10 May 1906, l. 2. *Ravnopravie zhenshchin*, 51–52. *Zhenskoe dvizhenie poslednykh dnei* (Odessa, 1905); *9-e ianvaria: Po dannym "anketnoi komissii"* (St. Petersburg, 1905); *Pochemu nuzhno dat' zhenshchinam vse prava i svobody* (St. Petersburg, 1906); and *Zhenskii vopros v Gosudarstvennoi Dume* (St. Petersburg, 1906). The Trudovik (Laborers') Party primarily represented the peasants, was the second largest group in the first Duma, and in overall outlook was closest to the Socialist Revolutionaries.
47 *Zhenskii vopros v Gos. Dume* describes the law project.
48 "Zhenskie delegatsii v parlamentskikh fraktsiakh," *SZh* 1 (June–July 1907): 8–11.
49 *ZhV*, no. 1 (September 1904).
50 M. I. Pokrovskaia, "Zashchitniki i protivniki ravnopraviia zhenshchin v pervoi Gosudarstvennoi Dume," *ZhV*, nos. 7–8 (July–August 1907): 174–76, 176.
51 Pokrovskaia, "Osvoboditel'noe dvizhenie v Rossii," *ZhV*, no. 12 (December 1905): 353–56, 356.
52 Ibid., 354.
53 "Programma zhenskoi progressivnoi partii," *ZhV*, no. 1 (January 1906): 26–29; *Ravnopravie zhenshchin*, 30–31. The Women's Party, the first such political party in the United States, was founded by a group led by Alice Paul in 1916.
54 "Programma," 26–29.
55 For Kollontai, see Alexandra Kollontai, *Sotsial'nie osnovy zhenskogo voprosa* (St. Petersburg, 1909), 314–15. For Chekhova's comments, see *SZh*, no. 3 (October 1907): 5.
56 M. I. Pokrovskaia, "Zadacha zhenskoi progressivnoi partii," *ZhV*, no. 3 (March 1906): 65–69; and "Klub zhenskoi progressivnoi partii," *ZhV*, no. 4 (April 1907): 123–25.
57 *ZhV*.

58 Chekhova's extensive autobiography has not been published. It is in TSGIA, f. 2251, o. 3, d. 1–4, and covers the period from 1866 to 1916.

59 TSGIA, f. 2251, o. 1–3, contain information about the Chekhov children. The delay may have in part been connected to the birth in late November 1906 of the Chekhovs' sixth child, Vladimir, as well as the internal politics of the Union.

60 The list of contributors is in *SZh*, no. 1 (June–July 1907): 24.

61 The first ads ran in the fourth issue of *SZh* and then sporadically after that. See *SZh*, no. 4 (November 1907): 22–23. For press run figures, see *Bibliografiia periodicheskikh izdanii Rossii, 1901–1916,* comp. L. N. Beliaeva, M. K. Zinov'eva, and M. M. Nikiforov, 4 vols. (Leningrad, 1958–1960), vol. 3, 270. For information on average wages of women workers, see Frosina, "Biudzhet semei rabotnits," in *Trudy pervogo vserossiiskogo zhenskogo s"ezda pri russkom zhenskom obshchestve v Sankt-Peterburge 10–16 dekabriia 1908* (St. Petersburg, 1909), 318–40; and Rose Glickman, *Russian Factory Women, Workplace and Society, 1880–1914* (Berkeley, 1984), 115.

62 *SZh*, no. 1 (June–July 1907): 1.

63 M. A. Chekhova, "Bor'ba za pravo, kak nravstvennaia obiazannost' zhenshchiny," *SZh*, no. 3 (October, 1907): 4.

64 *SZh*, no. 2 (August–September 1907): 1. Linda Edmondson, in commenting on the negative connotation of the word "feminist" in Russia, which persists to the present, has noted: "It seems to have been one foreign word that was *not* eagerly adopted by the intelligentsia." See "Women's Rights, Civil Rights, and the Debate over Citizenship in the 1905 Revolution," in *Women and Society in Russia and the Soviet Union,* ed. Linda Edmondson (Cambridge, 1992), 98.

65 Chekhova, "Bor'ba za pravo," 5.

66 Ibid.

67 Ibid.

68 M. I. Pokrovskaia, "Tol'stie zhurnali zhenskoe dvizheniie: *Russkaia mysl'*," *ZhV*, no. 10 (October 1910): 195–202, 199–201. M. A. Chekhova, "Khronika zhenskogo voprosa v Rossii," *SZh*, no. 5 (December 1907): 8–18. For excellent discussions of the context in which the prostitution debates took place, see Laura Engelstein, *The Keys to Happiness: Sex and the Search for Modernity in Fin-de-Siècle Russia* (Ithaca, 1992); and Laurie Bernstein, *Sonia's Daughters: Prostitutes and Their Regulation in Imperial Russia* (Berkeley, 1995).

69 Mariia Chekhova, "K chitateliam zhurnala *Soiuz zhenshchin*," *SZh*, no. 9 (December 1909): 1–2.

70 M. I. Pokrovskaia, "Muzh'ia i *Zhenskii vestnik*," *ZhV*, no. 10 (October 1906): 257–58, 257.

71 Pokrovskaia, "Provintsiia otkliknulas'," *ZhV,* no. 9 (September 1909): 165.
72 Ibid., 164–65.
73 Ibid., 165.
74 Chekhova, "K chitatel'iam," 2.
75 M. V. Orlovskaia, *O zhenskom dvizhenii v Rossii* (St. Petersburg, 1911), 5.
76 *ZhD* 14 (15 July 1912): 6–8.
77 A. V. Tyrkova, "Pervyi zhenskii s"ezd," in *Zarnitsy: Literaturno-politicheskii sbornik,* vol. 2 (St. Petersburg, 1909), 172–209, on the 1908 congress; "V provinstii," *SZh,* no. 5 (May–June 1909): 20–21.
78 Borman, *Tyrkova-Vil'iams,* 277, 278.
79 TSGIA, f. 2251, o. 1, ed. khr. 163, l. 34.
80 "Liubov' Iakovlevna Gurevich," 182. A collection of Gurevich's essays may be found in Liubov' Gurevich, *Literatura i estetika: Kriticheskie opyti i etiudy* (Moscow, 1912). Gurevich's *SZh* articles are "Vopros o ravnopravii zhenshchiny v krest'ianskoi srede," no. 1 (June–July 1907): 9–11; and "Otnoshenie k voprosu o zhenskom izbiratel'nym prave russkogo obshchestve zemstv i gorodov," no. 2 (August–September 1907): 3–5.
81 Liubov' Gurevich, "Vospominaniia," 117–76, 119; and *Modern Encyclopedia,* s.v. "Gurevich."
82 Tyrkova, "Voina," *SZh,* no. 3 (March 1909): 1–2.
83 Ivanova, "Otkrytie Ameriki," *ZhV,* no. 1 (January 1916): 1. For Pokrovskaia's views on wartime prohibition, see M. I., "Otnoshenie zhenshchin k zapreshcheniiu prodazhi spirtnykh napitkov" *ZhV,* no. 3 (March 1915): 91–93.
84 *ZhV,* no. 3 (March 1916): 60–61.
85 Liubov' Gurevich, *Pochemu nuzhno dat' zhenshchinam takie zhe prava, kak muzhchinam* (Petrograd, 1917), 2.
86 Ibid., 3; *ZhV,* no. 4 (April 1917): 49. There is not a word in Tyrkova's memoirs about this suffrage activity or her role in it.
87 Norman, "Tyrkova-Williams," 278.
88 Tyrkova-Williams, *From Liberty to Brest-Litovsk.*
89 Russian archival *fondi* exist for all four women. Gurevich's are located at Institut russkoi literatury-Pushkinskii dom, f. 19805, 20121, Rossiiskii gosudarstvennyi arkhiv literatury i iskusstva, f. 131, o. 1, and Gosudarstvennyi tsentral'nyi teatral'nyi muzei imeni A. A. Bakhrushkina, f. 82. Pokrovskaia's *fond* is located at Tsentral'nyi gosudarstvennyi istoricheskii arkhiv Sankt-Peterburga, f. 1037, o. 1. The archive has been closed for several years; its opening date is still uncertain. Tyrkova's is

located in Gosudarstvennyi arkhiv Rossiiskii Federatsii, f. 629, o. 1. Chekhova's has already been noted.

90 Tyrkova's second husband, Harold Williams, commented on the apathy of educated Russian women: "It is curious that while women students are greatly interested in general questions and flock to public lectures on literature and philosophy, they do not seem to be particularly interested in a specifically women's question and on the whole are indifferent to the suffrage movement." See Harold W. Williams, *Russia of the Russians* (London, 1914), 411.

Mariia Pokrovskaia and *Zhenskii vestnik*

Feminist Separatism in Theory and Practice

LINDA EDMONDSON

Mariia Ivanovna Pokrovskaia was a rather unusual phenomenon in Russia, both in the history of women's journalism and in the history of female emancipation. She was a dedicated feminist with a strong political awareness, who nevertheless refused to incorporate the women's movement into the wider political struggle against autocracy. As Rochelle Ruthchild has shown in the preceding essay, Pokrovskaia was firmly convinced of the natural moral superiority of women and believed that women, unlike men, were naturally cooperative, but in practicing her feminist philosophy, she tended to hold herself aloof from colleagues in the women's movement. Although little is known about her personal life, her journalism gives the impression of an unswerving and almost eccentric dedication to a cause, and a serious approach to life that allowed little hint of humor or irony; all the same, her stories and reports of everyday life reveal a compassionate and intelligent observer. Like so many reformers in Russia, as elsewhere, she was driven by an intense consciousness of the misery of those less fortunate than herself, but while her sympathy for the poor—and especially for poor women—was endless, she was less tolerant of moral failing, particularly when the failures were men.

Her single-mindedness can clearly be seen in the two aspects of her work that most concerned the "cause of women": her unremitting campaign, from the late 1890s to 1917, against state-regulated prostitution and the sexual morality that fed it; and her feminist journal, *Zhenskii vestnik (Women's Herald),* which she founded in 1904, at the height of the Russo-Japanese War, and maintained against all the odds until November 1917. Rochelle Ruthchild has described Pokrovskaia's development as a feminist activist, journalist, and campaigner in the context of women's political activity during and after the 1905 revolution. In this essay, I shall take up some aspects of Pokrovskaia's work and personality that marked her out from most of her contemporaries, and that drove her not only to set up her campaigning journal but to keep it going until it was forced out of circulation after the Bolsheviks took power. In the course of the discussion, I shall attempt to assess the place of Pokrovskaia in the history of Russian women's journalism and the significance of *Zhenskii vestnik* to the women's movement.

Assessing *Zhenskii vestnik* is not as simple as it might appear. Its longevity, when other publications were falling by the wayside, may imbue it with a significance that it did not possess, conveying the false impression that it played a prominent role in feminist politics before the revolution. There is some reason to doubt whether *Zhenskii vestnik*'s influence was ever very significant. At no point was it in tune with the dominant mood among politically active feminists, and throughout its existence, it suffered from such a restricted readership that on several occasions Pokrovskaia was tempted to cease publication.[1] There is no question that the journal is a mine of information about the movement for women's rights and an essential source for historians, but this may well lead us to exaggerate its importance to feminists at the time. All the same, whatever its actual impact on the women's movement, *Zhenskii vestnik* reveals a great deal about current preoccupations, particularly when read together with other feminist publications, such as its shorter-lived rival *Soiuz zhenshchin (Union of Women)*, which briefly became the voice of women's rights activists after the 1905 revolution. Taking a number of issues addressed by Pokrovskaia and her small group of collaborators, it is possible to delineate the journal's physiognomy and to suggest what was characteristic of Pokrovskaia's feminism.[2]

As so little has been written about her early life and experience, and as she seems to have left little autobiographical material, it is a complex task to plot the awakening of a feminist consciousness. Even the details of her professional career are unclear: though her fictional account of several years spent as a Duma doctor in St. Petersburg has always been taken as autobiographical, one résumé of her life in 1905 noted that after moving to the city, she worked in the hygiene laboratory at the Military-Medical Academy and "did not practice [medicine]."[3] Although it is evident from her choice of career that she possessed a strongly developed social conscience from her earliest years and that she had sufficient determination and self-confidence to step over conventional gender boundaries to train as a doctor, it is not so obvious that she had yet begun to ponder the woman question or had begun to think of herself as a feminist. Her first published writings were scientific pieces on her laboratory work and journal articles on aspects of public health, based on her years working as a doctor, followed soon after by accounts of workers' living conditions in St. Petersburg and popular pamphlets on hygiene and health care.[4] Though addressed to women as mothers and housekeepers, her pamphlets did not differ essentially from many similar publications of the period proffering advice on hygiene and nutrition to a "popular" readership. If she had continued to write in this vein, she would be remembered, if at all, as a prolific publicist on popular health issues, not as a feminist and campaigner against prostitution.

It was only in middle age, toward the end of the 1890s, that Pokrovskaia turned her attention specifically to an aspect of the woman question, when she took up arms against police-regulated prostitution. Besides her work in the Russian Society for the Preservation of Public Health, which Rochelle Ruthchild has described, Pokrovskaia became involved in the Russian Society for the Defense of Women (Rossiiskoe obshchestvo zashchity zhenshchin), the national branch of a prestigious and well-patronized international network established in 1899 to fight the "white slave trade."[5] Neither of these societies had any connection with feminism, however; the latter, in particular, benefited from official patronage and was established on a firm hierarchical (and male-dominated) structure. But within a few years, her crusade against prostitution had become explicitly feminist. While she remained adamant, like her fellow campaigners, that state-controlled "vice" encouraged sexual corruption and depravity, leading inevitably to the moral and physical degeneration of the Russian people, her critique of prostitution became increasingly preoccupied with the specific effects of "the trade in flesh" on women. Like other feminists, she was concerned both for the prostitutes themselves and for the "innocent" wives of the prostitutes' clients. Her target was as much society's tolerance of prostitution as it was the vice itself, and she made increasing use of journalism (and her own journal) to get the message across.[6]

At some point (it is not known exactly when), Pokrovskaia became a member of the Russian Women's Mutual Philanthropic Society (Russkoe zhenskoe vzaimno-blagotvoritel'noe obshchestvo), founded in 1895. This cumbersome name had been imposed on the society by the Ministry of Internal Affairs, which had insisted that women were legally disbarred from membership in any social organization lacking a clear educational or philanthropic purpose. Pokrovskaia's membership in the society—the first general women's organization to be permitted in Russia—suggests that she was well aware of women's unequal status in society and wished to change it.

Even so, it is still unclear whether she had yet developed the coherent feminist philosophy and campaigning energy that marked her years as editor of *Zhenskii vestnik*. In her preoccupation with issues of education and upbringing, and particularly with the moral development of children, her concern before 1904 seems, from her published writings, to have been mainly to inculcate an appropriate attitude to work, moral purity, and personal responsibility (not, after all, a uniquely feminist approach and one shared with much of Russia's intelligentsia and professional groups), rather than to draw attention to the unequal position of women. Although she had an explicit concept of gender difference (women, she believed, were less aggressive, more conciliatory, and more responsive to ethical values), she seems at this stage to have had quite a conventional viewpoint, revealed not so much in a developed argument as in passing comments about, for example, the ability of men of genius to overcome hardship and misfortune, or in assumptions about appropriate professions for men and for women.[7] Her observations (published in a journal aimed at parents and educators) reveals little awareness that sex roles may be stereotyped to the disadvantage of women, though as one of the first women doctors, she repeatedly had to overcome such stereotypes in her working life and commented on this fact in her fictional memoirs, written only a year later.[8] Equally striking in these early publications is the virtual absence of bitter antagonism toward men that later became a common feature of her writing in *Zhenskii vestnik*.

Pokrovskaia remained a member of the Mutual Philanthropic Society until the end of 1905. By the time she launched *Zhenskii vestnik*, however, she was already dissatisfied with the society's lack of dynamism and failure to break out of the official restrictions imposed on it.⁹ Along with many of those most active in the women's movement, she expressed an impatience to move on to a more direct involvement in the politics of women's rights. Unlike many, however, she does not appear to have participated in any of the unofficial associations working for political change that were coalescing into the self-styled Liberation movement after 1900. She was more at home in societies concerned with health issues and campaigns against regulated prostitution than she was with national politics; from everything that we know about her, she established a certain distance from opposition politics early on, and at no time up to 1917 did she attempt to draw closer. In this she makes a striking contrast to the activists who set up the Women's Equal Rights Union (Soiuz ravnopraviia zhenshchin) during 1905, all of whom were part of a cultural and political intelligentsia, with many ties and points of contact beyond the women's movement.[10]

Women's participation in the Liberation movement — a network of left-of-center liberals and moderate socialists — was quite marginal. Although a few were generally acknowledged to be at its center — most notably Ekaterina Kuskova — many achieved little recognition from their male colleagues, even though they considered themselves to be intimately involved in the movement's work and goals and, indeed, often performed many of the secretarial chores of the organizations.[11] Marriage to a liberal or socialist activist seems to have enabled some of these women to take a more prominent role in the movement (marriage to, and collaboration with, Prokopovich may have improved Kuskova's position vis-à-vis their colleagues), but women lacking this social advantage were far less likely to be taken seriously as political activists.[12] Indeed, it was their experience within the Liberation movement that released much of the energy that was directed into the struggle for women's equality during the 1905 revolution.[13] Although this campaign was addressed first and foremost to the government, much of the work during the revolutionary year was devoted to persuading male-dominated political unions to incorporate female suffrage into their programs.

Pokrovskaia's political activity went in a different direction. At the point when the Liberation movement was first taking coherent form and when open protest against both the autocratic system and the catastrophic conduct of the war with Japan was intensifying, she launched *Zhenskii vestnik*. It was certainly a brave undertaking; up to that time, no journal dedicated to the woman question had survived more than a few years, and there was no reason for Pokrovskaia to believe that her journal would be more enduring. On the other hand, the situation was more promising now. The growing strength of the political opposition naturally encouraged the setting up of new publications, even with the risk that the police would later close them down (as they did quite frequently during the 1905 upheaval).[14] The journal also stood a greater chance of surviving, as women were becoming restless to be more involved in politics and to claim political rights for themselves.

There is a certain irony, though, that the first and only feminist journal to survive for more than a few years should have been founded by someone whose open distrust of men in liberal and socialist politics kept her at a distance from the Liberation movement, at the very moment when the majority of active feminists were keen to identify with that movement.[15] Although Pokrovskaia's aims were much the same as those of the feminists who in 1905 set up the Women's Equal Rights Union under the umbrella of the left-liberal Union of Unions (Soiuz soiuzov), they were separated by their differing perceptions of the political situation and their differing assessments of men as allies. Yet the Union of Women was forced to depend on *Zhenskii vestnik* at least to some degree, as the organization lacked a journal of its own until 1907, by which time the revolutionary wave had subsided and the union itself was dying.[16]

At first glance, the response of *Zhenskii vestnik* to political developments in 1905 and its reporting of the movement for women's rights seem to have differed little from the union's. The journal followed the union's campaign for female suffrage closely and recorded a mass of information on women's issues from all over Russia (as well as abroad) for its monthly news summary. It poured scorn on men in the Liberation movement who made high-minded commitments to universal suffrage but excluded women, as when the Moscow municipal Duma decided that female suffrage was "inopportune," and it appeared to approve of the Union of Women's tactics on the issue.[17] The disagreements soon became evident, however. Nowhere was this more clearly expressed than in an article by one of the journal's contributors, entitled "To the Female Opponents of Women's Separatism," which challenged Union of Women members to defend their policy of working within the male-led opposition.[18]

Having so little information about Pokrovskaia's early years and personal life, it is impossible to say whether the increasingly caustic comments on men's morality and behavior that became noticeable as she grew older (she was fifty-two in 1904) were a response to her own experience, or whether it was simply that her true opinion was more openly articulated in the outspoken (and less censored) political and cultural environment during and after 1905. One can only speculate whether her decision to set up a journal was a long-term ambition made possible by her established reputation as a writer on health and hygiene and as a campaigner against the white slave trade, or whether it was much more a spontaneous reaction to the intensifying political and social crisis in Russia after the outbreak of the Russo-Japanese War. Equally one has to guess whether her disinclination to treat men as potential allies had always been part of her outlook, finding public expression once the women's movement abandoned its reticence at the end of 1904, or whether (as with many feminists in Russia) it was a process of disenchantment as it became increasingly clear that most of the men involved in liberal and socialist politics were unenthusiastic, to say the least, about committing themselves to women's political rights.

Whatever its source, there is no doubt that Pokrovskaia's particular brand of feminism was strongly, even passionately, felt. She became convinced that men were largely responsible for the evils of the world, that they had allowed their aggressive instincts and their urge toward domination to destroy the harmony of nature, bringing untold misery to human society. Her message, relayed in virtually every issue of *Zhenskii vestnik*, was that women must expect very little from men, that they should not depend on them in their struggle for their own emancipation and that they should refuse to subordinate their interests to any political movement led by men.[19] At the same time, however, she did not take the extreme position of refusing to work within the existing political system because it had been created by men for their own benefit and reflected their interests. She argued, as did many feminists all over the world, that women must be enfranchised, both for their own liberation and for the salvation of society.²⁰ Politics as currently defined and pursued by men could, and must, be transformed by women's equal participation. Indeed, as Rochelle Ruthchild points out, much of the frustration Pokrovskaia vented in her thirteen years' editorship of the journal was directed not against men but against women, because of their apparent indifference to their own fate, unwillingness to respond to the call of feminism (as defined by *Zhenskii vestnik*), and inability to recognize their power to bring about the regeneration of Russian society.

Her readiness to use a male political system while simultaneously berating the men who made it put her at odds with a considerable number of feminists who otherwise shared her skepticism of men's good faith and, like her, resisted the pressure to integrate the women's movement with the Liberation movement. Pokrovskaia's criticism of the strategy of the Women's Equal Rights Union during 1905 attracted these feminists to her new political venture, the Women's Progressive Party (Zhenskaia progressivnaia partiia), at the end of the year, but they soon withdrew after a stormy meeting in February 1906, when it became clear that the party would concern itself with general political issues rather than concentrating solely on those of direct concern to women.²¹

Whether this schism dealt a mortal blow to the new party is hard to say. The failure of the Women's Progressive Party to thrive may have had less to do with an initial split than with the change in political circumstances at the end of 1905. By that time (after the revolutionary uprising in Moscow in December), the tsarist authorities were regaining the political initiative. The scope for feminist political action during 1906 was increasingly limited; the Women's Equal Rights Union was already troubled by inner dissension and restrictions on its activities, and the Women's Progressive Party offered nothing that would make it more appealing to feminists trying to work within the system. Pokrovskaia had anticipated that the establishment of the State Duma would provide opportunities for women to directly influence its proceedings via their own political party. In this she was woefully optimistic, not only about the Duma's durability and the responsiveness of its electorate (exclusively male) to a fringe feminist organization but, perhaps most important of all, about feminists' willingness to work in a women's party that stood apart from the Liberation movement. In general, Pokrovskaia does not seem to have been very sophisticated politically, though her rather off-putting tendency to moralize may have disguised a useful pragmatism. In one respect, she may have been more astute than the leaders of the Equal Rights Union by taking advantage of the new laws on association and assembly and setting up a legally registered Club of the Women's Progressive Party in St. Petersburg.[22]

What, then, was most characteristic of Pokrovskaia's feminism, how was it distinguished from the politics of the Women's Equal Rights Union and its supporters, and what sort of impact did her journal have on the Russian women's movement? The most obvious difference between Pokrovskaia and the union was over relations with the Liberation movement and her insistence on remaining detached from it. Despite some of her barbed criticisms of men as allies in the struggle for equal rights, Pokrovskaia did not refuse to cooperate with them on principle. Indeed, a number of those who pledged their support for *Zhenskii vestnik* were men who had already written sympathetically about the women's movement.[23] She was happy to acknowledge the positive response of "the best people," supporters of women's suffrage in the first Duma, who "were able to rise above age-old prejudice and put human ideals and the good of the country in first place."[24] At the same time, however, she remained skeptical of the commitment of the political parties as a whole to ensuring the equality of women. In this she was by no means unique; feminists who had worked most intensively within the Liberation movement were among the most disenchanted in the years following the 1905 revolution, and a few leading figures in the Equal Rights Union were hardly less bitter than Pokrovskaia about liberal ambivalence on the issue.[25]

Nonetheless they continued to work with the new political parties and to criticize the "narrow separatism" of feminists like Pokrovskaia.[26] It is significant that she was one of the few in Russia to interpret the word "feminist" positively, and she wrote with apparent astonishment at others' refusal to class themselves as such. She insisted that contrary to common misunderstanding, feminists did not want to increase the isolation of one sex from the other. Instead they aimed to bring the two sexes together by ensuring women's equality. The issue of separation, she claimed, concerned only the methods by which this should be achieved. It was not simply because women alone knew the true burden of their own oppression. It was also because few men could be trusted to support the cause through thick and thin. In the same article, however, she made it clear that (contrary to hostile claims) feminism was not a war between the sexes. "Among men there are feminists, and among women antifeminists. Therefore feminism must be defined not as a struggle of women against men, but as a struggle for the equal rights of women."[27]

This conflict was undoubtedly damaging for the women's movement, at a time when unity would indeed have been a source of strength. Whatever the justice of the movement's aims, and the personal sympathies of considerable numbers of liberal and socialist men, female suffrage could easily be dismissed as a diversion from the "real" demands of political life, if suffragists like Pokrovskaia and members of the Equal Rights Union were themselves split not only on tactics but even on their own identification with the concept of feminism. In their failure to agree, they differed little from their male colleagues in the Liberation movement. But this was hardly a consolation, in a movement that was founded on the belief that women in the political life of the future would be more cooperative and constructive than men had proved to be.[28]

For all its significance, however, Pokrovskaia's separatism was not the sole feature of her feminism to alienate her from others in the women's movement. Possibly more profound were differences in personal outlook and philosophy. Although she paid close attention to political developments in Russia and devoted many column inches to the fate of the women's suffrage movement, both at home and abroad, she leaves the impression of a person whose interest in politics was secondary to an intense preoccupation with social and personal morality. This is not to say that she lacked a political instinct — her attack on the liberal Fedor Kokoshkin in the summer of 1905, when he justified the exclusion of women from the franchise, testifies to a real gusto for political polemics, which she retained right up to 1917.[29] The campaign for female suffrage suffered a sharp decline after the dissolution of the second Duma in 1907, but when it began to revive in 1912, *Zhenskii vestnik* was there to record and comment on the latest developments. All the same, she was driven by a concern for the spiritual and moral welfare of the Russian people to a degree that is not found in most of the feminists who identified with the Liberation movement. Though an ethical approach to life was a central element in their own feminist beliefs, most tended to be more pragmatic than Pokrovskaia. The dominant ethos in the Equal Rights Union was a left-leaning humanitarianism, a not very precisely defined mixture of egalitarian liberalism and ethical socialism, if with many variations in emphasis between the union's leading members. They were looking for civil and political equality and justice as ends in themselves, whereas Pokrovskaia trod the suffrage path in pursuit of personal and social perfectibility.

A clear example of her approach to politics can be seen in a piece that she wrote in response to Lev Tolstoi's verdict on the 1905 revolution.[30] Tolstoi, lamenting the rapacious violence of the upheaval, had condemned the opposition's pursuit of a legislative assembly as a harmful delusion. He believed that power of any sort "debauched" people.[31] If the masses, who had for so long been oppressed by tsarist force, acquired a voice in government, they too would become complicit in the use of force over their fellow human beings. This would be an evil. Pokrovskaia could not agree. She had enormous respect for "our great writer" and was in her own way as uncompromising in her beliefs as he was. But she had a different view of representative government; in those many instances where it existed on a foundation of violence, she argued, the fault lay not with the principle but with the "level of morality in modern civilized society." Representative government was not "power" (understood as legalized violence) but "a means of organizing society's affairs" on a new foundation. She also objected to Tolstoi's condemnation of the women's suffrage movement for aiming, as he so revealingly put it, to "inflict this debauchery on women too." On the contrary, she replied, the experience of women's suffrage in other countries showed that women had a "beneficial influence" on politics and raised the moral level of parliament.[32]

For all that she repudiated Tolstoi's attitude to liberal democracy, the attraction of his teachings remained strong. Personal morality must be the guide to behavior in every sphere of life. Society was striving toward the great ideals of fraternity, equality, freedom, and justice, but these could be achieved only by means of "the moral improvement of humanity." "We believe that hygiene, social and personal, has an immense significance here, as it alone can create that harmony of body and spirit which ought to exist in developed people and could create the perfect social system." Spiritual health was as important as physical, both for the individual and for society.[33]

What did Pokrovskaia mean by "hygiene"? At one level she was referring quite simply to basic issues of sanitation and the prevention of disease. In her medical practice, she had been horrified by her patients' ignorance and by the general absence of sanitation in their homes and at work. She became convinced that all her pharmacological training was useless in an environment where people did not have enough to eat and no knowledge of nutrition and sanitation, and where they had little defense against the spread of infectious disease.[34] The pamphlets that she wrote for a popular readership focused on these questions, in the hope that ordinary people would free themselves from the tyranny of sickness and premature mortality and thus be enabled to lead more rewarding and productive lives.

But as her comments on Tolstoi show, she saw physical well-being as inseparable from spiritual health and moral wholesomeness ("a healthy mind in a healthy body"). Morality for Pokrovskaia concerned every aspect of a person's thoughts and behavior, but it had a particular sexual connotation. She was by no means alone among feminists in her campaign against state-regulated prostitution, nor unique in her belief that women's emancipation was impossible without the creation of a "single moral standard" for men and women, based on sexual abstinence before marriage and self-control within it. She was at one with other feminists in detesting prostitution because it exploited women and exposed them to physical danger, disease, and social stigma.[35] But whereas others (for example, in the Equal Rights Union) argued that prostitution was above all a matter of economics and civil rights, dependent on women's depressed wages and low status, she believed that it was both a symptom and a cause of a corrupt culture, which exploited women but degraded both sexes, and put at risk the physical survival of the entire nation. She differed from many other feminists, too, in believing that sex was primarily for the procreation of the species, not for sensual gratification, even within marriage.[36]

Hygiene for Pokrovskaia, as for many eminent medical experts and social moralists, was as much about the purity of the species as it was about unpolluted water. Though she never made eugenics a central focus of her work, its influence can be seen in much of her writing, as well as in articles by some of her contributors to *Zhenskii vestnik*. Bad sanitation, infectious disease, sexual self-indulgence, prostitution, the collapse of moral standards—all endangered not only the health of the present generation but the future of the species. In her early article on the upbringing of children, she had claimed that young men's sexual promiscuity in France would lead to the degeneration of the French people.[37] In later writings she emphasized the dangers to the integrity of Russia that would result from the thriving sex trade and the abandonment of a strict moral code. She considered abortion a brutal way of limiting births and believed that "science" would find a more acceptable solution, but in existing conditions—and for the sake of future generations—she supported the growing campaign to decriminalize abortion.[38] Laura Engelstein suggests that Pokrovskaia's preoccupation with eugenics intensified in later years; if this was indeed so, it may have been a response to prevailing intellectual trends rather than a major shift in her own outlook.[39]

For all her passion on this subject, however, she was not so dogmatic as to bar differing opinions from her journal. Although none of her contributors preached unrestrained hedonism—all had an ethical purpose in what they wrote—she gave space to writers critical of her own views and encouraged debate about serious moral issues. One of her own short stories, concerning a young woman who rejects the man she loves when he takes sexual advantage of her, set off a heated exchange. In Pokrovskaia's view, the young woman has not only been sexually defiled; she is also completely misunderstood by her lover, who cannot see that she wishes above all to be a "human being" *(chelovek)* and not just a "female" *(samka)*.[40] The journal's Berlin correspondent M. Rogovich took issue with Pokrovskaia. Sexual love was normal, he argued; the abnormality lay in the repressive culture that educated "nice" women to believe that sex was bad. He disputed the claim of another correspondent, M. V. Orlovskaia, that women needed marriage to protect them from the irresponsibility and viciousness of men, and he argued that marriage gave women no protection at all from oppression and exploitation.[41]

Another regular contributor, M. L. Vakhtina, was of the same opinion. Marriage, she claimed, could only imprison women in an unequal relationship if it ceased to be founded on mutual love and respect. There must be a "spiritual bond" uniting a couple, but in love, as in all else, body and soul are inseparable: "Spiritual, platonic love without a relationship of the flesh is an idea; carnal love without spiritual oneness is debauchery."[42] This was an outlook that Pokrovskaia may well have found intellectually sympathetic; in her own writings, however, she tended to portray physical love as an obstacle to a woman's autonomy and energy, which would otherwise be devoted to rewarding work and the improvement of society.[43] At the same time, her concern for the health and welfare of mothers and their children, and her fears for the future of the human race, led her to place great emphasis on "sexual hygiene"; one feels that in her innermost soul, she wished sex did not exist, but as it did, she wished it to be wholesome, honest, and productive of healthy issue.

Sexuality and men's sexual exploitation of women were the dominating moral preoccupations that drove Pokrovskaia for the last twenty years of her career. Her campaign against prostitution, and her conviction that society was scandalously refusing to take the problem seriously, colored her perception of the work of others in the women's movement. In her verdict on the First All-Russian Congress of Women (Pervyi vserossiiskii zhenskii s"ezd) in December 1908, for example, she accused the organizers of paying insufficient attention to this burning topic, although an entire session had been devoted to the subject and it had featured prominently in debates on female poverty and exploited labor, women's rights, and sexual ethics.[44] As I have tried to show in this essay, her concept of morality was all-encompassing; she possessed a vision of a future society built on unshakable moral principles, guaranteeing social justice and equality, the protection of the weak, and the renunciation of violence. Her sympathy for Tolstoi's uncompromising opposition to the use of force, however, did not save her from a profound ambiguity in her response to actual conflict involving Russia and its enemies. Both during the Russo-Japanese War (the moment when she launched her journal) and ten years later, on the outbreak of the First World War, her pacifist principles were engaged in a losing battle with a vigorous patriotism, which during the war with Germany came close to the bellicosity she so deplored in men.

There was nothing out of the ordinary about her ambivalence. Few feminists (or their male colleagues in the opposition) demanded an end to the war with Japan until it had been raging for almost a year, in a succession of humiliating defeats for Russian troops and for

Russia's international prestige. The First World War imposed an even stronger pressure on feminists to render obeisance to patriotic duty. Those in Russia who could not do so chose silence or were censored; public opposition, when it did find an outlet, was rarely pacifist, but rather the militantly "defeatist" position of the "Zimmerwald Left," Lenin's Social Democrats, who denounced the capitulation of the Socialist International to patriotism and spent the war years attempting to turn the "imperialist war" into a war against "capitalist imperialism."[45]

Whatever their motives, feminists like Pokrovskaia, who believed women to be the world's natural peacemakers, exposed themselves to serious charges of inconsistency and hypocrisy when they offered their support to the government in time of war. It is not at all clear whether Pokrovskaia herself recognized this dilemma. In *Zhenskii vestnik* she adroitly maintained women's natural superiority to men while demonstrating women's equal commitment to the nation. In her first issue, in 1904, she rebutted the charge that women were doing nothing while men's lives were being sacrificed in the war with Japan, by citing the work of nurses and female doctors, the unpaid contribution of women in philanthropy, and the everyday routine of mothers caring for their families while their men were away at war. In doing so, she even managed to turn the tables on her male critic by implying that women were the more responsible and moral citizens by staying at home.[46]

The outbreak of the First World War elicited a more impassioned and complex response from Pokrovskaia.[47] She saw the conflict as a disaster for Europe, a return to barbarism, the deliberate self-destruction of a sophisticated culture that had taken centuries to develop and mature. It was a body blow for those who had believed that Europe's civilization would lead humanity to "the brotherhood of nations and eternal peace." At the same time, she derived a sort of masochistic pleasure from the catastrophe. This was a civilization that had depended on conquest and the overweening power of the few over the many, of the strong over the weak, enshrining the domination of men over women in the "natural" order of things. Like a "luxuriant and gaudy flower," Germany had blossomed in the fertile soil of modern civilization, but concealed within it was a "powerful venom that has slowly poisoned Europe and is quite capable of destroying it." The poison that had been eating away at human society "since immemorial" was "the lust for power."[48]

Germany was the aggressor in this war, but the underlying problem was "the megalomania and lust for power that to a greater or lesser degree has infected almost the entire male half of humankind, giving contemporary culture its particular quality." At certain moments in history, this "masculine disposition toward power and the rule of brute force" would find its expression in a particular individual—Alexander the Great, Attila, Genghis Khan, Napoleon I, and now the Emperor Wilhelm II.[49] But Pokrovskaia was clear that this was a characteristic shared exclusively by men. Her desire to blame men for the war and to absolve women of responsibility, however, collided with a sincere patriotism (quite unprompted by the censor) that would not allow her to see Russian soldiers driven by the same destructive impulses as their German enemies. This was a war for the defense of the Russian motherland, in which men and women must play an equal part. Although she saw women's contribution primarily as noncombatants, by 1917 she had modified her view, expressed during the Russo-Japanese War, that "women soldiers do not serve human progress,"[50] and she gave an unconditional welcome to the women's battalions when they were formed in 1917. By this time, she fervently supported the "knockout blow" launched by Russia and its allies to defeat Germany.[51] With the Provisional Government desperately trying to keep Russia in the war, she had moved as far from her earlier pacifism as it was possible to go. If women had possessed a "decisive voice" in the affairs of the nation, she proclaimed, this dreadful war would never have been waged. But having precipitated Europe into the conflict, men had proved incapable of bringing it to a successful conclusion. It was left to women to take on the responsibility. "History tells us that in ancient times, when Slav men refused to fight, the women would seize their swords and kill their husbands and sons as traitors. Women nowadays will not kill their own relatives. They would prefer to die themselves, as the women's battalions of death all over Russia have shown us."[52]

Although Pokrovskaia's belief in men's propensity for violence was compromised by her need to prove that women could be effective warriors in defense of their homeland, she remained rather more consistent in opposing the use of force for political ends. Rochelle

Ruthchild has discussed Pokrovskaia's hostility to strikes in 1905 and to the revolutionary violence of the Moscow uprising at the end of that year. Pokrovskaia's opinion did not change. Though she had boundless sympathy for the British suffragettes when they adopted violent tactics in their campaign for the vote during the succeeding decade, she did not advocate similar methods in her homeland, and she continued to look on the parties of the extreme Left in Russia with great unease.[53] Her negative attitude to the Social Democrats was fueled by their violent rhetoric of revolutionary upheaval and class warfare, not only because it threatened bloodshed and expropriation but also because it rejected the feminist belief in the solidarity of women across class lines.[54] On the woman question, feminists such as Pokrovskaia and the leading figures in social democracy maintained a state of mutual antipathy, which doubtless added to her anger at the Social Democrats' tactics overall. This was particularly marked during the critical months of mid-1917, when the Bolsheviks' determination to pull Russia out of the war and to overthrow the Provisional Government prompted a fierce rebuttal of the aims and methods of the revolutionaries.

Pokrovskaia took issue with their concept of freedom for being founded not on "strivings toward the ideal" but on "coarse materialistic motives." She demanded to know why it was necessary for the masses to use violence to defeat the minority. Invoking the authority of Jack London (one of Lenin's favorite writers), she claimed that the violent defeat of a once powerful minority would prove to be a hollow victory; the masses would not be able to create strong and enduring institutions; "by their 'arbitrary' actions they will create the right environment for the minority to seize back its power." The ensuing struggle "will awaken the wild beast of revenge, enmity, hatred, which will spare neither itself nor others, and usher in a terrible wild orgy of horrors, such as fill the chronicles of earlier revolutions."[55]

Reading Pokrovskaia's political journalism in the context of present-day feminist writing, one is struck by some remarkable similarities. In many ways, she could easily be categorized as a separatist feminist, with an emphasis on gender difference and a deeply felt distrust of men as allies. It is unclear, though, whether she believed masculinity and femininity to be innately differentiated, or whether she saw them as inculcated and reinforced by society; in all her writings there is a constant tension between her belief that men tended naturally toward violent domination and a more open-minded perception of human personality as infinitely malleable and perfectible. Her faith in women's natural pacifism, too, becomes increasingly unstable as the horrors of the First World War unfold. Her unambiguous approval of the women's battalions makes a particularly striking contrast to her refusal in the Russo-Japanese War to contemplate the idea of women fighting. Equally remarkable is her frequent invocation of bold and even bloodthirsty imagery in her writing; she evidently derives considerable pleasure from her verbal assault on men's brutality and destructiveness.[56]

Pokrovskaia's concept of gender roles is also somewhat ambiguous. In her own life, she appears to have led an independent and autonomous existence, unencumbered by personal ties and the practicalities of family life. She was emphatic that women should not be dependent, and her distrust of sexuality stemmed partly from a belief that women lost their autonomy when they made intense emotional attachments. Socially useful work and a responsible attitude toward others would provide a purpose in life: women were as capable as men intellectually and better suited emotionally to a wide range of occupations (such as her own field of medicine).

Coexisting with this quest for independence was her sincere concern for working women and their burden of child rearing, housework, and family health care. She tended to see other women, especially "women of simple rank," as mothers, while apparently eschewing that role for herself. One wonders whether she saw women as "natural homemakers," despite her own distrust of marriage. Is there a contradiction in her work and life between the ideal of the independent and unattached woman working usefully for the community, and an underlying belief that women belong above all to the home and private space?

It is difficult to know how to place Pokrovskaia among her contemporaries. Her writing is imbued with a concern for personal and social morality (above all, sexual morality) that is far more characteristic of her time than it is of ours, although she undoubtedly alienated other feminists by her single-minded pursuit of moral perfection, as well as by her separatism. She was as uncompromising in her distrust of the currently fashionable free love as she was in her detestation of the old duplicitous moral standards, but at the same time, she gave space in her journal to opposing views, provided that they were grounded in morality. Her critics argued for a liberation of sensual love from patriarchal repression, but she remained wary of sensual love altogether.

These debates clearly reflect the preoccupations of her contemporaries in the women's movement. All the same, the emphasis that she and some of her collaborators placed on the "sexual question" makes quite a contrast to the politically engaged feminist activism of the Women's Equal Rights Union. Even bearing in mind that the union did not long survive the collapse of the 1905 revolution, and that in the years of political reaction after 1907, personal politics and moral issues became more salient in the women's movement, Pokrovskaia still stands apart from her contemporaries in the Liberation movement as driven by moral imperatives and an unwillingness to engage in the subtleties of day-to-day political maneuvering.

If it is difficult to assess Pokrovskaia's influence in the women's movement, it is equally problematic to sum her up as a journalist. Running a campaigning journal for a cause that was so unappealing to the mass of educated readers and to the journalists who wrote for them, she and *Zhenskii vestnik* can easily be dismissed as marginal, even eccentric. It is hard to be inspired nowadays by the journal's moralizing certainties; one admires Pokrovskaia more for her perseverance and her commitment to sexual equality and social welfare than for her rather puritanical concept of the ideal society. It is tempting, nonetheless, to ask the unanswerable question: would she have been a more influential journalist if she had been a man? More hypothetically still: if women had not been working on the cultural margins, would she, as a woman journalist, have found a wider audience? She was a writer of strong convictions and confidence in expressing them, and she possessed a vivid and often impassioned prose style (if one tending to repetition and hyperbole). One can imagine her, in a different journalistic culture, writing with assurance about issues of the day, and being read as an "authority."

Instead she was a feminist campaigner editing and writing for a small readership and becoming embroiled in the politics and disagreements of the women's movement. By this I do not mean that her work was insignificant and without value, but rather that the exclusion of women from the mainstream of cultural life led her to devote a large period of her life to campaigning on behalf of women, and in doing so to slip into the category of the marginal. As a feminist campaigner, she was preaching to a large mass of the unconverted, not just because of what she had to say but also because she was a woman journalist lacking the voice of authority. Her passions seem eccentric at times, not only because of the vehemence with which they were expressed but as much because they *were* so far from the (masculine) center of the cultural world.

The problems that she had to face as a feminist journalist were not unique to her. But many of her contemporaries in the women's movement worked in other areas of journalism as well as feminism. Pokrovskaia was unique in devoting herself so unstintingly to "the cause of women." Her journal bears witness to a remarkable life and an extraordinary commitment to a set of values that were so generally undervalued by her own society.

Notes

This essay forms part of a research project funded by the Economic and Social Research Council in Britain: "Gender and Citizenship in Russia, 1860–1920: Issues of Equality and Difference."

1 For more detail, see Rochelle Ruthchild's essay in this volume.
2 I use "feminism" in the broadest sense to describe an awareness of a fundamental social inequality between the sexes and a belief that this inequality should be removed.
3 See *PZhK na 1905 god*, 395. Her "memoirs," set in the provincial town of X, were published as a separate pamphelt, *Kak ia byla gorodskim vrachom dlia bednykh (Iz vospominanii zhenshchiny-vracha)* (St. Petersburg, 1903). These are used by E. Ia. Belitskaia, in "Poliklinicheskaia pomoshch' v dorevoliutsionnom Peterburge i uchastie v nei zhenshchin vrachei," *Sovetskoe zdravookhranenie* 10 (1972): 64–68. I am very grateful to Rochelle Ruthchild for this reference. Belitskaia notes that Pokrovskaia's name is listed in a Petersburg yearbook as a Duma doctor, though she does not give the date (p. 64). She also refers to Pokrovskaia's clinical research. It seems quite possible that Pokrovskaia worked in the hygiene laboratory before being employed by the city. If so, there may have been a link: one woman doctor listed by Belitskaia

was M. P. Dobroslavina, sister of a noted professor of hygiene, A. P. Dobroslavin, Pokrovskaia's director at the laboratory. See also Pokrovskaia's article "Moia dumskaia praktika," *MirB*, no. 3 (1898): 17–27.

4 *PZhK*, 395.

5 Ibid., 395–96. For a detailed discussion of the police regulation of prostitution in Russia and information on its defenders and opponents, including Pokrovskaia, see Laura Engelstein, *The Keys to Happiness: Sex and the Search for Modernity in Fin-de-Siècle Russia* (Ithaca, 1992), especially 84–92. See also Laurie Bernstein, *Sonia's Daughters: Prostitutes and Their Regulation in Imperial Russia* (Berkeley, 1995).

6 Her pamphlets on the theme included *Vrachebno-politseiskii nadzor za prostitusiei sposobstvuet vyrozhdeniiu naroda* (St. Petersburg, 1902), and *O zhertvakh obshchestvennogo temperamenta: Chto delat' c prostitutsiei* (St. Petersburg, 1902). A common middle-class euphemism for a licensed brothel at that time was "house of tolerance" *(dom terpimosti, maison de tolérance)*.

7 See the chapter "O dushevnoi energii u detei," in M. I. Pokrovskaia, *Voprosy vospitaniia* (St. Petersburg, 1902), especially 29, 31.

8 *Kak ia byla gorodskim vrachom*, 6, 53, 57, 66–67.

9 For more information on the restrictions, see E. A. Chebysheva-Dmitrieva, "O russkom zhenskom vzaimno-blagotvoritel'nom obshchestve v S-Peterburge," in *Trudy 1-go vserossiiskogo zhenskogo s"ezda pri Russkom Zhenskom (Vzaimno-Blagotvoritel'nom) Obshchestve v S-Peterburge 16–19 dek. 1908 goda* (St. Petersburg, 1909), 586. This is summarized in Linda Edmondson, *Feminism in Russia, 1900–1917* (Stanford, 1984), 21.

10 Though Pokrovskaia had her own circle of colleagues, few are familiar from other contexts in the way that Ariadna Tyrkova, Liubov' Gurevich, Mariia Chekhova, and others such as Anna Miliukova are.

11 In her memoirs, Tyrkova writes, for example, that during the campaign for the first State Duma, "women shouldered the burden of most of the unskilled labor [chernaia rabota] of the elections," distributing leaflets, collecting money, arranging meetings, and so on, despite their continuing exclusion from the franchise. A. V. Tyrkova-Vil'iams, *Na putiakh k svobode* (New York, 1952), 257.

12 For an excellent discussion of Kuskova's ambiguous position, see Barbara Norton's essay in this volume.

13 Marriage to a prominent opposition activist by no means guaranteed access to political influence for women; in some cases, the relationship itself may have sharpened a feminist outlook.

14 For an all too typical example, see the fate of two publications, *NZ* and *Tovarishch,* described by Barbara Norton.

15 See Edmondson, *Feminism in Russia,* for a fuller discussion of feminists' relations with the political opposition in Russia.
16 The Union of Unions was a coalition of professional and special interest unions set up in spring 1905 to campaign for constitutional government. For a detailed history of the Liberation movement, including the Union of Unions, see Shmuel Galai, *The Liberation Movement in Russia, 1900–1905* (Cambridge, 1973).
17 See, for example, Pokrovskaia's indignant editorial after the Moscow Duma's decision and her attack on the liberal Fedor Kokoshkin for his recommendation to postpone the adoption of women's suffrage. "Ob izbiratel'nykh pravakh russkikh zhenshchin," *ZhV,* no. 7 (1905): 205–10. For a discussion of the liberals' response to the suffrage issue, see my article, "Women's Rights, Civil Rights, and the Debate over Citizenship in the 1905 Revolution," in *Women and Society in Russia and the Soviet Union,* ed. Linda Edmondson (Cambridge, 1992), 77–100.
18 A. Gorizontova, "Protivnitsam zhenskogo separatizma," *ZhV,* no. 7 (1905): 194–97.
19 For example, "Ob izbiratel'nykh pravakh russkikh zhenshchin," *ZhV,* no. 4 (1905): 124; "Feminizm," *ZhV,* no. 5 (1905): 132; "Ob izbiratel'nykh pravakh russkikh zhenshchin," *ZhV,* no. 7 (1905): 209–10; "Vopros o politicheskikh pravakh v Rossii," *ZhV,* no. 12 (1905): 371.
20 This is a constant theme in all her writing. For a representative sample, see "Kakie lozungy dolzhny ob"ediniat' zhenshchin?" *ZhV,* no. 1 (1907): 7–12, especially 11.
21 "Obshchee sobranie zhenskoi progressivnoi partii," *ZhV,* no. 3 (1906): 90–91. Ruthchild describes the party in more detail.
22 The decision of the Equal Rights Union not to apply for legal status, however, was taken only after repeated debate; the reason for not doing so was to maintain the union's independence from bureaucratic control. For the debates about the future of the union, see Edmondson, *Feminism in Russia,* 72–75; and *Ravnopravie zhenshchin. Tretii s"ezd soiuza ravnopravnosti zhenshchin. Otchety i protokoly 1906 g.* (St. Petersburg, 1906).
23 These included F. Iu. Levinson-Lessing, professor of geology at St. Petersburg University and author of several publications related to the woman question, including *O glavneishikh faktorakh zhenskogo dvizheniia: Idealisticheskie i ekonomicheskie stimuly* (St. Petersburg, [1904]) and "Materinstvo i umstvennyi trud," *MirB,* no. 9 (1902); M. V. Kechedzhi-Shapovalov, author of *Zhenskoe dvizhenie v Rossii i zagranitsei* (St. Petersburg, 1902), and E. I. Kedrin, Kadet deputy in the first Duma and supporter of women's rights.
24 "Zashchitniki i protivniki ravnopraviia zhenshchin v pervoi Gosudar-

stvennoi Dume," *ZhV,* nos. 5–6 (1907): 129–33, nos. 7–8 (1907): 174–76, quotation on 176. This was a paper delivered to the Petersburg Club of the Women's Progressive Party in March 1907. For a report of the session, see *ZhV,* no. 4 (1907): 123–24. The paper was also published as a separate pamphlet under the same title (St. Petersburg, 1907).

25 See, for example, Anna Kal'manovich's speech at the first national women's congress in 1908, "Zhenskoe dvizhenie i otnoshenie partii k nemu," in *Trudy 1-go . . . s"ezda,* 779–91. See also Mariia Chekhova's editorial in *SZh,* as quoted by Rochelle Ruthchild in this volume.

26 See Ruthchild's essay for Mariia Chekhova's and Ariadna Tyrkova's critical commentary on feminism.

27 "Feminizm," *ZhV,* no. 5 (1905): 129–32. I think it is significant that Pokrovskaia used the term *ravnopravnost'* (also *ravnopravie*), here and elsewhere. Its meaning in the context of the 1905 upheaval is not simply "equality" or "equal rights." It was the defining characteristic of the Liberation movement's political agenda, which envisaged a society founded on the equality of all citizens before the law. It was also the term taken by women suffragists for their organization, the Women's Equal Rights Union; in describing themselves as *ravnopravki,* they intended to be distinguished from narrowly focused *feministki.* Pokrovskaia, on the other hand, considered a feminist, ipso facto, to be working for equal rights.

28 See Edmondson, *Feminism in Russia,* for further illustrations of quarrelsome reality undermining the pervasive ideology of female cooperation and harmony.

29 See note 17.

30 "Sotsial'naia i lichnaia gigiena. L. N. Tolstoi i znachenie russkoi revoliutsii," *ZhV,* no. 3 (1907): 65–68.

31 Tolstoi's vocabulary clearly shows his train of thought—the verb *razvrashchat'* ("debauch," "corrupt," or "deprave") was most commonly used at the time, not least by Tolstoi himself, to describe and condemn sexual profligacy. Pokrovskaia used the same vocabulary in her attacks on self-indulgent sex and devoted some pages of her journal to an approving but somewhat misleading appraisal of Tolstoi's passionate morality tale, the "Kreutzer Sonata." *ZhV,* no. 9 (1908). For more on Tolstoi, and Pokrovskaia's misinterpretation of his story, see Engelstein, *Keys to Happiness,* 220–21.

32 "Sotsial'naia i lichnaia gigiena," 65–66.

33 Ibid., 68.

34 See, for example, her reflections in *Kak ia byla gorodskim vrachom,* 4–5, 32–35. In 1905 she established the St. Petersburg Women's Society

for Hygiene (Peterburgskoe zhenskoe gigienicheskoe obshchestvo), dedicated to improving the city's health, *ZhV*, no. 5 (1905): 158.

35 Prostitution and wider questions of sexual morality were discussed at some length at the 1908 women's congress (*Trudy 1-go . . . s"ezda*, 272–86, 343–86). Less than eighteen months later, a congress to discuss the "trade in women" was organized by the Russian Society for the Defense of Women; though not specifically a feminist event, feminists were heavily involved. *Trudy pervogo vserossiiskogo s"ezda po bor'be s torgom zhenshchinami i ego prichinami, proiskhodivshego v S-Peterburge s 21 po 25 aprelia 1910 goda* (St. Petersburg, 1911 and 1912).

36 See, for example, "K voprosu ob aborte," *ZhV*, no. 4 (1914): 105.

37 "O razvitii dushevnoi energii u detei," 45.

38 See, for example, "Vopros rasovoi gigieny," *ZhV*, no. 1 (1914): 1–4; "K voprosu ob aborte," 102–5.

39 Engelstein, *Keys to Happiness*, 225. See Engelstein also for an excellent account of the contemporary obsession with sexual continence and fears of degeneracy.

40 "Tragediia dushi sovremennoi zhenshchiny. Staroe i novoe. Psikhologicheskii ocherk," *ZhV*, no. 4 (1908): 97–104. Inessa Armand's real-life views on the demeaning concept of the *samka* are recorded in R. C. Elwood's biography *Inessa Armand, Revolutionary and Feminist* (Cambridge 1992), as Ruthchild has noted.

41 M. Rogovich, "Tragizm polozheniia zhenskoi molodezhi," *ZhV*, no. 10 (1908): 228–31. M. V. Orlovskaia, "K voprosu o tragizme zhenskoi molodezhi," *ZhV*, no. 12 (1908): 288–91. Orlovskaia was the author of a pamphlet, *O zhenskom dvizhenii v Rossii* (St. Petersburg, 1911), which was dismissive of the current apathetic state of the women's movement (p. 3). Rogovich's articles give no clue as to his sex; they are written in an impersonal voice, with no grammatical indication of gender. Orlovskaia clearly wished to make it unambiguous, opening her article with a reference to "Mr. M. Rogovich." "K voprosu o tragizme," 288. M. Rogovich, "K voprosu o tragizme zhenskoi molodezhi (Okonchanie)," *ZhV*, nos. 7–8 (1909): 151–55.

42 *ZhV*, nos. 7–8 (1909): 8. This was a speech Vakhtina had given at a contentious session of the First All-Russian Congress of Women, in December 1908. See *Trudy 1-go . . . s"ezda*, 374–78.

43 The article by Pokrovskaia that set off this debate, "Tragediia dushi," was motivated in part by this concern. See also her review of H. G. Wells's novel *Ann Veronica*, which appeared in a Russian translation in *VE*. This is the story of a beautiful, emancipated, and intellectually able young woman who capitulates to the charms of an unhappily married

man and runs off with him, abandoning her independence. The novel's ending greatly disappointed Pokrovskaia, who hoped for better things for the heroine. See *ZhV*, no. 9 (1910): 171.

44 Letter to the editor, *Novaia Rus'*, 7 January 1909, cited by E. Kuskova, "Zhenskii vopros i zhenskii s"ezd," *Obrazovanie*, no. 1 (1909): 36–37.

45 For the Zimmerwald Left, which grew out of an antiwar initiative of socialists in several belligerent countries, see R. Craig Nation, *War on War: Lenin, the Zimmerwald Left, and the Origins of Communist Internationalism* (Durham, N.C., 1989). A history of pacifism in Russia has yet to be written.

46 "Zhenshchiny i voina," *ZhV*, no. 1 (1904): 22. This article was a reply to "Homo Novus" in the newspaper *Rus'*, who had diagnosed women's hostility to war as arising from envy of men and had accused them of being incapable of doing anything useful for the war effort.

47 "Samoistreblenie Evropy," *ZhV*, no. 9 (1914): 170–73.

48 Ibid., 171.

49 Ibid. There are hints in the journal that Pokrovskaia was sympathetic to the international congress at The Hague in 1915, a brave and controversial attempt to protest against the war. See "Zhenskii mezhdunarodnyi kongress," *ZhV*, nos. 7–8 (1915): 140–41; and Edmondson, *Feminism in Russia*, 158–62.

50 "Zhenshchiny i voina," 22.

51 "Zhenshchiny zagovorili," 65–66. The battalions were formed in spring 1917 as a volunteer force of women. For a detailed study, see Richard Abraham, "Mariia L. Bochkareva and the Russian Amazons of 1917," in *Women and Society*, 124–44.

52 "Zhenshchiny zagovorili," 66.

53 The suffragettes were the militant wing of the British suffrage movement, led by the Women's Social and Political Union (WSPU). This had been formed in 1905 by a group of women's suffrage campaigners, dominated by Emmeline and Christabel Pankhurst, impatient with the moderate tactics of the National Union of Women's Suffrage Societies (NUWSS). In August 1914, the WSPU abandoned its campaign in order to support the war effort (a volte-face even more dramatic than Pokrovskaia's), though by no means all WSPU members accepted the Pankhursts' decision. See Andrew Rosen, *Rise Up Women! The Militant Campaign of the Women's Social and Political Union, 1903–1914* (London, 1974), 246–54. In the summer of 1917, Emmeline Pankhurst visited Russia in one of many vain efforts to bolster the Provisional Government's war effort. See Abraham, "Mariia L. Bochkareva," 125–34. For a discussion of the Russian feminists' (including Pokrovskaia's) response to the suffrage movement in Britain, see Edmondson, *Feminism in Russia*, 121–28.

54 Pokrovskaia's wariness of the Social Democrats dated from the beginnings of the Russian women's suffrage movement. The conflict between feminists and Social Democrats is most graphically revealed in several explosive debates at the 1908 congress. See, for example, *Trudy 1-go . . . s"ezda,* 456, 494, 523.
55 "Revoliutsiia i gumannost'," *ZhV,* nos. 5–6 (1917): 67–69.
56 For good illustrations, see the articles quoted earlier, "Samoistreblenie Evropy" and "Revoliutsiia i gumannost'."

Journalism as a Means of Empowerment

The Early Career of Ekaterina Kuskova

BARBARA T. NORTON

By the late nineteenth century, the pioneering efforts of the women journalists discussed in the preceding essays, as well as the growth of the commercial mass-circulation press, had combined to open new opportunities for women in the field of Russian journalism.[1] Nevertheless a career as a journalist was not something to which a young girl was likely to aspire. Despite increased opportunities for women, the emerging profession of journalism remained largely a male preserve. Men continued to predominate as publishers and editors, as well as writers and reporters — often, as Carolyn Marks and others have noted, even in the women's press.[2] In contrast to the majority of women profiled in this volume, most females who managed to surmount the gender barrier still labored in what has traditionally been considered the lower ranks of journalism, where employment was both uncertain and poorly paid, and where status was low.[3]

Yet women were steadily making their way into Russian journalism, as a look at the checklist of women journalists appended to this volume quickly reveals. Recent research indicates that in St. Petersburg and Moscow alone, "the last twenty years of the nineteenth century showed a sharp increase in the numbers of journals [and newspapers] women produced."[4] Intelligentsia women, in particular, continued to defy social convention to pursue lives as reporters and writers, editors and publishers. By the early twentieth century, these women — some of whom had served their apprenticeships in the revolutionary underground press — were clearly a force to be reckoned with, contributing importantly to the explosion of journalistic enterprise that occurred between the 1905 and 1917 revolutions. Among them was Ekaterina Dmitrievna Kuskova (1869–1958), a radical public activist *(obshchestvennaia deiatel'ia),* whose multifaceted career as author, editor, and publisher spanned more than six decades.

Although Kuskova was a prominent journalist in Russia and in emigration after 1922, this aspect of her biography has received only scant attention from scholars.[5] It is my aim to supplement the historiographic record by tracing her journalistic trajectory to 1917, examining Kuskova's early career as a source of both personal and political empowerment. It is my hope that this narrative of one woman's attraction to journalism, her professional work and relationships, and her role in accustoming the Russian reading public to women's voices will contribute something to the larger project of defining women's participation in journalism in late imperial Russia.

Kuskova's initial foray into the field of journalism in the early 1890s appears to have been wholly fortuitous. This, at least, is the impression she conveys in her memoirs.[6] I am wary, however, of following her into a biographical trap. As Carolyn Heilbrun has observed in another context, "well into the twentieth century," women's autobiographies tended to "report the encounters with what would be the life's work as having occurred by chance."[7] Nevertheless there seems little doubt that life circumstances, irrespective of life choices, played a critical role in prompting Kuskova's first journalistic endeavors.

The daughter of an illiterate Tatar woman and an impoverished Russian nobleman–civil servant, Kuskova spent her formative years in South Central Russia.[8] It was in the provincial capital of Saratov that she acquired most of her formal schooling and also encountered the radical ideas that were eventually to shape her socialist worldview. A principal source of these ideas was the thick journals that comprised much of the reading fare for the circles of "self-education" (*kruzhki "samoobrazovaniia"*) she attended. It may well have been from the pages of *Vestnik evropy (European Herald)*, *Otechestvennye zapiski (Notes of the Fatherland)*, and their like that Kuskova first came to know the power of journalism and appreciate its ability to stimulate action as well as ideas.[9] I can only speculate about this, however, for although she reports in her memoirs on her early reading habits—which, she says, included a passion for novels—she conveys nothing of the impression that journal reading made on her.[10] Nevertheless it is clear that such reading was an important part of her political education during her adolescence and teenage years and that it constituted a crucial component of her intellectual development.

Kuskova's early adult life began according to a "conventional marriage plot," or so it initially appears.[11] In 1885, at age sixteen, she married her former *gimnazium* science teacher and immediately began a family. Yet this marriage, which rescued her from a life of impoverishment and drudgery following the death of her parents, was far from conventional.[12] It was, in fact, a companionate marriage based on a strong mutual affection. Her husband, Ivan Iuvenaliev, encouraged her further education and facilitated her participation in local radical circles. "Life was quiet," Kuskova later recalled, "and it was possible to devote myself wholly to intellectual occupations."[13] Iuvenaliev's untimely death in 1889 disrupted her tranquility, however, and confronted her suddenly with the need to support a family. In these circumstances, she decided to train as a midwife — a decision motivated more by her limited options for employment than by any particularly strong attraction to midwifery.[14] Indeed, there was much in Kuskova's temperament that resisted traditional female roles. Already during her early teenage years, she had rejected the idea of working as a teacher or a governess, considering these servile female occupations a fate worse than death. Nevertheless, as she contemplated her future at the end of the 1880s, midwifery seemed to offer the economic security she required, as well as an opportunity to "serve society," a desire awakened in her by Saratov's oppositional intelligentsia.[15]

It was at this juncture that Kuskova first encountered the emerging profession of journalism. To provide for her family, she found temporary employment with the liberal newspaper *Saratovskii dnevnik (Saratov Journal)*. Some years later, she would recall this as a time when she "had to exist by newspaper work (translation and original)." Her memoirs, where she notes that *Saratovskii dnevnik* published her "first story," provide no further details. It seems unlikely that such work offered more than a subsistence living, however, as Kuskova's earnings could have been neither very substantial nor very steady.[16] It is tempting to speculate that she may already have recognized in journalism an opportunity to free herself from confinement to "women's work" and to translate her intellectual energy into stimulating independent activity. But this must remain a question. So, too, must the nature of her initial involvement with Russia's revolutionary underground press, which occurred soon after she moved to Moscow in 1891 to begin her midwifery course.[17]

Upon arriving in Moscow, Kuskova joined a student circle then organizing an illegal radical journal modeled on Aleksandr Herzen's *Kolokol (The Bell)*.[18] Police surveillance reports on the circle include only the sketchiest information about its activities, and Kuskova's own accounts of the group are vague and muddled.[19] It is clear, however, that by the early 1890s she had embarked on the path that would lead eventually to her life's work. Her experiences in Western Europe during the second half of the decade would propel her further along that path.

For reasons of both politics and health, in 1895, at the age of twenty-six, Kuskova left Russia for extensive travels in Western Europe. Her immediate concern was to recover from a debilitating tuberculosis, but she also wanted to acquaint herself more fully with the activities of Russian émigré Marxists and with the European labor movement.[20] The financial wherewithal for her travels was apparently provided by her traveling companion, Sergei Prokopovich, a young nobleman with a modest estate in Belorussia who was a member of the same Moscow circle and shared her newly found attraction to Marxism. The details of the couple's early relationship remain obscure; but their common-law marriage sometime after 1895 marked the beginning of a lifelong intellectual and emotional partnership that was to contribute importantly to Kuskova's development as a journalist.[21]

Once again, marriage gave her much-needed financial security and the opportunity to devote herself to intellectual pursuits. Prokopovich's money enabled the couple to live first in Switzerland and then in Belgium and Germany, where they resided for much of the next five years.[22] It was probably in Western Europe that Kuskova came to understand the full potential of journalism to promote radical change. Her conversion to social democracy during the early 1890s had been facilitated by the debate between Marxists and populists played out in part in the pages of the thick journals. But the debate, like all public political discussion in Russia, had been constrained by government censorship.[23] In Western Europe, Kuskova witnessed directly the power of a largely unfettered press to extend public consciousness and enlist public opinion in the discussion of critical political, social, and economic issues.[24]

In 1897 she and Prokopovich joined the Berlin branch of the Union of Russian Social Democrats Abroad (Soiuz russkikh sotsial-demokratov zagranitsei), an organization whose primary mission was to create illegal popular literature for workers in Russia. Kuskova quickly immersed herself in the union's publishing operations—to which Prokopovich contributed as well, including financially.[25] Much of her energy went into the technical aspects of production and distribution, but she also authored a number of articles for *Listok "Rabotnika" ("The Worker" Supplement)*, which chronicled the Russian and Western European labor movements.[26]

It is in connection with her writing for this underground Marxist journal that we get our first, brief glimpse of Kuskova's personal experience of journalism. In the winter of 1897–1898, Pavel Aksel'rod—liaison for the union's parent organization, the Emancipation of Labor Group (Gruppa "Osvobozhdenie truda")—pointed out certain "literary-stylistic defects" in her writing. Kuskova readily confessed to an inability to compose rough drafts, "a great deficiency," she allowed, that might prevent her "from developing into a 'genuine writer' [nastoiashchuiu pisatel'nitsu]."[27] Whether this confession was genuine or merely an attempt to disarm her critic is difficult to tell. Very likely it was both. Kuskova surely had some doubts about her abilities as a writer—what woman author in a patriarchal society has not? At the same time, she also recognized the value of self-deprecation before an émigré leader with whom significant ideological differences were emerging.

Because of political differences with Aksel'rod and other members of the Emancipation of Labor Group, at least three of Kuskova's articles for *Listok "Rabotnika"* remained unpublished.[28] This was not the only obstacle in her path to publication, however. The Marxist leaders clearly viewed Kuskova as little more than Prokopovich's helpmeet and thus showed no serious inclination to nurture her talents as a writer.[29] Nevertheless her period of apprenticeship with the Marxist underground press contributed importantly to her personal and intellectual self-confidence. While it may well have been Prokopovich's money rather than Kuskova's own abilities that provided her entrée into the world of émigré journalism, her literary skills and aptitude for the technical aspects of publication soon revealed themselves. Kuskova now knew that journalism had much to offer her and that she had much to offer Russian society as a journalist. There would rarely be a time from this point forward when she was not directly involved in some aspect of creating, managing, or supporting a newspaper or journal.

At the end of the 1890s, although still a convinced Marxist, Kuskova broke with organized social democracy. Persuaded by the ideological battle then raging that Russia's Marxist leaders were dangerously authoritarian and woefully out of touch with the country's real needs, she vigorously denounced narrow partisan politics in favor of cooperation between radicals and liberals. If her disillusionment with social democratic politics had its origins in her personal experience, so too did her newly expressed desire for cooperation among all elements of the oppositional movement. Kuskova's years in Saratov had exposed her to a uniquely nonsectarian brand of radicalism, making her aware of an alternative to narrow political partisanship.[30] But there was also the matter of her gender. While I feel on shakier ground here, it seems to me that her socialization as a Russian woman may have contributed to her preference for a politics of inclusion rather than exclusion, and to her inclination toward cooperation and compromise rather than conflict in resolving political differences.[31]

In any event, soon after the turn of the century, Kuskova placed her journalistic skills in the service of this broadened political perspective. In 1901, along with her husband, she joined a small group of radicals and liberals to found the illegal oppositional journal *Osvobozhdenie (Liberation),* around which the clandestine Union of Liberation (Soiuz osvobozhdeniia) would soon coalesce. Published in Germany by Petr Struve, the journal was intended "to awaken broad public opinion, to organize public forces" in support of Russia's transformation from autocracy to representative government.[32] Kuskova shared responsibility with Ariadna Tyrkova and others for the journal's transportation to Russia and its distribution there. She also wrote for *Osvobozhdenie,* one of the few women to do so.[33] Her articles, which dealt largely with the condition of the working class, appeared under the pseudonyms "Vsegda nekogda" (Always Never) and "Kredo" (Credo). In contrast to women who wrote for the legal press, Kuskova adopted these pseudonyms not as gender camouflage but as a means of maintaining her anonymity with tsarist authorities.[34]

The formation of the Union of Liberation in 1903 and 1904 provided the impetus for Kuskova, now living in St. Petersburg, to expand her journalistic activities still further. Toward the end of 1904, emboldened to act openly by Russia's disastrous war with Japan undertaken earlier that year, she and other union members launched the St. Petersburg daily *Nasha zhizn' (Our Life)* to promote their demands for civil liberties and constitutional government. Kuskova at last had a legal forum for her political views. Although not the paper's "responsible" editor, she was "almost the sole editor of *Nasha zhizn'*."[35] She threw herself into her new duties so completely that the usually supportive Prokopovich (also a contributor to the paper) complained of being neglected.[36]

As Russia's defeats in the Far East multiplied in the spring and summer of 1905, *Nasha zhizn'* grew bolder in its demands. The paper quickly availed itself of every opportunity to expand the nation's political consciousness and mobilize broad elements of society on behalf of democratic change. In October, just before the announcement by Nicholas II of his October Manifesto granting Russia a limited constitution, a number of prominent editors and publishers gathered in the paper's editorial office to organize a united front in defense of freedom of the press.[37] During the "days of freedom" that followed the October Manifesto, Kuskova and others at *Nasha zhizn'* took full advantage of the collapse of censorship authority to impress on readers the importance and urgency of a popularly elected representative government. In so doing, the paper contributed significantly to the politicization of the mass-circulation press, which in turn served to expand considerably the sphere of public discourse in Russia.[38]

It is significant that although Kuskova was an ardent champion of democracy, she made no special case in 1905 for women's right to vote. For her, as for socialists generally, women's rights were merely an aspect of the larger problem of human rights in a country where women and men were equally subjugated to autocratic authority. She assumed that sexual equality would go hand in hand with the achievement of freedom and democracy, and that female suffrage needed no special consideration. Unlike liberationist colleagues Tyrkova and Liubov' Gurevich, therefore, Kuskova did not join the newly formed Women's Equal Rights Union (Soiuz ravnopraviia zhenshchin).[39] Her attitude would soon change. But for the present, she attached no particular urgency to issues of gender.[40]

Kuskova's journalistic activities during this revolutionary period were not confined to the editorial office of *Nasha zhizn'*.[41] Toward the end of 1905, she and journalist colleagues organized a variety of professional and labor unions to promote the Liberation movement's program. These unions — including the Union of Russian Writers (Soiuz rossiiskikh pisatelei), the Union of Journalists (Soiuz zhurnalistov), the Union of Contributors to the Periodical Press (Soiuz sotrudnikov periodicheskikh izdanii), and the Union of Press Workers (Soiuz truzhenikov pechatnogo dela) — added their voices to the chorus demanding the right of free expression.[42] Their efforts were not in vain. After the October Manifesto, which had articulated the principle of press freedom, the government began revising censorship laws, finally eliminating most preliminary censorship as well as administrative controls over the press by the spring of 1906.[43] Publications would no longer have to be submitted for approval before printing and distribution, and the press was to be regulated exclusively by law, with punishments to be decided on and administered solely through the courts. Censorship had not been completely abolished, however. Preliminary censorship of articles on religious issues, court and military matters, and a number of other subjects remained in force. Additionally, all periodicals (and books) exempt from precensorship were still to be submitted for inspection after publication. Any journal or newspaper that violated the criminal code could be confiscated and proceedings instituted against the responsible editor.[44] Although Kuskova had hoped for more, this reform was nonetheless a significant victory.

An obvious measure of Kuskova's growing political influence was her election in October 1905 to the Central Committee of the newly created Constitutional Democratic Party — she was the first woman to join the Kadet inner sanctum. But political differences prompted her to withdraw from the party almost immediately.[45] Moreover, it was journalism, not organized politics, that best suited Kuskova's temperament and talents. And she recognized that journalists, because they were subject to fewer political, judicial, and administrative constraints, would be as important as parties in expressing and molding public opinion in and around Russia's soon-to-be-elected parliament.[46] In early 1906, therefore, together with Prokopovich, she established the weekly political journal *Bez zaglaviia (Without a Title)*, named to reflect the couple's nonaligned political stance and rejection of ideological labels. Kuskova was the publisher, Prokopovich the official editor.

Bez zaglaviia was intended to mediate among the factions into which the Liberation movement had fragmented in the aftermath of the 1905 revolution. As Kuskova explained to Georgii Plekhanov — a former political adversary from the Emancipation of Labor Group and now a potential contributor to *Bez zaglaviia* — the publication was "neither party nor sectarian" but "a literary undertaking that united all left elements."[47] At its editorial office, she gathered around her an impressive group of nonparty radical and left-liberal journalists, among them Liubov' Gurevich. It is worth noting that Kuskova does not appear to have made any particular attempt, either at this time or later, to attract women to her publishing projects.[48] This can be explained in part by the nature of her politics: there were relatively few women journalists who shared her particular ideological perspective. What additional factors influenced her attitude toward female colleagues may become clearer as we learn more about Russian women journalists.

With the launching of *Bez zaglaviia*, Kuskova obtained an important forum for her political agenda, an agenda that called for nothing less than "the transformation of the entire social order, the transition from capitalism to socialism."[49] In a section entitled "Press" (Pechat), she regularly analyzed the successes and failures of the 1905 revolution and outlined strategies for Russia's newly formed (or newly legal) political parties, then preparing for the country's first State Duma elections. *Bez zaglaviia* carried considerable clout in some radical and left-liberal circles, and it added importantly to Kuskova's growing reputation and influence as a journalist. Several years later, the idiosyncratic Christian philosopher-author Vasilii Rozanov, who crossed political swords with her more than once, recalled sarcastically how "everyone kissed the hand" of this "high-ranking lady" because "she published the highfalutin [vysokopostavlennyi] journal, *Bez zaglaviia*." And the liberal lawyer and politician Iosif Gessen would remark in his memoirs on what an unusually wide circle of friends and acquaintances she possessed.[50]

Once the Duma convened in the spring of 1906, the weekly publication schedule of *Bez zaglaviia* quickly proved inadequate to Kuskova's needs. "Now," she told her readers in mid-May, "the natural form for political thought is the daily press."[51] After just four and a half months of publication, she closed the journal to concentrate again on *Nasha zhizn'*, where she could respond instantly to the activities of the government and the Duma. She also assumed a key editorial position on *Tovarishch (Comrade)*, a new radical daily that, like *Nasha zhizn'*, enjoyed a broad readership, reaching workers and peasants as well as the educated elite. L. V. Khodskii, an economics professor at St. Petersburg University, was the founder and official editor of both newspapers, but it was Kuskova who largely determined editorial policy. Although *Nasha zhizn'* soon ran afoul of the censors and was closed in the summer of 1906, *Tovarishch* continued to publish for a short time longer.[52] In an irregular column called "Political Sketches" (Politicheskiie nabroski), Kuskova examined current political and social issues, with particular attention to party conflicts within the Duma and preparations for the forthcoming parliamentary elections.[53] Concerned, as always, with reviving Russia's liberal-radical democratic coalition, she also solicited contributions to the paper among a broad spectrum of political activists, from Kadets on the Right to social democratic Mensheviks on the Left.

Journalism had become an all-consuming passion for Kuskova. By 1907, if not earlier, she was devoting twelve to fifteen hours a day to her work, and this at a time when her health was again poor. "From morning to night I am occupied with *Tovar[ishch]*," she wrote Plekhanov, one of the paper's contributors, "and at night I am often at the printing press."[54] Such commitment and tireless dedication earned her the admiration even of those oppositional intelligentsia who did not share her political views.[55] When the government closed *Tovarishch* at the end of 1907, Kuskova continued her editorial work for its successor *Nash vek (Our Century)*. This paper was no better able to withstand the repression that had been mounting steadily since summer, when Prime Minister Petr Stolypin began reasserting some of the government's lost authority.[56] In fact, *Nash vek* survived barely a week. Following its cessation, Kuskova lamented privately:

The closing of *Nash vek,* and soon after *Stolichnaia pochta [Capital Post],* suggests that they [the government] do not intend now to tolerate even this type of newspaper—self-restrained and prudent. . . . Despite the fact that the systematic closings of the seemingly secure paper will ruin us in the end, we are making a last attempt to hold on, and [on] Sunday, 16 March, we will come out under a new name. If they close us a third time, it means it is impossible to hold on and it is necessary to lay down this weapon; it means a newspaper is impossible. The Right especially agitates against us, namely they press Stolypin and demand the "destruction" of such a "depraved" press.[57]

After the closure of *Nash vek,* Kuskova apparently worked on several other short-lived dailies, including *Nasha gazeta (Our Gazette), Pravda zhizni (Life's Truth),* and *Svobodnyi golos (Free Voice).* She was no longer satisfied to be working for someone else, however, and she and Prokopovich now made several attempts to acquire their own periodical. "We dream about a large daily newspaper," she wrote a friend sometime during the summer of 1908.[58] But the couple's efforts to purchase the weekly *Utro (Morning),* along with the prestigious thick journal *Obrazovanie (Education),* soon fell through.[59]

Journalism, whether Kuskova was conscious of it or not, provided an arena where she could function largely unhindered by male domination and where she could wield political influence as an equal (or nearly so) of her male colleagues. Although Prokopovich's constant presence beside her in her various journalistic endeavors might seem to belie such an assertion, the sources reveal quite clearly that the couple's professional relationship was collegial rather than paternalistic. Kuskova was always able to work independently, without direction or guidance from her husband. It was also true, of course, that their collaboration facilitated her journalism in numerous ways. It had gained her entrée into Marxist émigré circles and possibly also enhanced her position among the liberals and radicals who spearheaded the Liberation movement.[60] Prokopovich's money, moreover, may have remained a vital resource for her, even after she launched her own business (the publishing firm Izdatel'stvo E. D. Kuskovoi) early in the century.[61] Finally, and most importantly, the principal benefit of their collaboration throughout more than sixty years together was undoubtedly the intellectual and emotional support that her husband provided. Nevertheless Kuskova was clearly her own woman and, by all accounts, the dominant partner in this political-journalistic team.[62]

Sometime apparently during 1909, Kuskova relocated to Moscow, where the long-established liberal newspaper *Russkie vedomosti*, the city's second-largest daily, became the principal forum for her political message.[63] In the pages of this paper with its national distribution, as well as in other liberal and radical periodicals in Moscow and St. Petersburg, she examined a wide range of contemporary political, social, and economic issues in countless articles, editorials, and feuilletons. Her "fiery publicists," as one contemporary has described her writing,[64] not only served to promote her democratic cause but also helped accustom the Russian reading public to women's voices on traditionally masculine topics.

Kuskova's first contribution to *Russkie vedomosti* had appeared already at the end of 1908 and concerned the First All-Russian Congress of Women (Pervyi vserossiiskii zhenskii s"ezd), which she attended as a delegate. In her report on the proceedings, she had revealed an emerging feminist sensitivity, born of the changed political circumstances following the 1905 revolution.[65] The unusual degree of political equality that had existed previously between women and men — a consequence of everyone's lack of rights in Russia — had vanished with the promulgation of the 1906 electoral law that excluded women. Party politics during and after 1905, moreover, had quickly put the lie to the assumption that sexual equality would go hand in hand with freedom and democracy. Indeed, few women besides Kuskova had been able to penetrate the masculine inner sanctum of the country's oppositional parties, and support for extending women's rights was halfhearted at best from all but one or two of those parties.[66]

No doubt the heightened political activism of Russian feminists in this period, described by Rochelle Ruthchild and Linda Edmondson in the preceding essays, also played a role in Kuskova's new awareness of gender issues. It is likely that her new vantage point of professional success and political influence may also have contributed to a recognition of the special burdens imposed on women by their second-class status in Russian society. Regardless of its source — and Kuskova is frustratingly silent on the matter — a maturing feminist consciousness was very much in evidence in her journalism after

1908. Her *Russkie vedomosti* report on the Women's Congress, as well as her articles for the journals *Soiuz zhenshchin (Union of Women)* and *Obrazovanie,* emphasized the importance of women's participation in Russian political life. And although she sharply criticized much that had gone on at the congress, she was convinced that "this women's parliament . . . underscored the full preparedness of women to participate in representative institutions."[67]

Women's rights continued to be important to Kuskova, and she would return more than once to issues of political disenfranchisement, economic oppression, and educational needs.[68] Yet feminist concerns remained a comparatively small part of her journalism. There were probably several reasons for this. Women's emancipation was among the subjects still proscribed by the censors; thus other topics constituted easier vehicles for her political message.[69] I suspect also that she may have feared marginalization, both as a journalist and as a political activist. Too close an identification with women's issues would have meant risking the loss of credibility with male colleagues in the oppositional movement. Indeed, for all Kuskova's success and the respect she enjoyed, she still had to contend with the likes of Menshevik Iulii Martov, who referred to her dismissively as an "old broad in trousers" [baba v briukakh].[70] The status she had achieved and the influence she wielded were at the same time too precious and too precarious to jeopardize by assuming the mantle of feminist crusader.

Most important, however, women's rights were of interest to Kuskova primarily in the context of the oppositional movement's struggle for democracy. Thus she had observed in her *Russkie vedomosti* piece that the Congress of Women was a "remarkable phenomenon, not only as the first step in the development of an organized women's movement and women's struggle for equal rights, but also as a demonstration of the inexhaustible force of the general Russian liberation movement."[71] Still a committed Marxist, she also shared, at least to some extent, the view of most socialists that feminism was a self-interested "bourgeois" phenomenon.[72] She certainly shared the fears of many on the Left that feminism could lead to political separatism.[73] For all these reasons, although her feminist consciousness continued to develop, her journalism focused more often on matters other than women's rights.

In the years from 1911 to 1914, Kuskova remained a frequent

contributor to a variety of Mosow and St. Petersburg periodicals, including the prestigious thick journals *Golos minuvshego (Voice of the Past)* and *Sovremennyi mir (Contemporary World)*, the cooperative movement's *Kooperativnaia zhizn' (Cooperative Life)* and *Vestnik kooperatsii (Cooperative Herald)*, and the pedagogical journals *Svobodnoe vospitanie (Free Education)* and *Vestnik vospitanii (Education Herald)*. Her closest association was apparently with the radical *Sovremennik (The Contemporary)*. From its inception in early 1911, one of the journal's founders, Aleksandr Amfiteatrov, involved her in discussions about its direction and sought to draw her into its circle of contributors. Kuskova initially resisted because *Sovremennik* had "a political section without a definite political line."[74] When the journal began to reveal radical populist leanings, she was equally uncomfortable with its rejection of parliamentary government and its support of terror as a political tactic.[75] Amfiteatrov, disappointed at his failure to make headway with Kuskova, expressed his regret to Maksim Gor'kii, another of the founders, observing that she was "a valuable rarity" among "the absolutely bankrupt Russian intelligentsia."[76] Finally, in 1912, after a further shift in the journal's political orientation — this time in the direction of social democracy — Kuskova joined *Sovremmenik*'s staff of writers. Soon she was working with the editors to recruit other Marxist intelligentsia.[77]

But it was *Russkie vedomosti* that remained Kuskova's principal public forum in the years immediately preceding the First World War. Her articles revealed a wide range of social concerns along with a consistent political message. Here she examined the contemporary crisis of faith that had drawn Russia's youth away from the oppositional movement, analyzed the election results for the fourth Duma and the gains made in parliament by the oppositional elements, and contemplated the changing mood of society.[78] She also considered the precarious status of legality in Russia.[79] Kuskova's participation in the burgeoning consumer cooperative movement in these years was reflected in her discussion of the importance of the "cultural-enlightenment work" of the cooperatives, and her aversion to anti-Semitism expressed itself in a passionate attack on this "ulcer" that "festered daily" in the body of Russian society.[80] Her commitment to maintaining a free press was apparent in an article on the anti-democratic implications of a press bill before the Duma in early

1914.[81] In these and her other writings, Kuskova's advocacy of social and political cooperation, as well as her profound desire for a more democratic Russia, came through in a clear and certain voice.

With the outbreak of the First World War, Kuskova like many other socialists moderated her quarrels with the imperial regime in the interests of Russia's self-preservation. Yet her writing in this period was never chauvinistic, and she always maintained reservations in her support for government policies. In both word and deed, Kuskova continued to pressure the emperor to grant further concessions to society and allow greater popular initiative in the country's political and economic life. As an activist in the cooperative movement and a member of the recently formed Union of Towns (Soiuz gorodov), she was especially interested in seeing the so-called voluntary organizations assume a greater role in the war effort. This was a time when the distribution and consumption of goods at home and at the front were increasingly a matter of life and death. For Kuskova, the cooperative societies, in particular, constituted an obvious and essential mechanism for mobilizing Russia's resources; many of her articles were devoted to arguing this case.[82]

Russian military reversals in mid-1915 and mounting hardships imposed on the country by the war soon prompted Kuskova to resume a more active antigovernment stance. In concert with other prominent oppositional figures, including her husband, she now sought to launch a newspaper that would serve as a rallying point for a new democratic coalition. For reasons that are not yet clear to me, this project collapsed toward the end of the year.[83] But her attempts to unite Russia's democratic intelligentsia did not end there. By 1916, the country's growing disillusionment with the regime of Nicholas II and mounting popular unrest convinced Kuskova that "it was necessary to change the chauffeur of the automobile rapidly heading for the precipice."[84] Hoping to forestall a popular uprising, she assumed a pivotal role in bringing together many of Russia's most important public figures behind a "government of public confidence." Philosopher Nikolai Berdiaev described later what he witnessed: "In the last year before the revolution, closed meetings of Society [i.e., Russia's educated elite] took place in Moscow. Left elements of the intelligentsia, but not extremists, took part in them. There were the more moderate Social Democrats and Socialist Revolutionaries and the more left Kadets. E. Kuskova and S. Prokopovich were at the center."[85] According to Kuskova, it was at meetings such as these, many of them held in her apartment, that the future Provisional Government was organized on the eve of 1917.[86]

News of the uprising in Petrograd (formerly St. Petersburg) that sparked the February revolution of 1917 reached Kuskova in Moscow through the editorial offices of *Russkie vedomosti.* Quickly she set to work to report on as well as take part in the rapidly unfolding events.[87] By now Kuskova's reputation as a journalist was second to none, female or male. Her staunch commitment to democracy and her determination to defend the press as a place where critical issues could be put before the public had won her the respect and admiration of broad segments of progressive Russian society. It was a measure of her journalistic stature that Moscow's newly created Committee of Public Organizations (Komitet obshchestvennykh organizatsii) selected her to head the city's Commissariat for the Protection of the Freedom of the Press (Kommissariat po obespecheniiu svobody pechaty), a post for which there was no dearth of qualified men available.[88] In this capacity, Kuskova would assume responsibility for ensuring that the press continued to function amid the turmoil of war and revolution. This was the vantage point from which she would settle in to report on and guide what she hoped would be Russia's long-awaited transition to full political and social democracy.

In April Kuskova helped establish the aptly named cooperative daily *Vlast' naroda (Power of the People),* for which she soon assumed much of the editorial responsibility. But the promise of the February revolution was short-lived. Kuskova's outspoken opposition to the Bolsheviks, both before and after they seized power in October, meant that it was not long before her freedom of expression was curtailed once again. Arrested in 1921, along with Prokopovich (who had served in the Provisional Government), she was allowed to emigrate to Western Europe. There — first in Berlin, then in Prague, and finally in Geneva — she would spend the remainder of her life, contributing regularly to the émigré political press, an indefatigable champion of democracy for Russia.

Drawn to journalism in the 1890s, first by economic necessity and then by the potential of the press to promote radical change, Kuskova discovered a means of both personal and political empowerment. What had begun as temporary employment eventually became a vocation and a passion. In journalism she found a self-actualizing endeavor that provided not only independence but also influence beyond the boundaries that traditionally circumscribed the lives of women in Russian society. Through her writings, she gave voice to her wide-ranging social concerns and became an important advocate for equality and democracy in Russia.

Rejecting a gender ideology that emphasized self-sacrifice and quiet, demure behavior, Kuskova contributed to the definition of new gender roles for Russian women. Whether she was aware of her female journalist precursors remains unclear. The evidence available thus far would suggest that her journalistic models were not women such as Evgeniia Tur or Anna Volkova but rather the male publicists whose work she read in the radical circles of her youth, and, later on, her male colleagues in the oppositional movement. Nevertheless women precursors had helped make possible her career in journalism, and Kuskova's career, in turn, undoubtedly eased the way both for her contemporaries and for women in generations to come.

There is much still to be learned about Russia's women journalists. Yet there can be no doubt that the role of women in journalism in late imperial Russia was a good deal more significant than has traditionally been thought, and that women such as Ekaterina Kuskova contributed in a fundamental way to shaping the politics and society of their time.

Notes

I am indebted to Jehanne Gheith, whose thoughtful readings of this essay have been invaluable to its evolution.

1. On the role of the mass-circulation press in expanding opportunities for women, see Louise McReynolds, "Female Journalists in Prerevolutionary Russia," *Journalism History* 14, no. 4 (1987): 104–10.
2. In arguing that journalism was a male preserve, I am thinking not so much of numbers as of visible authority and influence.
3. Hence Linda Edmondson's observation that women's contribution to the prestigious thick journals "was confined almost entirely to the literary and review sections . . . even in these their names featured mainly as authors of short reviews, poems, and short stories and, above all, as translators of foreign authors." See "Women's Rights, Civil Rights, and the Debate over Citizenship in the 1905 Revolution," in *Women and*

Society in Russia and the Soviet Union, ed. Linda Edmondson (Cambridge, 1992), 80. The situation in the daily press has led Louise McReynolds to comment: "If we search . . . for luminaries to hold up as examples of what talented and ambitious women might achieve in tsarist Russia, . . . we might well be forced to conclude that women were of little importance in newspaper offices" ("Female Journalists," 104).

4 Rhonda Lebedev Clark, "Claiming Voice, Profession, Livelihood: Women Periodical Publishers and Editors of Moscow and St. Petersburg, 1860–1905," paper presented at the summer workshop on Slavic women, University of Illinois, Urbana-Champaign, 21 June 1995.

5 Thus previous biographical treatments mention her journalism only in passing, viewing it as incidental to other defining characteristics. See, for example, G. Aronson, "E. D. Kuskova: Portret obshchestvennogo deiatelia," *Novyi zhurnal* 37 (1954): 236–56. I am guilty of similar neglect in my earlier work on Kuskova. It is significant that, while Kuskova's name can be found in the major journalism reference works (in contrast to many other Russian women journalists), even the most recent and detailed entry on her is far from comprehensive. See *Russkie pisateli: 1800–1917gg. Biograficheskii slovar'*, ed. P. A. Nikolaev, vol. 3 (Moscow, 1994), s.v. "Kuskova, Ekaterina Dmitrievna."

6 See below for further discussion of this point. Kuskova's memoirs, "Davno minuvshee," were written at the end of her life and published in *Novyi zhurnal* between 1955 and 1958; they remained incomplete at the time of her death, covering the period up to the early 1890s only.

7 Carolyn Heilbrun, *Writing a Woman's Life* (1988; London, 1989), 24–25. Although Heilbrun's focus is on American and British women, the point holds true for Russian women also.

8 The information on her family and early years is from her memoir, "Davno minuvshee," *Novyi zhurnal* 43 (1955): 96–119. Kuskova was born into a minor branch of the noble Esipov family. The surname "Kuskova" was acquired later through marriage. See note 18 below. Fuller discussion of her early biography can be found in Barbara T. Norton, "The Making of a Female Marxist: E. D. Kuskova's Conversion to Russian Social Democracy," *International Review of Social History* 34 (1989): pt. 2, 227–47.

9 One of the circles she attended at the end of the 1880s or perhaps the early 1890s was conducted by V. A. Balmashev, a librarian for a local merchants' club, who provided the group with back numbers of various thick journals and guidance on what to read. See Kuskova, "Davno minuvshee," *Novyi zhurnal* 47 (1956): 169–70, 173–74.

10 Ibid., 43 (1955): 118. This passion for novels, reported by so many Russian women memoirists (see Miranda Remnek's discussion of women

readers in this volume), requires further attention from scholars. Were all these women as truly absorbed by literature as they report, or are we dealing here with some kind of memoiristic convention?

11 The "conventional marriage plot," in contrast to the "quest plot" characteristic of men's lives, "demands not only that a woman marry but that the marriage and its progeny be her life's absolute and only center" (Heilbrun, *Writing*, 48, 51).

12 Both parents had died by late 1884, and Kuskova was left to care for a younger sister. See Kuskova, "Davno minuvshee," *Novyi zhurnal* 45 (1956): 169–77.

13 Ibid., 47: 160ff.

14 Ibid., 48 (1957): 162, and 49 (1957): 145. Employment opportunities for a young widow with children remained exceedingly limited. For a description of the problems needy women encountered with jobs, wages, and lodging during the second half of the century, see Barbara Alpern Engel, *Mothers and Daughters: Women of the Intelligentsia in Nineteenth Century Russia* (Cambridge, 1973), 71–72. One of Kuskova's two children died of diphtheria soon after her husband's death. See "Davno minuvshee," *Novyi zhurnal* 49 (1957): 148.

15 Kuskova, "Davno minuvshee," *Novy: zhurnal* 45: 174, and 49: 149–50. Midwifery *(akusherstvo)*, in contrast to medicine, was regarded as an extension of the proper female role in society. See Engel, *Mothers and Daughters*, 157–58. Kuskova did not share the enthusiasm for midwifery of some young women who turned to it as a means of "serving society," a phrase commonly heard in radical circles of the period.

16 Hoover Institution on War, Revolution, and Peace (HIWRP), Nicolaevsky Collection, no. 209, folder 1, Kuskova to P. B. Aksel'rod, 9 January [1898]; and Kuskova, "Davno minuvshee," *Novyi zhurnal* 45 (1956): 179. Economic necessity, as we have seen elsewhere in this volume, is a recurring theme in Russian women's accounts of their attraction to journalism. Translation was a common task assigned to women. Regarding pay, see Louise McReynolds, *The News under Russia's Old Regime: The Development of a Mass-Circulation Press* (Princeton, 1991), 155–57.

17 Gosudarstvennyi arkhiv rossiiskogo federatsii (GARF), f. 102, 3 d-vo, 1894, d. 19, l. 1.

18 Through her subsequent marriage to a member of this student circle, P. I. Kuskov, Kuskova acquired the surname she used throughout most of the rest of her life. Herzen established *Kolokol* in 1857 to promote a "critical attitude" among Russia's educated elements.

19 GARF, DP III, 1893, d. 217, l. 45 ob, 46; and L. P. Men'shchikov, *Okhrana i revoliutsiia*, vol. 1 (Moscow, 1925), 292. Typical of Ku-

skova's recollections of the circle is "Davno minuvshee," *Novyi zhurnal* 50 (1957): 179–82.

20 Kuskova, "Davno minuvshee," *Novyi zhurnal* 51 (1957): 170–71; and "Nadpol'e i podpol'e marksizma," *Novoe russkoe slovo*, 24 July 1954. Her departure for Western Europe in the spring of 1895 was recorded by the Okhrana (political police) (GARF, f. 102, 3 d-vo, 1894, d. 19, l. 44).

21 Kuskova mentions her early relationship with Prokopovich without providing much detail. It appears that she and Kuskov were never divorced and that her "marriage [to Prokopovich] without the possibility of legalizing it" occurred after the pair went abroad. See "Davno minuvshee," *Novyi zhurnal* 54 (1958): 117.

22 Kuskova did not remain abroad uninterruptedly during this period but returned to Russia frequently, as the Okhrana duly noted. See, for example, GARF, f. 102, 3 d-vo, 1894, d. 19, ll. 50, 75, 90, 95.

23 On the legal authority of the government over the press in this period, see Jacob Walkin, *The Rise of Democracy in Pre-revolutionary Russia* (New York, 1962), 111–15.

24 From Kuskova's later recollections, particularly those found in articles published in emigration after 1922, it is clear that she attended carefully to the various mechanisms by which European socialist parties and labor organizations spread their messages and argued their causes.

25 HIWRP, Nicolaevsky Collection, no. 209, folder 1, Prokopovich to Aksel'rod [late December 1897 or early January 1898] and Kuskova to Aksel'rod [late March 1899]; and Arkhiv Dom Plekhanova (ADP), no. 2994, Kuskova to Aksel'rod, 7 February 1898. As far as I have been able to determine, Kuskova had little or no income of her own in these years.

26 She also penned two pamphlets under the union's imprimatur: *Stachka lzhi* (Geneva, 1898) and *Son pod pervoe maia* (Geneva, 1898). Her role in union publishing operations appears to be somewhat unusual, as women involved in Russia's revolutionary underground press more typically worked with printers and typesetters, served as couriers, or provided cover for these illegal operations. For a fuller discussion of Kuskova's involvement with the Union Abroad, see Barbara T. Norton, "*Esche raz ekonomizm*: E. D. Kuskova, S. N. Prokopovich, and the Challenge to Russian Social Democracy," *Russian Review* 45 (1986): 183–207.

27 HIWRP, Nicolaevsky Collection, no. 209, folder 1, Kuskova to Aksel'rod, 9 January [1898].

28 One concerned a Belgian miners' strike, another the Belgian politician Emile Vandervelde's parliamentary activities, and a third France's 1848 revolution. "Pis'mo k Aksel'rodu," 22; ADP, no. 2994, Kuskova to Aksel'rod, 7 February 1898; HIWRP, Nicolaevsky Collection, no. 209,

folder 1, Kuskova to Aksel'rod, 22 [February 1898], 15 [March 1898], and [late March or early April 1898]; and "Pis'mo S. N. Prokopovicha," 164.

29 The émigré leaders largely ignored Kuskova as a political actor not only in their private correspondence with one another but also in their public polemics, after disagreements with the Union Abroad erupted into the so-called Economist Controversy. There is no evidence that Kuskova was cognizant of the sexism in this. Like many women in the ranks of the Russian oppositional movement, she seems to have taken her equality with men so much for granted that it never occurred to her that anyone would question it.

30 On the unusual nature of Saratov radicalism, see Donald J. Raleigh, introduction to *Revolution on the Volga* (Ithaca, N.Y., 1986).

31 I certainly do not wish to suggest a crude essentialism, nor am I inclined to support the notion of a "woman's way of thinking." But I would argue that a variety of factors in the socialization process in any patriarchal society may incline women to particular attitudes and behaviors.

32 E. Kuskova, review of *Iz istorii rabochego dvizheniia i sotsial-demokratii v Rossii 1900–1904 gg.*, by F. Dan, *Byloe* 10 (1906): 325; and "Zigzagi pamiati (Po povodu vospominanii g-zhi Tyrkovoi-Vil'iams)," NRS, 17 and 18 July 1952.

33 Kuskova, "Zigzagi pamiati." Tyrkova and Liubov' Gurevich also contributed to *Osvobozhdenie*. See K. F. Shatsillo, "Novye svedeniia o psevdonimakh v zhurnale 'Osvobozhdenie," in *Arkheograficheskii ezhegodnik za 1977 god* (Moscow, 1978), 111–14.

34 Kuskova remained under police surveillance at the beginning of the twentieth century. Regarding her pseudonyms, see Shatsillo, "Novye svedeniia," 113. "Kredo" is an illusion to an infamous statement she penned during the course of the Economist Controversy. The use and meaning of pseudonyms for women journalists is another aspect of Russian women's journalism that requires more attention from scholars.

35 Archive of Russian and East European History and Culture, Columbia University, A. F. Damanskaia Collection, box 41, folder 2, Kuskova to Damanskaia, 9 July 1949. L. V. Khodskii, publisher of *Nasha zhizn'*, was the paper's "responsible" or official editor, that is, the individual registered with the local censorship committee.

36 International Institute for Social History (IISH), Lidiia O. Dan Archive, packet 15, folder 11, Kuskova to L. O. Dan, 29 April 1995. Recounting this episode years later, Kuskova recalled that Prokopovich had presented her with an ultimatum: the newspaper or him. From what I know of the couple's relationship, as well as of Kuskova's epistolary style, I suspect this was simply an exaggeration for dramatic effect.

37 See *Svoboda pechati pri obnovlennom stroe* (St. Petersburg, 1912), 46–48.
38 During the "days of freedom" in October and November 1905, press laws and directives from the censor were completely ignored in the capitals and were largely ineffective in the provinces. See Walkin, *Rise of Democracy*, 116, 123–34. For a discussion of the role of the press in this period, see McReynolds, *News*, 199ff.
39 Regarding attitudes toward women's suffrage, see Linda Harriet Edmondson, *Feminism in Russia, 1900–1917* (Stanford, 1984), 27–57. Tyrkova's and Gurevich's participation in the Equal Rights Union is discussed briefly in Rochelle Ruthchild's essay.
40 Like all Marxists, Kuskova was acquainted with the work of Friedrich Engels and August Bebel. As the police discovered, she had also been exposed to Russian writing on the oppression of women. See GARF, f. 102, 3 d-vo, 1894, d. 19, l. 1. The extent of her interest in the woman question in these years is difficult to gauge, however.
41 Nor was her political involvement in the 1905 revolution confined to journalism. She remained one of the Union of Liberation's most active members, playing a key role, for instance, in founding the Union of Unions. On this organization, see the preceding essay by Linda Edmondson, note 16.
42 On the formation of these unions, which contributed importantly to the further professionalization of journalism in late imperial Russia, see V. P. Leikina-Svirskaia, *Russkaia intelligentsiia v 1900–1917 godakh* (Moscow, 1951), 140–42. Kuskova was also instrumental in establishing the Union of Book Publishers (Soiuz knigoizdatelei). See "Sredi knigoizdatelei," *Nasha zhizn'*, 1 November 1905, 4. A subsequent report indicates that she provided 200 rubles to support its activities ("Ot biuro soiuz knigoizdatelei za osushchestvlenie svobody pechati," *Nasha zhizn'*, 12 November 1905, 4). Because Kuskova, rather than Prokopovich, is identified as the source of this money, it is likely that she now had income of her own, probably from her recently established publishing firm. Regarding the professionalization of journalism in Russia, see Jehanne Gheith's introduction, note 10.
43 The revision of the law for the periodical press came on 24 November 1905 and was supplemented on 18 March 1906; new rules were set for books, pamphlets, and brochures on 26 April 1906. For the revised statutes, see "Ustav o tsenzure i pechati," *Svod zakonov Rossiiskoi Imperii*, vol. 14, supplement (St. Petersburg, 1906). Press reform had been under discussion in government circles even before the events of 1905 forced the emperor's hand. See Charles Ruud, *Fighting Words: Imperial Censorship and the Russian Press, 1864–1917* (Toronto, 1982), 212–13.

44 Additionally, the new press law applied only to periodicals published in cities; the rural press continued to be regulated as before. Statistics on the number of publications and editors who ran afoul of the censorship regulations in and after 1905 and 1906 can be found in Leikina-Svirskaia, *Russkaia intelligentsiia,* 142; and Daniel Balmuth, *Censorship in Russia, 1860–1905* (Washington, D.C., 1979), 136.

45 See Kuskova and V. Ia. Bogucharskii's letter to the editor, *RVed,* 4 November 1905, 4. Prokopovich, also a member of the Central Committee, withdrew from the party as well.

46 On the special role of the press after 1905, see Caspar Ferenczi, "Freedom of the Press under the Old Regime, 1905–1914," in *Civil Rights in Imperial Russia,* ed. Olga Crisp and Linda Edmondson (Oxford, 1989), 191–214.

47 T. A. Bogdanova, "G. V. Plekhanov i gazeta 'Tovarishch,'" in *Knizhnoe delo v Rossii vo vtoroi polovine XIX-nachale XX veka* (Leningrad, 1989), pt. 4, 149. Kuskova defined the journal's position in "Otvet na vopros: kto my?" *Bez zaglaviia,* no. 3 (1906): 81–89.

48 I say "does not appear to have" because I am well aware of the limitations of my source base and that further research could reveal such a conclusion to be unfounded.

49 Kuskova, "Otvet na vopros," 89.

50 V. V. Rozanov, "Opavshie list'ia," in *Uedinennoe* (Moscow, 1990), 290 (the comment was penned in 1912); and I. V. Gessen, "V dvukh vehakh: Zhiznennyi otchet," *Arkhiv russkoi revoliutsii* 22 (1937): 377.

51 *Bez zaglaviia,* no. 16 (1906): 150.

52 According to a colleague at the papers, "Kuskova gained a certain influence on Khodskii, which led to the radicalization of the views of this, in essence, conservative professor" (V. F. Totomiants, *Iz moikh vospominanii* [Sofia, 1943], 72). Both papers ran into difficulty with the censorship authorities on numerous occasions before their final closure. See S. R. Mintslov, "14 mesiatsev 'svobody pechati': 17 oktiabria 1905g.–1 ianvaria 1907g," *Byloe,* no. 3 (1907): 131–32.

53 I have yet to examine this rare periodical. A brief description of Kuskova's *Tovarishch'* column can be found in *Russkie pisateli,* s.v. "Kuskova." The focus of her *NZ* articles, which appeared pseudonymously under her initials, was similar. See, for example, "Vybor sredi rabochikh," *NZ,* 21 March/3 April 1906, and *NZ,* "Vybor i partii," 28 April/11 May 1906.

54 From a letter of 15 April 1907, reproduced in Bogdanova, "G. V. Plekhanov," 158. Kuskova noted here that she would soon leave for Switzerland for a "rather serious operation."

55 Thus the Menshevik Aleksandra Kollontai observed to Plekhanov: "I personally respect Ekaterina Dmitrievna very much; I admire her energy" (Bogdanova, "G. V. Plekhanov," 149). Plekhanov responded: "I know Kuskova and also, like you, have respect for her energy." See *Filosofskogo-literaturnoe nasledie G. V. Plekhanova,* vol. 1, *G. V. Plekhanov i ego rol' v rasprostranenii marksistskogo mirovozzreniia v revoliutsionnom dvizhenii Rossii* (Moscow, 1973), 219.

56 After June 1907, the government restored some of the administrative controls on the press eliminated in 1905 and 1906.

57 These thoughts were directed to Plekhanov in the spring of 1908 (Bogdanova, "G. V. Plekhanov," 170). Kuskova also had some connection with *Stolichnaia pochta*. The practice of changing a periodical's name to get around the censorship was a common one. Regarding this genealogical dimension of Russian journalism, see Ferenczi, "Freedom of the Press," 197–98.

58 HIWRP, Nicolaevsky Collection, no. 109, box 5, folder 51, undated letter to B. N. Krichevskii (probably September 1908).

59 At one point, the couple wrote as if already in possession of both publications. HIWRP, Nicolaevsky Collection, no. 109, box 51, folder 51, Kuskova and Prokopovich to Krichevskii, 13 September [1908]. However, subsequent correspondence indicates that this was premature. Ibid., Kuskova to Krichevskii, 11 October 1908; and no. 19, box 1, folder 1, A. N. Potresov to Iu. O. Martov, 28 September 1908 (the letters in this file are copies). During 1909 the couple would discuss creating a daily paper, but that project, part of an attempted rapprochement with organized social democracy, never materialized. Ibid., no. 19, box 1, folder 1, Potresov to Martov, 7/20 August 1909, and Potresov to Martov, 31 October 1909; and a letter from Martov to Aksel'rod, 27 September 1909, in *Pis'ma Aksel'roda,* 199, and HIWRP, Nicolaevsky Collection, no. 93, A. Martynov (A. S. Piker) to Martov, 29 September [1909] (the letters in this file are copies).

60 I am not as persuaded as Linda Edmondson (see the preceding essay) that marriage to Prokopovich significantly facilitated Kuskova's access to, or enhanced her standing in, the activist community that would establish *Osvobozhdenie* and the Union of Liberation. By the turn of the century, Kuskova was already well-known in radical circles and counted many prominent liberals among her friends as well.

61 Although I have not yet examined the archival records of this firm — in business from 1902 or 1903 until at least 1907 — it is evident from the socioeconomic nature of the books issued under Kuskova's imprimatur (listed on the back cover of each publication) that her first priority was

not profit but politics. It would be interesting to know how many other women owned publishing houses in imperial Russia and what these women's priorities were.

62 Acquaintances (including N. E. Andreyev, S. N. Pushkarev, Boris Sapir, and Leonard Schapiro) who knew the couple in Russia and in emigration after 1922 consistently reported to me in interviews in the mid-1970s that Kuskova was intellectually the stronger partner. How unique this partnership may have been in the annals of Russian journalism is not clear. Certainly there were other wife-and-husband teams, as Jehanne Gheith and Mary Zirin remind us in their essays in this volume. Most of these relationships have yet to be examined by scholars. A preliminary list of such teams can be culled from the checklist of women journalists in the appendix.

63 Kuskova always lived an extremely peripatetic life, and it is often difficult to determine precisely where she called home. The move to Moscow may not have come until the following year.

64 Aronson, "E. D. Kuskova," 242.

65 E. Kuskova, "Zhenskii s"ezd," *RVed,* 20 December 1908, 7. Her nascent feminism was already apparent in April 1906, when she signed an appeal for women's rights published in *NZ,* 29 April 1906, 3–4. I use "feminist" here to denote an individual consciously concerned with expanding the rights and improving the welfare of women.

66 See Edmondson, *Feminism in Russia,* 58. (The penetration metaphor is deliberate.)

67 Kuskova, "Zhenskii s"ezd," 7. For her criticism of the congress, see also "Zhenskii vopros i zhenskii s"ezd," *Obrazovanie,* no. 2 (1909): 36–38, 43, and no. 1 (1909): 97, and "Zhenshchiny i ravnopravie (Po povodu prevogo vserossiiskogo zhenskogo s"ezda)," *SZh,* no. 12 (December 1908): 1–3.

68 In 1913 or 1914, she would author the entry on the woman question *(zhenskii vopros)* for the *Entsiklopedicheskii slovar'* (Granat), 7th ed., vol. 20 (Moscow, nd), s.v. "Zhenskii vopros." Publication in this prestigious reference work is another indication of Kuskova's stature in the publishing world.

69 The situation of factory workers, strikes and demonstrations, political prisoners, the "Jewish question," and anti-Semitism were among the topics still prohibited by the government. See Ferenczi, "Freedom of the Press," 200.

70 Letter from Martov to Aksel'rod, 1 November 1907, in *Pis'ma Aksel'roda,* 173. Whether Martov's remark, made in connection with Kuskova's editorial position at *Tovarishch,* was anything more than

sexism, I cannot say; I have found no indication that she broke with social convention over the matter of prescribed female attire.

71 Kuskova, "Zhenskii s"ezd," 7.
72 Kuskova had obviously overcome some of this attitude, as she began to recognize the value of gender issues in attracting working women into oppositional activity.
73 *Trudy 1-go vserossiiskogo zhenskogo s"ezda pri Russkom Zhenskom (Vzaimno-Blagotvoritel'nom) Obshchestve v S-Peterburge 16–19 dek. 1908 goda* (St. Petersburg, 1909), 767.
74 Kuskova to A. V. Amfiteatrov, 26 January 1911, quoted in *Literaturnoe nasledstvo*, vol. 95, *Gor'kii i russkaia zhurnalistika nachala XX veka*, ed. I. S. Zil'berstein and N. I. Dikushina (Moscow, 1988), 304–5.
75 See Kuskova's comments to Amfiteatrov from 6 May 1911 and 19 June 1911, quoted in *Liberaturnoe nasledstvo*, 305 and 309 respectively.
76 Amfiteatrov to Gor'kii, 23 June 1911 [NS], *Literaturnoe nasledstvo*, 320. Despite a friendship with Kuskova stretching back to the early 1890s, Gor'kii was not so regretful. (See his letter from mid-July 1911, 319). My sense is that he thought Kuskova was a pain in the neck.
77 See, for example, ADP, no. 2994, Kuskova to Plekhanov, 15 February 1912 and 18 May 1912.
78 E. Kuskova, "Ranenye," *RVed*, 17 July 1911, 2–3; "Shelest biulletenei," *RVed*, 31 October 1912, 3; and "Probuzhdenie," *RVed*, 4 November 1912, 3.
79 Kuskova, "Koshmarnye fanty," *RVed*, 6 February 1913, 2; and "Izlishnii spor," *RVed*, 16 June 1913, 2.
80 Kuskova, "Kulturno-prosvetitel'nye zadachi russkoi kooperatsii," *RVed*, 25 November 1913, 6; and "Utikhnut li strasti?" *RVed*, 5 November 1913, 3.
81 Kuskova, "Trudnyi put'," *RVed*, 22 April 1914, 2.
82 The Union of Towns was organized shortly after the war's outbreak to coordinate local initiative. Regarding Kuskova's membership, see IISH, Dan Archive, 15, p. 12, Kuskova to Dan, 14 February 1956. For Kuskova's views on the role of the voluntary organizations, see for example her "Otdykh kooperatorov," *RVed*, 4 January 1915, 6, and "Voenno-promyshlennykh komitety i rabochie," *RVed*, 15 October 1915, 5. With the outbreak of the war, Kuskova also took part in an ill-fated attempt to establish a cooperative newspaper. See Iu. N. Emel'ianov, *S. P. Mel'gunov: V Rossii i emigratsii* (Moscow, 1998), 40.
83 Gor'kii mentions the project in a letter to Vladimir Voitinskii, written apparently in early November 1915 (*Literaturnoe nasledstvo*, 932). See also S. P. Mel'gunov, *Vospominaniia i dnevniki*, vol. 1 (Paris, 1964), 192.

84 E. Kuskova, "Puti ternistye . . . ," *Poslednie novosti*, 3 April 1936.
85 N. Berdaiev, *Samopoznanie (Opit filosofskoi avtobiografii)*, 2d ed., vol. 1 (Paris, 1988), 261.
86 S. P. Mel'gunov, *Na putiakh k dvortsovomu perevorotu* (Paris, 1931), 171–72. For more on these efforts to create a democratic coalition, see Barbara T. Norton, "Russian Political Masonry and the February Revolution of 1917," *International Review of Social History* 28 (1983), pt. 2, 240–58.
87 E. Kuskova, "Mgnovenie 27 fevral'ia 1917g.," *Dni*, 15 March 1923.
88 *RVed*, 18 March 1917, 3.

Sources for the Study of Russian Women Journalists

A Bibliographic Essay

JUNE PACHUTA FARRIS

The topic of Russian women journalists is a difficult one to research for several reasons. Materials on the history of Russian journalism are diffuse, sometimes found in literary sources, sometimes in historical sources, rarely in separately published titles devoted solely to the subject of journalism.[1] In most histories of Russian journalism, as several of the essays in this volume have noted, women contributors are given only a passing mention, a paragraph here, a page or two there. And although nineteenth-century sources on women, women writers, women in the professions, and the history of the women's movement in Russia are numerous,[2] a mere handful focus specifically on women journalists. The last twenty years have seen a renewed interest in topics concerning women and their contributions to Russian society and culture and have produced another surge in publications on women in Russia, not only in Western languages but in Russian and the various languages of the former Soviet Union. Nevertheless, identifying women journalists and their activities is still a slow and difficult process; printed sources specifically on this topic remain remarkably scarce.

The net must be cast as widely as possible to capture even the smallest bits of information; this often requires approaching the topic obliquely, through memoirs, papers, and archives of friends, colleagues, and family, as well as through the published histories and archival materials of specific journals and newspapers known to employ women. Both general and specialized reference sources in history and literature can prove valuable, whether their focus is on journalism, the development of the popular press, or topics relating specifically to women. Whether researchers use printed or electronic resources, key word and subject searches need to be formulated carefully and inclusively to bring together all relevant materials. It is also important to remember the differences and discrepancies encountered in research that cuts across languages, countries, and traditional subject classifications. Although the words "journalism" and "the press" are sufficient to identify most applicable material on the topic in English-language sources, *zhurnalistika-zhurnalist/zhurnalistka* and *publitsistika-publitsist/publitsistka*, with their important differences in meaning and scope,[3] along with *pressa, gazety, zhurnaly,* and *reportazh,* must be used to extract the full range of Russian language materials available.

Women's names themselves create an additional series of problems in accessing information about various writers; some women are best known by their family names, others by the names of their husbands. The use of pseudonyms (often gender neutral) further complicates the situation. The compiler of each reference source or index selects one form of entry from among many possibilities, perhaps without a set of cross-references. Although there is a great deal of standardization of name entries, cataloging rules change, particularly regarding the use of pseudonyms in a bibliographic entry. Even in an electronic environment, cross-references (if they exist at all) are far from foolproof and rely on the knowledge and expertise of indexers for their effectiveness and comprehensiveness.[4]

General Reference Aids and Bibliographies

The field of Russian bibliography has a long and rich history that has produced a vast number of retrospective and current reference sources on Russian history, literature, and culture. From this abundance, the following works have been carefully selected as the most potentially useful to those wishing to pursue research on Russian women journalists. All items referred to in the text of the essay and in the notes are followed by a bracketed number [] referring to the full bibliographic citation given for each title in the corresponding list of works cited.

Bibliographies of Serial Publications

Among the many bibliographies of prerevolutionary Russian serial publications, the most authoritative and comprehensive is N. M.

Lisovskii's *Russkaia periodicheskaia pechat' 1703–1900 gg.* [3]. Entries are arranged by first year of publication and include all known changes in title, subtitle, frequency of publication, and editorship. Cross-references to earlier, later, and merged titles are also given so that the complete history of a publication can be traced. In addition to title, name, and geographic indexes, a series of bibliographic tables present the history of Russian periodical publishing in a succinct and graphic way. L. N. Beliaeva's *Bibliografiia periodicheskikh izdanii Rossii, 1901–1916* [1] updates Lisovskii's volume and includes information about all available indexes to a given title, as well as an issue-by-issue, year-by-year enumeration of volumes published. The two companion volumes of *Russkaia periodicheskaia pechat': Spravochnik* [4 and 5], compiled by M. S. Cherepakhov and others, give detailed bibliographic information about hundreds of eighteenth-, nineteenth-, and twentieth-century Russian journals and newspapers, and the extensive annotations provide a publication history, highlighting important events (incidents of censorship, closure, etc.) and a summary of the periodical's contents and organization, as well as mention of important contributors. Entries are arranged by date of first publication, and name, title, and geographic indexes are included, as well as a list of important underground publications *(nelegal'naia pechat')*. When available, journal indexes can be of enormous help to the researcher in pursuing elusive publications by and about a given writer. Iu. I. Masanov's comprehensive *Ukazateli soderzhaniia russkikh zhurnalov i prodolzhaiushchikhsia izdanii* [2] provides important and hard-to-identify information about indexes to both prerevolutionary and Soviet periodical publications. The first section (pp. 8–189) lists indexes to journals published between 1755 and 1917. Included are separately published indexes and indexes found in the journals themselves or published in other periodicals. A detailed description of the coverage, scope, and length of each index is provided.

General Bibliographies, Dictionaries, and Encyclopedias

Among currently published ongoing bibliographies, the annual *Bibliografiia rossiiskoi bibliografii* [7] provides access to innumerable Russian bibliographies published separately or in books and periodical publications, and covering the entire range of subject fields within the humanities, social sciences, and sciences, arranged in broad subject categories. In the earlier volumes, bibliographies pertinent to journalism were listed under the heading "Pechat'. Knigovedenie"; the most recent volumes list journalism entries under "Sredstva massovoi informatsii i propagandy." No detailed subject index is provided, but name, corporate author, and title indexes help to identify bibliographies relevant to individual persons or journal titles. The Russian Academy of Sciences Institute of Scientific Information on the Social Sciences (Institut nauchnoi informatsii po obshchestvennym naukam, or INION) publishes *Novaia otechestvennaia i inostrannaia literatura po obshchestvennym naukam,* a series of comprehensive monthly bibliographies citing the most current research published in Russia, as well as selected citations from North American and Eastern and Western European publications. Its history and literature subseries, *Istoriia, arkheologiia, etnografiia* [12] and *Literaturovedenie* [13], include citations to journal and newspaper articles, books, conference proceedings, chapters of books, dissertations, and unpublished manuscripts deposited in the institute's library. Although there is no annual cumulative index, since the mid-1980s, each issue has a detailed subject index that provides access to materials on journalism, journalists, and related topics, as well as specific individuals. The history subseries lists articles having to do with the history of journalism and the press and includes citations on women and the women's movement (*zhurnalistika, publitsistika, pressa, zhenschiny,* etc.), and the literature subseries contains materials on the journalistic activities of individual authors (see *publitsistika* in the subject indexes). The annual *American Bibliography of Slavic and East European Studies* [6] and the *European Bibliography of Soviet, East European, and Slavonic Studies* [8] provide the same comprehensive coverage of materials published in the United States, Canada, and Western Europe. In addition to citations to books, dissertations, chapters, journal articles, and government reports, each has a separate section devoted to book reviews. Both bibliographies are arranged by broad subject categories, and several sections should be scanned to identify pertinent citations to women and journalism (Communications and the Media, History, and Literature). The *European Bibliography,* which was formed by merging the earlier British and French bibliographies, contains primarily English, German, and French publications, although each successive volume expands coverage of publications from the Netherlands, Belgium, Scandinavia, and other areas. The sections on Russian biography, history, culture, literature and arts, publishing and censorship, and politics (mass media and propaganda) contain citations to material on women and journalism.

Retrospective bibliographies of particular usefulness include *Istoriia dorevoliutsionnoi Rossii v dnevnikakh i vospominaniiakh* [9], a truly monumental listing of more than 24,500 entires to books and periodicals containing diaries, memoirs, necrologies, and reminiscences by and about the men and women of pre-1917 Russia, providing the broadest possible picture of the country's social, political, and military history through Russian governmental, religious, educational, and cultural institutions. Although only a few subsections deal exclusively with topics relating to women ("Vysshie zhenskie kursy [1857–1894]," vol. 3, pt. 2, pp. 331–32; "Zhenskoe dvizhenie," vol. 4, pt. 2, p. 138; "Vysshie zhenskie kursy [1895–1917]," vol. 4, pt. 3, pp. 276–81), through the use of each volume's name index, there is access to hundreds of entries to material by and about individual women—journalists, writers, artists, actresses, scientists, teachers, revolutionaries, wives of priests and merchants, women of the nobility—all those who have written about themselves and the times they lived in. Additional sections, "Pechat'. Zhurnalistika. Izdatel'skoe delo" (vol. 3, pt. 2, pp. 251–73; vol. 5, pt. 1, pp. 21–31; vol. 5, pt. 2, pp. 238–48), provide citations to the memoirs of journalists and publishers,[5] including M. S. Skovronskaia, V. N. Tsekhovskaia (Ol'nem), A. I. Sokolova, N. A. Belozerskaia, A. A. Davydova, I. A. Grinevskaia, L. I. Gurevich, L. K. Tugan-Baranovskaia, M. V. Iamshchikova, T. P. Passek, and M. N. Sleptsova (Lavrova). In addition, works by and about other women journalists are cited throughout other sections and subsections (A. V. Tyrkova, V. M. Velichkina, A. N. Peshkova-Toliverova, for example). See the systematic index (vol. 5, pt. 1, p. 325) for a complete list of journalism entries. Extensive annotations are given, often supplying detailed contents notes.

Another retrospective bibliography of great import and usefulness is N. A. Rubakin's massive *Sredi knig* [14], comprising a series of lengthy bibliographic essays on the critical social, political, religious, and literary topics and movements abounding in late-nineteenth- and early-twentieth-century Russia; each essay is followed by a bibliography of materials recommended for further reading. Two sections are particularly relevant to the study of women and journalism in Russia, the first being "Publitsistika i kritika v sviazi s istoriei iziashchnoi literatury i drugikh iziashchnykh iskusstv i s istoriei literaturno-obshchestvennykh techenii" (vol. 1, pp. 204–351). The section begins with an extensive bibliographic essay (see especially pp. 315–17 for a history of journalism in Russia), followed by a select bibliography of related titles. "Stroi semeinyi i ego istoriia" (vol. 2, pp. 340–61) also begins with a lengthy bibliographic essay followed by an extensive bibliography on the family, marriage, and women, with subdivisions for the topics of the woman question, the history of women, the abilities of women and their right to an equal education, their intellectual activities, their legal, economic, political, and social position in Russian society, and ending with women as prostitutes and criminals. An additional section, "Stroi narodnogo obrazovaniia i vospitaniia," contains a subsection devoted to women's education (pp. 375–76). All citations, including translations of Western European sources, refer to separately published monographic works and are without annotations.

Among the many general encyclopedias and biographical dictionaries available, *Russkie pisateli 1800–1917* [15] provides the most comprehensive coverage of Russian women authors, with detailed entries for both well-known and relatively obscure prose writers, reporters, editors, translators, and publishers. As well as biographical information, a brief analysis of individual works is given, and entries are often accompanied by a portrait of the author. Included in the bibliographies are detailed references to archival *fonds* that contain substantial holdings of the authors' papers and manuscripts. Two English-language encyclopedias, *The Modern Encyclopedia of Russian and Soviet History* [10] and *The Modern Encyclopedia of East Slavic, Baltic, and Eurasian Literatures* [11], also include articles on a wide variety of topics related to journalism, journalists, and writers. The accompanying bibliographies can be very helpful as a guide to further research. In the history encyclopedia, see the index section "Publications and Press" (vol. 57, pp. 196–203) for a list of all entries dealing with specific periodicals, and with journalists (no women cited), editors, and publishers. The literature encyclopedia is only partially completed; coverage of women writers, although not extensive, includes some authors who were journalists, editors, and publishers (Al. Altaev [Iamshchikova], A. N. Annenskaia, Dashkova, Gurevich, for example). Entries for various literary genres and topics are also useful ("Feminism in Russian Literature," "Feuilleton, Russian").

Electronic Information Sources

The world of electronic resources (full-text reference works, indexing, and abstracting services, full-text databases and library catalogs and information servers) is in a continuous stage of development and change. A profusion of new sources appears each year, some replicating printed sources, others entirely new. Specific information about coverage and scope is likely to alter within months as publishers and individuals develop and refine their electronic products. There are often several options and formats available for providing access to a database (compact discs available at a single workstation or cluster, locally networked as databases or system-wide databases). Electronic sources may offer complete or partial coverage, which may require the use of retrospective print volumes for comprehensive coverage. To become aware of the full range of electronic resources available at any given time and at any given institution, it is best to contact appropriate reference staff. Two primary advantages of electronic sources are their currency (often with weekly, monthly, quarterly, or semiannual updates that are immediately accessible) and their multiple access points, through which one can construct specific or broad search strategies. As more and more of these electronic databases become available in vendor-supplied packages, the necessity of learning a variety of complex and unique commands is disappearing, simplifying and facilitating the search process for each database.

Among the electronic sources most useful to the study of women and journalism in Russia are *ABSEES On-line* [16], *Dissertation Abstracts* [18], *Historical Abstracts* [20], the *MLA International Bibliography* [21], and *RAS-Russian Academy of Sciences Bibliographies* [22]. *ABSEES Online* is the electronic counterpart to the annual printed volume of the *American Bibliography of Slavic and East European Studies* and begins its coverage with the material found in the 1990 volume of *ABSEES;* it is updated monthly. There are multiple points of access (by author, title, place and date of publication, publisher, series, and notes, and by formal subject headings or keyword/Boolean searching), and results can be downloaded to a printer or sent to an electronic mail address.[6] Available only since 1998 through the collaboration of eight major European research institutions, *EBSEES Online* [19] is the electronic counterpart to its printed volumes. Coverage has begun with 1991 to 1993, with plans to become current as quickly as possible. This database will be a particularly rich resource for the less widely indexed publications of Austria, Belgium, Finland, France, Germany, the Netherlands, Switzerland, and the United Kingdom. *Dissertation Abstracts Online* (or *OnDisk*), the electronic counterpart of *Dissertation Abstracts International,* is updated quarterly as well as offering complete retrospective coverage from 1861 to the present. Likewise, *Historical Abstracts Online* (or *OnDisk*) provides bibliographic coverage of the world's historical literature on modern history (1450 to the present). The print version began in 1955 and includes articles on journalism, journalists, individual periodicals, editors and editing, the press, and reporters and reporting, as well as works on women, the women's liberation movement, and feminism, cross-referenced with Russia. A publication of the Modern Language Association, the *MLA International Bibliography* (available on-line and on compact disk), was first published in 1921 and includes articles, essays, dissertations, and books on language, linguistics, folklore, and literature in all languages, with moderately comprehensive coverage of Russian authors and topics. Another important electronic source is *ArcheoBiblioBase* (ABB) [17], an integrated archival information retrieval and publication system, which combines the display of vital data about individual Russian archival repositories with a structured bibliography of their finding aids, using a Macintosh-based program in 4th Dimension. The project is coordinated in the United States by Patricia Kennedy Grimsted in collaboration with a team of Russian compilers and editors and is maintained on the Web site of the International Instituut voor Sociale Geschiedenis in Amsterdam. The *Russian Academy of Sciences Bibliographies* corresponds, in part, to the monthly printed subject bibliographies of the Academy's Institute of Social Sciences [12, 13]. The 200,000-plus citations and abstracts (from 1990 to the present, with monthly updates) cover materials in archaeology, anthropology, demography, economics, folklore, history, international relations, law, linguistics, literary studies, philosophy, political science, religion, sociology, and scientific policy, with citations primarily to Russian language material, but with increasing numbers of citations to publications in the other languages of the Soviet successor states, the countries of Eastern and Western Europe, and American publications. This is likely to become the most comprehensive and useful database available to researchers in Russian studies.

Reference Aids and Bibliographies on Women in Russia

Among the earliest specialized reference sources on women in the Russian empire is N. N. Golitsyn's 1889 *Bibliograficheskii slovar' russkikh pisatel'nits* [24], a comprehensive biobibliographical dictionary of more than 1,200 women writers, most having written only in Russian or in Russian and other languages, with seventy-three entries for authors who wrote exclusively in languages other than Russian. Information is provided not only for authors of belles lettres but also for those writing on historical social, political, and scientific topics. Entries range from a few lines to six or seven pages (Catherine II requires eighteen pages) and often include biographical information and information about pseudonyms and other name variations. Citations include books, articles, translations, separately published poems, and dissertations. A bibliography about a given author and her works, including citations to reviews, necrologies, and memoirs, is provided whenever possible. The first section of S. I. Ponomarev's *Nashi pisatel'nitsy* [28] consists of an analysis of women authors and their works as reflected in Golitsyn's *Bibliograficheskii slovar' russkikh pisatel'nits*. Because the Golitsyn work is a straight listing of authors without indexes of any sort, Ponomarev, in effect, creates a subject index, in which he classifies the writing activities of these authors by type and topic of their writing and by the nature of their activities (pp. 3–11). Included among the categories are journalists/publicists (seventeen women), publishers and editors (eighty-four), critics and reviewers (nine), memoirists (twenty-seven), writers of belles lettres, bibliographers, dramatists, historians, mathematicians, physicians, teachers, translators, and bookstore managers, with many names appearing in more than one list. The second section (pp. 23–78) consists of a supplement to Golitsyn's bibliography and includes 419 entries, either for authors not listed in the Golitsyn dictionary or for additions and corrections to earlier entries. Many of the new works cited date from the late 1880s through 1890. A contemporary English-language update to the Golitsyn/Ponomarev volumes is the *Dictionary of Russian Women Writers* [23], with more than 450 entries, from the earliest women writers such as N. B. Dolgorukaia (1714–1771) to the most contemporary living authors. This work brings together an enormous amount of information about women writers — poets, prose writers, essayists, publicists, journalists, editors, memoirists, biographers, translators, playwrights, and literary critics. All known forms of an author's names are given (birth name, married name[s], pseudonyms), followed by a biography and general analysis of her literary oeuvre. A bibliography of works by and about the author accompanies each entry, including citations to other biographical reference works listing the author and locations for any archival materials. A detailed index of names (with extensive cross-references) and subjects is included, as well as a bibliography, chronology, and time line, altogether providing not only a useful and straightforward ready reference source but also a guide to further research.

Among the earliest and most important bibliographies on Russia and the woman question is "Ukazatel' literatury zhenskogo voprosa na russkom iazyke" [30], a comprehensive bibliography of 1,785 citations of monographs and journal articles in Russian pertaining to all aspects of women and the family. Categories include the history of women, the contemporary position of women, female literary types, the woman question, the upbringing and education of women, and female labor and public activities (including women in war, in industry and agriculture, in medicine, in the arts, and the pedagogical activities of women). Many translations of Western-language sources are included, and the articles are taken from a wide variety of popular, scholarly, and professional journals. Subject and author indexes are included. Roberta Manning's "Bibliography of Works in English on Women in Russia and the Soviet Union" [27], Yedlin and Wilman's *Women in Russia and the Soviet Union* [31], Ignashev and Krive's *Women and Writing in Russia and the USSR* [26], and Ruthchild's *Women in Russia and the Soviet Union: An Annotated Bibliography* [29] provide additional coverage of English-language materials on various aspects of women in Russia. Manning's bibliography of nearly 400 citations in nine roughly chronological categories (from women in pre-Petrine Russia to Soviet women) lists journal articles, monographic works, and relevant periodical titles and includes both original works and translations from Russian and other languages. The material ranges from scholarly research, law codes, and legislative projects to folklore, memoirs, diaries, and travel accounts. Brief critical annotations are given for the majority of citations. In the Yedlin-Wilman compilation, more than 600 citations to journal articles, monographs, and dissertations are listed in one alphabetic sequence. Although citations are primarily to English-language materials, items in other Western European languages and Russian are well represented. Citations cover both scholarly and popular materials and include many general works on Russian history, family history, education, law, art history, literature, folklore, and sociology, providing a broad range of secondary material. Also included are citations to fictional works that portray various aspects of women's lives, as well as biographies, memoirs, and correspondence. Works about non-Slavic women of the Soviet Union are also represented. Brief annotations are included for many items, and an author index is provided. The first supplement, compiled by Janet Hyer [25], contains additional citations. Ruthchild's bibliography, arranged primarily under broad chronological headings from the ancient and medieval periods through the end of the Soviet era in 1991, not only updates the earlier bibliographies but broadens its coverage by the comprehensive inclusion of relevant dissertations, pamphlets, and translations. Particularly useful are the detailed critical annotations, not only to monographic works but also to individual journal articles.

Reference Aids and Bibliographies on Journalism in Russia

Specialized bibliographies and reference sources on journalism in Russia are rare indeed; most form only a section of some larger work, as is the case with the bibliographies found in the Institute of Russian

Literature's authoritative volumes. V. P. Stepanov and Iu. V. Stepnik's "Periodicheskaia pechat' i kritika" [35] covers the eighteenth century, and K. D. Muratova's "Istoriia zhurnalistiki" [32] covers the nineteenth century, and her "Zhurnalistika" [38] covers the thirty years preceding the Soviet era. Although the coverage of each volume varies, their arrangement is identical; citations to books, articles, and pertinent reference works (bibliographies, guides, handbooks, indexes) are provided. Other sections of interest include "Istoriia kritiki" and "Tsenzura." In each of these three bibliographies, the large "Personalia" section lists only a few women journalists (E. Ardov-Apreleva, Dashkova, Gurevich, Ol'nem, O. A. Shapir, T. L. Shchepkina-Kupernik, P. S. Solov'eva, E. Tur); however, a careful examination of the detailed name and subject indexes produces a great many relevant citations to other women journalists (correspondence with other authors, literary and theatrical criticism, etc.). N. M. Somov's *Sistematicheskii ukazatel' knig i statei po zhurnalistike* [37] covers material from both the prerevolutionary period and the early Soviet period. It contains more than 600 entries on the history, theory, and practice of journalism, both in Russia and abroad ("Inostrannaia zhurnalistika"). Included in the section "Russkaia zhurnalistika" (pp. 11–85) are articles, monographs, encyclopedia entries, and conference papers on topics ranging from bibliography, Russian émigré journalism, publishing and the law, individual journalists, journals and newspapers by category, provincial journalism, journalism in the capital (Moscow), and censorship to sections on N. M. Lisovskii, the Museum of the Russian Press, and the State Institute of Journalism. E. P. Prokhorov's "Russkaia zhurnalistika, publitsistika, kritika vtoroi poloviny XIX veka" [36] lists 375 Soviet articles and books of the early 1960s on nineteenth-century Russian journalism, and N. I. Navolotskaia's "Materialy k bibliografii po istorii russkoi zhurnalistiki 1966–1970" [34] lists an additional 783 citations to Soviet works covering all aspects of nineteenth-century Russian journalism and the activities of individual writers. D. Kuz'min's "Alfavit sotrudnikov gazety *Narodnaia volia*" [33] is a list of staff and contributors to the newspaper, among whom are a number of women. When available, references to articles by and about each individual and his or her contributions to the publishing of *Narodnaia volia* are given, whether through writing or editing or in the more technical areas such as typesetting.

Archival Guides

Archival research is particularly important when little has been published on a given topic, as is the case with women journalists in Russia. Physical access to Russian archives is now a reality undreamed of even a decade ago; however, there is still an enormous distance to travel before detailed and accurate information about the holdings in Russia's elaborate system of state archives is easily available.[7] Old guides, even if grossly incomplete and sorely out-of-date, must still be used in conjunction with various newer finding aids (also out-of-date almost at the point of publication) to determine the location of materials relevant to a research topic. Archival research strategies must be as carefully developed as those used for printed sources, always remembering that important information is apt to be found not only in the archives of women journalists themselves but also in the papers of family members and male colleagues.

Patricia Kennedy Grimsted's various handbooks on Russian archives are, without a doubt, the most useful sources to review in preparation for research in Russian archives. Her *Archives and Manuscript Repositories in the USSR: Moscow and Leningrad* [43 and 44], although out-of-date in many particulars, still provides the most comprehensive descriptions of archives in Moscow and St. Petersburg; the indexes are detailed enough to give preliminary location information for a variety of prerevolutionary journals such as *Nabliudatel'*, *Russkaia starina*, *Vestnik Evropy*, *Sovremennik*, *Severnyi vestnik*, *Studencheskii mir*, and other periodicals found in the Manuscript Division of the Academy of Sciences' Institute of Russian Literature (Pushkinskii dom). Grimsted's *Handbook for Archival Research in the USSR* [45] provides straightforward information about the general organization and description of archives and information regarding access to them. The later chapters deal with research strategies and general reference aids for archival and library research, as well as information about the duplication of archival materials. Perhaps most useful are the appendixes, which include basic information and citations to published research guides for Russian archives outside of Moscow and St. Petersburg and for state archives of the non-Russian republics of the former Soviet Union, areas not yet covered in any of Grimsted's major archival guides (aside from Ukraine, Belarus, and the Baltic States).

The collaboration between Patricia Kennedy Grimsted and archivists of Rosarkhiv and other Russian archival institutions has produced *Arkhivy Rossii: Moskva i Sankt-Peterburg* [40], an immense compilation that is both a directory and a detailed bibliographic guide, combining in one volume the most up-to-date information available on federal, academic, and special archives, with detailed bibliographies of sources by and about each archive and its holdings. In its most recent incarnation, an English language edition entitled *Archives of Russia* [39], Grimsted, Repulo, and Tunkina further expand and update information about Moscow and St. Petersburg archives and trace in detail the constantly merging and splitting of archival depositories that has become the hallmark of postsoviet institutional reorganization. As in all of Grimsted's guides, the annotations are dense with information, and the citations to published and unpublished guides and finding aids are particularly useful. The online *ArcheoBiblioBase* [17], a much pared down version of the print sources, can also be a very quick and useful reference tool, especially for those without access to the very expensive originals. Among other recent Russian language archival guides is *Gosudarstvennye arkhivy SSSR* [42], which is, of course, outdated, but still useful, offering information about all of the Soviet Union's state archives, their organization, and a brief description of their holdings and coverage. *Dokumenty GAF SSSR v bibliotekakh, muzeiakh i nauchno-otraslevykh arkhivakh* [41] gives basic descriptions of archival holdings in libraries, museums, and other institutions formerly under the jurisdiction of the USSR and republic Ministries of Culture and the USSR and republic Academies of Science. A name index offers additional points of access.

Among the older archival guides, two are still of particular importance in the study of journalism and journalists, the first being *Lichnye arkhivnye fondy v gosudarstvennykh khranilishchakh SSSR* [46], which lists personal and family papers found in state archives throughout the former Soviet Union. The third volume, published seventeen years after volume 2, contains a supplement of 8,481 additional names, as well as a variety of indexes. The second guide of primary relevance to research on journalism is *Tsentral'nyi gosudarstvennyi arkhiv literatury i iskusstva SSSR: Putevoditel'* [48], published over a span of thirty-nine years. It is a seven-volume guide to Russia's main state repository for literature and art, commonly known as RGALI (formerly TSGALI). The first two (unnumbered) volumes, published in 1959 and 1963, covering art and literature respectively, describe the basic holdings of the archives; volumes 3–6 describe fonds received in later years. Along with the papers of many individual writers, editors, and journalists of the prerevolutionary and Soviet periods (including A. I. Volkova, A. F. Damanskaia, and Shchepkina-Kupernik), the archives of numerous journals and newspapers are located in this repository, including such titles as *Russkii vestnik, Delo, Russkoe bogatstvo, Russkaia mysl', Sovremennik, Russkie vedomosti, Russkoe slovo, Kur'er, Rech'*, and *Sovremennoe slovo. Russian State Archives of Literature and Art — the Complete Archive Guide* [47] is a recent CD-ROM product that has combined the contents of all six printed volumes of the RGALI guide into one electronic database, searchable through multiple access points. Although a bit awkward to use, it nevertheless brings together under one entry detailed information about the contents of each person's or institution's fond gathered during the course of several decades or more.

Select Sources on Women and Journalism in Russia

In contrast to the relatively abundant material published on the lives and work of women writers involved in the revolutionary movement of the nineteenth and twentieth centuries, little has been published on the other Russian women journalists of the imperial period. A selection from the few books, articles, and memoirs that constitute the main body of work on this topic is discussed hereafter.

Monographs, Articles, Essays, Memoirs

Effie Ambler's *Russian Journalism and Politics, 1861–1881* [50] uses A. S. Suvorin's long and varied journalistic and literary career as the setting for the study of the development of journalism in Russia, particularly within the context of continual clashes with censors and involvement in the political and social movements of the last half of the nineteenth century. Women's issues and women journalists are mentioned only in passing. In *The News under Russia's Old Regime* [65], Louise McReynolds's study of the development of the mass-circulation press and its competition with the thick journals of the intelligentsia, women figure only slightly in the discussion of journalism's leading figures. Sokolova (pp. 77–78), Ol'nem (pp. 150–51), N. A. Lukhmanova (p. 191), and O. Gridina (p. 231) are among those who are mentioned.

Published in 1900, as a report on the International Women's Congress in Paris, E. Chebysheva-Dmitrieva's "Russkaia zhenshchina v iziashchnoi literature i zhurnalistike" [52] may be the first article written on the topic of Russian women journalists. It presents a brief history of Russian women writers, whom the author considers to be comparatively as successful as men in their literary endeavors. However, Chebysheva-Dmitrieva views women's achievements in journalism from a more negative perspective. M. K. Tsebrikova alone is acknowledged as a serious journalist writing about important social and literary questions. Women editors and publishers have fared somewhat better, and Chebysheva-Dmitrieva briefly discusses the careers of A. O. Ishimova and others—particularly Peshkova-Toliverova and her efforts (through the *Obshchestvo izdatel'nits*) to professionalize the work of women journalists (and women involved in the technical aspects of publishing and printing) to provide them with living wages. Rhonda Lebedev Clark's 1996 dissertation "Forgotten Voices: Women in Periodical Publishing of Late Imperial Russia, 1860–1905" [53] examines the activities of more than 230 almost forgotten women editors and publishers, assessing their impact on Russian journalism and intellectual life in the late imperial period.

In his article "Zhenshchiny osvaivaiut professiiu zhurnalista" [54], B. I. Esin examines the entry of Russian women into journalism in the 1860s, owing primarily to the rise in literacy, coupled with the significant increase in the number of periodicals being published; many new jobs were created, and literate women were able to fill them in substantial numbers, not only as correspondents, publicists, and writers of belles lettres but also in the more "technical" areas of editing, translating, publishing, proofreading, typesetting, and bookselling. According to Esin, from 1847 to 1866, approximately fifteen women were connected to *Sovremennik,* and between 1868 and 1884, forty or more worked for *Otechestvennie zapiski* in some capacity.[8] All told, Esin specifically names more than fifty women very active in

Russian journalism in the last half of the nineteenth century. Current research has already expanded that number considerably.[9]

In her article "Female Journalists in Prerevolutionary Russia" [64], Louise McReynolds briefly discusses the careers of Sokolova, Toliverova, Ol'nem (Menshikova), and Gridina, four women who enjoyed considerable success as writers and journalists. In "Evgeniia Konradi-Bochechkarova" [63], G. S. Lapshina examines Konradi's involvement in the women's movement, particularly as it pertained to the education of women, and briefly touches on her journalistic career and her contributions to *Zhenskii vestnik, Russkoe slovo, Nedelia, Znanie,* and *Zagranichnyi vestnik.* Jehanne Gheith's dissertation, "In Her Own Voice: Evgeniia Tur, Author, Critic, Journalist" [55], presents an in-depth analysis of Tur's literary and journalistic writings and her place within the literary history of Russia, especially among its female writers. Chapter 1 provides a biography of Tur, and chapter 4 discusses her activities as an editor and publisher (of *Russkaia rech'*). S. V. Karavashkova's *Publitsistka A. M. Kollontai, I. F. Armand, L. N. Stal', A. I. Ul'ianovoi-Elizarovoi v bor'be za ukreplenie mezhdunarodnogo rabochego dvizheniia* [59] examines the activities of four prominent woman journalists involved in the international worker's movement and the international women's movement. The author devotes a good deal of her study to the problems of female workers, their activities (particularly between 1905 and 1917), their political organizations, and the writings produced about them. A bibliography is included. N. Mostovskaia's article on the journalistic activities of A. N. Engel'gardt [67] focuses primarily on the importance of Engel'gardt's translations of Zola and the wide array of other contemporary Western European and American authors whose works she brought to the Russian reader. It also describes Engel'gardt's extensive ties to the important Russian literary figures of her time and her editorial and literary influence, both formal and informal, on their work.

Although myriad articles and books have been written about the history and influence of various Russian periodicals (*Otechestvennye zapiski, Sovremennik, Narodnaia volia,* for example), as might be expected, little has yet been written about the history of women's journals. Barbara Heldt Monter's "*Rassvet* (1859–1862) and the Woman Question" [66] provides a detailed discussion of the contents and influence of one of imperial Russia's earlier women's publications. It was aimed at young women in their teens and hoped to encourage them in interests beyond fashion and domestic science by including articles on a wide variety of general interest topics in literature, history, geography, and the natural sciences, as well as a wide range of reviews and commentary on recent publications. In "Zhurnal *Zhenskii vestnik* (1866–1868 gg.)" [60], M. Klevenskii provides a description and history of an important and influential journal, discussing its staff (formerly with *Russkoe slovo* until its closure by the government) and its impact on the social and political movements of the day. Included is a list of the contributors to each of the various sections, as well as highlights from a number of particularly important articles printed in the journal's pages. In "Nachalo *Rabotnitsy*" [62], A. I. Leiberov discusses the founding of a much later, if very short-lived, journal for women; there were seven issues in all (three of them confiscated), one of which played a significant role in organizing women workers in the years immediately preceding the 1917 revolution.

Memoirs and reminiscences are without a doubt the most abundant source of published material on women journalists of imperial Russia. F. F. Fidler's *Pervye literaturnye shagi,* a collection of autobiographies of writers of the late nineteenth and early twentieth centuries, contains the autobiographies of I. A. Grinevskaia [56], Gurevich [58], Shapir [70], and Shchepkina-Kupernik [71]. The memoirs of Ardov-Apreleva, a writer for *Russkie vedomosti* [51], Ol'nem, a reporter for *Kievskoe slovo* and an editor of *Russkie zapiski* [68], Volkova, a contributor to and editor of *Drug zhenshchin* [72], and E. D. Kuskova, another contributor to *Russkie vedomosti* [61], are among those works important to the study of women journalists. The critic V. Zotov's recollections of Nadezhda Dmitrievna Khvoshchinskaia [73] are one of a number of memoirs about that prolific writer and essayist. Gurevich's reminiscences about her years at *Severnyi vestnik* [57] provide information about not only her own life and work but the lives of her colleagues, including A. M. Evreinova, a coeditor of *Severnyi vestnik*. Stanley Rabinowitz's article [69] also examines Gurevich's early years as editor and contributor to *Severnyi vestnik* and her influence on Russian literary journalism in the 1890s. The reminiscences of M. V. Iamshchikova [49] contain numerous references to the many publishers and editors with whom she worked in her long and varied career, including Peshkova-Toliverova, O. N. Popova, Davydova, and Annenskaia, among many other important literary, journalistic, and pedagogical figures of the last decades before the revolution.

Serial Titles

From the publication of *Damskii zhurnal* (1823–1833) to *Zhenskoe delo* (1910–1917), serial publications primarily intended for the woman reader were a steady presence in the periodical press of imperial Russia, whether as short-lived as the seven issues of *Rabotnitsa* or lasting as long as the thirteen years of *Zhenskii vestnik*. Most of the titles published in the latter half of the nineteenth century up until 1917, if not entirely staffed by women, certainly had a large number of women contributors involved in every aspect of publication.

Drug zhenshchin (1882–1884) [74] had as its main focus the religious and moral upbringing of women, particularly supporting the right of women to obtain a higher education. Each issue contains a selection of stories, poems, and articles on a wide range of literary, social, legal, and political topics, written predominantly by women authors. Included on a regular basis are sections devoted to women's education ("Po uchebnomu delu"), to bibliography and reviews of current publications, often but not necessarily on women's topics ("Bibliografiia"), and a chronicle of pedagogical activities pertinent to women in Russia and abroad ("Raznye izvestiia").[10]

Pervyi zhenskii kalendar' (1899–1915) [75] had the dual function of a general handbook of information useful to women, as well as a medium for journalistic commentary. Each volume contains a section of general information (church calendar, postal, telephone, and telegraph information, foreign currency exchange rates, etc.), sections on medical advice ("Meditsinskii otdel"), legal aid ("Iuridicheskie svedeniia"), information about museums, libraries, and other public offices ("Svedeniia i spravki"), and a listing of educational institutions open to women ("Zhenskoe obrazovanie"). The final section ("Iz proshlogo i nastoiashchogo") concerns itself with the activities and events of the women's movement in Russia and abroad, providing biographies and necrologies of important figures, a chronology of the year's events, and a calendar of important dates. There is a subsection on female employment statistics ("Iz statistiki zhenskogo truda") and a chronicle of women's educational events for the year. Also included is a listing of the many and varied women's social and political societies and circles and brief reports on their activities. By 1907, the volume had expanded considerably to include such categories as a list of establishments providing lodging and food for women and children ("Ubezhishcha i deshevye komnaty i obedy dlia zhenshchin v S.-Peterburge i Moskve"), as well as a series of essays and reports on important topics ("Zhenshchina i politika," "Novye techeniia v zhenskom dvizhenii v Rossii") found in the final section.

Rabotnitsa (1914) [76] was published in a printing of 12,000 copies, with the first issue printed on International Women's Day, 23 February (8 March) 1914. Although it contained a variety of articles on topics of general interest, the greater portion of each issue was devoted to issues of women's labor, employment, and insurance (the sections "Zhenskii trud" and "Rabotnitsy i strakhovanie").

Rassvet (1859–1862) [77] was specifically aimed at young women age fourteen or fifteen and is generally considered to be the first Russian journal for women to venture beyond the realms of fashion and domestic science in order to encourage women to acquire a broader education and help them to become good citizens. Each issue (400–600 pages in length) includes a wide variety of articles of general interest, both original and translated, on literature, history, geography, the natural sciences, and pedagogy. Within these categories are a substantial number of articles specifically about women (biographies of famous Russian and Western European women, women writers, women's education, etc.). The bibliography section, which includes lengthy reviews and commentary on a wide range of current publications, was headed by D. I. Pisarev and includes his first published writings of more than one hundred reviews and articles. For a more detailed discussion of the journal's contents and influence, see Barbara Heldt Monter's article [63].

Russkoe zhenskoe vzaimno-blagotvoritel'noe obshchestvo: Otchet (1895–1917) [78] comprises the annual reports of the Russian Women's Mutual Philanthropic Society, founded in 1895 and continuing through 1917. Each volume is a collection of reports of the various sections, bureaus, circles, and commissions sponsored by the society, and taken as a whole, the volumes provide an extraordinarily detailed picture of the society's activities. In particular, the reports of the society's governing council *(sovet)* illustrate the dual role of the society as both a political and charitable organization. The society annually sponsored lecture series on all aspects of the woman question, founded a section on voting rights ("Otdel izbiratel'nykh prav"), produced hundreds of petitions in favor of giving the vote to women, and was the main organizing force behind the 1908 All-Russian Women's Congress (Pervyi vserossiiskii zhenskii s"ezd), all documented in the various divisional reports. Hostels, shelters, and lunchrooms for women and children are also noted among the society's programs, as are libraries and literary and musical circles. Each volume lists in full the administrators and officers of the society as well as the membership at large.

Soiuz zhenshchin (1907–1909) [79] deals with all aspects of the woman question and the women's movement in Russia and abroad and includes reports on various Russian and international conferences and congresses, texts of speeches and reports presented to the Duma, and so forth. Particularly interesting is the section "Khronika zhenskogo voprosa v Rossii," which lists the activities of various women's institutions and organizations throughout the Russian empire. A similar section is devoted to the activities of women's organizations abroad. Most issues also include a bibliographic section that contains short reviews of important new publications or a subject bibliography on some aspect of the women's movement.

Zhenskaia mysl' (1909–1910) [80] contains articles on the women's movement and the woman question, with particular emphasis given to reports on various conferences and meetings relating to women. Also included is a selection of poetry and short fiction by and about women. Position papers and texts of reports of organizations such as the Woman's Progressive Party (Zhenskaia progressivnaia partiia) are also published, and a section entitled "Khronika" offers news briefs on a variety of topics, including legal developments relating to women. A bibliographic section provides reviews of two or three current books on topics of particular interest to women.

Zhenskii vestnik (1904–1917) [81] was edited and published by M. I. Pokrovskaia, a prolific author of articles, pamphlets, and books on the problems of prostitution and other topics relating to women. She herself is a major contributor to the journal. The longest lived of the serial publications devoted to political issues concerning women, *Zhenskii vestnik* had as its goal the support and encouragement of all efforts to attain full equality for women in the family and in society. Articles are short and include many translations from Western European sources. Although some works of fiction are included, articles generally focus on the civil, political, and legal rights of women—as well as their education and employment. The activities of the Women's Progressive Party Club (Klub zhenskoi progressivnoi partii v S.-Peterburge) are reported on in some detail, and many of the letters, petitions, and other documents produced by the party were published in the pages of the journal. The bibliography section includes one or two brief reviews of contemporary titles, and each issue also contains information and news about women in Russia and abroad ("Izvestiia i fakty, kasaiushchiesia zhenshchin," later called "Khronika").[11]

Zhenskoe delo (1910–1917) [82] was envisioned as a journal having wide appeal, meant to be neither a strictly feminist journal with lengthy political articles nor a women's magazine devoted to fashion and home economics, but a combination of both. Contributors were both male and female. Included in each issue was a wide range of articles about the women's movement in Russia and Western Europe, as well as articles on legal, educational, and literary topics. Necrologies and short biographies of a wide variety of women were often included, along with selections of poetry and prose. Every issue also contained sections entitled "Zagranichnaia khronika" and "Khronika 'Zhenskogo dela,'" listing important and interesting events and activities pertaining to women. A supplement devoted to fashion, crafts, and the home accompanied each issue. By the end of 1914, articles reflecting the war began to appear, and in the last few years of publication, articles about feminist issues had all but disappeared, replaced by articles on women and the war effort. Literary pieces, stories, and poems also began to appear more frequently in the latter years of its publication.

Zhenskoe obrazovanie (1876–1891) [83] supported the right of women to participate actively in society. Although the journal's format varied over the years, it was basically divided into an "official section" concerned with curricula, new programs, and official decrees, and an "unofficial section" consisting of a wide range of historical and methodological articles on women and children's education and the general state of women's education in Russia and abroad. Sections concerned with bibliography (lists and reviews of new textbooks and books for general reading) became an increasingly important part of each issue.

Notes

1. Because this essay is intended primarily as a research tool for specialists, Russian titles are not translated into English.
2. Golitsyn's 1889 *Bibliograficheskii slovar'* [24] has 1,286 entries, whereas the first comprehensive bibliography on the woman question, published in issues no. 7–8 (1887) of *SevV* [30], has 1,785 citations.
3. See p. 184 n. 1 of Effie Ambler's *Russian Journalism* [50] for a brief discussion of *zhurnalistika* and *publitsistika* within the context of nineteenth-century Russian society.
4. An example of the confusion that names can generate is that of Elizaveta Vasil'evna Salias de Turnemir [Sailhas de Tournemire], born Sukhovo-Kobylina and writing under the pen name of Evgeniia Tur. In various reference sources, she is entered under Tur, Salias, Salias de Turnemir or Turnemir, or even Sukhovo-Kobylina, sometimes with cross-references, sometimes without! For more on Tur's journalism, see Jehanne Gheith's essay in this volume.
5. Although the term "journalist" has been employed throughout this volume in the broadest sense to include reporters, writers, editors, publishers, and others involved in the production of periodicals, bibliographic references maintain a distinction among various types of journalistic activity. In general, "journalist" here refers to correspondents and writers for journals and newspapers.
6. Boolean searching makes use of AND, OR, and NOT to combine words or phrases to expand or limit a search in an electronic database, providing much more precision than a general keyword search.
7. See pp. i–lxxxix of *Archives in Russia 1993: A Brief Directory*. P. K. Grimsted, comp. (Washington, DC: IREX, 1993) for an excellent summary of the physical and intellectual changes which occurred in Russia's archives in the early 1990s and a detailed description of the country's new archival administration (the State Archival Fond of Russia) and its impact on archival research. See pp. xxxix–xlviii of *Archives of Russia* for a status report on Russian archives at the end of the decade.
8. See p. 62 of Esin's essay "Zhenshchiny osvaivaiut professiiu zhurnalista" [54].
9. See the appendix to this volume.
10. For more on this journal, see the preceding essays by Carolyn Marks and Adele Lindenmeyr.

11 For more on this journal, see the preceding essays by Rochelle Ruthchild and Linda Edmondson.

Works Cited

General Reference Aids and Bibliographies

Bibliographies of Serial Publications

1. *Bibliografiia periodicheskikh izdanii Rossii, 1901–1916.* Beliaeva, L. N., Zinov'eva, M. K. i M. M. Nikiforov, sostav. V. M. Barashenkov, glav. red. Leningrad: Gos. publichnaia biblioteka im. Saltykova-Shchedrina, 1958–1961. 4 t.
2. Masanov, Iu. I., Nitkina, N. V. i Z. D. Titova. *Ukazateli soderzhaniia russkikh zhurnalov i prodolzhaiushchikhsia izdanii 1755–1970 gg.* Moskva: Izd-vo "Kniga," 1975. 439 s.
3. *Russkaia periodicheskaia pechat' 1703–1900 gg.: Bibliografiia i graficheskie tablitsy.* Lisovskii, N. M., sostav. Petrograd: Izd-vo avtora, 1915. 267 s.
4. *Russkaia periodicheskaia pechat' (1702–1894): Spravochnik.* A. G. Dement'ev, A. V. Zapadov i M. S. Cherepakhov, red. Moskva: Gos. izd-vo politicheskoi literatury, 1959. 835 s.
5. *Russkaia periodicheskaia pechat' (1895–oktiabr' 1917): Spravochnik.* M. S. Cherepakhov i E. M. Fingerit, sostav. Moskva: Gos. izd-vo politicheskoi literatury, 1957. 351 s.

General Bibliographies, Dictionaries, and Encyclopedias

6. *American Bibliography of Slavic and East European Studies.* Bloomington, Ind., Columbus, Ohio, Washington, D.C., Urbana, Ill.: American Association for the Advancement of Slavic Studies, 1957–1994. The 1994 volume is the last to be published in paper format. See no. 16 for information on the electronic version ABSEES-Online.
7. *Bibliografiia rossiiskoi bibliografii.* Moskva: Rossiiskaia knizhnaia palata, 1992–. Called *Bibliografia sovetskoi bibliograffi*, 1939–1991. (Not published 1940–1945.)
8. *European Bibliography of Soviet, East European, and Slavonic Studies/ Bibliographie européene des travaux sur l'URSS et l'Europe de l'est/ Europäische Bibliographie der Sowjet- und Osteuropastudien.* Birmingham, England: University of Birmingham, 1975–, vol. 1–. See no. 19 for information on the electronic version EBSEES Online. A merging of *Soviet, East European and Slavonic Studies in Britain, 1971–1974,* and

"Bibliographie des travaux parus en français sur la Russie et URSS," published annually in *Cahiers du monde russe et soviétique*, 1968–1974.

9. *Istoriia dorevoliutsionnoi Rossii v dnevnikakh i vospominaniiakh. Annotirovannyi ukazatel' knig i publikatsii v zhurnalakh*. Nauchnoe rukovodstvo, redaktsiia i vvedenie P. A. Zaionchkovskogo. Moskva: "Kniga," 1976–1989. 5 t./13 ch.

10. *The Modern Encyclopedia of Russian and Soviet History*. 58 vols. Gulf Breeze, Fla.: Academic International Press, 1976–1994. Vols. 56–58 entitled *The Modern Encyclopedia of Russian, Soviet, and Eurasian History. The Supplement to the Modern Encyclopedia of Russian, Soviet, and Eurasian History*. Vol. 1–. Gulf Breeze, Fla.: Academic International Press, 1995–.

11. *The Modern Encyclopedia of East Slavic, Baltic, and Eurasian Literatures*. Vol. 1–. Gulf Breeze, Fla.: Academic Press International, 1977–. Vols. 1–9 entitled *The Modern Encyclopedia of Russian and Soviet Literature*.

12. *Novaia otechestvennaia i inostrannaia literatura po obshchestvennym naukam: Bibliograficheskii ukazatel': Istoriia, arkheologiia, etnografiia*. Moska: INION, 1993–. Called *Novaia sovetskaia literatura po obshchestvennym naukam. Istoriia, arkheologiia, etnografiia*, 1976–1992, and *Novaia sovetskaia literatura po istorii, arkheologii i etnografii*, 1949–1975.

13. *Novaia otechestvennaia i inostrannaia literatura po obshchestvennym naukam. Literaturovedenie*. Moskva: INION, 1993–. Called *Novaia sovetskaia literatura po obshchestvennym naukam. Literaturovedenie*, 1976–1992, and *Novaia sovetskaia literatura po literaturovedeniiu*, 1953–1975.

14. Rubakin, N. A. *Sredi knig: Opyt obzora russkikh knizhnykh bogatstv v sviazi s istoriei nauchno-filosofskikh i literaturno-obshchestvennykh idei*. Izd. 2-oe, dop. i per. Moskva: KnigoIzd-vo "Nauka," 1911–1913. 3 t.

15. *Russkie pisateli 1800–1917: Biograficheskii slovar'*. P. A. Nikolaev, glav. red. Moskva: Izd-vo "Sovetskaia entsiklopediia," 1989–, t. 1–.

Electronic Information Sources

16. ABSEES Online. American Association for the Advancement of Slavic Studies. Maria Gorecki Nowak, Managing Editor. Access through personal or institutional subscription. Contact ABSEES Online at the University of Illinois at Urbana-Champaign by E-mail (absees@uiuc.edu or mgnowak@uiuc.edu) or through the internet: (http://www.library.uiuc.edu/absees).

17. ArcheoBiblioBase Online (ABB). International Instituut voor Sociale Geschiedenis (IISG). Free Internet access at: http://www.iisg.nl/~abb/.
18. Dissertation Abstracts Online/OnDisk. Check with local library to determine availability by network or compact disk.
19. EBSEES Online. (European Bibliography of Slavic and East European Studies Online). 1991–1993+. Currently free of charge. For further information, contact Mme. Monique Armand of the Ecole des Hautes Etudes en Sciences Sociales (armand@ehess.fr). Accessible on the Internet at: http://dodge.upmf-grenoble.fr:8001/fra/themes/bee.html.
20. Historical Abstracts Online/On Disk. Check with local library to determine availability by network or compact disk.
21. MLA International Bibliography Online/On Disk. Check with local library to determine availability by network or compact disk.
22. RAS/Russian Academy of Sciences Bibliographies. A CitaDel database with networked access by subscription only with the Research Libraries Group (RLG). For subscription information contact RLG by E-mail (bl.ric@rlg.org) or on the Internet at http://www.rlg.org/cit-ras.html.

Reference Aids and Bibliographies on Women in Russia

23. *Dictionary of Russian Women Writers.* Edited by Marina Ledkovsky, Charlotte Rosenthal, and Mary Zirin. Westport, Conn.: Greenwood Press, 1994. 869 pp.
24. Golitsyn, N. N. *Bibliograficheskii slovar' russkikh pisatel'nits.* S.-Peterburg: Tip. V. S. Balasheva, 1889. 308 s.
25. Hyer, Janet, ed. *Women in the Soviet Union.* Ottawa: Carleton University, 1988. 40 leaves. (Institute of Soviet and East European Studies. *Bibliography,* no. 3, sup. 1).
26. Ignashev, Diane Nemec, and Sarah Krive. *Women and Writing in Russia and the USSR: A Bibliography of English-Language Sources.* Garland Reference Library of the Humanities 1280. New York: Garland Publishers, 1992. 328 pp.
27. Manning, R. T. "Bibliography of Works in English on Women in Russia and the Soviet Union: A Guide for Students and Teachers." *Slavic and European Education Review* 1 (1979): 31–62.
28. Ponomarev, S. I. *Nashi pisatel'nitsy.* S.-Peterburg: Tip. Imp. Akademii nauk, 1891. 78 s. (*Sbornik otdeleniia russkogo iazyka i slovestnosti Imperatorskoi Akademii nauk,* t. 52, no. 7).
29. Ruthchild, Rochelle Goldberg. *Women in Russia and the Soviet Union: An Annotated Bibliography.* New York: G. K. Hall; Toronto: Maxwell Macmillan Canada, 1993. 203 pp.

30. "Ukazatel' literatury zhenskogo voprosa na russkom iazyke." *Severnyi vestnik* 7 (1887): 1–33; 8 (1887): 34–56.
31. Yedlin, T., and J. Wilman, comps. *Women in Russia and the Soviet Union: A Select Bibliography*. Institute of Soviet and East European Studies *Bibliography* no. 3. Ottawa, Canada: Carleton University, 1985. 80 pp.

Reference Aids and Bibliographies on Journalism in Russia

32. "Istoriia zhurnalistiki." In *Istoriia russkoi literatury XIX veka: Bibliograficheskii ukazatel'*, red. K. D. Muratova, 75–85. Moskva; Leningrad: Izd-vo Akademii nauk SSSR, 1962.
33. Kuz'min, Dmitrii. "Alfavit sotrudnikov gazety *Narodnaia volia*." In *Narodovol'cheskaia zhurnalistika. S poslesloviem V. Figner*. Moskva: Izd-vo Vsesoiuznogo obshchestva politkatorzhan i ssyl'no-poselentsev, 1930: 175–202. (*Istoriko-revoliutsionnaia biblioteka*, 1930, no. 2, 51).
34. Navolotskaia, N. I. "Materialy k bibliografii po istorii russkoi zhurnalistiki 1966–1970 gg." In *Russkaia zhurnalistika i literatura XIX v.*, red. E. G. Babaev i B. I. Esin, 146–82. Moskva: Izd-vo Moskovskogo universiteta, 1979.
35. "Periodicheskaia pechat' i kritika." In *Istoriia russkoi literatury XVIII veka: Bibliograficheskii ukazatel'*. V. P. Stepanov i Iu. V. Stepnik, sostav. Leningrad: Izd-vo "Nauka," Leningradskoe otdelenie, 1968: 86–100.
36. Prokhorov, E. P. "Russkaia zhurnalistika, publitsistika, kritika vtoroi poloviny XIX veka. Materialy dlia bibliografii. Literatura 1961–1965 gg." In *Iz istorii russkoi zhurnalistiki kontsa XIX–nachala XX v.: (Stat'i, materialy, bibliografia)*, red. B. I. Esin, 246–66. Moskva: Izd-vo Moskovskogo universiteta, 1973.
37. Somov, N. M. *Sistematicheskii ukazatel' knig i statei po zhurnalistike: (Bibliografiia zhurnalizma)*. 2-oe dop. izd. [s.l.]: Izd. Gos. instituta zhurnalistiki, 1924. 86 s.
38. "Zhurnalistika: (Obshchie raboty, istoriia otdel'nykh zhurnalov)." In *Istoriia russkoi literatury kontsa XIX–nachala XX veka: Bibliograficheskii ukazatel'*, red. K. D. Muratova, 41–46. Moskva/Leningrad: Izd-vo Akademii nauk SSSR, 1963.

Archival Guides

39. *Archives of Russia: A Directory and Bibliographic Guide to Holdings in Moscow and St. Petersburg*. Edited by Patricia Kennedy Grimsted; compiled by Patricia Kennedy Grimsted, Lada Vladimirovna Repulo,

and Irina Vladimirovna Tunkina; with an introduction by Vladimir Petrovich Kozlov. Armonk, N.Y.: M. E. Sharpe, c2000. 2v.

40. *Arkhivy Rossii: Moskva i Sankt-Peterburg: Spravochnik-obozrenie i bibliograficheskii ukazatel'*. Russkoe izdanie. Glav. red. V. P. Kozlov, P. K. Grimsted. Otv. sostavitel' L. V. Repulo. Moskva: Arkheograficheskii Tsentr, 1997. 1,070 pp.

41. *Dokumenty GAF SSSR v. bibliotekakh, muzeiakh i nauchno-otraslevykh arkhivakh: spravochnik*. N. V. Avtokrator et al., red. Moskva: Mysl', 1991. 590c.

42. *Gosudarstvennye arkhivy SSSR: Spravochnik*. N. M. Andreeva et al., sostav. Moskva: Mysl', 1989. 2 t.

43. Grimsted, Patricia K. *Archives and Manuscript Repositories in the USSR: Moscow and Leningrad*. Princeton, N.J.: Princeton University Press, 1972. 436 pp.

44. Grimsted, Patricia K. *Archives and Manuscript Repositories in the USSR: Moscow and Leningrad. Supplement 1: Bibliographical Addenda*. Zug, Switzerland: IDC, 1976. 203 s.

45. Grimsted, Patricia K. *A Handbook for Archival Research in the USSR*. Washington, D.C.: Kennan Institute; New York: IREX, 1989. 430 pp.

46. *Lichnye arkhivnye fondy v gosudarstvennykh khranilishchakh SSSR: Ukazatel'*. E. V. Kolosova et al., sostav. Iu. I. Gerasimova et al., red. Moskva: Glavnoe arkhivnoe upravlenie; Gos. Biblioteka SSSR im. V. I. Lenina; Arkhiv AN SSSR, 1962–1980, 3 t.

47. *Russian State Archive of Literature and Art—the Complete Archive Guide [RGALI]/Rossiiskii gosudarstvennyi arkhiv literatura i iskusstva [RGALI]—putevoditel' po arkhivu*. Edited by Klaus W. Waschik and Natalia B. Volkova. Bochum, Germany: Lotman-Institute of Russian and Soviet Culture; Moscow, Russia: RGALI, 1996. 1 CD-ROM computer file.

48. *Tsentral'nyi gosudarstvennyi arkhiv literatury i iskusstva SSSR: Putevoditel'*. Moskva: GAU, 1959–1998. 7 t.

Select Sources on Women and Journalism in Russia

Monographs, Articles, Essays, Memoirs

49. Altaev, A. (Iamshchikova, M. V.) "Moi starye izdateli: (Iz vospominanii). Publikatsiia N. A. Letovoi i B. D. Letova." In *Kniga: Issledovaniia i materialy*, t. 26, 154–82. Moskva: Izd-vo "Kniga," 1973.

50. Ambler, Effie. *Russian Journalism and Politics, 1861–1881: The Career of Aleksei S. Suvorin*. Detroit: Wayne State University Press, 1972. 239 pp.

51. Ardov-Apreleva, E. "Iz vospominanii o sotrudnichestve v *Russkikh vedomostiakh*." In *Russkie vedomosti, 1863–1913: Sbornik statei*, 160–63. Moskva: Tip. "Russkikh vedomostei," 1913.
52. Chebysheva-Dmitrieva, E. "Russkaia zhenshchina v iziashchnoi literature i zhurnalistike: Doklad E. Chebyshevoi-Dmitrievoi na zhenskom mezhdunarodnom kongresse v Parizhe 5 (18)–10 (23)-go iiunia 1900 goda." *Zhenskoe delo* 8–9 (avgust–sentiabr' 1900): 186–94.
53. Clark, Rhonda Lebedev. "Forgotten Voices: Women in Periodical Publishing of Late Imperial Russia, 1860–1905." Ph.D. diss., University of Minnesota, 1996. 208 pp.
54. Esin, B. I. "Zhenshchiny osvaivaiut professiiu zhurnalista." In *Puteshestvie v proshloe: Gazetnyi mir XIX veka*, by B. I. Esin, 59–64. Moskva: Izd-vo Moskovskogo universiteta, 1983.
55. Gheith, Jehanne M. "In Her Own Voice: Evgeniia Tur, Author, Critic, Journalist." Ph.D. diss., Stanford University, 1992. 234 pp.
56. Grinevskaia, I. A. "Izabella Arkad'evna Grinevskaia." In *Pervye literaturnye shagi: Avtobiografii sovremennykh russkikh pisatelei*. F. F. Fidler, sostav, 243–64. Moskva: Tip. T-va I. D. Sytina, 1911.
57. Gurevich, L. "Istoriia *Severnogo vestnika*." In *Russkaia literatura XX veka: 1890–1910*, red. S. A. Vengerov, to 1, 235–66. Moskva: T-va Mir, 1914.
58. Gurevich, L. "Liubov' Iakovlevna Gurevich." In *Pervye literaturnye shagi: Avtobiografii sovremennykh russkikh pisatelei*. F. F. Fidler, sostav, 182–98. Moskva: Tip. T-va I. D. Sytina, 1911.
59. Karavashkova, S. V. *Publitsistika A. M. Kollontai, I. F. Armand, L. N. Stal', A. I. Ul'ianovoi-Elizarovoi v bor'be za ukreplenie mezhdunarodnogo rabochego dvizheniia: Uchebno-metodicheskoe posobie dlia studentov fakul'tetov i otdelenii zhurnalistiki gosudarstvennykh universitetov*. Moskva: Izd. Moskovskogo universiteta, 1973, 19 s.
60. Klevenskii, M. "Zhurnal *Zhenskii vestnik* (1866–1868 gg.)." In *Russkaia zhurnalistika*, t. 1, 107–29. Moskva-Leningrad: Academia, 1930.
61. Kuskova, E. D. "Davno minuvshee." *Novyi zhurnal/New Review* 43 (1955): 96–119; 44 (1956): 124–42; 45 (1956): 149–80; 47 (1956): 154–76; 48 (1957): 139–62; 49 (1957): 145–70; 50 (1957): 173–97; 51 (1957): 147–72; 54 (1958): 117–47.
62. Leiberov, A. I. "Nachalo *Rabotnitsy*." *Voprosy istorii* 9 (1985): 174–77.
63. Lapshina, G. S. "Evgeniia Konradi-Bochechkarova." *Voprosy istorii* 7 (1988): 124–30.
64. McReynolds, Louise. "Female Journalists in Prerevolutionary Russia." *Journalism History* 14, no. 4 (1987): 104–10.

65. McReynolds, Louise. *The News under Russia's Old Regime: The Development of a Mass-Circulation Press.* Princeton, N.J.: Princeton University Press, 1991. 313 pp.
66. Monter, Barbara Heldt. "Rassvet (1859–1862) and the Woman Question." *Slavic Review* 36, no. 1 (1977): 76–85.
67. Mostovskaia, Natal'ia. "A. N. Engel'gardt—Russkaia zhurnalistika i perevodchitsa." In *Russkie pisatel'nitsy i literaturnyi protsess v kontse XVIII-pervoi treti XX vv.: Sbornik nauchnykh statei.* M. Sh. Fainshtein, sostav, 115–25. Wilhelmshorst: Verlag F. K. Göpfert, 1995. (*FrauenLiteraturGeschichte: Texte und Materialien zur russischen Frauenliteratur*, 2).
68. Ol'nem, V. N. "Iz reporterskikh vospominanii." *Golos minuvshego* 7 (1913): 123–59; 8 (1913): 119–51. Part 2 entitled "*Iz zapisok reportera.*"
69. Rabinowitz, Stanley J. "No Room of Her Own: The Early Life and Career of Liubov' Gurevich." *Russian Review* 57, no. 2 (April 1998): 236–52.
70. Shapir, O. A. "Ol'ga Andreevna Shapir." In *Pervye literaturnye shagi: Avtobiografii sovremennykh russkikh pisatelei.* F. F. Fidler, sostav, 46–55. Moskva: Tip. T-va I. D. Sytina, 1911.
71. Shchepkina-Kupernik, T. L. "Tat'iana L'vovna Shchepkina-Kupernik." In *Pervye literaturnye shagi: Avtobiografii sovremennykh russkikh pisatelei.* F. F. Fidler, sostav, 69–73. Moskva: Tip. T-va I. D. Sytina, 1911.
72. Volkova, Anna Ivanovna (Vishniakova). *Vospominaniia, dnevnik i stat'i.* Ch. Vetrinskii (V. E. Cheshikhin), red. S prilozheniem biograficheskogo ocherka, dvukh fototipicheskikh portretov A. I. Volkovoi i trekh ukazatelei. Izdanie A. S. Vishniakova. Nizhnii-Novgorod: Tipo-Litografiia "Nizhegor. Pechatnoe delo," 1913.299 s.
73. Zotov, VI. "Nadezhda Dmitirievna Khvoshchinskaia: (Iz vospominaniia starogo zhurnalista)." *Istoricheskii vestnik* 10, no. 38 (1889): 93–108.

Serial Titles

74. *Drug zhenshchin: Ezhemesiachnyi zhurnal.* Moskva, 1882–1884. Thirty issues published in all; edited by M. Boguslavskaia. A chronological listing of the contents of the 1883–1884 issues was published in A. I. Volkova's *Vospominaniia, dnevnik i stat'i.* N.-Novgorod, 1913: 266–70.

75. *Pervyi zhenskii kalendar'*. P. N. Ariian, sostav. S.-Peterburg, 1899–1915. Seventeen volumes published in all.
76. *Rabotnitsa: Dvukhnedel'nyi zhurnal*. Peterburg: Tsentral'nyi Komitet bol'shevistskoi partii, 1914. Seven issues published in all; edited by F. V. Martsinkevich (no. 7 by A. A. Bychikhin). Published by D. F. Petrovskaia (no. 7 by L. I. Loorberg).
77. *Rassvet: Zhurnal nauk, iskusstv i literatury dlia vzroslykh devits*. S.-Peterburg: Izd-vo V. Krempin, 1859–1862. Fourteen volumes published in all; edited by V. A. Krempin (1859–1862) and N. N. Firsov (1862).
78. *Russkoe zhenskoe vzaimno-blagotvoritel'noe obshchestvo: Otchet* S.-Peterburg: 1895–1917.
79. *Soiuz zhenshchin: Zhurnal, posviashchennyi voprosam, sviazannym s bor'boi za ravnopravie zhenshchiny i, glavnym obrazom, za ee izbiratel'nye prava*. S.-Peterburg, 1907–1909. Twenty-nine issues published in all; edited and published by M. A. Chekhova. Annual subject indexes are found in no. 12 (1908) and no. 12 (1909).
80. *Zhenskaia mysl': Dvukhnedel'nyi khudozhestvenno-literaturnyi zhurnal, posviashchennyi ravnopraviiu i uluchsheniiu ekonomicheskogo polozheniia zhenshchin*. Kiev, 1909–1910. Five issues published in all (15 November 1909 to 15 January 1910); edited and published by Mariia Petrova-Svobodina.
81. *Zhenskii vestnik: Ezhemesiachnyi obshchestvenno-nauchno-literaturnyi zhurnal, posviashchennyi zhenskomu voprosu*. M. I. Pokrovskaia, red. S.-Peterburg: 1904–1917.
82. *Zhenskoe delo: Ezhenedel'nyi illiustrirovannyi zhurnal*. Moskva, 1910–1917. Edited from 1910 to 1915 by L. M. Rodionov and from 1915 to 1917 by G. A. Iovenko.
83. *Zhenskoe obrazovanie: Pedagogicheskii listok dlia roditelei, nastavnits i nastavnikov izdavaemyi pri S.-Peterburgskikh zhenskikh gimnaziiakh*. S.-Peterburg, 1876–1891. Edited by V. D. Sipovskii. "Ukazatel' statei zhurnala *Zhenskoe obrazovanie* za 10 let ego sushchestvovaniia," a ten-year chronological index of some 900 entires, is found in no. 10 (1885): 1–33.

Appendix

Checklist of Women Journalists in Imperial Russia

JUNE PACHUTA FARRIS

(with Rhonda Lebedev Clark, Barbara T. Norton, and Mary F. Zirin)

This compilation is a work in progress, a starting point for further research on women journalists in early as well as late imperial Russia. Although it aims at comprehensiveness, it is by no means complete in any category. The majority of women listed are almost entirely unknown, and for the handful of recognizable names, it is often the case that we are much more familiar with their literary, political, or other professional activities than with their journalistic efforts. With the exception of publishers and editors, there are no published sources that systematically list those who worked for the (legal and illegal) periodical press in imperial Russia. The net must be cast wide and deep to identify women journalists of prerevolutionary Russia and to link them to the specific journals and newspapers to which they contributed.

The various bibliographies of prerevolutionary serial publications cited in the preceding bibliographic essay [1, 3, 4, 5], as well as other sources such as *Svodnyi katalog russkoi nelegal'noi i zapreshchennoi pechati XIX veka: Knigi i periodicheskie izdaniia*, 3 t. (Moskva: Gosudarstvennaia biblioteka SSSR, 1982), provide systematic access to women registered as editors and publishers. The name index to Beliaeva's *Bibliografiia periodicheskikh izdanii Rossii, 1901–1916*, for example, lists more than 850 women active in publishing and editing. In the course of research for her dissertation "Forgotten Voices" [53], Rhonda Lebedev Clark has extracted much of the relevant data found in these bibliographies and contributed it to this checklist.

No such straightforward access is available to aid in identifying women journalists who were neither editors nor publishers but were on the staff of various periodical publications (*sotrudnitsy, perevoditsy*, etc.) or contributed freelance articles. Reference sources such as Ponomarev's *Nashi pisatel'nitsy* [28], Golitsyn's *Bibliograficheskii slovar' russkikh pisatel'nits* [24], *Dictionary of Russian Women Writers* [23], *Russkie pisateli 1800–1917* [15], and *Pisateli sovremennoi epokhi: Bio-biograficheskii slovar' russkikh pisatelei XX veka* (Moskva: Gosudarstvennaia akademiia khudozhestvennykh nauk, 1928) were consulted, as were several collections of memoirs and biographies, such as *Slavnye bol'shevichki* (Moskva: 1958) and *Revoliutsionerki Rossii: Vospominaniia i ocherki o revoliutsionnoi deiatel'nosti rossiiskikh bol'shevichek* (Moskva: Sovetskaia Rossiia, 1983). Indeed, snippets of information were culled from almost all the sources under review for inclusion in this volume's bibliographic essay, as well as from Mary Zirin's residual cache of names collected for the *Dictionary of Russian Women Writers*. Thus the list of women journalists in imperial Russia presented here is the most comprehensive to date. What is needed now, to make it more comprehensive, is an exhaustive and systematic review of the full runs of individual journal and newspaper titles, their published indexes, and their archival records. It is hoped that the current checklist will serve to encourage such work by scholars, as it facilitates further research on Russian women journalists.

Establishing consistent entries for women journalists is a difficult and complex process. Simply determining what name should head an entry is complicated, particularly if a woman is best known under a pseudonym or was married more than once. In this checklist, entries have been made according to the most recognizable form of a woman's name, that is, the form found most frequently in the reference sources cited in the foregoing paragraphs. Additional names are provided whenever known: birth and married names are in parentheses, followed by birth and death dates, with pseudonyms in brackets. Where relevant, entries also include information on journalistic activities after 1917. Because more information was available on some journalists than on others, the entries in this checklist are uneven. It is important to note, therefore, that there is no obvious correlation between the length of an entry and the extent or significance of a journalist's work.

Abramova, M. [M. Ab——va]   Worked for *RVed* (1897).

Agreneva, Z. A. Contributor to *Golos*.

Agrinskaia, N. [N. Agr——kaia] Worked for *Saratovskii dnevnik*.

Akhmatova, Elizaveta Nikolaevna, 1820–1904 [Leila] Founder, publisher, and editor of the journal *Sobranie inostrannykh romanov, povestei i rasskazov v perevode na russkii iazyk* (1865–1885); publisher, editor, and contributor to *Delo i otdykh* (1864–1865) and *Sbornik perevodov dlia legkogo chteniia* (1867–1868).

Alekseeva, Mariia Danilovna Founder and publisher of *Peterburgskaia zhizn'* (1890).

Aleksinskaia, T. Publisher of *Bez lishnikh slov* (1917).

Alferova, Aleksandra Samsonovna Worked for *RVed*.

Alektorova, N. E. Publisher of *Astrakhanskii vestnik* (1896–1907).

Ananieva, Elizaveta Emil'ianovna Editor and publisher of *Mody i rukodeliia* (1875).

Andreeva, A. P. Editor and publisher of *Smolenskii listok ob"iavlenii* (1900–1901).

Andreeva, Aleksandra Alekseevna, 1853–1926 Literary and theatrical critic who later wrote on social-educational topics; contributor to *VE, Kosmopolis, RM, Russkii kur'er, SevV,* and the postrevolutionary *Narodopravstvo, Krasnaia Niva, Rabochii i krestianin,* and others.

Andreeva, Mariia Editor of *Kaleidoskop* (1860–1862).

Andronikova, Tat'iana Pavlovna Editor and publisher of *Kostromskoi listok ob"iavlenii* (1888–1898) and *Kostromskoi listok* (1898–1906).

Annenskaia, Aleksandra Nikitichna, 1840–1915 Contributor to *SS* (1871–1878), *Rodnik,* and *Vskhody;* translator for *BVed*.

Antipova, Mariia [M——iia An——p——va] Worked for *Zhural dlia milykh* (1804).

Ardov-Aprelevna, Elena Ivanovna, 1846–1923 Contributor to historical and educational journals, including *SS* (editor); an editor of *RVed* (1878).

Ariian, Praskov'ia Belenkaia, 1864–1944 Editor of *PZhK* (St. Petersburg, 1899–1915).

Aristova, V. [V. Ari——va] Worked for *SemV*.

Arkadieva, Iuliia Andreevna Publisher of *Luch* (1886–1889).

Armand, Inessa, 1874–1920 Coeditor of *Rabotnitsa* (1914), along with other women Bolsheviks.

Arsen'eva, Anna Sergeevna, 1897–? Worked for *Utro Rossii* (1914).

Bakh, Tat'iana [T. V.] Worked for *TvK*.

Bakhareva, Natal'ia Dmitrievna [N.B., S.K.] Managed the theater section of *Peterburgskii listok*.

Bardakova, M. M. [Marina] Worked for *Zadushevnoe slovo, Detskaia gazeta, Detstvo, Otrochestvo, Iuzhnyi zapad, Zhurnal nachinaiushchikh* (Kishinev), *Vera i zhizn'* (Chernigov), *Odesskii listok, Russkaia zemlia, Russkaia rech'*.

Bazhina, Ekaterina Nikolaevna Publisher of *RB* (1880–1882).

Bazhina, Serafima Nikitichna (Alymova), 1849–1894 [S. Nikitina, K. G— —va, L. N——va, S. Ni——na, Ni-ni, S. N.] Worked for *ZhV, Peterburgskii listok, Vaza, Novosti, Slovo, RB*.

Beketova, Elizaveta Filaretovna Publisher of *S.-Peterburgskie teatral'nye vedomosti* (1910).

Beketova, Elizaveta Grigor'evna, d. 1902 [E.B.] Contributor to *RV*; worked for *Russkii invalid*, in charge of its foreign department (Inostrannyi otdel), also writing some of its music reviews; published poetry translations in *Sovremennik*.

Beketova, Mariia Andreevna, 1861–1938 Published numerous translations of the works of European authors for *Rodnik, Vestnik inostrannoi literatury, Vskhody, VV, NV*, and others; wrote articles on geography and biography for *ChNS* and *Solnyshko*.

Belaventseva, Ol'ga. [O. B.] Worked for *Shut* (1910–1911).

Belozerskaia, Nadezhda Aleksandrovna, 1838–1912 Contributor to *Illiustrirovannyi zhurnal, IV, RStar*, editor of *VO* (1877–1880).

Bel'skaia, Vera Aleksandrovna Editor and publisher of the newspaper *Krest'ianskoe delo* (1906).

Berchanskaia, Avgusta [A. B——aia] Worked for *Nedelia khristianskogo voskhoda* (1889).

Berdiaeva, Elena Grigor'evna Editor and publisher of *Po moriu i sushe* (1891–1893).

Berner, Anna Vasil'evna Publisher of *Teatral'nyi kur'er* (1903–1904).

Bestuzheva, Sof'ia Pavlovna Publisher of *Vestnik ob"iavlenii* (1885).

Beznina, Anna Aleksandrovna (Trubesska), ?–1805 [A. B., Murinon Murinov]   Contributor to *Zhural dlia milykh*.

Bezobrazova, Elizaveta Dmitrieva (Maslova), 1834–1881 [E. Vasil'evskaia, Tatiane Swetow]   Regular contributor to *Journal des débats, La nouvelle revue, Journal des économistes, Contemporary Review*; regular contributor to *Journal de St. Pétersbourg* (1896–?).

Bittenbinder, Sof'ia G.   Publisher of *Russkii vestnik strakhovanii* (1890–1897) and *Strakhovye vedomosti* (1890–1904).

Blagoveshchenskaia, O.   Editor of *NRB* (1870–1872).

Blavatskaia, Elena Petrovna (Gan), 1831–1891   Published various theosophical journals such as *Theosophical Review* (London) and *Lotus* (Paris); contributed articles to *OZ, RV*.

Blinova, M.   Worked for *ZhV* (1905).

Bliummer, Aleksandra Vasil'evna   Publisher of *Volga* (1883–1884).

Bobrinskaia, Varvara Nikolaevna   Worked for *Severnoe siiane* (1908) and became its publisher and editor (1909).

Bobrova, Aleksandra Ivanovna [A. B.]   Worked for *Rebus* (1900s).

Bogdanova, F. I.   Publisher of *Kievskaia mysl'* (1906–1918).

Bogdanova, Nadezhda Fedotovna   Worked for *RVed* (1896).

Bogdanovich, Tat'iana Aleksandrovna (Krol'), 1872–1942   Translator and contributor of original articles to *MirB, RB, Obrazovanie*; correspondent for *Parus*; editor of the literary section of *Sovremennoe slovo*.

Bogushevich, Ekaterina Aleksandrovna   Publisher and editor of *Biblioteka luchshikh inostrannykh romanov i povestei* (1865–1868).

Boldyreva, Elizaveta Ivanovna   Publisher of *Kaspii* (1889–1900) and *Bakinskii torgovo-promyshlennyi listok* (1890–1895).

Borozdina, Elizaveta   Publisher of *DS* (1869–1876).

Braun, Evgeniia Mikhailovna (Shershevskaia, Studenskaia)   Worked for *IV* (1903).

Broido, Eva L'vovna (Gordon, Edel'man), 1876–? [E. L'vova]   Worked for *Luch*.

Bubnova, Lidiia Aleksandrovna   Contributor to *RVed* (1909–1911).

Burche, Elizaveta Andreevna   Publisher of *Golos zhizni* (1905–1906).

Bulanova, M. V. Translator for the newspapers *NV, Birzhevaia gazeta,* and *Sankt-Peterburgskie vedomosti* and for the journals *ZhivO* and *VE.*

Bulanova-Trubnikova, Mariia Vasil'evna Worked for *Zhurnal aktsionerov* (1858), *Peterburgskie vedomosti* (1869), *ZhivO;* translated French, German, and English news for *NV* (1876–?); member of the editorial staff of *BVed* (1863–1869), working in its literature, bibliography, and translation sections; London correspondent for *VE* (1871–1884); worked for the English daily *Now a Day;* along with A. N. Engel'gardt and N. V. Stasova, organized the first women's publishing cooperative *(zhenskaia izdatel'skaia artel').*

Burinskaia, Aleksandra Konstantinovna Editor and publisher of *Zhenskii trud* (1882–1883).

Burnasheva, Ekaterina Pavlovna, 1819–1875 Wrote articles, translated for *Severnaia pchela, BdCh, Zvezdochka, Luchi* (1853–1856); wrote on women's education for *Zhurnal dlia vospitaniia.*

Burnasheva, Sof'ia Petrovna, 1818–1883 [Devista Esbe, Glafira Mikhailovna Shchigrovskaia] Editor and publisher of the children's magazine *Chas dosuga* (1858–1863) and editor of the children's newspaper *Kaleideskop* (1860–1862).

Bykovskaia, E. L. Worked for *RVed* (1890s).

Ekaterina II, empress of Russia, 1729–1796 (reigned 1762–1796), also Catherine II Founder and contributor to *Vsiakaia vsiachina* (1769); published *Sobesednik liubitelei rossiiskogo slova* (1783–1784).

Charnolusskaia, Ekaterina Matyshevna Publisher and editor of *Listok knizhnogo dela i ob"iavlenii* (1899–1902); worked for *Shkola i zhizn'* (1911–1913).

Charnova, Anna Ivanovna Publisher and editor of *Baian* (1888–1890) and *Detskii muzykal'nyi mirok* (1887–1888).

Chebotarevskaia, Anastasiia Nikolaevna, 1876–1921 Worked for *Zhurnal dlia vsekh* and *Tovarishch* (1905); editor of *Otechestvo* (1914); contributed articles to *RM, Narodnyi put', Rech',* and *RVed* (1906–1908).

Chebysheva-Dmitrieva, Evgeniia Aleksandrovna, 1859–1923 Contributor to *Obrazovanie, ZhD, ZhO.*

Chekhova, Mariia Pavlovna Publisher and editor of *SZh* (1907–1909).

Chernysheva, Mariia Matveevna, 1873–? Editor and publisher of *Bal-*

alaika (1910–1911); contributor of poems and articles to many Arkhangel'sk regional periodicals (1911–?).

Chichinadze, Mariia Vasil'evna   Publisher and editor of *Iuridicheskaia gazeta* (1898–1906).

Damanskaia, Avgusta Filippovna, 1875–1885   Translator for *Vsemirnaia literatura;* wrote prose, poetry, and criticism for both the Russian and émigré press, such as *Narodnoe delo, Dni, Segodnia.*

Dan[n] Charnova, Anna Ivanovnaenberg, Mariia Aleksandrovna, 1820–1891 [Sosnogorova]   Wrote articles about Crimea for *Odesskii vestnik.*

Danilova, Vera Aleksandrovna (Erakova) [Andreev]   Worked for *RV.*

Dashkova, Ekaterina Romanovna (Vorontsova), 1743–1810   With Catherine II, published *Sobesednik liubitelei rossiiskogo slova* (1783–1784); founded *Novye ezhemesiachnye sochineniia* (1786–1796); a publisher of *Nevinnoe uprazhnenie* (1763).

Davydova, Aleksandra Arkad'evna (Gorozhanskaia), 1848–1902   Founder, editor, publisher of *MirB* (1892–1902); worked for *SevV* (1880s); publisher of *Vskhody* (1896–1899).

De-Veki, Feodosiia Anatol'evna   Publisher of *Sudebnaia gazeta* (1904–1905).

Dostoevskaia, Anna Grigorevna   Copublisher with her husband, Fedor Dostoevskii, of the journal *Dnevnik pisatelia* (1876–1877, 1880–1881).

Dragomanova, Liudmila   Worked for *VE* (1874).

Drashusova, Elizaveta Alekseevna (Karlgof), 1816?–1884   Wrote articles for *MVed, Sovremennik, Zvezdochka.*

Durnovo, Natalia Ivanovna   Publisher of *Delo* (1887–1888).

Dzhavrova, Ol'ga Dmitrievna   Publisher of *Askhbad* (1905–1916).

Efimenko, Aleksandra Iakovlena (Stavrovskaia), 1848–1918   Wrote articles on a wide variety of economic, historical, and ethnographic topics for *Delo, Znanie, Slovo, RM, Nedelia.*

Engel'gardt, Anna Nikolaevna (Makarova), 1838–1903   For more than twenty-five years, a regular contributor of articles and translations to *VE* (1871–?), as well as to a variety of other journals, including *Golos, BVed, OZ, VE, RV,* and *SPVed* (1882); an editor of *Vestnik inostrannoi literatury* (1891–1893) and *Novyi zhurnal inostrannoi literatury;* along with M. V. Trubnikova and N. V. Stasova, organizer of the first women's publishing cooperative (*zhenskaia izdatel'skaia artel'*).

Enkvist, Anna Aleksandrovna [Al'bert, A. Belov]   Worked for a number of agricultural journals between 1890 and 1910.

Esaulova, Ekaterina Ivanovna   Publisher of *Literaturnyi sbornik* (1881–1882); editor and publisher of *MM* (1881–1882).

Eval'd, Liubov' Nikolaevna   Publisher of *Vseobshchaia gazeta* (1883–1886).

Evfratova, Lidiia Petrovna   Worked for *Damskii mir* (1914).

Evinogradskaia, T. V.   Publisher of *Ekho* (1883).

Evreinova, Anna Mikhailovna, 1844–1919   Contributor to *Kriticheskoe obozrenie, DZh*; an editor (1885–1890) of *SevV*, as well as its publisher (1889–1890).

Evropeus, Aleksandra Konstantinovna (Pavlovna), 1837–1895 [Vladimirova]   Regular contributor to the children's journal *Igrushechka* (1887–1895), as well as one of its publishers (1888); proofreader for *BVed* (1865–1866).

Fedulaeva, Vera Ivanovna   Publisher of *Teatral'nyi mirok* (1885–1886).

Figner, Vera Nikolaevna, 1852–1942   Worked for *RVed* (1912–1913); contributor to *Rech'*.

Florova, Ekaterina E.   Editor and publisher of *Samarskii spravochnyi listok* (1876–1888).

Florovskaia-Figner, O. N.   On the editorial staff of *Samoupravlenie: Organ sotsialistov-federalistov* (Geneva, 1887–1889).

Fomina, Mariia   Worked for *Ippokrena* (1799).

Fon-Gel'freikh, Ol'ga Vsevolodovna   Publisher of *Peterburgskii listok* (1867–1870).

Fon-Iunk, Nadezhda   Publisher of *Kievskii telegraf* (1871–1874).

Galenkovskaia, O.   Regular contributor to *Igrushechka*.

Gal'person, Anna Mikhailovna, 1856–1902   Editorial worker for many newspapers and journals in Moscow and St. Petersburg, including *RVed*; worked for the foreign department (Inostrannyi otdel) of *SPVed*.

Gan, Elena Andreevna (Fadeeva), 1814–1842   Translator; contributor to *BdCh* in the late 1830s.

Garshina, Ekaterina Stepanovna, 1828–1897 [E. Zatrapeznikova]   Writer of nonfiction articles on feminist subjects published in periodicals such as *SPVed, Iskra*.

Gedeonova, Zhosefina Karlovna   Editor and publisher of *Vaza* (1869–1879).

Gedik, Nadezhda Andreevna [N. A. G.]   Worked for *Ulei* (1811–1812).

Gel'freikh, Ol'ga Vsevolodovna von   Publisher of *Peterburgskii listok* (1867–1870).

Gelliman, Elizaveta Petrovna   Publisher and editor of *Russkoe sadovodstvo* (1897).

Genkel', M. G.   Publisher and editor of *Detstvo* (1899).

Gerlakh, Anna Nikolaevna   Publisher and editor of *Modnaia masterskaia* (1904–1906).

Giliarovskaia, Nadezhda Vladimirovna (Lobanova), 1886–? [Nina Giliarovskaia, Maugli]   Poet, prose writer, art critic, and translator who wrote for a wide variety of periodical publications, including *RSlovo*, *RM*, *Niva*, *Nova*, *Segodnia*, *Na vakhte*, *Vecherniaia Moskva*.

Gladkova, Mariia   Worked for *Damskii zhurnal* (1827).

Glagoleva, Tat'iana Matveevna, 1885–?   Educator, journalist, critic, with articles in *RM* and *Izvestiia Akademii nauk*.

Gogotskaia, Evdokiia Ivanovna, d. 1888   Publisher and editor of *Kievskii telegraf* (1874–1876).

Golitsyna, Sof'ia Alekseevna (Korsakova), ?–1858   Cofounder and publisher of the almanac *Molodik* (1843–1844).

Gol'dshtein, Natal'ia Dmitrievna   Publisher of *Voronezhskii telegraf* (1873–1876).

Golokhvastova, Ol'ga Andreevna, 184?–1897
Wrote the section "Oblastnoe obozrenie" for the newspaper *Rus'*.

Gol'tseva, Natal'ia Alekseevna   Contributor to *RVed*.

Golubeva, E.   Editor and publisher of *Pskovskaia gazeta* (1886–1887).

Gonzal', Marianna Dmitrievna   Publisher of *Shkol'noe obozrenie* (1889–1893).

Goppe, Adel' Germanovna   Publisher of *NRB* (1895–1900), *MSMM* (1895–1900), *Vsemirnaia illiustrtsiia* (1895–1898), *Modistka* (1895–1898).

Goppe, Adel' Pavlovna   Publisher of *MSMM* (1895–1900), *Vsemirnaia illiustratsiia* (1886–1895), *Trud* (1889–1895), *NRB* (1886–1895), *Parizhskaia moda* (1893–1895); editor and publisher of *Modistka* (1889–1895).

Goppe, Luisa Germanovna   Publisher of *NRB* (1895–1900), *MSMM* (1895–1900), *Vsemirnaia illiustratsiia* (1895–1898), and *Modistka* (1895–1898).

Goppe, Mariia Germanovna   Publisher of *NRB* (1895–1900), *MSMM* (1895–1900), *Vsemirnaia illiustratsiia* (1895–1898), and *Modistka* (1895–1898).

Gorbatova-Dobrovol'skaia, Natal'ia Iakovlevna (Pervukhina) [E. D. I.]   Worked for *TvK*.

Gorbunova, M. K.   Contributed to *OZ*.

Gotovtseva, Mariia Ivanovna [Avdot'ia Stepanovna Gul'pinskaia]   Worked for *RV* (1853).

Govorskaia, Lidiia Nikolaevna [Lidiia G.]   Worked for *Vestnik iugo-zapadnoi Rossii*.

Grech, Evgeniia Ivanovna (Shvidkovskaia) [Serafima]   Worked for *Severnaia pchela* and other journals in the 1850s.

Gridina, Ol'ga   Wrote for *Gazeta kopeika*.

Grigor'eva-Sidorova, S. A.   Editor and publisher of *Kurskaia gazeta* (1897–1899).

Grinevskaia, Izabella Arkad'evna, 1864–1944   Prose writer, playwright, literary critic, and translator who wrote for a wide variety of periodical publications, including *NV, ZhivO, Trud, Obrazovanie,* and *Zhivopisnoe obozrienie*.

Groman, Ol'ga [Ol'ga]   Worked for *Iskra* (Geneva, 1903).

Grot, Natal'ia Petrovna (Semenova), 1828–1853   Wrote for *Zhurnal dlia vospitaniia, Nashe vremia, Sovremennaia letopis',* and other periodicals.

Grushentskaia, E. M.   Editor and publisher of *Penzenskii spravochnyi listok* (1904).

Gudvilovich, Ekaterina K.   Editor and publisher of *Zhurnal inostrannykh perevodnykh romanov* (1877–1880).

Gurevich, Liubov' Iakovlevna, 1866–1940   Editor (1895–1898) and publisher (1891–1898) of *SevV*; contributor to the illegal journal *Osvobozhdenie* (Stuttgart-Paris), *RVed* (1907–), and a variety of other periodical publications such as *Apollon, Niva, Zhizn', NZhdV*; writer of literary and theatrical criticism for *Slovo* and *Rech'* (1908–), as well as

RM (1909–); editor of the literary-artistic-criticism section of *RM* (1912–1914); editor of the "foreign section" of the publishing house Mospoligraf (1924).

Gurskaia, M. K.   Editor and publisher of *Zdravyi smysl* (1907).

Gurskaia, Neonila Pavlovna   Publisher of *Batum* (1888–1905).

Guseva, Nina Ivanovna, 1876–? [N. Arkhipova-Moreva, Sestra Nina] Worked for *RB, Peterburgskaia zhizn', ZhD*.

Gvozdikova, Lidiia Nikolaevna   Publisher and editor of *Rosinki* (1868–1870); editor and publisher of *Kroshka* (1870).

Iadrintseva, Adelaida Fedorovna, ?–1888   Contributed articles on popular education in Siberia and authored the "Khronika" section for *Vostochnoe obozrenie* (1882–?), a newspaper edited and published by her husband N. M. Iadrintsev; special correspondent for *Volzhsko-kamskoe slovo* (early 1870s).

Iakovleva-Karich, E. F.   Editor and publisher of *Otdykh* (1899–1903).

Iamshchikova, Margarita Vladimirovna (Rokotova), 1872–1959 [A. Altaev, Al. Altaev, Aleksandr Altaev, Chuzhoi]   Published prose and biographical sketches in a wide variety of popular journals, including *Rodnik, DCh, Iunaia Rossiia, Vskhody,* and *IuCh*; edited the literary section of *Igrushechka*; served on the editorial board of the newspapers *Soldatskaia pravda* and *Derevenskaia bednota* (1917); wrote a daily column in *Bednota* (1918); edited the section "Derevnia" for *Litagit* (1919–1921); served as secretary of the journal *Krasnyi pakhar'* (1921–1922); edited the "Agitprop" section of *Trudovoi put'* (1922).

Ianchevetskaia, Varvara Pompeevna   Editor and publisher of *Revel'skie izvestiia* (1893–1910).

Ianzhul, Ekaterina Nikolaevna (Veliasheva)   Contributor to *RVed* (1889–1902).

Iavorovskaia, Anna Karlovna [Boane, A.]   Publisher and editor of *NZhdV* (1913–?).

Il'iashenko, A. G.   Publisher of *Kazanskii telegraf* (1894–1916).

Il'inskaia, Lidiia Appolonova   Editor and publisher of *Russkii muzykal'nyi vestnik* (1880–1882).

Il'inskaia, Nina Vladimirovna   Worked for *Krest'ianskoe delo* (1910).

Iordanskaia, E. I.   Worked for *Doshkolnoe vospitanie* (1916).

Ishimova, Aleksandra Osipovna, 1804–1881 Publisher and editor of *Zvezdochka* (1842–1863) and *Luchi* (1850–1860), in which were published more than 600 of her own articles and translations.

Istomina, Natal'ia Aleksandrovna Publisher of *DO* (1881–1887).

Iur'eva, N. N. Worked for *ZhivO* (1878–1879).

Ivanova, Anna Iosifovna, 1852–1931 Worked for *TvK* (1913–1914).

Ivanova, Elena Konstantinovna Editor and publisher of *Stolichnye ob"iavleniia* (1898–1901).

Ivanova, Mariia Trokhorovna Editor and publisher of *Ukazatel'kvartir* (1893–1894).

Ivanova, Zinaida Sergeevna, 1865–1913 [N. Mirovich] Wrote articles on self-education for *RVed* (1896) and articles on the woman question in *RM, VE, Obrazovanie, VV*.

Kalmykova, Aleksandra Mikhailovna (Chernova), 1849–1926 Contributor to *Iuzhnyi krai* and *Posrednik* and to the children's journals *Igrushechka* and *Zhavoronok*.

Kairova, Anastasiia Vasil'evna, 1845–1888 [A. K., N. S., A. V.] Contributor to the newspapers *NV* (1876) and *Golos* (1876–1880) and to the journals *VE, RM,* and *Delo* (1880s).

Kalitskaia, Vera Pavlovna, 1882–? [V. Abramova-Kalitskaia, V. Alien] Worked for *ChNS, Protalinka, DO, Tropinka, Vskhod,* and other publications.

Kirova, E. I. [Rodrigo] Worked for *Sibirskaia zhizn'* (1900s).

Karaffu-Korbut, Iuliia, 1831–1911 [Iu. Vladimirova, Iu. Vladimirtseva] Correspondent for *Golos*.

Karatygina, Raisa Genrikhovna Publisher of *Molochnoe khoziaistvo* (1902–1907).

Kardo-Sysoeva, Sof'ia Petrovna Publisher of *Luch* (1880–1881).

Kartamysheva, Mariia Fedorovna Editor and publisher of *Sibirskii vestnik politiki, literatury i obshchestvennoi zhizni* (1887–1905).

Kashpirova, Sof'ia Sergeevna Publisher and editor of *SemV* (1870–1891).

Kasitsyna, O. V. Publisher of *Dushepoleznoe chtenie* (1902–1913).

Kaspari, A. A. Publisher of *Dlia detei* (1901–1903) and its editor (1901–1916).

Katkova, S. P. Publisher of *RV* (1887).

Kazakevich-Stefanovskaia, E. P. Publisher of *IuCh* (1899–1906), along with A. Ia. Ostrogorskaia-Malkina and E. K. Pimenova, and publisher of *Po belu svetu* (1904–1905).

Khersonskaia, Ekaterina Pavlovna (Kunaeva), 1876–? Editor of the illegal newspaper *Golos truda* (1905) and *V poezde Kalinina* (1919–1920); editor of the pedagogical section of the publishing house "Lengiz" (1923); coeditor of *Vestnik prosveshcheniia* (1924–?).

Kholeva, Aleksandra Vikent'evna Publisher of *LO* and *Rostovskii na Donu listok ob"iavlenii* (1879–1888).

Khvoshchinskaia, Nadezhda Dmitrievna (Zaionchkovskaia), 1824–1889 [V. Krestovskii, V. Porechnikov, N. Vozdvizhenskii]
Literary critic; contributor to *OZ, Golos, RVed, ZhivO*.

Kirkhner, Liubov' Vasil'evna Publisher of *Amurskaia gazeta: Politicheskii, obshestvennyi i literaturnyi organ* (1904–1905), *Amurskaia gazeta: Prilozhenie literaturnoe i illiustrirovannoe* (1904–1905), and *Amurskaia gazeta: Telegrammy rossiiskogo telegrafnogo agenstva* (1904–1906).

Klirikova, L. N. Publisher of *Kolos* (1913) and *Krest'ianskoe delo* (1912).

Kniazhevich, Mariia Dmitrievna Worked for *RStar* (1888).

Kollontai, Aleksandra Mikhailovna (Domontovich), 1872–1952
Wrote articles for *Obrazovanie, Sovremennyi mir, Vpered, Sotsial-demokrat*, among many others.

Kolokolova, M. G. Worked for *Obrazovanie* (1893).

Koltonovskaia, Elena Aleksandrovna (Sas'ko), 1871–1952
Contributor to *MirB, IuCh, Zhizn', Obrazovanie, NZhdV*, as well as author of reviews for *Syn otechestva* and *Novosti*.

Konradi, Evgeniia Ivanovna (Bochechkarova), 1838–1898 Wrote for *ZhV* (1866–1868) and *Zagranichnyi vestnik;* with others, published the newspaper *Nedelia* (1870–1874); worked for the journal *VO;* contributed to *ZhD, RM, Vestnik innostrannoi literatury*.

Konstantinova, A. O. Editor and publisher of *Khudozhestvenno-remeslennyi zhurnal* (1895–1896).

Kop'eva, Elena Worked for *Moskovskii telegraf* (1830).

Korelina, Nadezhda Petrovna Worked for *RM* (1897–1900).

Korovitskaia, E. V. Publisher of *Volyn* (1892–1896).

Korvin-Krukovskaia-Zhaklar, A. V. Contributed to the French paper *La sociale* and to *SevV;* together with her husband, Zhaklar, composed the political survey for *Delo*.

Koshelevskaia, Mariia Publisher of *Vestnik parizhskikh mod* (1836–1850?).

Kovalevskaia, E. [Marina] Worked for *Novoe slovo* (1897).

Kovalevskaia, Sof'ia Vasil'evna (Korvin-Krukovskaia), 1850–1891 [Sof'ia Niron] Wrote scientific articles for *NV, RVed, VE*, and a variety of other Russian and Western European journals.

Kozhdanskaia, Iu. I. Editor of the Odessa *Studencheskaia mysl'* (1906).

Kozhevnikova, Lidiia Mikhailovna Editor and publisher of *Kozlovskaia zhizn'* (1912–1913).

Kozlovskaia, E. F. Publisher of the Rostov-on-Don *Fugas* (1916).

Kozlovskaia-Oginskaia, E. M. Editor and publisher of *Polnoch'* (1914–1916).

Krapivina, Tat'iana P. Editor of *LO* (1875–1877).

Krukovskaia, Sof'ia Karlovna Editor and publisher of *Tovarishch* (1900–1904).

Krupskaia, Nadezhda Konstantinovna, 1869–1939 Worked for the illegal Bolshevik newspaper *Vpered,* in charge of all correspondence with its journalists, editors, and the staff of its various local bureaus scattered throughout Russia; shared editorial responsibility for *Rabotnitsa* (1914); served on the editorial staff of *Proletarii* (Geneva, 1905); contributed to *Prosveshchenie;* worked for *Soldatskaia pravda* (1917–1918).

Krzhizhanovskaia, Z. P. [Vozhanskii, Z.] Worked for *Volna* (1906).

Kudasheva, Elikonida Ivanovna Worked for *Putevodnyi ogonek* (1900s).

Kudelli, Praskov'ia Frantseva, 1859–? Involved in publishing *Rabotnitsa* (1914).

Kugul'skaia, M. I. Publisher of *Novosti sezona* (1898–1916).

Kulitskaia, Olimpiia Vasil'evna Editor and publisher of *Professional'naia shkola* (1891–1892).

Kumanina, Olimpiada Karpovna   Publisher of *Teatral'naia biblioteka* (1896–98), *Teatral'* (1896–1900), *Chitatel'* (1896–1900).

Kuskova, Ekaterina Dmitrievna (Esipova, Iuvenalieva, Prokopovicha), 1869–1958 [M. M., Credo, Vsegda nekogda, E. K.]
Contributor to the illegal journals *Listok "Rabotnika"* (Geneva, 1896–1898) and *Osvobozhdenie* (Stuttgart-Paris 1902–); translator for, and contributor to, the newspaper *Saratovskii dnevnik;* coeditor and contributor to *NZ* (1904–1906) and the short-lived dailies *Tovarishch, Novyi put', Nash vek, Nasha gazeta;* publisher and coeditor (with her husband S. N. Prokopovich) of the weekly journal *Bez zaglaviia,* for which she also wrote; contributor to *RVed* (1908–1918) and to the journals *Byloe, Professional'noe dvizhenie, SZh, VE, VV, Vestnik kooperatsii, Kooperativnaia zhizn', Obrazovanie, Sovremennyi mir, Golos minuvshego,* among others; coeditor of, and contributor to, the newspapers *Vlast' naroda* (1917) and *Pomoshch'* (1921); in emigration published in numerous periodicals, including *Dni* (Paris), *NRS* (New York), *Novoe vremia* (Belgrade), *NZh* (New York), *Poslednie novosti* (Paris), and *Vozhrozhdenie* (Paris).

Lalosh, V.   Editor and publisher of *Parizhskie modnye vykroiki* (1876–1878).

Lashmanova, M. N.   Editor and publisher of *Kaluzhskii vestnik* (1896–1897).

Laskos, Izabella L'vovna (Griunberg), 1830?–1877   Wrote musical and theatrical criticism for the newspaper *Vest'* (1862–1869), as well as articles on women, their education, and place in society; reported from Vienna on musical events and art exhibitions in Austria for *Grazhdanin* (1874), *MVed* (1875–1876), and *RV* (1876–1877).

Laskovskaia, Mariia Fedorovna   Editor and publisher of *Biblioteka inostrannykh romanov i povestei* (1881).

Latysheva, Evgeniia Vasil'evna   Editor and publisher of *Russkii nachal'nyi uchitel'* (1905–1911).

Lavrent'eva, Sof'ia Ivanovna, 1836–1918?   Prose writer, translator, and essayist, writing extensively for a variety of children's journals *(Detskie zabavy, DCh, SemV, VO),* as well as publications for adults (*NV, SPVed, Den', RB, IV,* and others); assisted T. P. Passek, the founder of *Igrushechka,* in the first year of that journal's publication (1880).

Lavrova, Polina Matveevna   Worked for *Rebus* (1906).

Lebedeva, Ekaterina Epaminondovna   Editor and publisher of *POIR* (1880–1891).

Leont'eva, Mariia Platonovna   Worked for *Staryi Vladimirets* (1911).

Lenkevich, Lidiia   Editor and publisher of *LO* (1875–1877).

Lepkovskaia, Stefaniia K.   A publisher and editor of *Avrora* (1875–1878); publisher of *Vaza* (1882–1884).

Lermontova, Iuliia Vsevolodovna, 1846–1919   Book review editor for *Zhurnal russkogo khimicheskogo i fizicheskogo obshchestva* (mid-1870s).

Levitskaia, F. [F. L.]   Worked for *IV* (1900).

Levitskaia, Sof'ia Aleksandrovna [Russkaia soldatka]   Correspondent for the Galician newspaper *Slovo* (1878–1881).

Lidert, Mariia Fedorovna   Editor and publisher of *Svetliachok* (1902–1916).

Likhacheva, Elena Osipovna (Kosinskaia), 1836–1904   Wrote on women's topics for *OZ* and other journals.

Lipskerova, P. E.   Editor and publisher of *Sem'ia* (1905).

Lishke, Amal'ia Andreevna   Publisher of *NRB* (1872–1878).

Lisovskaia, Emiliia Fedorovna   Publisher of *Bibliograf* (1885–1914).

Litvinova, Elizaveta Fedrovna, 1845–1919 [E. El']   Wrote numerous articles for *ZhO* and *ZhD*.

Liubomudrova, Anna Fedorovna (Konovalova)   Worked for *Spiritualist* (1913).

Lopatina, Ekaterina Mikhailovna, 1865–1935 [K. El'tsova]   Published stories and sketches in a variety of newspapers and journals, including *RM* and the émigré *Poslednye novosti* and *Sovremennye zapiski*.

Lukanina, Adelaida Nikolaevna, 1843–1908 [A. N. Paevskaia]   Contributor to *VE*, *SevV*, and *RB*.

Lukhmanova, Nadezhda Aleksandrovna (Baikova), 1840–1907 [Baron F., Drozd., Drozd-peresmeshnik, N. Lukh., Neschastnyi muzh, Ptitsa-mukha, Revizor, Trech, Turist, Tsirkul']   Correspondent for *Peterburgskaia gazeta* during the Russo-Japanese War; editor and publisher of *Vozrozhdenie* (1899–1900).

Lund, Sofiia   Took over as publisher of *Moda* (1851–1852) from her mother, Elizaveta Safonova.

Lupandina, N. R.   Editor and publisher of *Krymskii kur'er* (1898–1907) and *Ezhednevnoe pribavlenie k gazete "Ialta"* (1894–1898).

L'vova, Mariia Nikolaevna   Publisher of *POIR* (1878–1880).

L'vova, Natal'ia Ivanovna   Publisher of *POIR* (1875–1878).

Lystsova, Sof'ia Valentinovna   Worked for *RM*.

Mak-Gakhan, Varvara Nikolaevna (Elagina), 1850–1904 [Pavel Kashirin]   Contributor to the *New York Herald* and the *Sidney Herald*; foreign correspondent for the newspapers *Golos* (1878–1883), *RVed* (1883–1898), *NV*, and *MVed* (1899–?), and for the journals *VE* (1882–1891), *SevV* (1889–1894), *RM* (1895–1897), *Russkoe obozrenie* (1895–1897), and *Nabliudatel'* (1901–1903).

Makarova, Sof'ia Markovna (Vepritskaia), 1834– 1887 [Avarova]   Editor of *Zadushevnoe slovo* (1879–1885).

Maksimova, Ol'ga Ivanovna   Editor and publisher of *Uchitel'-lingvist* (1890–1891).

Mal'neva, E.   Publisher of *Slovo* (1880–1881).

Mal'skaia, Anna Iakovlevna   Publisher of *Bessarabets*.

Malysheva, Agniia N.   With Zoia Travlinskaia, publisher and editor of *Guvernantka* (1862).

Malysheva, Mariia Ivanovna, 1830–1906   Contributor to the newspaper *Voronezhskie gubernskiea vedomosti*, edited by her brothers; member of the Stasova-Trubnikova women's translating and publishing cooperative *(zhenskaia izdatel'skaia artel')*; contributed translations to *Niva*.

Malysheva, Sof'ia Karlovna   Editor of *Zhenskii trud* (1880).

Manaseina, Natal'ia Ivanovna, 1869–?   Along with P. S. Solov'eva, a co-editor and publisher of *Tropinka* (1906–1912).

Mansvetova, Raisa Mikhailovna   Publisher of *Derevnia* (1898–1899) and *Krest'ianskoe khoziaistvo* (1899–1900).

Mar, Anna (Brovar), 1887–1917   Wrote articles for *Zhenskaia zhizn'* and *ZhD*, and an advice column in *Zhurnal dlia zhenshchin*.

Markova, M.   Editor of *Vestnik ptitsevodstva* (1894–1896).

Mei, Sof'ia Grigor'evna (Polianskaia, Rekhnevskaia), 1820–1889   Founder, editor, publisher, and contributor to *MM* (1862–1883); editor of *Literaturnyi sbornik: Prilozhenie k zhurnalu "Modnyi magazin"* (1881–1882).

Mel'nitskaia, A. V.   Editor of *Drug detei* (1902–1903).

Messarosh, Anna Borisovna   Publisher of *ZhV* (1866–1868).

Metaska, Elena Spiridonovna   Editor and publisher of *Artisticheskoe illiustrirovannoe obozrenie kafe-kontsertov, teatrov, var'ete i tsirkov* (1898–1899).

Mezentseva, Zinaida M.   Worked for *Zvezdochka* (Rostov-on-Don, 1907–1908).

Mikhailovskaia, Nadezhda Valerianovna   Publisher of *RB* (1892–1900).

Miller, N. F.   Publisher of *Razvlechenie* (1881–1884).

Miratova, Margarita   Worked for *Teatral'nyi mirok* (1892).

Miropol'skaia, Ol'ga Nikolaevna   A publisher and editor of *Avrora* (1875–1876).

Mordovina, Mariia Vasil'evna   Worked for *Zvezda* (1911).

Mordukhai-Bolotovskaia, Mariia Ivanovna [L. Mitina, M. Mitina]   Worked for *Niva* (1898).

Moskaleva, Vera Aleksandrovna   Publisher of *Nauchnoe obozrenie* (1902–1903).

Mukhina, Elena Borisovna   Editor and publisher of *Penzenskii spravochnyi listok* (1900–1902).

Murav'eva, A. Z.   Editor and publisher of *Baian* (1905–1906).

Napalkova, Evgeniia Viktorovna   Editor and publisher of *DO* (1888–1895).

Nazar'eva, Kapitolina Valer'ianovna, 1847–1900   Edited the section on provincial news for *Syn Otetechestva*; wrote literary reviews for the periodicals of the publisher M. O. Vol'f.

Nekrasova, Ekaterina Stepanovna, 1841–1905   Contributed numerous articles to a wide variety of newspapers and journals (1880–1900), including *RVed*, *VE*, *OZ*, *Kievskaia starina*, and *MirB*, primarily on major contemporary Russian authors as well as on many women authors of the 1820s to 1840s.

Nesvitskaia, Ekaterina Andreevna   Editor and publisher of *Zhurnal dlia detei* (1886–1890).

Nikitina, Lidiia Ivanovna   Publisher of *Derevnia* (1895–1898) and *Krest'ianskoe khoziaistvo* (1898–1899).

Nikoladze, Olga Andreevna   Publisher of *Novoe obozrenie* (1888–1891).

Novgorodskaia, I.   Editor and publisher of *Telegrammy severnogo telegrafnogo agentstva i vladimirskii listok ob"iavlenii* (1893) and *Vladimirskii listok ob"iavlenii* (1894).

Novikova, Ol'ga Alekseevna (Kireeva), 1850–1925 [Ol'ga Kireeva, O. K., O. N.]   Contributor to British newspapers, including *Northern Echo* (1877–1880) and *Pall Mall Gazette* (1884–1891); and to French and Belgian periodicals; foreign correspondent for *MVed* and *Rus'*; contributor to *NV, Sovremennyi izvestiia, Svet,* and *Russkoe obozrenie*.

Novosil'tseva, Ekaterina Vladimirovna, 1820–1885 [T. Tolycheva]   Wrote for *SemV, RV, Russkii arkhiv*.

Okreits, Vera Andreevna   Publisher of *Luch* (1881–1885).

Olinko, N. P.   Editor and publisher of *Kavkazskie ob"iavleniia* (1890–1891).

Orlova, M.   Publisher of *Tsaritsynskii listok ob"iavlenii* (1893–1897).

Oshanina, Mariia Nikolaevna (Olovennikova), 1853–1898 [M. N., Mar. Nik. Polonskaia]   On the editorial staff of *Narodnaia volia* (1881–1882) and *Vestnik Narodnoi voli: Revoliutsionnoe sotsial'no-politicheskoe obozrenie* (Geneva, 1883–1886).

Ostrogorskaia-Malkina, Anna Iakovlevna   Editor and publisher of *IuCh* (1899–1906), *Po belu svetu* (1904–1905), and *Biblioteka iunogo chitatelia* (1907–1908), along with E. P. Kazakevich-Stefanova and E. K. Pimenova.

Ovsianiko-Kulikovskaia, Z.   Worked for *VE* (1911).

Ozmidova, Zinaida Konstantinovna (Nevolina), 1851–1899   Editor and writer for *Novorossiiskii telegraf* (1870–?) and its copublisher (1889–?).

Panaeva, Avdot'ia Iakovlevna (Brianskaia), 1819–1893   Editor and contributor to *Sovremennik* (1848–1864), managing the fashion section ("Otdel mod"); published her memoirs in *IV*.

Panova, Evgeniia Alekseevna   Editor and publisher of *Dal'nii vostok* (1894–1916).

Parnok, Sof'ia Iakovlevna, 1885–1933   Literary critic; reviewer for *SevV* (1913–1917) and *Russkaia rech'* (1913–?).

Passek, Tat'iana Petrovna, 1810–1889   Editor, publisher, contributor to *Igrushechka* (1880–1887); publisher of *Zadushevnoe slovo*.

Pazukhina, Varvara Mikhailovna, ?–1894   Worked for *Razvlechenie* (1887).

Pechorina, M.   Worked for *RB* (1890–1893).

Peiker, Aleksandra Ivanovna   Editor and publisher of *Russkii rabochii* (1882–1886).

Peiker, Mariia Grigor'evna   Editor and publisher of *Russkii rabochii* (1875–1880).

Pel't, Aleksandra Nikolaevna   Publisher of *Narodnyi listok* (1879); editor and publisher of *Vseobshchaia gazeta* (1880–1883).

Pelitsaro, Ioganna Norbertovna   Publisher of *Noveishie mody muzhskikh plat'ev* (1887–1912).

Peregudova, A. F.   Editor of the Chita newspaper *Zabaikal'e* (1905?–1906).

Peshkova-Toliverova, Aleksandra Nikolaevna (Iakobi), 1842–1918   Editor and publisher of *Igrushechka* (1888–1910), *ZhD* (1899), and *Na pomoshch' materiam* (1894–1904); contributor to *RStar*; editor and publisher of the newspaper *Novoe delo* (1901–1903) and of the literary journal *Novoe delo* (1902).

Petrovich, Ol'ga Ivanovna   Editor and publisher of *Spravochnyi listok* (1893–1897) and *Teatral'nye izvestiia* (1894–1896).

Petrovskaia, Kaler'ia Andreevna   Editor and publisher of *Ukazatel' kvartir* (1892–1893).

Pikhno, Mariia Konstantinovna (Popova), 1846–1883   Regular contributor to *Kievlianin* (1864–1878) and, after the death of her first husband, V. Ia. Shul'gin, its publisher (1879–?).

Pimenova, Emiliia Kiril'evna   Editor of *IuCh* (1899–1903).

Pisareva, M. Ia.   Editor of *Izvestiia sibirskogo otdela Imperatorskogo russkogo geograficheskogo obshchestva* (1885–1887).

Platonova, Aleksandra Fedorovna   Worked for *Russkii palomnik* (1911).

Pogodina, Elizaveta Ivanovna   Editor and publisher of *Moskovskaia gazeta* (1883–1884) and publisher of *Zhizn'* (1885).

Pogosskaia, Ernestina   Publisher of *Dosug i delo* (1874).

Pogozheva, Nadezhda   Contributor to *Repertuar i Panteon* (1850s).

Pogozheva, Vera   Contributor to *Repertuar i Panteon* (1850s).

Pokrovskaia, Mariia Ivanovna, 1852–?   Editor and publisher of *ZhV* (1904–1906).

Polivanova, Elizaveta Mikhailovna   Editor and publisher of *ZhV* (1901–1906).

Polkova, A.   Publisher of *Ekaterinburgskaia nedelia* (1879–1883).

Polushina, Ol'ga   Worked for *Iskra* (1906).

Pomerantseva, Iuliia Petrovna   Editor of *MS* (1868–1873).

Popova, Aleksandra Martinovna   Publisher of *Russkii sport* (1884–1895).

Popova, Evgeniia Aleksandrovna [Zh. Linskaia, Zh. A. Linkskaia]   Worked for *RSlovo*.

Popova, Ol'ga Nikolaevna, 1848–1907   Founder and publisher of *Novoe slovo* (1895–1897); publisher of *Biblioteka nashikh detei*; publisher of *DS* with M. K. Tsebrikova and of *RB* (1894–1895), as well as contributor of many articles; coeditor of *VO*, along with Tsebrikova and N. D. Shelgunova; shareholder in the Marxist journal *Zhizn'*; publisher of books and pamphlets by many European and Russian revolutionaries.

Popova-Lavrova, Elizaveta Vasil'evna   Publisher (1899–1907) and editor (1903–1907) of *DO*.

Prokope, Anna Nikolaevna   Editor and publisher of *Modnaia masterskaia* (1903–1905).

Protopova, Ol'ga Andreevna   Editor and publisher of *Sevastopol'skii spravochnyi listok* (1886–1888) and publisher of *Krym* (1888–1889).

Pribylova-Korba, Anna Pavlovna, 1849–1939   Editor of *Narodnaia volia* for a brief period in 1881.

Pustoshkina, Anna Dmitrievna   Publisher of *Znamia* (1901).

Putiatina, Iuliia Feodorovna   Editor and publisher of *Pervoe izdanie vykroek* (1872).

Rakhmaninova, Kh.D.   Worked for *IV* (1899).

Rassokhina, Elizaveta Nikolaevna   Worked for *Budil'nik* (1895).

Reingardt, L. P.   Publisher of *Kazanskaia sel'sko-khoziaistvennaia gazeta* (1897–1903).

Reisner, Larisa Mikhailovna, 1895–1926 [Leo Rinus, M. Larin, I. Smirnov, L. Kharpovitskii] Along with her father, edited *Rudin* (1915–1916); wrote literary criticism for *Letopis'* and *Novaia zhizn'*.

Remizova, M. K. Editor and publisher of *Sever* (1894–1895).

Rikker, Ol'ga Aleksandrovna Publisher of *Russkii vrach* (1901).

Riumina, Olimpiada Grigorevna Publisher of *Moda* (1852–1854).

Rodionova, Ekaterina Petrovna Publisher of *Vestnik remesl i obshchedostupnyi tekhniki* (1904–1905) and *Remeslennik* (1904–1905).

Romanovskaia, Florentina Ignat'evna Publisher of *Vechernye izvestiia* (1904).

Romanovskaia, M. Worked for *RSlovo* (1905–1908).

Rostovskaia, Mariia Feodorovna (L'vova), ?–1872 Founder and publisher of *SemV* (1864–1869).

Rozanova, A. Worked for *Russkii palomnik* (1892).

Rudneva, E. Worked for *Russkaia shkola* (1912–1913).

Rumiantseva, Elizaveta Iakovlevna Publisher of *Luch* (1880).

Runova, Ol'ga Pavlovna (Meshcherskaia), 1864–1952 A regular contributor of prose to *Nedelia, RM, Obrazovanie, MirB,* and *SS*; a publisher of the newspaper *Volzhanin* (1905–1906).

Ryzhkova, Evgeniia Nikolaevna (Faleeva) Worked for *Zritel'* (1905).

Sabashnikova, Anna Vasil'evna An editor and publisher of *SevV* (1885–1888).

Safonova, Elizaveta Frantsovna Publisher of *Zhurnal noveishego shit'ia* (1836–1838), which became *Sanktpeterburgskii zhurnal raznogo roda shit'ia i vyshivan'ia* (1838–1847) and then *Vaza* (1857–1869?); publisher of *Listki dlia svetskikh liudei* (1840s), which eventually became *Moda* (1851); publisher of *Zhenskie raboty* (1872–1874).

Sakharova, A. G. Contributor to *ZhivO* (1878–1879).

Sakharova, Varvara Iosifovna Publisher and editor of *BdCh* (1875–1885).

Samoilova, Konkordiia Nikolaevna, 1876–1921 [Natasha Sibiriakova, N. Sibirskii, N. Sibiriakova, N. Simbirskii] A secretary for *Pravda* (1912–?), and in conjunction with the first International Women's Day, became director of *Pravda*'s special section "Zhenskii den' i rabotnitsa" (1913);

on the editorial staff of *Rabotnitsa* (1914); regular contributor to *Kommunistka*.

Saracheva-Freiberg, Elena Vladimirovna   Publisher and editor of *DO* (1888–1895).

Savich, Aleksandra Frantsevna   Publisher of *RB* (1878).

Savinkova, Vera Viktorovna   Worked for *RB*.

Savitskaia, P.   Editor and publisher of *Delovoi korrespondent* (1890–1893).

Selekhova, Klavdiia Fedorovna   Worked for *Moskvitianin* (1843).

Selenkina, Mariia Grigor'evna (Myshkina)   Worked for *Delo* (1869).

Selezneva, Ekaterina   Publisher of *Russkii kur'er* (1879–1880).

Semenova, Nadezhda Alekseevna (Sentiapina)   Editor and publisher of *Orlovskii vestnik* (1886–1899).

Semevskaia, Elizaveta Nikolaevna   Publisher of *RStar* (1892).

Serdobinskaia, M. P.   Worked for *RV* (1818).

Serova, Valentina Semenovna   Publisher of *Muzyka i teatr* (1867–1868).

Shaginian, Marietta Sergeevna, 1888–1982   Critic; contributed to a variety of journals and newspapers from 1906 to 1919, including *Priazovskii krai, Baku, Kavkazskoe slovo*.

Shamonina, Nadezhda Dmitrievna   Worked for *RV* (1858).

Shapir, Ol'ga Andreevna (Kisliakova), 1850–1916   Contributor to *Otechestvenye zapiski, VE, SevV, Obrazovanie, RB, Zhenskaia mysl'*.

Shaposhnikova, E. F.   Editor and publisher of *Penzenskii listok ob"iavlenii* (1899).

Shaposhnikova, S. F.   Editor and publisher of *Penzenskii spravochnyi listok* (1900).

Sharapova, Zinaida Fedorovna   Editor and publisher of *Listok dlia materia* (1902–1905) and *Mirok* (1902–1905).

Shcheglova, V. D.   Editor and publisher of *Kaluzhskii listok ob"iavlenii* (1900–1901).

Shchepkina-Kupernik, Tat'iana L'vovna, 1874–1952   Wrote for a wide variety of journals and newspapers of the popular press. Her nonfiction works included a large number of articles on the theater.

Shcherbatova, Mariia Nikolaevna   Editor and publisher of *Voskresnaia beseda* (1895–1896).

Shelgunova, N. D.   Publisher of *Nasha pishcha* (1894–1896); coeditor of *VO*.

Shents, Liubov' Nikolaevna   Editor and publisher of *Grammofon i fonograf* (1903).

Shirokikh, S. D.   Editor and publisher of *Mirok* (1905–1906).

Shishmareva, Sof'ia Ivanovna   Editor of *NRB* (1872–1900) and of *Parizhskaia moda* (1893–1898).

Shkapskaia, Mariia Mikhailovna, 1891–1952   Wrote for *Den'*.

Shreider, Klavdiia Nikanorovna   Editor and publisher of *Sbornik obshchedostupnykh ob"iavlenii* (1875–1876).

Shtyl'ko, A. A.   Editor and publisher of *Astrakhanskii vestnik* (1906–1916) and publisher of *Astrakhanskii vestnik: Illiustrirovannoe prilozhenie k gazetu "Astrakhnskii vestnik"* (1901–1912).

Shukina, Avgusta   Worked for *Monastyr'* (1908).

Shul'gina, A. I.   Publisher of *Zhivopisnoe obozrenie stran sveta* (1882).

Shuvalova, Praskov'ia   Worked for *Zhurnal zemlevladel'tsev* (1858).

Simonovich, Adelaida Semenovna   Publisher and editor of *DS* (1866–1868), to which she contributed numerous articles on the upbringing of young children.

Skavronskaia, Mariia Savel'evna (Boguslavskaia)   Worked for a variety of Moscow newspapers, including *Sovremennye izvestiiakh* and *Kur'er* (1870s); editor and publisher of *DZh* (1882–1884).

Skibinevskaia, Amal'ia Ivanovna   Editor of *Zhenskii trud* (1880–1882).

Sleptsova, Mariia Nikolaevna (Lavrova), 1861–1951   Contributor to the children's journals *Rodnik* and *DCh*; along with her husband, managed the journal *ChNS*; publisher of popular books for young people in the series *Knizhka za knizhkoi* (1889–1906).

Soboleva, Sof'ia Pavlovna, 1840–1884   Worked in the editorial office of *OZ*; worked for the children's journals *SemV* and *DCh*.

Sobolevskaia, S.   Worked for *Russkii palomnik* (1895).

Soedova, A. A.   Publisher of *Razvlechenie* (1891–1904).

Sokolova, Aleksandra Ivanovna, 1836–1914   Contributor to *IV*, *SPVed*,

Moskovskii listok, MVed; writer of music reviews; publisher of *Russkii listok* (1875–1895).

Sokolova, Elizaveta Sergeevna   Editor and publisher of *Bessarabskii vestnik* (1889–1892).

Sokolova, M.   Worked for *ZhO* (1888–1889).

Soldatova, A. G.   Editor of the Chita newspaper *Zabaikal'e* (1901–1906).

Solov'eva, Poliksena Sergeevna, 1867–1924 [Allegro]   Editor and publisher of the children's journal *Tropinka* (1906–1912).

Spasovskaia, Anna Vasil'evna (Chemodanova), 1895–1915
Publisher of *Veshnye vody* (1914–1915).

Stal', Liudmila Nikolaevna, 1872–1939   Worked for the Omsk newspaper *Stepnoi krai* (1895); edited *Kronshtadtskaia pravda*; shared editorial responsibility for *Rabotnitsa* (1914); edited *Soldatskaia pravda* (1918), *Viatskaia pravda*, *Bor'ba,* and a variety of other army newspapers and bulletins during the years of revolution and civil war.

Staniukovich, M.   Publisher of *Damskii al'bom rukodel'nykh rabot* (1855–1856) and *Severnyi tsvetok* (1857–1861).

Stepanova, Aleksandra Grigorevich, 1845–? [Iurik]   Wrote reviews and articles on the woman question for the newspapers *Sovremennoe slovo* (1862) and *SPVed* (1864–1865, 1869); contributed regularly to *Budil'nik* (1868–1870).

Stolina, Ekaterina Fedorovna   Publisher of *Razvlechenie* (1881–1884).

Strekalova, Aleksandra Nikolaevna   Editor and publisher of *Voskresnie rasskazy* (1875–1877) and *Sobranie povestei i romanov dlia iunoshestva* (1884–1888).

Stupina, Mariia Vladimirovna   Editor of *Sputnik zdorov'ia* (1904).

Sukhomlina, Ol'ga Andreevna   Editor and publisher of *POIR* (1874–1875).

Sviatlovskaia, Raisa Samoilovna   Worked for *Sovremennye izvestiia* (1880s).

Sushkova, Mariia Vasil'evna (Khrapovitskaia), 1752–1803   Wrote articles for *Truten'* and *Vsiakaia vsiachina.*

Sysoeva, Ekaterina Alekseevna, 1829–1893   Children's writer, translator; editor and publisher of *VO* (1881–1893) and editor of *Rodnik* (1882–1894); publisher and editor of *ChNS* (1887–1889).

Taube, Sof'ia Ivanovna (Anichkova), 1888–1960   An editor of *Ves' mir* (1912–1919); worked for *NV* (1904–1916); in emigration, worked for *Vozrozhdenie, Rossiia i slavianstvo, Morskie zapiski, Vestnik Riv'ery,* and *Novoe vremia* (Belgrade), as well as for a variety of Czech newspapers.

Tenisheva, Mariia Klavd'evna   Publisher of *Mir iskusstva* (1899–1900).

Tikhomirova, Elena Nikolaevna   With I. V. Borisov, publisher of *DCh* (1894–1900); publisher of *Iunaia Rossiia* (1906–1916) and *Pedagogicheskii listok* (1894–1916), as well as its editor (1915–1916).

Tikhonova, Ol'ga Stepanovna   Publisher of *Narodnoe blago* (1900–1901).

Tilli, Ida Avgustovna   Publisher of *LO* (1876).

Timofeeva, Vera Vasil'evna   Proofreader, contributor to *VE*.

Timofeeva, Zinaida Vasil'evna [Kholmskaia]   Publisher of *Biblioteka "Teatr i iskusstvo"* (1897–1916), *Dnevnik teatra i iskusstva* (1903–1905), and *Teatr i iskusstvo* (1896–1916).

Tkhorzhevskaia, Nadezhda Karpovna   Editor and publisher of *Voskresenie* (1896–1905).

Travlinskaia, Zoia   With Agniia Malysheva, publisher of *Guvernantka* (1862), as well as its editor.

Trubesska, Elizaveta Petrovna   Editor and contributor to *Zhural dlia milykh*.

Trubnikova, V. K.   Editor and publisher of *Russkii ekonomist* (1884–1886).

Tsebrikova, Mariia Konstantinvna, 1835–1917 [M. Artem'eva, M. Nikolaev, M. Nikolaevna]   Shared editorial responsibility for *VO* (1878); publisher of *DS*, along with N. V. Shelgunov and O. N. Popova; contributor to *OZ*.

Tseidler, A.   Editor of *Zabavy i rasskazy* (1863–1867).

Tsekhovskaia, Varvara Nikolaevna (Menshikova), 1872–1941 [Ol'nem, O. Ol'nem, O. N. Ol'nem, V. Tse-skaia, V. Ts-skaia N.]   Worked for *Kievskoe slovo* as a correspondent (1889–1895); an editor of *RB/Russkie zapiski* (1914–1916).

Tsivinskaia, Emiliia Aleksandrovna   Editor and publisher of *Peterburgskie izvestiia* (1901–1902).

Tsvetkova, Anna Iakovl'evna   Editor and publisher of *Maliutka* (1886–1910).

Tsvetkova, Elena.   Worked for *Vesy* (1906).

Tugan-Baranovskaia, Lidiia Karlovna (Davydova), 1869–1900
Edited the section "Na rodine" of *MirB* (1892–1900) and managed its foreign department (Inostrannyi otdel); wrote reviews and a wide variety of articles on social and economic questions for *MirB* and other periodicals.

Tur, Evgeniia (Elizaveta Vasil'evna Sukhovo-Kobylina, Saliás de Turnemír), 1815–1892   Founded, edited, and published the newspaper *Russkaia rech'* (1861); edited the belles lettres section ("Literaturnaia deiatel'nost'") of *RV* (1856–1860); contributed articles and prose to *BdCh*, *OZ*, *RSlovo*, *Severniaia pchela*, *Vremia*, *Golos*, *Sankt-Peterburgskie vedomosti*.

Turba, Lidiia Pavlovna   Editor and publisher of *Illiustrirovannyi mir* (1887–1889).

Tyrkova, Ariadna Vladimirovna, 1869–1962   Contributor to the illegal journal *Osvobozhdenie* (Stuttgart-Paris), and to *Rus'*, *Rech'*, *BVed*, *NZhdV*, *SZh*, and *Zarnitsy*, among others.

Ul'ianova, Mariia Il'inichna, 1878–1937   Secretary of the editorial board of *Pravda*.

Ul'ianova-Elizarova, Anna Il'inichna, 1864–1933?   Correspondent for *Vpered* (Geneva), *Proletarii* (Geneva), and *Nasha mysl'*, the Bolshevik newspaper *Zvezda*, *Prosveshchenie*, and *Pravda*; shared editorial responsibility for *Rabotnitsa* (1914).

Umanets, Mariia Pavlovna   Publisher of *Rossiia* (1884–1885).

Umnova, Aleksandra Vasil'evna   Editor of *Spravochnyi listok raiona morshansko-syzranskoi Zheleznoi dorogi* (1876–1880).

Utilova, Nadezhda Vladimirovna   Editor and publisher of *Moda* (1859–1861).

Utkina, Lidiia Nikolaevna   Along with her husband A. I. Utkin and others, a publisher and editor of *Budil'nik* (1875–1883).

Vagner, Ekaterina Aleksandrovna   Editor of *Molochnoe khoziaistvo* (1902–1907).

Vannovskaia, Ol'ga Alekseevna (Belova, Fedoseeva), 1875–1822? [M. A. Bern]   Worked for *Severnyi krai*.

Vasil'eva, Aleksandra Vasil'evna   Publisher of *Blagovest* (1884–1894).

Vasil'eva, Mariia Rolandovna   Editor and publisher of *Niva* (1903).

Vavilova, E. N.   Worked for *Kooperativnaia zhizn'* (1914).

Veis, Anna Germanovna   Publisher of *Vserossiiskii vestnik ob"iavlenii po torgovle, promyshlennosti i tekhnike vsekh otraslei* (1903).

Velichkina, Vera Mikhailovna (Bonch-Bruevich), 1868–?   On the editorial staff of *Zhizn'* (1902), which had been closed by the government in 1901 and later reopened "abroad"; regularly contributed articles to *Iskra*, *Vpered*, and *Proletarii*; served on the editorial staff of *Proletarii*; involved in editing the illegal journal *Rassvet* (1904); worked for the newspapers *Zvezda* and *Pravda*.

Velichkovskaia, Anna Nikolaevna, 1854–19? [Volkovich-Vel']   Wrote for *RV, NV, BVed, ZhD, ZhV*.

Vengerova, Zinaida   Covered Western European art and music for *SevV* in the 1890s and contributed to *VE*.

Verderevskaia, S. A.   Worked for *Niva* (1888).

Vergun, Vera Nikolaevna   Worked for *Slavianskii vek* (Vienna, 1902–1903) and *Slavianin* (1913).

Vernadskaia, Mariia, 1831–1860   Coeditor (with her husband Ivan Vernadskii) and contributor to *Ekonomicheskii ukazatel'*.

Veselovskaia, Aleksandra, 1840–1910   Contributor to *RVed*.

Veselovskaia, Varvara Iakovlevna   Publisher of *Don* (1884–1888).

Vezenkova, Vera Georg'evna [Vez]   Worked for *MVed* (1914–1916).

Vinogradova, Elizaveta Vasil'evna, 1870–? [Ef. Vasil'kov, Efim. Vasil'kov]   Worked for *Permskii krai*.

Vitalina, Vital'ia Grigor'evicha, ?–1917   Worked for *RSlovo*.

Vlas'eva, Evgeniia Valentinovna   Publisher of *Peterburgskii telefon* (1904–1906).

Vodovozova-Semevskaia, Elizaveta Nikolaevna (Tsevlovskaia), 1844–1923 [E. Ts— —skaia]   Contributed many articles on education and educators to *DCh*, *Golos uchitelia*, *Narodnaia shkola*, *Pedagogicheskii sbornik*, *Uchitel'*, *MirB*, *RB*, and *RStar*; published her memoirs in *Minuvshie gody*.

Voeikova, Anna Aleksandrovna   Editor and publisher of *Nachalo* (1899).

Volkova, Agrippina Aleksandrovna   Publisher of *Maliar* (1873–1878).

Volkova, Aleksandra Konstantinovna   Editor and publisher of *Teatral'nye izvestiia* (1895–1896).

Volkova, Anna Ivanovna (Vishniakova), 1847–1910   Editor of *DZh*; wrote hundreds of articles on the education of women and children for a wide variety of journals, including *Bibliograficheskii kruzhok, Deiatel', Detskaia pomoshch', Dlia narodnogo uchitelia, DZh, Drug zhivotnykh, Etnograficheskoe obozrenie, Gorodskoi i sel'skii uchitel', Kur'er, Moskovskaia illiustrirovannaia gazeta, Molochnoe khoziaistvo, Narodnyi uchitel', Na pomoshch' materiam, Pskovskaia zhizn', Pedagogicheskii listok, Remeslennaia gazeta, RVed, Russkii nachal'nyi uchitel', Shkol'noe khoziaistvo, Slepets, Svobodnoe vospitanie, Tavricheskii narodnyi uchitel', Teknicheskii sbornik i vestnik promyshlennosti, Tekhnicheskoe obrazovanie, Trezvost' i berezhlivost', Vestnik blagotvoritel'nosti, VV, Vestnik trezvosti, Voskhod, Zemledelets, ZhV,* and *ZhD*.

Voronova, Elizaveta Petrovna   Editor and publisher of *Zhurnal inostrannykh perevodnykh romanov* (1876–1877).

Voronova, Zoia Leonidovna   Editor of *Naborshchik* (1903–1905).

Vovchok, Marko (Mariia Aleksandrovna Vilinskaia, Markovich, Lobach-Zhuchenko) 1833–1907   Editor of *Dlia detskogo chteniia* (1871–1872) and *Illiustrirovannyi zhurnal* (1871–1872).

Vystavkina, Ekaterina Vladimirovna [Brovtsyna]   Worked for *Drug detei, SS, VV, ZhD, Kur'er, Rul', Put'*.

Zaika, Kleopatra N.   An editor of *Avrora* (1876–1878).

Zakrevskaia, Mariia [Mariia A . . . skaia]   Worked for *Sovremennik* (1837).

Zasulich, Vera Ivanovna, 1849–1919 [A. Bulgina, V. Ivanov, N. Karelin]   Correspondent for the newspaper *Znamia* (New York); articles published in *Sotsial-demokrat* (Geneva); coeditor of *Rabotnik* (Geneva, 1896–1899) and its supplement *Listok "Rabotnika"* (Geneva, 1896–1898); instrumental in publishing *Na rodinu* (Geneva, 1882–1883); on the editorial staff of the illegal Marxist newspaper *Iskra*.

Zborzhevskaia, V.   Editor and publisher of *Illiustrirovannyi zhurnal dlia detei* (1881–1882).

Zelenskaia, Elizaveta   Publisher of *Astrakhanskii vestnik* (1889–1896).

Zhandar, Aleksandra Vasil'evna, ?–1883 Correspondent for *MVed*.

Zhavoronkova, M. Editor and publisher of *Ural'skii listok* (1892–1896).

Zhelikhovskaia, Vera Petrovna (Gan), 1835–1896 Contributor to *Kavkaz, Tifliiskii listok, Igrushechka, Rodnik, DCh, Grazhdanin, Sever*, and many other newspapers and journals.

Zhukova, Mariia Worked for *Sel'skoe khoziaistvo* (1861).

Zhukovskaia, Adelaida Kazimirovna (Gertsyk) [Sirin] Worked for *Vesy* (1905–1906).

Zrazhevskaia, Aleksandra Vasil'evna, 1805–1867 Contributor to *Maiak, Moskvitianin*.

Zuichenko, Evgeniia Aleksandrovna Editor and publisher of *Ekaterinoslavskii listok ob"iavlenii* (1885–1902).

Contributors

Linda Edmondson, ESRC Research Fellow at the Centre for Russian and East European Studies, University of Birmingham, England, is the author of *Feminism in Russia, 1900–1917* (1984). Editor of *Women and Society in Russia and the Soviet Union* (1992) and coeditor of *Civil Rights in Imperial Russia* (1989), she is currently compiling an anthology, *Gender in Russian History and Culture.*

June Pachuta Farris, Bibliographer for Slavic and East European Studies, University of Chicago, is the author of numerous bibliographic articles in history and literature, and is editor and compiler of "Current Bibliography" for *Dostoevsky Studies.* She has recently finished a manuscript, *Women and Children in Imperial Russia: An Annotated Bibliography.*

Jehanne M Gheith, Associate Professor of Russian Literature, Duke University, has published articles on Russian women's prose, including introductions to *The Memoirs of Princess Dashkova* (1995) and the Evgeniia Tur novel *Antonina* (1996). Coeditor of *A History of Women's Writing in Russia,* she is author of *(Not) Writing like a Russian Girl: Evgeniia Tur, V. Krestovskii, and Nineteenth-Century Prose* (forthcoming).

Adele Lindenmeyr, Professor and Chair of History, Villanova University, has published numerous articles, principally on the nineteenth century, and is the author of *Poverty Is Not a Vice: Charity, Society, and the State in Imperial Russia* (1996). Her current research is on the life and work of philanthropist and liberal political leader Countess Sophia Panina.

Carolyn R. Marks, Ph.D. candidate in Russian History at the University of North Carolina, is completing her dissertation, "The Women's Press: A Look at How the Educated Elite Sought to Fashion Middle Class Values in Russia, 1860–1917."

Barbara T. Norton, Professor of History, Widener University, is the author of articles on Ekaterina Kuskova and on the role of Russian Political Masonry in the February 1917 revolution. She is presently engaged in an oral history project, "An Ordinary Life in Extraordinary Times: A Russian Woman Remembers Stalinism."

Miranda Beaven Remnek, Russian and East European Studies Bibliographer, University of Minnesota, is the author of numerous bibliographical essays on the history of publishing in prerevolutionary Russia. She has recently completed her dissertation, "The Expansion of Russian Reading Audiences, 1828–1848."

Christine Ruane, Associate Professor of History, University of Tulsa, is the author of numerous articles on nineteenth-century Russia and *Gender, Class, and the Professionalization of Russian City Teachers, 1860–1914* (1994). She is currently preparing a history of the fashion industry in imperial Russia.

Rochelle Goldberg Ruthchild, Professor of Graduate Studies, Norwich University, is the technical editor of *Women and Russia: Feminist Writing from the Soviet Union* (1984) and the compiler and editor of *Women in Russia and the Soviet Union: An Annotated Bibliography* (1994). She is now completing a monograph on the feminist movement in Russia from 1859 to 1917.

Mary F. Zirin, independent researcher-translator, Altadena, Calif., is translator of *The Cavalry Maiden: Journals of a Russian Officer in the Napoleonic Wars* (1988), and coeditor and contributing author for *Dictionary of Russian Women Writers* (1994). The author of numerous articles on Russian women's prose fiction, she is presently translating the autobiography of the writer Nadezhda Sokhanskaia.

An additional "contributor" to this volume is our editor at Duke University Press, Valerie Millholland, who, like our authors, has from the beginning displayed an enthusiasm for this project and an infinite patience with its editors, essential ingredients in making this book what it is. To her and to our authors we offer our considerable thanks. (BTN and JMG)

Index

Aksakov, Ivan, 146
Aksel'rod, Pavel, 226
Alexander I: cultural life during reign of, 29
Alexander II, 93, 143
Alexander III, 93
Almanacs, 48n17; and censorship, 28; circulation figures, 28; contents of, 38–39; cost of, 50n50; and female readership, 45; female subscribers to, 35–37, 50n51; history of, 29; subscription rates and lists, 28, 35
Alovert, Nikolai Pavlovich, 98; biography of 108; and breaking Goppe monopoly of women's magazines, 108; and *Vestnik mody,* 108–11
Amfiteatrov, Aleksandr, 235

Balkan crisis, 143–44
Bashkirtseva, Mariia, 190n30
Belinskii, Vissarion, 59
Bestuzhev courses, 169, 170, 188n9, 189n16
Bez zaglaviia. See Kuskova, Ekaterina Dmitrievna
Biblioteka dlia chteniia, 27, 29, 36
Boguslavskaia, Mariia, 104–5
Bolsheviks: and *Rabotnitsa,* 183; and women's rights, 175
Britain: relations with Russia, 145–48
Bulgaria: 1876 revolt in, 156
Bulgarin, Faddei, 30, 32

Catherine II, 11, 24n30, 55
Censorship, 72n58, 77, 101, 103, 104, 117n45, 132, 134, 135, 141, 225; administration, 76, 96, 105, 108, 109; and almanacs, 28; appeal by Adel' Goppe, 109–10; changing periodicals name to avoid, 245n57; collapse of after October Manifesto, 228, 243n38; history of 10; post-publication penalties, 151; procedure for establishing a periodical, 96; revision of laws, 141, 229; and Temporary Press Laws of 1882, 95; and women, 11
Chekhova, Mariia: family background and education of, 169–70; and feminism, 176; and League of Women's Equality, 182; marriage of, 170–71, 182; and October Revolution, 185; and Pokrovskaia, 181; and *Soiuz Zhenshchin,* 179, 182–83; and Women's Equal Rights Union, 179; and women's rights, 180; work in education, 171
Circulating Libraries, 50n46
Club of the Women's Progressive Party in St. Petersburg, 179, 204
Congress of Berlin, 154
Constitutional Democrats, xi, 174–75, 229
Court of Honor, 158
Crimean War, 144; impact on fashion in Russia, 83–86

Damskii zhurnal, 29, 31
Dashkova, Ekaterina, 11–12, 23n29, 55
De Genlis, Stephanie Felicite: popularity of in Russia, 41–42
Detskaia pomoshch, 129, 138n38
Divorce: and pre-revolutionary Russia, 171
Dobroliubov, Nikolai, 58–59
Drug zhenshchin, 97, 98, 126, 130, 131, 267; closure of, 106, contents of, 105–6; contrast with *Vestnik mody*, 111; and education of women, 106; founding of, 104; mission of, 104; and request for subsidy from Ministry of Internal Affairs, 104–5; and Anna Ivanovna Volkova, 105–7
Drug zhivotnykh, 127
Duma, xi; and women's rights, 175
Durova, Nadezhda, 11, 23n29, 36, 41

Education: access to in Russia, 106; and gentry women, 158; higher education for women in Russia, 63, 73n61, 124, 131, 170; and merchant class, 122, 124; professional education and women, 112
Emancipation of Labor Group, 226
Engel'gardt, A. N., 265

Fashion: columns in thick journals, 90n2; and female journalists, 74–75; history of fashion press in Russia, 74–92; influence of Crimean War on, 83–86; influence of Peter I on, 85; and nationalism, 85–86; pages in *Sovremennik*, 58; readership of fashion magazines, 75; Russian fashion industry, 82

February Revolution, 237
Female medical students in Russia, 131–32
Feminism: in Russia 6; view of prostitution, 198. *See also* Chekhova, Mariia; Gurevich, Liubov', Kuskova, Ekaterina Dmitrievna; Pokrovskaia, Mariia Ivanovna; Tyrkova, Ariadna
Fiction: access to, 35–37; and female readership, 27, 32–34; foreign novels in translation, 29–30; history of Russian fiction, 30; publication of, 27; reading of during reign of Nicholas I, 31–34; social class of readers, 37–39; subscription lists for, 31, 33–34; works by women, 36
Figner, Vera, 185
First All-Russian Congress of Women, 183, 209, 233, 234

Gan, Elena, 36
Golos, 141, 149, 150, 156; print run of, 160n3; suspension of, 151; women's contribution to, 143, 144
Golos rabotnitsy, 183
Golubkova, A. E. ('Lialia'), 141
Goppe, Adel', 109–10, 112, 119n71
Goppe, Herman Dmitrievich: biography of, 102; competition with Alovert, 108–9; and *Modnyi svet*, 102–4; and monopolization of women's magazine market, 108; success of, 107; and technological change, 104
Gor'kii, Maksim, 235, 247n76
Great Reforms, xi; effect on magazine subscription rates, 87; effect on Russian society, 87

Grech, Nikolai, 29
Grot, Natal'ia, 68n17
Gurevich, Liubov': and *Bez zaglaviia*, 230; daughter of, 170; and Duma, 175; family background of, 169; and Moscow Art Theater, 184; and politics, 175; reminiscences of, 266; and *Severnyi vestnik*, 172; and Women's Equal Rights Union, 175; and women's rights, 180–81

International Telegraph Agency, 151–52, 156

Jews in Russia, 147–48, 165n49
Journalism in Britain, 7, 22n18, 22n20
Journalism in Russia: and gender, 2–5, 7, 54–56, 64; history of, 1–2, 55; and politics, 7–8; as profession, 57; relationship with fiction, 8; and salons, 8–9
Jury system, 148

Kadets. *See* Constitutional Democrats
Kairova, Anastasiia Vasil'eva: and anti-Semitism, 154; biography of 148; and Constantinople conference, 153; death of, 155; and feuilletons, 152; and *Golos*, 149–52, 54; and Imperial Russian Historical Society, 155; and *Novoe vremia*, 149–50; obituary of, 155; relationship with Fedor Koni, 148–49, 164n37, 164n40; and *Russkaia mysl'*, 154; and Serbian-Bulgarian War, 154–55; trial of, 148–49; use of male voice in writing, 150, 159; and *Vestnik Evropy*, 154

Karaffa-Korbut, Iuliia, 144
Karamzin, Nikolai, 11–12, 27, 32, 41
Katkov, Mikhail, 13, 141
Khodskii, L.V., 231
Kireev, Nikolai, 162–63n24
Koni, Fedor. *See* Anastasiia Kairova
Koshelevskaia, Mariia, 94
Kraevskii, Andrei, 30, 141, 149, 151
Krupskaia, Nadezhda, 170
Kruzhki, 223
Kuskova, Ekaterina Dmitrievna: Askel'rod's criticism of, 226; and *Bez zaglaviia*, 230–31; and the Bolshevik government, 237; break with organized Social Democracy, 227; and Commissariat for the Protection of the Freedom of the Press, 237; and Committee of Public Organizations, 237; employment as journalist, 224–25; family background and education, 223–24; and feminism, 234; and First All-Russian Congress of Women, 233–34; and Kadet Party, 229; marriage of, 224; memoirs of, 239n6; and *Nasha zhizn'*, 228, 231; and *Nash vek*, 231–32; and *Osvobozhdenie*, 174, 227–28; and radical activities, 225; relationship with Sergei Prokopovich, 225–26, 228, 230, 232–33, 236, 237, 241n21, 242n36, 245n60; and *Russkie vedomosti*, 233, 235; and *Sovremennik*, 235; and *Tovarishch*, 231; training as midwife, 224, 240n15; and Union of Liberation, 243n41; and Union of Russian Social Democrats Abroad, 226; and women's

Kuskova, Ekaterina (*cont.*)
  rights, 228–29; and World
  War I, 236–37

Lazhechnikov, Ivan, 30
League of Women's Equality, 182
Liberation movement, xi, 15, 230, 232; and creation of professional and labor unions, 229; and feminists, 204; women's participation in, 200
Lieven, Dorothea, 162n20
Likhachev, Elena, 144
Likhachev, Vladimir, 141
Listok "Rabotnika," 226

MacGahan, Januarius Aloysius. *See* Mak-Gakhan, Varvara Nikolaevna
Mak-Gakhan, Varvara Nikolaevna: and anti-Semitism, 158; conflict with E. N. Matrosov, 157–58; death of, 158; and 1876 revolt in Bulgaria, 156; family life of, 155–56; and *Golos*, 156; marriage of, 155–56; and *Russkie vedomosti*, 156; and *Severnyi vestnik*, 156–57; and *Vestnik Evropy*, 156; and women readers, 159; and writings about America, 157, 159
Martov, Iulii, 234
Mass-circulation newspapers: and censorship, 141; history of in Russia, 140–41; and Russian women, 141–42
Matrosov, E. N. *See* Mak-Gakhan, Varvara Nikolaevna
Medicine: discrimination faced by female physicians in Russia, 173
Mei, Sofiia Grigor'evna, 98; biography of, 100; marriage of, 100, 101; and *Modnyi magazin*, 100–101; salon of, 100–101
Mensheviks: and *Golos rabotnitsy*, 183; and women's rights, 175
Middle class in Russia, 111–12
Midwifery, 240n15
Miliukov, Pavel: disagreement with wife over suffrage, 174, 191–92n41
Miliukova, Anna: disagreement with husband over suffrage, 174, 192n41
Ministry of Internal Affairs, 96, 104–5
Mir Zhenshchin, 183
Moda: Zhurnal dlia svetskikh liudei, 75; advertisements in, 78–80; agenda of 77–78; contents of, 77–81; and French fashions, 81–82; history of, 76–77; illustrations in, 79; inclusion of sewing patterns, 79; and marketing strategies, 88–89; merger with *Severnyi tsvetok*, 86; and promotion of Russian fashion industry, 82; publishers of, 63; readership of, 78, 88; and Russian influence on French fashion, 82; subscriptions to, 78–79
Modnoe ezhemesiachnoe izdanie, ili Biblioteka dlia damskogo tualeta, 94
Modnyi magazin, 95, 98, 100–101, 102, 108
Modnyi svet, 89, 97–98; and advertising, 103–4; and censorship, 103; circulation figures of, 102–3; establishment of, 102; fashion prints in, 103; and feuilleton, 103; and miscellany, 103
Moscow Slavic Benevolent Committee, 146

Moskovskie vedomosti, 141, 144, 146
Moskovskii al'manakh dlia prekrasnogo pola, 31
Moskovskii nabliudatel', 29–30
Moskovskii telegraf, 29

Nadezhdin, Nikolai, 60, 64
Nasha zhizn'. *See* Kuskova, Ekaterina Dmitrievna
Nash vek, 231–32
Nekrasov, Nikolai, 69n24, 69n25. *See also* Panaeva, Avdot'ia
Nicholas I, 145; social and cultural life during reign of, 26–45
Nicholas II, 228
Novikov, Nikolai, 94
Novikova, Ol'ga Alekseevna: biography of, 145; and *Moskovskie vedomosti*, 146; and Nicholas I, 145; pamphlets of, 147; and Pan-Slavism, 145–46, 148; pseudonym of, 146; and religion, 145; and treatment of Russian Jews, 147–48
Novoe vremia, 141, 149
Novosil'tseva, Ekaterina, 144
Novyi russkii bazaar, 102, 108, 118–19n69

October Manifesto, 228
Osvobozhdenie, 227
Otechestvennye zapiski, 30; women working at, 264–65

Panaeva, Avdot'ia: biography of, 56; and Dobroliubov, 58–59; fiction of, 57–58; relationship with Nekrasov, 56–59; and Reshetnikov, 59; salon of, 56, 59–60; and *Sovremennik*, 13, 56, 57–60
Pan-Slavism, 143, 146, 162n15

Pervyi zhenskii kalendar', 185, 267–68
Peter I: influence on Russian fashion, 85
Pisarev, Dmitri: and Panaeva, 58, 62; work at *Rassvet*, 268
Plekanov, Georgii, 230, 231
Pogodin, Mikhail, 29
Pokrovskaia, Mariia Ivanovna, 269; and abortion, 208; attack of Fedor Kokoshkin, 205, 217n17; biography of, 169–70, 197–98; and Chekhova, 181; and Club of the Women's Progressive Party in St. Petersburg, 204; concern for living conditions of poor peasants and proletariat, 172–73; definition of feminism, 204–5; and discrimination against female doctors, 173; and feminism, 176–78; and First All-Russian Congress of Women, 209; and Liberation movement, 201, 204, 214; membership in Russian Women's Mutual Philanthropic Society, 199; and prostitution, 173, 181, 198, 207, 209; and revolutionary violence, 177; and Russian Society for the Defense of Women, 198; and Russo-Japanese War, 209–11; and sexuality, 179; and Social Democrats, 212; and stereotypes of women doctors, 199; and Tolstoi, 206, 209, 218n31; and view of Duma, 203; and view of men, 202–3, 204, 210–12; and Women's Economic Union, 184; and Women's Equal Rights Union, 203, 214; and Women's Progressive Party, 178, 203; and women soldiers, 211; and World

Pokrovskaia, Mariia (*cont.*)
War I, 184, 209–11; and *Zhenskii vestnik*, 15, 173–74, 176–77, 181–82, 201–3. See also *Zhenskii vestnik*
Polevoi, Nikolai, 29
Poliarnaia zvezda, 29
Popova, Elizaveta, 40, 42
Prechistenskie courses, 171
Press Laws, 243n43, 244n44
Professions: restrictions on female participation in Russia, 171
Prokopovich, Sergei. *See* Kuskova, Ekaterina Dmitrievna
Prostitution, 173, 196; euphemisms for brothels, 216n6; feminists view of, 198, 207; and First All-Russian Congress of Women, 219n35; and Russian Society for the Defense of Women, 198, 219n35
Provisional Government, xi, 184, 237

Rabotnitsa, 183, 266, 268
Radcliffe, Ann: popularity of in Russia, 43
Rassvet, 94–95, 100, 265–66, 268
Raznochintsy: definition of, 68n19
Readership in Russia: and fashion magazines in Russia, 75, 78–79, 87–88; female readers and fiction, 31–34; and mass-circulation press, 148; motivations for female readers, 39–44; and provincial women, 78; reading aloud, 37; social class and subscription lists, 28, 37–39, 48–49n25, 49n39, 49–50n40, 50–51n52; thick journals and female readers, 90n2; and urban women, 104; and women's magazines, 95
Reshetnikov, Fedor Mikhailovich, 59, 70n35
Riumina, Olimpiada Grigorevna, 76–77, 81
Russian Society for the Defense of Women. *See* Prostitution
Russian Society for the Preservation of Public Health, 173
Russian Women's Mutual Philanthropic Society: annual reports of, 268–69; history of, 199
Russian Writers' Union for Mutual Aid, 158
Russkaia khoziaika, 62–63
Russkaia rech', 57, 60–63. *See also* Tur, Evgeniia
Russkie vedomosti, 128, 141, 144, 156, 233; women's contribution to, 143
Russkii vestnik, 60–61
Russo-Japanese War, 228; and feminists, 209
Russo-Turkish War, 144; end of, 154; and female journalists, 144; and women, 144

Safonova, Elizaveta Frantsova, 94; and fashion magazines, 76; and *Moda: Zhurnal dlia svetskikh liudei*, 76
Salons, 8, 56, 57, 59–60, 68n19, 100–101, 130, 145
Sand, George: popularity of in Russia, 43–44
Serbian-Bulgarian War, 154–55
Serbian-Turkish War, 143–44
Severnye tsvety, 29
Severnyi tsvetok: Modnyi zhurnal dlia svetskikh liudei, 86–88; cost of subscription, 86; merger with

Moda, 86; publication schedule of, 86
Severnyi vestnik, 156, 172
Shapir, Olga, 191n31
Skvortsov, Nikolai, 141
Slavic Benevolent Committees, 143
Slavophiles, xi, 84. *See* Pan-Slavism
Social Democrats, 212
Soiuz zhenshchin, 197, 269; advertising in, 180; contents of, 180; cost of, 180; demise of, 182–83; and feminism, 180; and funding, 181; history of, 179; press run of, 180; support for, 182; and Women's Equal Rights Union, 180; and women's rights, 180, 186; and *Zhenskii vestnik*, 181
Sokhanskaia, Nadezhda, 32–34, 36–37, 40–41, 61, 71n47
Sokolova, Aleksandra, 55, 141; and anti-Semitism, 165n49
Sovremennik: and fashion pages, 58; history of, 60, 69n25; and Kuskova, 235; subscription figures of, 70n31; women working at, 264–65. *See also* Panaeva, Avdot'ia
Specialized Publications in Russia, 128–30
Stanislavskii, Konstantin, 184
Struve, Petr, 174, 184, 227
Suffrage, 205; in Britain, 212, 220n53; fight for in Russia, 167–77; in Finland, 187n5; and Kadet Party debates, 174; and Miliukov, 191n41; and Provisional Government, 184–85
Suvorin, Aleksei, 61, 71n53, 141, 149
Syn otechestva, 29, 36

Table of Ranks, 31, 49n27
Tatlina, Praskov'ia, 32, 33, 42–43
Telegraph: invention of, 152
Teleskop, 60
Thick journals, xi–xii, 27, 47n8, 90n2, 223
Tolstoi, Lev: and female suffrage, 206
Tovarishch. *See* Kuskova, Ekaterina Dmitrievna
Trudovik Party, 192n46
Tsebrikova, Marina, 68n17, 264
Tur, Evgeniia, 265; biography of, 56–57; and censorship, 72n58; and female readers, 72n56; and *Russkaia rech'*, 13, 57, 61–63; and *Russkii vestnik*, 13, 60–61, 64; salon of, 57, 60; and *Teleskop*, 60; and women writers, 61, 62
Tyrkova, Ariadna, 227; arrest of brother, 170; and émigré life, 185; family background and education of, 169–70; and First All-Russian Congress of Women, 183–84; and journalism, 171; and Kadet Party, 174–75; marriage of, 171–72; memoirs of, 185; and *Osvobozhdenie*, 174; and Petrograd city soviet, 185; and *Russkaia molva*, 184; and women's rights, 180; and World War I, 184

Union of Liberation, 227–28
Union of Russian Social Democrats Abroad, 226
Union of Towns, 247n82
Union of Unions, 217n16
Utilova, Nadezhda Vladimirovna, 13, 77

Vaza, 94, 100, 102, 108, 114n9
Vengerova, Zinaida, 191n31
Vernadskaia, Mariia, 55, 56, 67n9, 68n17
Veselovskaia, Aleksandra, 144
Vestnik Evropy, 11–12, 32, 154, 156, 172–73
Vestnik mody, 96, 98; contents of, 109, 110–11; and nationalism, 108–9; and readership, 111; and "woman question," 111
Vestnik parizhskikh mod, 94
Volkova, Anna Ivanovna: biography of, 105; and censorship, 132, 134, 135; and child welfare, 129; criticism of capitalism, 134; diary of, 121, 133; and *Drug zhenshchin*, 14, 105–7, 126–27, 30; and *Drug zhivotnykh*, 14, 127; education of, 123–24; family life of, 120, 122–25; and female medical students, 131–32; and higher education for women, 107, 124; 131; intellectual life of, 124–25; journalistic output of, 127–28; marriage of, 123–24, 128; memoir of, 124; and moral obligations of journalists, 129; salon of, 130; and specialized publications, 128–30; and translation of *La Baronne Miroel*, 125–26; and women's rights abroad, 132–33; work methods of, 130–31
Vsiakaia vsiachina, 24n30, 55

Westernizers, xii, 71n51, 84
"Woman question" in Russia, 88, 94, 111
Women: in Muscovite era, 85; nineteenth-century view of, 140
Women's Economic Union, 184
Women's Equal Rights Union, 175, 204, 206, 214, 217n22, 218n27, 229; and inner dissension, 203; organizers of, 179, 200; and prostitution, 207; and revolutionary violence, 177; and *Soiuz zhenshchin*, 180
Women's magazines in Russia: and advertising, 98, 116n23; and censorship, 95; circulation figures of, 95–96, 117n43; contents of, 97, 101–2; history of, 93–119; number of, 96–97, 104; personal financing of, 98; publishers and editors of, 99, 112; readership of, 95; subscription rates of, 97; and technological change, 95, 112
Women's Press: definition of, 19n6
Women's Progressive Party, 203; founding of, 178; membership of, 178–79; and *Zhenskii vestnik*, 178
Women's Rights Organizations in Russia. *See* Women's Equal Rights Union; Women's Progressive Party
World War I, 236–37; and feminists, 210

Zagoskin, Mikhail, 30, 32
Zhandr, Aleksandra Vasil'evna, 142
Zhenskaia mysl', 183, 269
Zhenskaia zhizn', 183
Zhenskii vestnik, 95, 196–97, 208, 266, 269–70; contents of, 179; demise of, 185; and funding, 181–82; launching of, 173–74, 201; male supporters of, 204; readership of, 197; relationship with Women's Equal Rights

Union, 201–2; and *Soiuz Zhenshchin,* 181; and suffrage, 201, 205; view of men presented in, 199, 202, 210; and woman question, 176–77; and Women's Progressive Party, 178–79; and World War I, 184. *See also* Pokrovskaia, Mariia Ivanovna

Zhenskoe delo, 183, 270

Zhenskoe obrazovanie, 97, 270–72

Zinov'ev, Fedor Alekseevich, 77, 86

Library of Congress Cataloging-in-Publication Data

An improper profession : women, gender, and journalism in late Imperial Russia / edited by Barbara T. Norton and Jehanne M Gheith.

p. cm.

Includes bibliographical references and index.

ISBN 0-8223-2556-X (cloth : alk. paper) — ISBN 0-8223-2585-3 (pbk. : alk. paper)

I. Norton, Barbara T., 1948–. II. Gheith, Jehanne M.

PN5277.W58 I48 2001

070'.082'094709034—dc21   00-046259